The Trainer's Handbook

THE AMA GUIDE TO EFFECTIVE TRAINING

Third Edition

Garry Mitchell

AMACOM
American Management Association
New York • Atlanta • Boston • Chicago • Kansas City • San Francisco • Washington, D.C.
Brussels • Mexico City • Tokyo • Toronto

This publication is designed to provide accurate and authoritative
information in regard to the subject matter covered. It is sold with the
understanding that the publisher is not engaged in rendering legal,
accounting, or other professional service. If legal advice or other expert
assistance is required, the services of a competent professional person
should be sought.

Library of Congress Cataloging-in-Publication Data

Mitchell, Garry.
    The trainer's handbook : the AMA guide to effective training /
Garry Mitchell.—3rd ed.
        p.   cm.
    Includes bibliographical references and index.
    ISBN 0-8144-0341-7
    1. Employees—Training of.   I. Title.
HF5549.5.T7M58   1998
658.3'124—dc21   97-33473
                                                          CIP

Printing number

10   9   8   7

Contents

Preface to the Third Edition

DURING his 1996 election campaign, President Bill Clinton repeatedly promised that his education policy would make a college education possible for every American. This sounds like an admirable goal, but it is not. Some of the reasons people don't go to college are that they don't want to, have no talent for studying, are unable or unwilling to master the skills needed to graduate, and, consequently, don't see the need to study for college entrance. But what alternatives do they have? With the President's current thrust, public schools will become even more college-preparation–oriented, denying any effective alternative training to those who don't want to go to college.

In my youth I chose to attend a technical high school rather than a college-track one because I wanted to learn the manual skills offered in technical school. I was still taught English literature, writing, history, science, and mathematics (the best math class I ever had, in fact), but, in addition, I got to learn cabinetmaking, electrical wiring, plumbing, and the basics of house construction, as well as the proper use of a number of power tools and machines.

I did go on to attend college anyway, learned to love it, and now hold three degrees including a Ph.D., but to this day I have used the technical skills I learned in high school far more and with as much or more pleasure than I have used my science, history, or mathematics. There are still a few good technical schools (my own has long since closed), but they are rare and fail to get the funding that the college-track schools receive.

We have become culturally fixated on the idea of a college education. It is demanded of even entry-level jobs, most of which require no college skills at all. I know many executives who do not have college degrees—some of whom had to lie about their education in order to get that first job. Yet they are excellent managers and a credit to their companies and their industries. I also know many people who are working successfully at jobs that are totally unrelated to their college education: The national sales manager for a very pricey, upscale import automobile company has a Ph.D. in medieval history. A large part of the education problem in the United States is this requirement of a college education.

The theories of John Dewey shaped American education in this century. Dewey helped America respond to the major economic shift from a largely agrarian society with a rural majority population to a largely industrial, urban-centered society. He envisioned a system of subject-centered education carefully structured into growing levels of difficulty that would bring children to full literacy and prepare them for life as adults. His system modernized education in his day and for decades thereafter and made American education the envy of and model for the world. The United States reached the ideal of a nearly universally literate society for the first time in history.

Not wanting to stop at mere literacy, for the last fifty years we have assumed that a broader curriculum in high school followed by four years of college was the next natural step in fulfilling Dewey's plan. It should be abundantly clear at this point that this was a wrong assumption.

That once enviable universal literacy is declining. American students consistently rank among the lowest of those from advanced countries in tests of high-school–equivalent academic skills. Corporations complain of the increasing difficulty they have in finding entry-level employees who can read and follow simple instructions or perform elementary arithmetical calculations. More and more managers are finding that literacy in the workplace cannot be taken for granted, even among long-term employees. To compound the problem still further, the demographic makeup of the American workforce is changing radically as we near the end of the century. Yet our elected leaders still promote a college education as the sine qua non of necessary preparation for the adult world of work. Instead, we need to rethink college as a universal job requirement, re-create and beef up technical training opportunities, and create work-study cooperation between industry and education, much as the Germans have done (see Chapters 13 and 14).

In this third edition of *The Trainer's Handbook* I have tried to cover all of the training skills such an approach would require for two reasons: First, there may be a realization that the workforce needs more than a college education as proper preparation, and those who are adept at training will be in even greater demand. Second, corporate training will need to become more and more the prime source of teaching job-related skills. This is particularly true with the continued exciting growth in technology that is forcing all workers to continually upgrade their skills. *The Trainer's Handbook* should help.

Finally, I continue to receive quite a lot of feedback on the first and second editions, which has helped me to focus on areas that need more clarification and additional examples. It is a rare and pleasurable treat to be able to reshape and fine-tune something written years ago. I've enjoyed the task tremendously.

Acknowledgments

I BEGAN the first edition of *The Trainer's Handbook* in 1987 by saying:

> Knowledge and skill are inseparable from the training that engendered them, no less for me than for all who read this book. So I must express my gratitude to my trainer Beverly Hyman, who has taught me much of what is written here. My four-year degree in education from the University of Alberta, Canada, gave me a basic framework that made twenty years of teaching everything from fourth grade to postgraduate seminars meaningful. But it was not until I met Beverly that I learned about training. It was she who taught me the power of Socratic dialogue; it was she who taught me the value of training objectives; and it was she who taught me program design. I can no longer separate what else I've learned from her, what I brought already formed to our professional relationship, and what I've learned from the thousands of trainers, secretaries, salespeople, and executives that I've trained in the past six years. I do know, however, that Beverly remains my model—the best trainer I know. Thanks, Bev. And thanks to Chris Nystrom for bringing us together.

This is as true now as it was when I wrote it two editions ago, but much has happened in the intervening years, and new players have joined many of the familiar ones in the process of getting the work into print for the third time.

Renewed editions of a book, the second and third and so forth, are seldom the author's choice. New editions occur when two conditions are met: Sales of the previous edition are so good that the publisher feels assured that there will be a market for a new version; and events or techniques in the subject area have changed to the extent that the book must be updated in order to stay current. Both of these conditions have been amply met even since the second edition. So

I'm thankful once again for the opportunity to express my gratitude to all those thousands of trainers and managers worldwide who have purchased *The Trainer's Handbook* and who use it to help shape successful training.

Once again I owe thanks to my editor, Adrienne Hickey, for asking me to update the book to incorporate the changes that are taking place almost daily, and for her very helpful suggestions and supportive background pieces.

Finally, for the pleasure of working with them and learning from them, I'd like to thank all of my trainees, past and future.

Introduction

ALL books have a purpose. Some entertain, some teach, some act as references, and some make excellent doorstops, shelf fillers, and booster seats. This book is a desktop reference, meaning that I envision it as a book to be kept next to the dictionary as an immediate and constant source of information.

It is possible to read this book from beginning to end (it was written that way, after all), and everything will make perfect sense. However, the basic structure is not sequential, nor is it climactic. Instead, it is centered around three major functions of training, with brief fourth and fifth sections newly added to discuss the most frequently asked questions about applications of training. The functions are: the face-to-face act of training other people; the planning for that training; and the management of training facilities, personnel, and operations. The applications are: team training, on-the-job training, and technical training, with a separate consideration of sales training as well. A new chapter has been added to what is now Part 5. It discusses the need for the trend toward integrating training into corporate objectives. The new material throughout the book is a direct response to readers who have generously provided feedback to me on the previous versions.

Part 1, The Nature of Training, covers the essential interaction skills required of a trainer—skills such as maintaining leadership, creating learning associations, planning lessons, controlling training groups, analyzing trainees, and establishing credibility. It outlines the steps in handling resistance to training and for building environments that encourage a change in trainee behavior on the job. In essence, Part 1 provides a perspective, a methodology, and a rationale for the role of training in the organization.

Part 2, Planning and Preparing for Training, details the day-to-day steps involved in performing needs analyses, writing training programs, and conducting evaluations. There are sample questionnaires and examples to illustrate clearly the content and process of needs analyses and task analyses. These areas are both expanded to include a brief and useful description of the role of statistical analysis in defining and evaluating training needs as well as some tips for application. This part includes evaluating outside sources, such as off-the-shelf training packages, consultants, and commercial seminar organizations. It addresses the care, uses, and creation of audiovisual aids. There is a chapter on the impact and uses of technology on training that explores ways to make the best use of them. In short, Part 2 provides detailed, step-by-step descriptions of how to carry out the basics of training.

Part 3, Special Applications in Training, is a detailed discussion of several special aspects of training. We look at specific considerations and tools for building and training effective teams, how to train supervisors to perform effective on-the-job training, special problems encountered and differences that become apparent between managerial training and technical skills training, and finally we explore the key elements in making sales training more effective.

Part 4 is about management concerns, not in general terms but, rather, in those matters germane to training. It deals with the task of marketing and selling internal training programs as well as the usually neglected areas of writing skills, negotiation techniques, financial management and budgeting, and human resources development.

In Part 5, Chapter 18 examines problems that training managers will face in the closing decade of this century and the first few years of the new one. Topics include literacy in the workplace and the changing demographics of the workforce. Chapter 19 discusses in detail the trend toward enlarging the traditional role of training to include strategic planning and posttraining follow-up services. Chapter 20 updates the discussion in the second edition on several major issues in the current training scene and further into the year 2000 and beyond.

The list of training resources in the Appendix has been updated for this third edition and several more sources have been added. Finally, in the spirit of this as a work to be used to train others, a set of application assignments has been added to each chapter so that the reader/learner can perform specific tasks using the material just read in order to help to master the skills discussed. This feature should prove very useful for training managers who use the book to train their people.

A word of warning is necessary. This book is not intended to be the benchmark of training against which all other efforts must be measured. Instead, it contains a compendium of workable solutions to most training problems. At no time should you view these solutions as necessarily the only answer to a problem. Training is in large measure an art. As in any art, there are many ways to approach a problem, some better than others. All the ideas presented here are effective, well worn by years of use. If you haven't already found a solution of your own, try one of these.

Finally, in accordance with the principle of redundancy, concepts are presented in two forms: first in detail within each chapter and then in a brief summary at the end of each chapter. Many key ideas are also repeated for emphasis in checklists, figures, and sidebars. If you are an experienced trainer, first read the summary to see what is covered in the chapter. If you are familiar with the material or have no problems in that particular area, move on. Readers who desire somewhat more detail should skim the chapter and peruse the figures and checklists, which present, in a quick-to-read fashion, the basic precepts and guidelines of the training process. Those of you who want a thorough treatment of the topic should read the entire chapter to consider the subject in detail.

Yet another help to readers is the table of contents. A glance at the breakdown of chapters by major headings gives a good overview of the various areas covered. After you have read the book, or portions of it, the table of contents helps refresh your memory. The chapter summaries are again helpful for reviewing, and the checklists and figures can be used at any time to bring back to mind important procedures and techniques.

Although not intended as a benchmark, this book *is* intended as a manual for the training of trainers. A training manager can assign readings from it and build practical experiences around its various topics. Indeed, this is the intent behind the newly added applications at the end of each chapter. When the book is used for training, such practical assignments are vital. The emphasis here is on detailing the procedures, not on theory or even on skills mastery. Intended as a backup when mastery is incomplete, the book allows those who are as yet unskilled in any of these various training areas to tackle unfamiliar tasks with proven techniques.

This is a book for trainers at all levels. For the novice it is a daily procedural manual. For the expert trainer newly appointed to a management position, it is a practical guide to new perspectives on familiar material. And for the experienced training manager, it is a field reference for getting back to basics, keeping on track, refreshing your knowledge, training new trainers, and developing new managers.

Those who have read and used the first and second editions will find much of value that is new in this third one. Those who come to *The Handbook* for the first time will find in it a wealth of practical training tools. To both: Good luck and good training!

Part 1

The Nature of Training

Introduction to Part 1

Part 1 is the most theoretical of the four major parts of this book. That is not to say it isn't practical. This first part gives you an orientation to the theory behind training and also introduces you to many of its practices. Chapter 1 establishes the role of the trainer as an agent for structuring change and growth in a company. This concept sets the tone for the rest of the book, so for those learning the craft, this beginning chapter is essential for grounding all other necessary skills solidly within the basic concepts of training excellence.

Consequently, Chapter 1 encompasses the basics of adult learning theory, how to cope with resistance to learning, and the dynamics of group behavior. The person or group to be trained is the focus here, with a discussion of how people learn, the role that the senses play in receiving input, differences in learning ability, and ways to discover what trainees know and what they want and need to know. Also included are some effective techniques for handling groups, including the roles members assume and how decisions are made.

Chapter 2 examines the structure of training. We look at the bedrock of training—objectives. We examine the cultural need for live training and discuss the importance of maintaining a learning dialogue and patterns of redundancy. Structural patterns are examined, and finally the four basic steps to creating effective lessons are discussed.

In Chapter 3, the function of the trainer is examined, especially with regard to personal skills. We look at all the ways a trainer can assume a leadership role, and we consider the various tasks a training leader must perform. We explain ways of controlling distractions in the classroom, including the handling of difficult trainees. There are also specific instructions on improving your listening skills and heightening and varying your question-forming abilities. We provide guidelines for making effective responses to trainee questions and give tips on projecting a positive nonverbal image. Credibility is discussed, including how to establish it and how to use it effectively.

This part is, therefore, both a compendium of solid training techniques and a theoretical underpinning for the novice or the expert; indeed it is for anyone who wants to better understand the nature of training.

Chapter 1
The Function and Purpose of Training

WHY would a company hire a trainer? You can probably think of a dozen or so specific problems that a company might try to solve by setting up a training program. But no matter how many you might think of, there is only one basic reason: A company hires a trainer to produce a change in its operation. The sole function of training is to produce change. When it does, it is successful; when it doesn't, it fails. Regardless of other results a trainer or training manager may accomplish, the bottom line is a measurable change in performance. The trainer is an agent for change, and this book concentrates on ways of achieving that change.

The Nature of Change

We would all happily have others change to suit our needs or habits or desires, but none of us, not even the managers who demand the change, wants to change how *we* do things. Our society pays great lip service to change. We call ourselves the most progressive and advanced society. Indeed, technologically we are advanced. But if that technology causes us to change the way we do things, we resist it (unless, of course, it palpably makes the task easier). We want to think faster and work more efficiently, but not if that means having to break habitual patterns of work to learn new ways of doing things. We like the idea of American business being leaner and more competitive internationally, but not if it means being paid lower wages or losing our jobs. People love the status quo. It is a very human trait. To change is to risk losing what we already have, and few people are willing to run that risk.

Of course there are exceptions. Many people welcome change in any direction. But most people are, at best, concerned with what the future may bring, and, when learning new job skills, they are apprehensive about their ability to make the change. They resist the required change, often in subtle ways, and it is this resistance that the trainer must anticipate, recognize, and reduce.

The Motivation to Change

Change is neither good nor bad, only constant. Individuals respond constantly to various combinations of elements in the environment. These elements can be as diverse as pressure from a family or peer group, the temperature of the room, a recent illness, traffic conditions, a working situation, feelings of indigestion, attitudes about age, concerns about inflation, or fears for the world economic condition. Or these elements can be a host of other factors that affect us. We are constantly adjusting to a shifting environment, changing to meet new demands. Trainers cannot create that change, but they can guide it.

Educators talk a great deal about motivation—the desire to learn—but, in the end, an individual either does or does not want to learn. An instructor cannot create motivation where none exists. We are all familiar with the old saying "You can lead a horse to water but you can't make it drink." What can be done, however, is to work the horse hard before leading it to the water, so that it will be much more likely to want a drink. In other words, a trainer shapes the environment to make it conducive to learning. The how-to's of this book are all directed toward shaping and controlling the learning environment to facilitate change.

Changing People's Behavior

Anyone who has ever tried to diet or to stop smoking knows how difficult it can be to break a habit. Yet no change can take place until the old way is given up. Thus, the first step in making a change is to "unfreeze" the present habit. Once the habit is broken, the second step is to replace it with a new one, that is, to change the behavior. The third step is to "refreeze" the new behavior, usually through a reward system. The reward helps the person to perceive a benefit in the change and to feel good about it.

One of the most successful applications of this three-step method is the U.S. Marine Corps' induction system. New recruits are taken to a place where they have never been, talked to in a manner to which they have never been subjected before, and stripped of their old wardrobe and given an ill-fitting new one (including underwear). They receive a closer-than-close haircut; must sleep in narrow, public conditions; are denied all contact with old friends and family; and must submit to complete control over their vital functions such as sleeping, eating, and exercising. In effect, the Marine Corps disposes of all old habits. Life as it was known before induction into the corps is completely unfrozen. The recruits have no choice but to change.

Now the Marine Corps creates its change. In six weeks, recruits learn an entirely new way of life. They lose weight, become much more physically fit, learn detailed new skills, obey instructions, experience group living, and take on a host of other behaviors necessary to survive in that organization. As each step is mastered, recruits are rewarded with a sense of pride, accomplishment, and self-worth that refreezes the new behavior, making it seem right, proper, and worthwhile. In my experience, most marines remain loyal to the corps and value its training for the rest of their lives.

Change is a constant; it is always with us. It happens to us all, all the time. As writer Alvin Toffler has pointed out, not only is change continuing to happen, but the rate of change is increasing and will continue to increase well into the twenty-first century and beyond. However, most people tend to resist change unless they can perceive an immediate, definable benefit. For trainers, the process of change is further complicated by the fact that training alone cannot accomplish most organizational changes. But training can help. What a trainer changes is skills; and, insofar as new skills bring about the desired changes in an organization, training can achieve far-ranging results. Training itself cannot motivate a workforce. It cannot change the economic system. But training can and should be—indeed must be—an important part of change efforts in any organization.

Even on the most basic, straightforward skills level, learners will tend to resist change. Whether their training is part of an overall corporate change or an entry-level assessment, they will not want to change unless that change is both easy and attractive. Trainees need to be motivated to learn. You as trainer must set up an

---

Ten Steps to Making Effective Changes

1. Assess the corporate status quo. Determine the climate for change.
2. Define the objectives of your proposed change in terms of end result, not method.
3. Devise methods for unfreezing present procedures.
4. Develop methods for teaching the new, desired procedures.
5. Devise methods for rewarding (refreezing) the new procedures.
6. Put the methods you devised in step 3 into practice.
7. Implement the training planned in step 4.
8. Utilize the methods devised in step 5.
9. Evaluate the effectiveness of your changes so far. Make necessary adjustments.
10. Repeat the process until you achieve your desired results.

---

environment that is conducive to change. And to ensure that such an environment is conducive, you must organize your training sessions around the following basic principles of learning.

The Three Laws of Adult Learning

In the early 1900s, Edward L. Thorndike, a pioneer of educational psychology, did some of the most definitive work on learning. He concluded that there are three laws that govern how we learn:[1]

The Law of Readiness

Simply stated, the law of readiness means we only learn when we are ready to learn. Readiness includes seeing a need to learn, feeling a desire to learn, being interested in the subject, and having sufficient skills to both comprehend and utilize the new information.

The Law of Effect

Nothing succeeds like success. This law points out that the more success we feel in learning, the more excited we get about learning. We need to gain pleasure from our learning, and the successful performance of a formerly difficult task is one of life's greatest pleasures.

The Law of Exercise

In essence, practice makes perfect. This means that hands-on drill is necessary. It also means that the more personally we are involved in learning—that is, the harder we work at it—the more it engages us and the more we learn.

To take advantage of Thorndike's findings, you must ask yourself the following questions and evaluate your training methods accordingly:

1. *Are the trainees ready to learn the material?* This question really has two parts: (a) Are they motivated to learn it? If not, what can I do or say to move them? If they are, how can I best encourage that desire and align my material with it? (b) Do they have sufficient background to understand and proficiency to perform the new skills? If not, how can I best bring them to the readiness level? If they have sufficient proficiency, how can I present the material to be studied so the trainees will be both challenged and able to perform the new skills?

2. *Have I provided sufficient opportunities for the trainees to succeed?* Have I created enough feedback mechanisms for them to be able to see their success? Have I created opportunities for constructive failure? Can those failures be transformed effectively into successes?

3. *Have I built in sufficient practice phases?* Is each group given hands-on practice? Is there a practice drill to ensure skills improvement? Have I created enough practice and built enough conceptual bridges to engage and hold their interest?

If your answer to any of these questions is no, you need to familiarize yourself with the principles of learning.

Principles of Learning

There are ten recognized priciples of adult learning. Build your lessons around the following concepts:

1. People learn only what they are ready to learn.
2. People learn best what they actually perform.
3. People learn from their mistakes.
4. People learn easiest what is familiar to them.
5. People favor different senses for learning.
6. People learn methodically and, in our culture, systematically.
7. People cannot learn what they cannot understand.
8. People learn through practice.
9. People learn better when they can see their own progress.
10. People respond best when what they are to learn is presented uniquely for them. Each of us is different.

Each of these principles is a complex idea of critical importance to your training objectives. In the pages that follow, these topics are discussed with special attention to how they relate to the training situation.

Readiness and Resistance

As mentioned earlier, little or no positive learning takes place without a readiness to learn. In fact, the learner merely learns how to resist more effectively, and the training becomes confrontational and ineffective. The first step in responding to resistance is to ventilate it; encourage the trainees to express their resistance. Once you know what form their resistance is taking, you can respond to it. According to management and training consultant Dr. Beverly Hyman, there are seven sources of resistance to training:

1. *Parochial self-interest.* This is a "what's in it for me?" attitude. Trainees ask, "Why should we learn this?" Your best response is to sell them on the idea of what the training will do for them. Don't be coercive. Rather, structure your response in positive terms. Empathize with their resistance, but show them how they will benefit from the training. Give them reasons for wanting to at least try to learn.

2. *Lack of trust.* You, as the trainer, are always perceived as management and so your motives will be suspect if employees are in any way suspicious of management. Again, sell them on the benefits of the training. This may mean redefining the purpose of training. For example, suppose a trainee's supervisor said, "Get in there and get trained or else!" The trainee might feel you are there merely to evaluate him or her. You will have to earn that employee's trust. Be frank and open, talk about the trainee's resistance, and ask questions. Listen to the answers, then sell the benefits of the program. Incidentally, any promises you make *must* be kept if you want to maintain that trust.

3. *Different assessments of different information.* In this case, the trainee is resisting because he or she perceives the purpose or value of the training to be quite different from what you propose. If you carefully define your plan and explain the purpose right at the beginning, it should ease this form of resistance. You may have to redefine why the trainees are there, choosing your words with care to allay any fears or misgivings. Again, it is vital to talk over the resistance and get them to explain how they feel before you begin clarifying the situation for them. I have found this to be the most common form of resistance to training and one of the easiest to deal with.

4. *Low tolerance for change.* This form of resistance is common in shy people, people with a low self-opinion, and those who are slow learners. It is a hopeless attitude, not usually expressed openly but, rather, indirectly through nonverbal attitudes, lack of participation, shrugs, nervous behavior, or uncertain laughter. These people simply are afraid they lack the skills or correct behavior patterns to

---

The Seven Forms of Resistance

1. Parochial self-interest
2. Lack of trust
3. Different assessments of different information
4. Low tolerance for change
5. Fear of losing face
6. Peer-group pressure
7. Mistaken first impressions

---

learn the new material. To ease such resistance, give them something they will succeed at right away, something they *will* be able to do. Show them that they can do it, and build on each success. Go slowly. Let them gain self-confidence.

5. *Fear of losing face.* This is a much stronger fear than the previous one. No one wants to look foolish, and it takes a lot of courage to perform an about-face to admit having been wrong. Most of us are reluctant. To deal with the fear of losing face, you must build bridges that allow such people to modify their former opinions. Avoid either-or formulations. Define the terms so that everyone agrees on the end result, and shape that end result so that it is within the parameters of their original position. In other words, give them large opportunities to save face.

6. *Peer-group pressure.* This, too, is a powerful source of resistance. Despite Thoreau's admiration for those who do, it is very hard to march openly to the sound of a different drummer. Most of us do not want to look foolish in front of our peers. This is particularly true for those who define themselves socially. They see themselves as a part of an ethnic group, labor union, community, religious group, or sexual minority. "What will they think of me?" becomes a powerful motivator. If peer-group opinion is against you, you have a hard task. To handle such resistance, you must win over the group rather than the individual. To do that, you will need to persuade the group leader(s) of the value of the training. Again, ventilate the problem first, then work out a joint solution with the key group influencer(s). Finally, sell the entire group on the merits and benefits of the training program.

7. *Mistaken first impressions.* According to Edward DeBono, a noted researcher on creativity, we tend to make snap judgments about new things and then invest all our energies defending those initial judgments.[2] If the judgment is against you, you have a problem. The best tactic to counter such an eventuality is to ensure a positive first impression. This means carefully "positioning" the training in your initial advertising or selection process. It also means having a positive physical environment and creating a good initial impression. If you fail to give a favorable first impression, then you'll have to ventilate the resistance, empathize with it, and negotiate a modus operandi for carrying on cooperatively despite the trainees' first impressions.[3]

In all seven cases, the basic approach is to ventilate the resistance by bringing it out into the open, establish a low-threat environment by empathizing with that resistance, and then sell the trainees on the need for training. Stress the innovation and indicate the benefits they will reap from what you plan to train them to do.

Active vs. Passive Learning

We learn by doing. Recall how you learned to drive a car. You learned by actually driving it, didn't you? All the classroom work and book study couldn't really teach you to drive. Certainly no lecture could. You needed to get your hands on the wheel. In short, we need to get our hands on whatever it is we will learn. This is why 75 percent of the training in America takes place on the job.

To take advantage of this basic principle in your training, remember two things:

1. Minimize passive learning experiences such as lectures, films, slides, video presentations, or demonstrations.
2. Maximize active learning experiences such as case studies, workshops, projects, panel discussions, and hands-on activities.

Without active sessions to lock in the learning, people will not transfer that information—that is, they will not put the new learning to work on the job.

We retain roughly 10 percent of what we read, 20 percent of what we hear, 30 percent of what we see, and 50 percent of what we both see and hear. But if we become active, those percentages jump to 70 percent of what we say and 90 percent of what we both say and do. Get your trainees to report back to you what they've learned. After all, the best way to master a skill is to teach it.

Trial and Error

We learn best by making mistakes. Edward Thorndike's law of effect, which was discussed earlier, tells us that nothing succeeds like success. Success motivates us and makes us want to learn more, but it is the errors we make that we remember and learn to correct. To learn we must have a chance—indeed, several chances—to fail (or succeed). The problem is that errors on the production line or in the field can be very costly; this is why training facilities exist. The training climate must allow for errors and invite challenges. Medical technicians practice on plastic dummies, airline pilots polish their skills in cockpit simulators, and lawyers hold formal debates and mock trials in law school. Our errors teach us far more than our successes. Build the chance for errors into your training.

Association

Training doesn't take place in a vacuum. No one comes to your session with an empty mind waiting to be filled. We learn by connecting the new material we meet with the things we know already. Each person learns the same things differently because he or she brings a different background to the learning. When learning fails to take place, often it is because the learner had no internal reference with which to connect the new material. He or she failed to understand because the context in which the material was presented did not strike a responsive chord in his or her memory.

One of the core skills of training is building bridges that relate new material to the familiar. Few people can make a quantum leap into the unknown. We must relate new information to the known in order to understand it at all. The trainer, by discovering what trainees already know, can build upon that knowledge. (This is discussed further in Chapter 4, in connection with needs analysis.) You can ask questions of the trainees early in the seminar so that you can zero in on key elements they already know and on how they feel about the material to be learned. In addition, pretests reveal a great deal of what trainees know. Among the best ways to begin is with a group exercise or management game so that all trainees have a common experience to draw upon later. Teach by using stories or parables and personal examples; give each individual a reference point to which he or she can relate new material.

Multisensory Input

All of our senses are sources of learning. Everything we know comes to us through one or more of them. Yet, as industrial psychologist Jard DeVille points out, we are a product of the traits we inherit, the experiences we receive through our senses, and the choices we make throughout our lives.[4] These last two factors combine to produce sensory biases—that is, each of us tends to favor (choose) one sense and make it dominant for learning. The other senses continue to function, but the dominant one is our preferred way to learn.

Let's review the sensory biases and how they affect learning.

Sight. Many cannot follow a complicated description but can instantly grasp the same process when it is diagrammed. From childhood onward we love "picture books." This is why computer manufacturers and software developers are touting CD-ROM technology and the Internet offers the World Wide Web. The old saying "A picture is worth a thousand words" is true for many of us. Architects not only describe and draw schematic diagrams but construct scale models and sketch representational perspectives for what they plan to build. Our eyes inform us greatly.

Hearing. We learn of other people's experiences because they tell us about them. The sense of hearing is a particularly important one because it relates back to the distant (and sometimes not so distant) heritage of all peoples. All human cultures were at some time oral. That is, they did not have a written language or, if they did, it was only for an elite few and was not used extensively. Many cultures today still have a predominantly oral tradition. In such oral cultures, sound and language play huge roles. Spoken communication is oral and repetitive; memory becomes paramount. Ballads, poems, and legends abound. Social events and ritu-als take on deeper meanings. In modern America, we retain at least two major vestiges of our oral past: religion and education. We like to learn by hearing others (teachers) speak to us, and we like to worship communally. The oral tradi-tion is the deep-rooted, powerful learning tool you use in creating learning through discourse. (Note that it is *discourse* that teaches, not lectures. We need to hear the sound of our own voices in order to learn.)

Touch. Through touch we understand the size, shape, smoothness or rough-ness, texture, and temperature of objects. Touch is our measure of physical com-fort, and, therefore, it controls a potentially negative response to training. If the room is too hot or cold, or if the seats are too hard or soft, such sensory input interferes with the learning environment and must be corrected.

Kinesthesia. This sense is often confused with touch, and, indeed, the two work together closely. Kinesthesia is the sense through which we determine the degree of hardness or softness of an object, the direction and amount of muscular movement, and the amount of effort we have to exert to move it. Manipulative skills depend heavily on this sense. It is kinesthesia that is involved directly in hands-on training. We use it to gauge where to move our fingers to strike the keys of a typewriter or computer; we use it to determine how much force to exert when lifting a tool or lever. This sense, when engaged in learning, is very power-ful. Whenever possible, utilize the kinesthetic sense as a direct pathway to under-standing and retention.

Smell. Though potent in creating memories, the sense of smell is not really vital to most training situations. It gives the learner a strong sense of being there—a sense of place. If trainees are working where odors are pervasive, capi-talize on this aspect of the workplace and emphasize its positive nature to moti-vate them. Certainly anyone who has worked at sea or in a printing shop, furniture finishing room, coffee plant, or lumber mill will recognize the evocative power of odors to awaken and sharpen the memory. Of course, the same is true for negative smells. Once experienced, the odor of a building on fire can never be forgotten.

Taste. The sense of taste is, unfortunately, not very useful in training, except in the food and drug industries. Still, if it can be utilized, you can lock in learning as surely as with the other senses.

The three senses most commonly and most easily involved in training are sight, hearing, and kinesthesia. Work the following methods into your training, so you are using these senses to encourage learning:

Sight

- Diagrams
- Charts and graphs
- Training manuals
- Flip charts
- Reference materials
- Lists of parts or definitions
- Sample transactions
- Films
- Slides
- Actual situations to be observed
- Demonstrations
- Interactive computer sessions (CD-ROM, etc.)
- Virtual reality sessions

Sound

- Discussions
- Demonstrations
- Question-and-answer sessions
- Definitions
- Panel discussions
- Group projects
- Lectures
- Films
- Audiovisuals
- Interactive computer sessions (CD-ROM, etc.)
- Virtual reality sessions

Kinesthesia (Hands-On)

- Supervised practice on the job
- Simulations
- Paper and pencil tests
- Flowcharting
- Case histories
- Group projects
- Role playing
- Interactive computer sessions (CD-ROM, etc.)
- Virtual reality sessions

Create a variety of sensory input because what isn't clear when received by one sense often crystallizes through another. This is particularly true when you remember that people show a bias toward one sense as the easiest or most trust-worthy.

One Thing at a Time

Most trainers have the dangerous tendency to overload their learners. As experts on the subject, we see all the problems and their ramifications. We forget that the learner is completely new to the subject and cannot grasp *all* of it. We tend to go too fast and to give trainees too much material at one time. When we do this, we lose them.

We want to rush ahead because we are under time constraints. But the train-ees may not yet have grasped some key element. We cannot afford to lose them. Information overload is as critical a problem in training as it is in computers. Given more information than they can process, learners' minds simply shut down.

To prevent information overload, practice the slogan of the 1920s Bauhaus School of Design: LESS IS MORE. The simpler you can make the material, the more effectively it can be learned. This means taking even the most complex technical material and breaking it into manageable chunks of instruction. Set up a simple structure or pattern or model, then build your lesson around the pattern you've created. Enhance the pattern with stories (parables), analogies to material with which they are already familiar, and audiovisual aids.

Understanding

Learning takes place only with understanding. This is why, even in a how-to book such as this, we must cover some key elements of theory. Learning by rote, with no understanding, produces inferior performance, at best, and very quick loss of memory and skills. On the other hand, if trainees can comprehend why they need to learn something and how that information fits into the overall picture, it will make a great deal more sense and be much easier to learn. Therefore, when-ever possible, take your trainees with you on the road to understanding. Explain what they are doing and why. Give them a map of the territory, so they will know both where they have been and where they are headed. Use agendas, summaries, progressive diagrams, and flowcharts.

In addition, define in advance the level of understanding at which you are aiming. When necessary, let the trainees know what level is required of them. As a rule, aim at one or all of the four most commonly recognized levels of under-standing:

1. *Simple recognition.* Do learners recognize the correct answer when they see it (as in a multiple-choice question)? Can they tell when something is wrong? Do they recognize the correct tool or the need for the step being taught?

2. *Specific recall.* Can learners describe the process involved? Can they delineate the steps? Fill in the blanks? Repeat the formulas? Recite the uses?

3. *Discrimination.* Can learners pick the appropriate responses from among several choices (multiple choice)? Can they choose the correct method or response to match the situation (as in emergency training, budgeting, and so on)? Can they select an appropriate applicant? Recognize incorrect usages?

4. *Judgment.* Can learners use the material to solve problems? Case histories? Role playing? Can they create new formats? Judge between two appropriate responses and analyze which one would be preferable? Troubleshoot the system?

Practice

We all know the saying "Practice makes perfect." Always allow time for some form of practice. The more opportunity learners have to practice, the greater their retention rate will be. Practice should be as close to on-the-job situations as possible, and initially it should follow the instruction as soon as possible. Make practice sessions an integral part of learning.

Feedback

People need to know how they are doing. It is impossible to learn in a vacuum, yet testing newly acquired knowledge can also create problems. Many of us experienced test anxiety in school. We knew we would be judged, so we put great pressure on ourselves to do our best. If test anxiety is a problem for your learners, sell them on the idea (a true one for adult learning) that the purpose of the test is not for you to judge them but, rather, for them to evaluate what they have learned and compare it to what you expect them to learn. Tests are merely a form of feedback. They let the trainees know how they are doing.

You'll need other forms of feedback as well, though. Create lessons that invite dialogue. Provide opportunities for evaluating their work. And offer chances for trainees to make self-evaluations. This is particularly important for jobs in which trainees are unsupervised for part of the time. Help the trainees perfect the skill of self-evaluation.

Uniqueness

Individual differences are always a factor in learning. Each person is a unique individual, and each learns differently. People come to training with different backgrounds, abilities, skills, knowledge, and personalities. For your training to succeed, you need to recognize and respond positively to each individual's different perceptions, habits, and manners. Typical areas of difference include the following:

Sources and Kinds of Resistance. People resist learning for different reasons. We've already covered the seven forms of resistance and what to do about each. Remember, however, that until you've dealt with all the forms of resistance, the only learning that will take place is how to be an effective resister. There may be several different forms of resistance among your trainees. You will have to recognize, ventilate, and deal with all of them in order to successfully train the group.

Personal Temperament. People vary. Some bubble with enthusiasm, and others' tempers flare up easily; still others remain easygoing and affable under all circumstances. As a rule, positive traits such as affability, enthusiasm, and willingness to try are helpful and need encouragement whenever they appear. Negative traits and habits such as a quick temper, a complaining nature, gossiping, apathy, boredom, sloth, or suspicion hinder learning. Make every effort to avoid triggering these negative responses. In addition, you should:

1. *Make suggestions rather than give orders.* Telling people what to do implies a superior-inferior relationship, which can trigger negative responses. It is usually better with adults to lead by suggesting. If resistance occurs, ask what the problem is rather than polarize the situation by responding to what seems to be a challenge to your authority. Besides, asking is a courtesy most of us respect.

2. *Sell the learners on the benefits of the training.* Tell how they can grow and develop in their respective jobs by using the skills you are teaching. Even when there is no resistance, it is a good idea to specify how they will benefit. Learning done with a personal purpose locks in more easily. Also, sell the idea that their work is improved with an understanding of the theory and concepts behind that work.

3. *Define necessary strictures (rules for behavior) as regulations, not as punitive rules.* Make it clear (if necessary) that some regulations are always necessary to allow a group to function. Otherwise, you'll have chaos and anarchy—fun, perhaps, but tedious after a while and very unproductive.

4. *Maintain leadership.* In essence, the group should be guided toward learning through clear directions, suggestions, agendas, questions, and focused instruction, rather than coercion.

As a trainer, you have no authoritarian right to control. The most punitive thing you can do is have an offending individual removed from your class. The second most authoritarian action is to report the individual to his or her boss.

Even in the military, there are limits to disciplinary action. If you use even these heavy-handed actions, you will lose the offenders as learners, the respect of the rest of the group, your effectiveness as a teacher, and, possibly, your own job. Force and coercion are simply not effective, or even viable, tools for training.

You must lead the group by winning its respect. You are dealing with adults who demand to be treated as such. You may suggest, urge, persuade, even cajole, but if you command or try to dominate an individual or a situation, you risk losing far more than you gain. It is partly for this reason that I stress discussing any problems of resistance. If you ask the difficult person(s) to explain the problem, you create a forum for discussion. Summarily ordering them to behave creates a confrontation that you may lose.

In summary, you must be tolerant of individual differences and find ways to help those who need help. Utilize the good traits of others. Regard your trainees as colleagues rather than as subordinates. Build trust rather than resentment, even among those whose personalities lean toward mistrust or anger.

Background Experience and Level of Education. When you are faced with a relatively homogeneous group, simply follow your agenda. Watch for two variations: (1) any individual form of resistance, and (2) any need for extra explanation or coaching. If either appears, respond appropriately (usually privately) and solve the problem. On the other hand, when you have a group that varies in experience, education, and skills, you will need to consider one of these three steps:

1. *If possible, use the more experienced people as part of your teaching team.* Ask them to illustrate some of your points from their own experience; for instance, they can share their own war stories. Appoint them as skills resources for some practice exercises so each becomes responsible for the practice of one or more novices. Create group projects in which experienced people function as expert resources for the rest of the group. Assign them to make presentations to the rest of the group in their areas of interest and expertise.

2. *Divide the class into groups by level of experience and then give each group an assignment commensurate with its ability.* This is the classic approach of the one-room schoolhouse. It's not as efficient, perhaps, as a giant consolidated urban system, but the method has been effective for more than one hundred years.

3. *Instruct each trainee individually.* This tactic is necessary when you use the one-room schoolhouse approach, particularly when individual differences are very great. It is the most time-consuming and, therefore, the most inefficient. It is, however, the most effective way to learn, which is why so much training in America takes place on the job. It is also the medieval guild system of training via apprenticeship to journeyman to master. Artists have always found this the best approach to excellence. They study with the masters.

Learning Ability. Although people learn at their own rate, it is usually convenient and useful to group trainees into three types: slow, regular, and fast. Most instruction is aimed at regular learners, the middle group. Even in a group of the most gifted learners, there will be some who are faster, some who are slower, and most who are just fast. Aim your lesson plans at the majority in the group. This will always leave a few for whom the work is easy and a few for whom the work is difficult. To be fully effective, you cannot ignore either extreme.

To help the slow learner keep pace, first diagnose what the difficulty is. All too often, it is merely a problem of finding a bridge—some connecting link between the new material and the old. The more familiar the material, the closer the parallel, and the more easily and quickly the learner will grasp the concept.

Another difficulty might stem from insufficient prior education. This can be approached two ways: (l) assign related remedial work to bring learning up to par, and (2) provide extra attention or individual instruction.

Poor reading ability (or eyesight) may also be a problem. If the problem is reading ability, assign remedial work with minimum reading demand and maximum oral or manual involvement.

If the problem is simply that individuals are slow learners, give extra attention and individual instruction. Also, build confidence by asking them questions that can be answered easily. Show sincere interest in them and their work. Provide clear, vivid explanations in simple terms. Use visual aids whenever possible. Lastly, group slow learners with average learners rather than with fast ones.

When working with slow learners, remember that they are capable of grasping concepts and improving skills. The problem is reaching the level of understanding they presently have and then building bridges to what they must learn, creating the necessary maps, and taking them at their own rate across those bridges through the solid groundwork they need to progress. Patience is vital.

To help superior learners, you must devise ways to challenge them. People who learn fast, who grasp concepts quickly, are often ahead of you and get bored or impatient. In such situations they tend to become critical and evaluative, and you open the door to potential resistance and challenge to your authority.

You must engage and challenge superior learners. To engage them, create challenging assignments. Such assignments can be case histories, additional reading, or problem solving. Have fast learners complete specific research or design exercises that can be used by the entire group (such as developing a flowchart, devising specific figures to work through an example, or creating critical-incident case histories). Have them become group facilitators or resource people; use them as group observers or evaluators. Have them prepare and present material to the rest of the group or participate in panel discussions and plan agendas. All of these give quick learners enough stimulation to keep them active in the learning environment.

In making special assignments, however, be careful they don't appear to be punitive or mere busywork. Position the extra work as an opportunity to expand learning for the adventurous, or as an aid to you personally, or merely as a challenge, but never as an added chore. Be careful, also, not to create animosity toward those you've assigned more challenging material. No one likes the idea of favored treatment, especially when they're not among the favored. Most people are reasonably tolerant of personality differences—such as the flamboyant learner who is always first to volunteer or the shy one who says little—and they extend their tolerance both to those who learn more quickly and to those who are slower. But minimize the differences and make everything as normal and low-keyed as possible, because the range of tolerance is limited. Most people feel embarrassed by too much or too obvious special attention, and all people feel resentment when they perceive that someone else is getting more than they.

Whom Are You Training?

Whom you are going to train is far more important than what you are actually training them to do. Of course, what you train people to do is your overall objective. If you are a change agent, then your effectiveness is measured by the changes you bring about—in other words, what they learn. But before you can bring about those changes, you must establish a baseline, a point from which to start. If you don't, you'll have no way of measuring the changes you've caused, and so will create only chaos—change for its own sake, without direction or meaningful function. A major part of that baseline is who it is you are training.

Let's say that you are about to instruct a group of trainees in some rather technical skill. The skill is demanding, difficult to master, and yet not really intellectually challenging. The skill is treated as routine by those who know how to do it but is considered rather intimidating by people who first encounter it. Suppose you need to teach that group a new computer program. The course would be completely different, depending on who was in the group. Your learners could be a seventh-grade science class, a twelfth-grade class of business majors, a college class in plasma physics, members of a doctoral research seminar, newly hired secretarial trainees, senior executive secretaries, recently hired robotics engineers, or fifteen-year production-floor veterans. Each group would demand a completely different approach.

Remember, you cannot create learning. You can only create an environment that is conducive to learning. Each group of trainees just mentioned would respond best to a different environment. The content—how to set up and run the new computer program—remains the same. But whether you succeed in bringing about a change ultimately is a function of how skillfully you have analyzed the group's makeup and its needs and how well you have created an environment that encourages them to learn. Therefore, who you train is as important, perhaps even more important, than what you are training them to do.

There is a fundamental question you should ask about a group before you begin training: "How will the group have changed because of this training?" After all, this is the question you were hired to answer. As you will see in Chapter 19, an important part of your job is ensuring that the company—workers, middle management, supervisors, support system people, senior management—recognizes that training gets results. If you don't remind them how effective your training is, you'll constantly be on the defensive, justifying every dollar you spend. Training is always on the wrong side of the ledger. To avoid being considered an expensive frill, use every opportunity to show the positive changes your training has brought about. Start, therefore, by answering the initial question. How will they have changed because of this training?

Once you begin thinking about it, you'll realize that the answer does not come quickly. In order to answer it, you need to ask three other questions about the participants in the training:

1. What do they know about the subject?
2. What do they want to know about the subject?
3. What do they need to know about the subject?

Let's consider each of these questions.

What They Know

In accordance with one of the learning principles discussed earlier, you must move from the known to the unknown, from the familiar to the new. Begin by finding out what the group knows, so you can guide them from that place to where you want them to be.

Perform a formal needs analysis as described in Chapter 4. Ask the group for information about themselves and their experience. Conduct a preclass survey or give an assignment asking them to describe their personal objectives—what they would like to get from the class. Give a pretest of the material at the beginning of the first class and study the results.

Engage the group in discussion by asking questions about why they are in the class. Ask questions that establish a common ground. Open up the floor for a gripe session, or ask the trainees to list things that bother them.*

Create or administer a game or event that you can use later as a common experience. This is one of the main uses for management games. Set a task for them to accomplish and evaluate their performance. Ask them to describe a critical incident that has just happened and then discuss it.

*I have had great success with this technique when training clerical staff in better communications and customer service techniques. Many participants tell me that they are thrilled to find that others have the same problems.

Any or all of these approaches will tell you a great deal about what the group knows. Of course, several of the techniques just listed can't be used in advance. Start with those that can be used in advance—for example, a needs analysis—then build your course around the results and later bring in the others to verify your original analysis. In any event, stay flexible and adapt your course to the level of knowledge you discover.

What They Want to Know

This question addresses the problems of motivation and resistance. Most of the techniques just mentioned also answer the question of what they want to know. In particular, the most effective techniques are performing a needs analysis (records and supervisors' input on each trainee), holding a gripe session, asking them for their objectives, taking a preclass survey, asking questions about why they are there, and using a critical incident.

What They Need to Know

Of course, this has already been established by a subject matter expert (probably yourself), but it has been expressed only in terms of the end result—the change desired—not in terms of the starting place. What does this particular group need to know in relation to what they already know and in relation to what they want to learn? Combine what you know they need to know with what they already know and with the new material they are willing to learn. For example, if N = the need to learn, O = the desired change (your objective), K = what they already know, and W = what they want to learn:

$$N = O - K + W$$

The techniques for discovering the answer to this third question are all the previous ones used to answer the first two questions, but in particular they are:

- A needs analysis
- Preclass surveys
- A pretest
- Management games
- Discussion or role-playing of critical incident
- A preclass assignment

Principles of Group Behavior

In this chapter we have been looking at elements that affect individual trainees. But you don't always train individuals. In fact, most trainers are involved with groups of people from three to three hundred at a time. There are some key training factors that involve group interaction, so we need to look at them, too.

Characteristics of a Group

In most group situations, people interact with those around them. But they also have the opportunity to act as a group. For example, strangers in an elevator or at a corner waiting for a traffic light, managers at a meeting, people in a movie theater, or trainees in a seminar can ignore the others and remain alone, can casually interact with one or more of the others, or can interact with all the others as a unit and create a group that behaves in several special ways.

Once a decision is made to interact as a group, several things happen. In training groups especially, these distinct features play an important role. The first distinction is that all groups have a purpose. Individuals can be purposeless, but a group without a purpose simply isn't a group. The feeling of being a group arises out of a sense of purpose, of what is to be done. Consequently, if you wish to create learning groups (a highly recommended tactic), break up any preexisting groups before establishing new ones. People who begin a class as a preexisting group tend to sit together, stay together, fulfill the purposes of their own group (some positive, perhaps, some not), and tend to exclude others. They constitute an independent power base in the training room, and these functions are in no way conducive to a learning environment. At best, they are irrelevant—at worst, a detriment. Whenever possible, break up preexisting cliques by (1) assigning seats or seating people by a random alphabetical or numerical system, and (2) placing people in new learning groups.

All groups have norms. Norms are informal, often unspoken, rules of conduct. Some things are acceptable to the group, some things are not. It is usually advisable to ask for input in making procedural rules. This is particularly important in cross-cultural training situations where group norms may differ widely. We will discuss this cross-cultural situation in more detail in Chapters 18 and 20. To go against any norm, however, is to create resistance; whereas, to ally your purposes with the group's norms is to enhance the chances for cooperation and to lessen resistance.

Frequently, the old ways you are training people to change may be perceived as norms. "That's the way we've always done it," is an all-too-frequent comment. If you arbitrarily dismiss such comments, you will polarize the group and lessen or even negate the effectiveness of your training. It is essential that you understand the wants and habits of your trainees.

If you have to change their group norms, follow the procedures discussed in this chapter concerning breaking habits. Also, there are key opinion- or norm-molders in any group. These are the people whose support you need to gain, whom you need to convince. They, in turn, will influence the rest of the group.

Three events occur in a sequence when a group is confronted with a problem that needs a decision. First, each member with status voices his or her opinion and tries to rally support for it. In a group dominated by one individual, this may be a very short discussion. In more loosely structured groups the discussion can go on interminably (as, for example, in congressional or parliamentary debates). Second, those who have been strongly opposed by one or more of the others will make an effort to rethink or adapt their positions to the majority or to those they perceive as most powerful; where they are not threatened, they will adopt what appears to them to be the most rational position. If they can accept the other position or persuade the others to accept some compromise, the decision is made and the group adopts the agreed-upon concept. If the concept proves successful or remains unchallenged, it will become a new norm for the group.

But there is a third step that occurs when no agreement can be reached. That is, both sides have tried to persuade each other, both have tried to reevaluate and compromise, and both have failed. At this point one or both (or more, if there are more factions) will redefine the group. Each will exclude the other; or, if that is not possible, each will agree only on the surface but will hold back privately. If the group does this to one individual, that person is ostracized, blackballed, and/or made into a scapegoat. If the individual does it to the group, he or she simply goes another way, seeking some other affiliation but usually downgrading the value or the members of the group. When whole parts of the group exclude entire other parts, we get factionalism: splinter groups, fanatics, moderates, or cliques.

Change in Groups

Training creates change, as we have seen, and means "unfreezing" the old way. You do this in step one of the group process, but you must reach step two to cause them to rethink their current norms. You cannot push them to step three or they will drop out and resist learning anything (a syndrome we have probably all observed in our high school days). The members of the group must be allowed to air their opinions in step one, or they will feel resentment at being force-fed a new way of doing things and will resist that, too. This is why building an environment that is conducive to learning is so important.

You'll win the first part of the battle for learning when you reach the members' minds and give them cause to rethink their comfortable old ways. This is also why, as will be seen in Chapter 3, there must be an effort to prepare them for learning. It's why dealing with resistance is so important. Unless each trainee comes to realize the worth of the material you are teaching—that it is worth changing for—he or she will redefine the situation to exclude you from the group and will dismiss the norms of management in favor of the norms of whatever subgroups he or she can create or join. To be conducive to learning, the environment must:

- Allow and encourage the airing of trainees' problems, habits, and doubts.
- Encourage interaction and the discovery of ideas.
- Encourage testing of both opinions and skills so that people are motivated and learn from their mistakes.
- Engage and challenge learners, rather than bore them.
- Stimulate thought, effort, discussion, and new ideas.
- Encourage openness rather than private withdrawal.
- Demand commitment through action.
- Provide an abundance of practice and evaluation.

Obviously, some of us train groups that are prepared to learn, and so the task is easier. These groups already recognize the need to change. But with groups that are reluctant, you must deal with the three stages of group dynamics.

Roles Within the Group

There are several easily recognizable roles that members of a group may adopt. If you recognize these roles, you can move with them and lessen the amount of change required. To fight these naturally elected roles is to court resistance, but to engage them—by tailoring requests and assignments to the norms of the group—is to encourage and motivate members to learn.

Leader. In most groups the leadership emerges informally. Leadership is always present to some degree when a group of people is undecided about what to do. In a theater after a spectacular performance some people will lead a standing ovation, jumping spontaneously to their feet. Others will wait to follow their lead. A group of friends standing around with nothing to do always inspires suggestions for activity; those who suggest are bidding for leadership. In a classroom, if the trainer fails to arrive on time, sooner or later (usually after about twenty minutes) at least one person will appeal for support in doing something about it.

Such moves are bids for leadership. If several bids are made at once or early on, discussions and possibly arguments will occur until the members of the group go through the three steps outlined earlier. Then they choose to follow one leader or break into several factions. These bids for leadership are largely a result of the frustration level individuals can tolerate. Those who can least tolerate the frustration will move toward what they perceive as an easement.

Usually these early bidders will ask for support from others. If they get none, they will either act alone or capitulate, following someone else's bid for leadership. If they get some support, they will usually measure its strength by demanding immediate action or inviting discussion directly or indirectly. Eventually they gather their supporters, having gone through the argue, rethink, redefine cycle. Leadership usually grows from three actions: (1) suggesting or demanding courses of action, (2) monitoring progress, and (3) evaluating performance or other calls to action.

Authority/Reference/Adviser. Another almost mandatory position is that of the authority. This is the person everyone respects and listens to because of his or her experience or special expertise. In a group of strangers it is anyone who can gain credibility by appearing to know what he or she is talking about. Often the authority is self-proclaimed (*I read a book once* . . . , or *I know a fellow who* . . . , or *My uncle was once* . . .). This person can be appointed, but then must prove he or she is worthy of respect. The authority can bid for leadership but just as often maintains a power position by having prospective leaders seek his or her endorsement. The authorities in groups sometimes become the scheming force behind the leader.

Entertainer. We are all familiar with the quick wit who can make a funny remark about almost anything. Such people need an audience and readily find one in their social and business groups. They are important to their groups because their humor provides a relief from tension and often prevents a confrontation. Consequently, even the most serious groups will have a member who makes wry remarks.

Peacemaker. Peacemakers hate confrontation. They are often excellent facilitators or negotiators, and they strive to iron out difficulties among those bidding for leadership. They are harmonizers. They try to work out rational, mutually beneficial solutions to problems. In doing so, they sometimes end up in leadership roles themselves, sometimes effectively and sometimes not so effectively. This is particularly true in parliamentary systems such as those in Great Britain, Israel, and France, where coalition governments are led by prime ministers who, to keep the peace and get the job done, negotiate shaky compromises between fighting factions. In fact, this leadership option—the role of peacemaker—is available to the trainer even in the most difficult groups.

Worker-Follower. The workers are the people who carry out what the leaders, authorities, and peacemakers want done. They are the power base upon which leadership is based, and they are usually the majority in any group. Because they don't relish change and would rather go along with their friends than create an issue, they are easily swayed as a group. To change their opinions, persuade the leader and the group will follow. Such a statement may sound crass, but there is considerable evidence that it is true. In a series of studies done by psychologist Solomon Asch, a significant number of people would deny their own perceptions of a geometric figure projected on a screen rather than disagree with a planted observer who intentionally lied about what he had seen. When there was more than one person disagreeing with them, an even larger number of individuals falsified their own observations to more closely align themselves with the distortions of others.[5] It seems that when we perceive ourselves to be part of a group, we have a strong urge to conform to what appears to be that group's norms—even if it means compromising our own beliefs.

Most people do not feel comfortable acting alone. If you can recognize the roles and patterns of group behavior, you can take advantage of such mental states. You can establish a learning environment that harmonizes with the natural behavior of the group to create a learning situation that leads to positive change. If you are unaware of a group's dynamics or intentionally at odds with it, you court friction, resistance, confrontation, and, ultimately, the likelihood that little will be learned.

Summary

In this chapter we looked at the trainee, both as an individual and as part of a group. We began with the realization that, while you, as a trainer, are a change agent, the changes you can bring about are largely limited to the skills you can train others to perform. In doing so, you are likely to face resistance because most people prefer to do things the way they've always done them. Resistance can take many forms, but it stems from seven basic causes, each of which you should recognize and deal with. Once you have uncovered the cause of resistance to change, you can eliminate it by ventilating the resister's need and motivating the learner toward a desired change in behavior. To deal with resistance, you must create an open environment that is conducive to the ventilation and discussion of the problem. To accomplish this, you must be aware of, and structure your learning sessions around, the psychological principles of adult learning. These principles are Thorndike's three laws: the law of readiness, which states that people can learn only what they are ready to learn; the law of effect, which says that succeeding at a task motivates people to work still harder; and the law of exercise, which demands that people practice what they've learned. These laws brought us to the ten principles of adult learning, which provide the basic framework for all training. We also covered in some detail how to create learning environments that use these fundamentals, particularly in handling resistance, using multisensory approaches, building conceptual bridges between old and new material, and handling individual differences among trainees.

To apply these principles to your training programs, you must recognize the needs of the group you are training. We examined ways of analyzing trainees to discover what they already know and what they need to know. Lastly, one of the vital aspects of understanding your trainees is recognizing the interactions of groups. We looked at group behavior and norms, and saw how groups handle change. We also outlined the roles that emerge in most groups, and concluded the chapter with comments on using group dynamics to foster an effective learning situation.

Applications

1. Review each of the ten principles of adult learning. As you consider each one, think of an instance or situation from your own past learning experiences that involved that principle.
   - What role did the principle of learning play in this situation?
   - Was the siuation a positive instance of the principle?
   - How did the principle of learning help you to learn (or teach)?
   - Was it a negative example?
   - In what way or ways was the principle of learning violated or ignored?

2. Review the seven sources of resistance. Focus on a training situation that you are currently facing (or are about to face). For each of the seven forms of resistance, devise a strategy for responding positively to it in your training situation. Write each strategy down. Refine it and refer back to it whenever you are faced with a resistant situation.

3. Select a training situation. Write down the answers to the three identifying questons:
   - What do the trainees know about the subject?
   - What do they want to know?
   - What do they need to know?

Answer in detail. Answering these questions will focus your training and ensure that it satisfies a job-related need.

Chapter 2
The Structure of Training

WE have examined what the role of training is in the organization. We've looked at the aspects common to most trainee groups. We've studied the basic principles of learning, and stressed how whom you teach is more important than what you teach. Now it is time to turn to content, and discuss how to prepare and structure training.

Training Objectives

The single most important action for a trainer is to set clear, action-oriented objectives. Once you've defined the learning population and established the present level of performance, you must decide where you want to go, that is, what change you want to bring about. Your objectives will govern what you teach and how you teach it, how that training is evaluated, and how management will ultimately gauge your success. Clear objectives are the bedrock of good training. Training cannot be effective without clearly defined and specific objectives.

The Distinction Between Management Goals and Training Objectives

First, let's distinguish between management goals and training objectives. A management goal is a statement of purpose. It names targets and acts as a guide in efforts to hit those targets. It is an informed estimate of future necessary performance levels. It is an extremely effective tool but is limited to describing end results, not the specific skills used to achieve them, nor any of the means toward those ends.

A training objective, on the other hand, is both means and end. It states the end results (not of training, but of learning) by specifying what skill must be learned, how it will be taught, and how the learning will be evaluated. Because it describes the means, the end, and the evaluative feedback, the training objective is your single most important tool in training. Attaining your training objectives helps you to reach your management goals, so training objectives may be seen as a subset, a series of intermediate accomplishments that will contribute to the overall attainment of the larger management goals. Each time you meet a training objective you've taken a step toward attaining management's goals.

Criteria for Objectives

To be effective, a training objective needs to meet five criteria:

1. The objective must describe an action the trainee will perform.
2. The action must be stated specifically and in detail.
3. The action must be measurable (observable).*
4. The action must be realistic.
5. The action must be given a time frame for completion.

An easy way to remember these five criteria is to arrange them into an acronym:

Specific
Measurable (observable)
Action performed by the trainee
Realistic
Time frame

Let's look at each of these.

Specific Action. New trainers often fail to pin down the specific action in an objective. *The trainee will be able to operate the machine* is too general. It is much more effective to say *the trainee will perform the following tasks on the machine.* The objective is focused on the specific results to be accomplished, not on weak generalizations.

This approach is particularly effective when there are special conditions under which the tasks must be performed. In Coast Guard training, for instance, certain tasks must be completed under gale-force winds, in driving rain with lim-

---

*Measurable is the more frequently used term in defining objectives. However, many of the skills that you will be teaching are not really measurable (such as proper handling of tools or effective interaction with customers), so the author prefers *observable* as a more accurate term.

ited visibility, and on a pitching deck. It isn't enough to mention that special conditions may interfere with doing the tasks. In such cases, list the conditions as part of the objective.

If your training lesson is informational rather than strictly skill-oriented, then state your objectives in terms of grades on tests.

> The trainee will pass a final test with a grade of *x* or better.

Passing the test is not enough; the objective should point to exact performance. Whenever possible, quantify the objective:

> Trainee will perform XYZ within a 3 percent tolerance for error . . . with a 16 percent reduction in scrap.

> Trainee will perform eight tasks in running sequence with no errors in an allotted 4½-minute time span under full open-factory floor conditions.

Notice that when the conditions and criteria are spelled out carefully, the objective leaps into clear focus. Clear objectives give direction to the learners, the trainer, and management. They are businesslike because they are specific and action-oriented. They are professional because stating a clear objective demands results.

Measurable (Observable) Action. There are common words that we believe we know the meaning of and assume that the people we talk to understand. We are right in both cases. The problem is the other people understand the word differently than we do and so they (and we) become confused or misled. These words are simply too abstract for everyone to share the same meaning. Such words frequently pop up in poorly phrased training objectives. Probably the worst are *understand, know,* and *feel,* as in "The trainees will be able to understand the XYZ . . ." or "The trainee will know how to . . ." or "The trainees will feel better about. . . ." Such words tell us nothing. They are too abstract. A word like *understand* means different things to different people, and besides, there is no way to really *know* that they understand except to test for understanding. In that case, the objective verb should be *demonstrate* or *show* an understanding by *passing* the test.

The verb that drives an objective needs not only to describe a specific action but to be evaluable in some way as well, either by measurement or observation. "Knowing" and "understanding" are things that happen in the head. They are private. No trainer can see them happening. What a trainer can observe is behavior that indicates knowledge or understanding. The objective, therefore, must describe the behavior by which the trainer will recognize that the trainees have learned.

Avoiding nonmeasurable words is quite easy, fortunately. Ask yourself, *Is this measurable or observable? How will I know they've learned?* If the answer isn't expressed by the verb you've used, change it until you get one that tells you just how you'll know they've learned. When you do this, you will find that every objective contains the method for evaluating the training. Each such training objective not only sets the goal, it also suggests how to reach it and how to measure whether or not it has been achieved.

Evaluable Verbs for Writing Training Objectives

compare	explain	program
create	identify	show
defend	list	solve
demonstrate	make	state
describe	perform	use
discriminate	present	utilize

Trainee Action. I have seen objectives such as "I will teach the trainee to . . ." or "I will communicate the X principles of . . ." or "The trainer will instruct the trainees . . ." These are descriptions of what the *trainer* plans to do. They describe teaching, not learning. Trainers can teach perfectly, yet trainees might not learn, and so the objectives aren't met because learning has failed to take place. Indeed, this is what often happens in our public schools. Students are taught at, rather than taught with.

The company hires a trainer to achieve a change in work behavior. It is concerned about the ultimate change, not what the trainer does to bring it about (within reason, of course). An objective that states what the trainer plans to do is beside the point and of no interest to management. What the trainees will be able to do is the point, and it should be stated as the training objective.

The easiest way to write a trainee-oriented objective is to ask yourself, "If I teach them XYZ, what will they be able to do with it?" Concentrate on the verb that describes what they will be able to do, then construct a sentence or group of sentences that states clearly the objective using the verb you've selected.

Here are some examples:

The trainee will be able to perform ————————————————.
The trainee will be able to build ————————————————.
The trainee will be able to describe ————————————————.
The trainee will be able to measure ————————————————.

Note that these are actions that the trainee will have to learn to perform. They are not descriptions of the trainer's activity during the lesson.

Note also that the phrase *The trainee will be able to* . . . gets very repetitive when written out like this. The accepted format is to write it only once at the beginning and then list all of the things the trainees will be able to do. So the above list would look like this.

At the completion of this training, the trainee will be able to:

> *perform* _____.
> *build* _____.
> *describe* _____.
> *measure* _____.

Realistic Action. Sometimes trainers set goals that are desirable but beyond the capacity of the learners to master in the available time. You build in frustration with an unrealistic objective, and with frequent frustration comes despair. So, in addition to describing a specific action, in evaluable terms, the objective must also be attainable.

Time Frame. No objective is meaningful without a time frame. If you want trainees to learn how to operate a vehicle properly and safely, you cannot wait forever for them to learn. You must say at what point you will test them to see whether or not they can indeed perform the skills you've taught. If it takes them years to learn, you most likely will have failed to meet your commitment to management to create a meaningful change in trainee behavior. If you can get them to change—that is, to drive the vehicle correctly—in one three-hour lesson, then you will have met your goal. You need to specify in what time frame you expect them to learn the skill.

In summary, then, to ensure that your objective meets the criteria stated earlier, answer the following questions:

- How will trainees be able to use what I have taught?
- What verb precisely describes this action?
- Does the verb clearly state what the trainees will do?
- What simple sentence can describe the desired result?
- Does this sentence describe the specific activity and the conditions under which it must take place?
- Does the sentence clearly state the time by which the trainee must be able to perform the task?
- Is the means of evaluation implicit in this statement?
- Does the statement ask for realistic action? Can the objectives be met in the given time?

Measuring Affective Learning

So far we have been dealing with cognitive learning, that is, specific skills. Objectives for this learning tell us what tasks the trainees will know how to do. But there is another very important type of training objectives. These describe the attitudes we want from our trainees. They are called affective objectives. We are often asked to change both skills and attitudes. As will be seen in this chapter and Chapter 3, you need to influence the attitude of your trainees to ensure their participation in the learning process. Objectives to describe affective learning are more abstract. You must decide how you want your trainees to feel as well as how you want them to think and act.

Your problem with affective objectives is that feelings are not specific and measurable. Yet you must try for as much precision as possible. Fortunately, feelings usually lead to actions. By specifying and quantifying the actions to observe, you can evaluate affective learning. Observable types of actions that indicate attitudes include:

- Absenteeism
- Lateness
- Cleanliness in the workplace
- Frequency of confrontational situations
- Employee turnover rates
- Customer complaints
- Scrap rates
- Safety records
- Sales figures
- Service calls
- Numbers participating in company-sponsored community events
- Numbers participating in voluntary company programs

These and many more actions are legitimate means for evaluating employee attitude. Even simply asking trainees to explain the importance of learning a particular skill or procedure is asking them to make a commitment and thus express an attitude toward that learning. One observable indicator of an attitude shift is the willingness or confidence with which trainees approach a newly learned task. Another is the degree of self-empowerment they display in using their new learning on the job. Attitudes are evaluable when objectives are tied to specific, observable behavior. The key to framing affective learning objectives then is to define observable behaviors that, when the trainees perform them, will let you know how they feel about what they are learning or have learned.

Learning Patterns

We think in chronological patterns largely because we have been trained to do so from early childhood. As soon as we begin to read we get locked into a linear pattern as well. In Western culture, printing goes from left to right, from top to bottom, in numbered sequence. The pattern becomes second nature, and since much of what we learn is through reading, we tend to think in that same linear pattern. So when it comes to training others, we find it natural to follow a linear, chronological approach. This is not always the best way to communicate a subject, however. In fact, it is frequently the worst way.

Once you have set your objectives, decide on the most effective structure for achieving those objectives. Because you know your subject, you will likely think of *what* you are going to teach first. As we've just observed, don't slip thoughtlessly into a chronological pattern. The chronological approach is dull. It is common in novels and movies and on television, but these have been shaped to contain an element of suspense. Also, reality is compressed so you see only key, exciting parts. An unedited documentary is as lengthy and dull as life on a boring day. As a trainer you want to create an environment that makes learning easy, motivates the trainees, and involves them in the subject. Without suspense or condensing, a chronological pattern is demotivating and makes learning difficult.

Training Patterns

1. *Funnel.* From broad concepts to specific skills.
2. *Inverted funnel.* From specific skills to broad concepts.
3. *Tunnel.* Steady presentation of topics, needs strong substructure.
4. *Spool.* From initial concepts to specific skills back to broad concepts.

There are four basic patterns for presenting information: the funnel, the inverted funnel, the tunnel, and the spool. Try each one until you find the method that best suits your trainees, your subject, and your objectives. You are, in effect, creating a pattern for learning—a structure around which you will mold or model the content of your lesson.

Funnel Pattern

With the funnel pattern, you start with a broad concept and narrow it down until you are teaching the step-by-step how-to's of the subject. The effect is like a funnel, hence the name (see Figure 2-1).

For example, this is the overall structure of this book. We look first at the concepts—the whys of the topic—then proceed to the specifics. We follow this pattern when we learn from experience. It is the way we solve problems; design houses, clothing, and cars; make friends; and learn informally. Our interest is

Figure 2-1. Model of funnel training pattern.

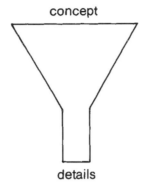

aroused by the concept of an idea, then we apply it to our specifics. It is the pattern of deductive reasoning.

Inverted Funnel Pattern

In the inverted funnel, you start with details and move gradually to the broad concept (see Figure 2-2). The inverted funnel is the pattern of traditional education. We begin with the ABC's and simple arithmetic and, as we gain proficiency, expand our understanding and tackle novels and essays, quantum mechanics and relative field theory. Or we learn the actual events of history, and, as we begin to understand them, we move on to why they happened and how one thing leads to another. The inverted funnel is the traditional approach to skills training, too.

Figure 2-2. Model of inverted funnel training pattern.

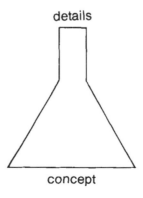

It is the way we learn music, math, and motor mechanics. We start with the parts, then gradually work up to the whole. This is the pattern of inductive reasoning.

Tunnel Pattern

The third pattern is the tunnel. As its name suggests, this method is a straight progression. In effect it is a linear arrangement of information (see Figure 2-3).

We travel in a linear sequence. We view our lives in a linear way. We move from point A to point B as directly as possible. It is how we read. Computer programming is usually taught in a linear pattern. Following a recipe is a matter of moving from one step to the next. Concepts are either ignored or incidental. It is the movement through the time frame or sequence that is the vital activity.

We have all had the experience of little children on a long car trip, either as parents, relatives, friends, or as children ourselves. What do all children begin to say fifteen minutes into the journey? "Are we there yet?" Straight chronological or sequential linear progressive experience is inherently demotivational. Be very careful when you use the tunnel format to maintain interest in the material.

Figure 2-3. Model of tunnel training pattern.

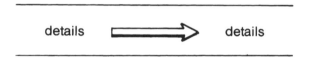

Spool Pattern

Each of these patterns has its application and you must decide which works for your group, your material, and your objective. For mastery of practical skills, the tunnel is likely to be efficient, if you maintain interest. If you are developing long-range planning abilities—for example, progressive management skills for future senior executives—the inverted funnel provides a growing sequence of challenges. The problem with these patterns, however, is that with the tunnel there is no motivation unless it's brought in by the learner, while with the inverted funnel all the motivation is in the later phases. Anyone who has ever taken lessons on a musical instrument knows the drudgery of the early lessons. Only the funnel method grabs the learner's mind at the start. It is most effective for creating a want-to-learn atmosphere.

As has been stressed throughout this book, you always need a want-to-learn atmosphere. It is inherent in any good training environment. The more appealing the learning, the more effective it will be. The ideal structure is a combination of the three, which I call the spool pattern (see Figure 2-4).

With the spool pattern, the learner is grabbed instantly by the concepts, then learns the application of those concepts to reach a new threshold of yet broader concepts. Whenever possible, make the spool your basic approach.

Figure 2-4. Model of spool training pattern.

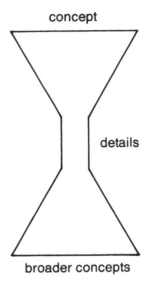

Using the Learning Patterns

Ultimately, you will choose an approach that opens with the initial funnel and motivates the trainee with a concept. You'll create bridges from what is already known to the new concept and then from the concept to specific skills. You'll break the skills into steps so learners can look back at the progress they've made. You'll challenge them with new ideas, and interweave concepts with skills at appropriate levels so that mastery of both the skills and the concepts produces independence and self-direction.

Recent neurological research has discovered that tiny infants are able to discern patterns to be distinct from the backgrounds on which such patterns are presented to them.[1] This seems to verify what many psychologists have long believed: that we perceive things by bringing them into the focus of our attention, which makes them distinct from the background information that surrounds them. This is referred to as distinguishing the figure against the ground. It means that we learn things by first isolating them and then making sense of them in terms of the unique mental background that each of us brings to learning.

There are six logical patterns in which you can present information in order to take advantage of this learning or perceiving behavior. From most powerful (that is, closest to the way we perceive) to least powerful they are:

1. Contrast
2. Problem/solution
3. Cause and effect
4. Anecdotal
5. Logical sequence
6. Chronological sequence

Let's look at each one in turn.

Contrast

Placing one idea or step or artifact in contrast to another very closely parallels the way we think. So, when you present material in which some elements are contrasted with others or compared to them, your learners will instantly grasp the relationship. It will come naturally to them. Any contrast will do: right/wrong, light/dark, front/back, left/right, or before/after. You see how familiar the pattern is to us.

Problem/Solution

This is a special, powerful variation on the contrast pattern. Few things motivate people more than tackling and solving problems. This format is one of the best for establishing concepts and setting a tone or environment for your training. Pose a problem and let the discussion lead to its solution, or present the training as an answer to a company problem. The closer you make the problem come to the trainees' personal needs, the more effective this format will be.

Cause and Effect

Another compelling variation on contrast is cause and effect. People do not learn in a void. Cause-and-effect relationships are strong bridges between the known and unknown and between concepts and practices. They provide a rationale for learning. They are particularly effective because the cause-and-effect relationship of a known example can be paralleled with an unknown case to clarify it. As with problem/solution and simple contrast, this is a dynamic form. Usually a cause-and-effect relationship is more memorable than the parts separately, because that relationship is an action and engages the learner's mind. Finally, a cause-and-effect relationship can be verified—put to the test—so trainees learn by doing and seeing the outcome.

Anecdotal

Everyone loves a story, and every culture is built on myths and stories. Simple chronology tends to be monotonous. Adding an anecdotal structure with a beginning and middle leading to a climax and denouement creates interest in the chronological format. The Judeo-Christian heritage is built upon parables and life histories from which we draw lessons. So are the ethical and moral teachings of all of our predecessors and contemporaries. Most moral training is through parables, fables, myths, or legends. Work them into your training. This is why case histories work. Parables, personal histories, war stories, and tales of the trail all serve to enlighten and enlarge us conceptually.

You can also use the literary device of allegory to develop a concept, endow it with symbolic names and characters, and then wander through a series of symbolic places to prove your point. People learn from such allegories and find them generally more interesting (and therefore easier to learn) than a dry recital of the facts themselves. When you need to work in concepts, use stories. They can be used to combine other relationships or patterns. A mystery is always fun—and effective. A joke (cause-and-effect relationship) is often dramatically effective for getting a point across. A case history transforms concepts into practical applications. Use stories, parables, and anecdotes to make your point memorable.

Logical Sequence

Another way to build mental bridges between the known and unknown is to create logical relationships between the elements. Both the funnel and the inverted funnel are classic patterns of logic. Other patterns may be combined to enhance and enliven your lessons. For instance, use a series of problems and solutions to lead the group to inductively or deductively find the solution to a much larger problem. Learning is exciting when logic is exercised.

A very effective logical structure is the topical pattern, which is simply a sequence of topics in some sort of order. Frequently the topics you need to cover are unrelated, which makes them hard to learn. If you have several only loosely related topics, look for—or create—similarities among them or link them by structure (such as stories or cause and effect). Acronyms are excellent. For instance, the five elements of a good training objective are made memorable with the word SMART. If the first letters of your elements don't make a word, create a sentence with them to make the sequence more interesting and the elements more memorable. For instance, those elements of good objectives could also be remembered as:

Sweet
Maiden
Aunts
Rarely
Tipple

The key here is *less is more,* one of the ten principles for learning (see Chapter 1). Simplify. The more a learner thinks there is to learn, the harder it is to learn it. It all seems overwhelming. Break up your material into consumable chunks. For instance, twenty-four steps for doing a particular task are very hard to remember; on the other hand, four steps, each with six substeps, are easier to remember and look far less intimidating. The more concentrated or complex the material, the more you should follow the *less is more* principle.

A common logical arrangement is based on spatial relationships. You can organize your material in such a way as to work with the physical relationships of articles in a given space, for example, the room in which you are teaching. This method is excellent when your materials can be flowcharted or explained with large diagrams that let you walk from Point A to Point B. Charts, graphs, layouts, and models are excellent for this.

Chronological Sequence

The straightforward chronological approach has already been discussed. It is useful only when you can create some sort of suspense using the other structural

---

Structural Planning

1. Choose the overall structure best suited to:
   - Your trainees
   - Your objectives
   - Your material
2. Choose a substructure that will engage trainee performance.
3. Choose substructures that build bridges from the known concept to the needed skill.
4. Structure learning plateaus that enable you to measure progress.
5. Keep in mind that the end result is to produce mastery and self-direction, and choose structures accordingly.

---

tools. It is probably inescapable when an exact step-by-step sequence must be followed, as in teaching complex computer programming. Counter its limitations by frequently using problem/solution, cause and effect, and anecdotes to break the monotony. By incorporating other structures to keep it lively, you can use the chronological format to great effect when it suits your group, your objectives, and your material.

Redundancy

Another structure essential to learning is repetition, or redundancy. In Chapter 1 we discussed briefly the effectiveness of oral behavior and its effect on our learning. We need now to take a more detailed look.

Human beings can talk. None of the animals around us seems to have the range, depth, or fluency of oral expression that we have. Many have surprisingly rich vocabularies, but none appears to have as many as the more than 250,000 words that humans have in just the English language. Even so, as we all know, it's not what you say but how you say it that gets meaning across.

When our power to communicate orally was combined with our ability to design and use tools that shape and control our environment, a written language developed. Then came printed language. Writing was a *time binder* that solved the problem of remembering. If people wrote it down, they would always have it. Printing was a *space binder* that gave that initial time-binding ability to everyone anywhere who could learn to read and write. Writing—and ultimately printing— changed people's lives and livelihoods in every culture that adopted them. They are still doing so.

Cultural anthropologists are exploring the changes that occur when a culture makes the transition from an oral pattern to a literate one. They have found many changes, including a decline in the credibility of the spoken word. People in a literate culture don't believe something until they see it in print, hence the need for written legal contracts and the power of the press. Another change is that listening attention spans shrink. Even as recently as one hundred years ago people in America would listen attentively to six hours of political debate. Today one hour seems far too long. Several radio stations have tried without success to revive old radio plays, but they find that their listeners today need visual stimulation, too. It is too hard today to listen attentively. A third change is a result of the increasing dependence on writing. People begin to revere the written word and use it as the final arbiter of truth. A fourth change is that the language shrinks. Poetic devices, colorful words, precise expression—all of these diminish in frequency in spoken language. Compare the crackling dialogue of Shakespeare's semiliterate society with that of our own more literate one. Speech loses mnemonic devices and parables, rhymes, strong metaphors, and richly descriptive adverbs and adjectives.

But these changes are not universal, nor are they evident in all facets of a culture. In several areas people retain their oral traditions. One such area is education. Any subject you wish to learn is available in books (including this one, of course). Yet thousands of people attend training seminars, many of which are largely talkfests. The public seminar business has become hugely successful in the United States and around the world. Despite strong leanings toward print, people still feel the need for oral stimulation when they wish to learn. Yet, nowadays people are less equipped to learn orally. They have shorter attention spans, weaker memories, and no ability to create their own rich metaphors that bridge the gap between the old and the new. They are used to passive entertainment, not active engagement. They like a good show but take little learning from it.

The trainer must compensate for culturally induced learner shortcomings by returning to some of the practices of oral culture. Redundancy is a key element in this return. In all myths and legends, the epic poems, and genealogies of peoples of ancient times, repetition of names, events, messages, and morals is central. In surviving oral cultures today, there are patterns of redundancy in rituals, dances, and songs, as well as in words and gestures. Anthropologists believe repetition enhances memory; it embeds learning in the subconscious. Therefore, repetition must become a part of any effective training lesson. Devise and use patterns of redundancy. They become the hooks on which to hang the memory.

Of course, repetition doesn't mean simply repeating things over and over. That shortens the attention span and dulls the mind. There is an old rule for effective public speaking: *Tell 'em what you're gonna tell 'em, tell 'em, and then tell 'em what you told 'em.* I like to shorten this to *Tell 'em³*. Metaphorically, it is telling them raised to the third power. As every math student knows, a number multiplied by itself three times is considerably larger than that same number multiplied by the number 3. The *Tell 'em³* rule calls for forecasting the material, covering the material, and reviewing the material. Each repetition takes a different form and serves a different purpose.

This is the recommended pattern for building redundancy into your lessons: forecast, teach, review. It is similar to old-fashioned writing drills in which you were asked to fill page after page with spirals. Learning progress is like that: two steps forward and one step backward. Several tools are available for creating redundancy. Any way you can cover the same material from different perspectives will enhance learning. What we are doing is using the multisensory principle of learning to lock in what has been taught with memory hooks provided by redundancy. Build redundant patterns into your content; relate each of the patterns to one of the principles of learning discussed in Chapter 1:

1. Share your training objectives with the learners before beginning.
2. Review the agenda with the group before beginning to teach.
3. Use a "kickoff" incident (for example, role-playing) to start a lesson, then refer back to it to draw out principles.
4. Assign material to be done and then go over it with the group.

5. Review what you have covered so far.
6. Summarize what has been taught.
7. Use visual aids (more than one where possible) to make your points clearer and to vary the presentation.
8. Devise practice sessions so trainees can apply what they have been taught.
9. Give both written and oral evaluations.
10. Administer tests and quizzes frequently.
11. Have refresher sessions.
12. Devise games in which material taught must be used to win.
13. Provide reading assignments that cover the same material from a different perspective.

Timing and Structure

There has long been controversy over whether first impressions (primacy) or most recent impressions (ultimacy) have the greater impact on an individual and are therefore more memorable. Currently, the consensus is that the first impression is stronger. In any event, both first and last impressions hold key positions for engaging the memory. One of your structural considerations, then, is the matter of primacy or ultimacy. Determine which key ideas need to be presented at points perceived to be starting places—first thing, first day, beginning of afternoon session, beginning of each day, and first session after each break. Remember that the first impression the learner receives will govern whether there is resistance to it and will also shape the learner's readiness to learn. Make those initial impressions highly memorable and influential. Give careful thought to how you will introduce topics. This means that your start-off positions should be keyed to a motivator. Examples of such motivators are:

- Demonstrations
- Stories
- Exercises
- Visual aids (e.g., films and charts)
- Projects
- Discussions
- Challenges

Or use other methods, as long as they engage the learners, have a degree of excitement (sales appeal), and set the stage for the material to come.

Timing also means making your strongest points first. There is an academic argument for approaching subjects chronologically and saving the big moment—for example, the solution to the problem—for last. But remember the *Tell 'em*[3]

Applying the Ten Principles of Learning to the Lesson Plan

1. *Readiness and resistance.* The preparation stage. Use funnel and inverted funnel patterns to structure the lesson. Ventilate resistance. Share objectives, use substructure formats to engage the learners.
2. *Active versus passive learning.* The practice stage. Set action-oriented, trainee-centered objectives for training. Use questions to introduce material. Include dynamic substructures (problems and solutions or cause and effect).
3. *Trial and error.* The practice and evaluation stages. Provide hands-on practice to reenforce learning and provide a means for evaluation.
4. *Association.* The preparation, presentation, and evaluation stages. Use questions to prepare learners and introduce material, repetition to reenforce learning, and practice sessions to provide a basis for evaluation.
5. *Multisensory input.* The presentation and practice stages. Use integrated Socratic method and lecture approach with audio and visual aids in patterns of redundancy.
6. *One thing at a time.* The four-step method is applied by topic for discrete time periods. Following the *less is more* principle, guard against information overload. Use acronyms, numbers, simplified chunks of topics, and patterns of redundancy.
7. *Understanding.* The preparation, presentation, practice, and evaluation stages. Set clearly defined, specific training objectives, which specify the level of understanding and learning you will demand. Use questions to prepare the group for learning. Following the *less is more* principle, introduce material in sequences. Use repetition to reenforce learning.
8. *Practice.* The practice stage. Set action-oriented, trainee-centered objectives. Use repetition to reenforce learning. Provide hands-on practice, simulations, and so forth.
9. *Feedback.* The practice and evaluation stages. Use questions, explain corrections, analyze errors, and provide learning maps.
10. *Uniqueness.* The preparation and practice stages. Use questions to bring out individual differences. Ventilate resistance. Engage the more advanced to help you work with those who need help. Use panels, projects, and special assignments.

---

format. Tell them what the exciting solution is at the beginning to grab their attention, then work through the problem in good order until you reach the solution again, this time in context. Because the final thing said is the second most memorable, repeat what you told them before. You'll begin by grabbing attention and end by reinforcing the concept. This way you will be taking advantage of both primacy and ultimacy.

Four Steps to a Good Lesson Plan

After setting your objectives, choosing your structure, building in patterns of redundancy, and taking advantage of the primacy-ultimacy phenomenon, you are ready to work on the specific content—the lesson plan itself.

Every learning sequence should be a separate lesson. It is usually convenient to break up the material into natural blocks of time, so each lesson corresponds to a time chunk, such as from the beginning of the day to the first break. The four-step lesson plan is the most effective method for structuring these blocks of time and topics. It is also the most effective format for ensuring that you provide sufficient opportunity for your trainees to practice their newly learned skills. The four steps are: preparation, presentation, practice, and evaluation. Let's look at each step.

Preparation

In the academic world, *preparation* refers to something the teacher does. Not so in training. Certainly the trainer also prepares, but in this book that activity is a learning one, not a teaching one, and as such it is part of the ten principles of learning discussed in Chapter 1. As mentioned in that earlier chapter, people cannot learn unless they are ready to learn. They must be prepared to learn—which is the meaning of the term *preparation* in the training context. The preparation you choose depends on your learners, your objectives, and your content. Even if the group is already motivated, their learning will be made easier, will be better focused, and will be more dynamic if you prepare them for it. If they are not motivated, the preparation will lay the groundwork for positive learning. Ways of handling the preparation stage are as follows:

1. *List the objectives to be learned.* When learners are already motivated and have come prepared to learn, this is an effective preparation. It puts the learning into perspective; it gives the learners a map to follow so they can build mental bridges for themselves between what they already know and what they will learn. In addition, it is the first part of the *Tell 'em³* formula.

2. *Ventilate resistance.* If you are concerned that there might be resistance to learning, it must be ventilated before learning can take place. Preparing them means getting rid of negative steam. Depending on what form the resistance takes, you can explain how they will benefit from the training and why they should learn. If the problem is lack of trust or misunderstanding, explain why

you are there by describing your purpose as you see it. If the group has a different assessment of the training, explain management's goals or redefine your goals.

If the resistance stems from a low tolerance for change, express confidence in the group and its ability to master the subject. Make it seem not hard at all. If there is a fear of losing face, again redefine the purposes to allow room for others to save face. If the problem is peer pressure, there is little you can do in this preparation phase. Allow group leaders to save face by keeping the options open.

Create a strong first impression with positive nonverbal behavior and enthusiasm. Make the surrounding environment attractive, and start your lesson with a "grabber."

3. *Ask challenging or engaging questions.* Start the group thinking and discussing. Good questions cause them to build mental bridges to the new material. They call for immediate active participation and help direct understanding. In addition, questions allow each participant to adjust uniquely to the learning environment.

4. *Administer a pretest.* Or have the group perform some skill (role-playing, for example). If you think some people feel they already know the material, the pretest tells them they don't know as much as they thought they did.

5. *Begin with an exercise or management game.* These games engage the group and create curiosity about what they are to learn. The activities are bridges made from common experience. They also foster group feelings early in the training. Furthermore, they can be fun; people love to play.

6. *Tell a story or set up a mystery.* Both draw people in, establish a common ground, and help to meld the trainees into a group. Of course, the story or mystery must make a point and must direct them to some element of the subject.

7. *Ask trainees for their objectives.* What would they like to gain from the session? This forces them to think about the program and to apply it to their unique situations. It also allows you to repeat your training objectives and to focus the group's attention on learning. Lastly, it provides them with a learning map of the course.

Presentation

There are two approaches to presenting information, each hundreds of years old. By far the most common was presented by seventeenth-century English philosopher John Locke, who described the mind as a tabula rasa, which means blank slate. In effect, the trainer assumes the learner knows nothing and proceeds to fill that mind with ideas and learning in much the same way one fills a chalkboard with writing or diagrams. The blank-slate approach assumes that the learner knows nothing and the trainer knows all and transmits the information to the learner, usually through words.

The other approach is called the Socratic method, after the fifth-century B.C. Greek philosopher Socrates, and made famous by the writings of his pupil Plato. Socrates didn't define his method, but Plato illustrated it by reporting the learning dialogues in which Socrates engaged. Socrates never voiced a point of view but, rather, challenged learners by asking them questions. The dialogue led the learner to discover for himself the truth that Socrates was teaching. The Socratic method assumes that the learner knows a great deal and can be guided by questioning to reach new understandings.

If we examine each approach in the light of the ten principles of learning (see Chapter 1) it is obvious that the Socratic method engages far more of them than does the blank-slate method. It is, therefore, the more effective approach to learning. Yet it is much less common. This is because when we are asked to *teach* someone, our first approach is simply to tell what we know. Leading a person to information through questioning is much more demanding. Besides, if a learner doesn't know the subject, how can he or she answer questions about it? We trust ourselves to know the material, but it is very hard to trust others to know it, especially when we assume that because they are in training they need to learn. Furthermore, the bulk of our own education came to us by the blank-slate method, which makes it seem the natural way to teach.

We will discuss other benefits of the Socratic method and illustrate how to structure Socratic interactions in Chapter 3 when we discuss leadership. For now, it is important to recognize that, despite the effectiveness of the Socratic method, both approaches are usually necessary. In highly technical fields learners cannot know what has not been explained to them, though even with this type of training the more Socratic you can be, the better the learning. A blending of active participation (Socratic) with passive absorption of information (blank slate) will likely constitute the presentation stage of your lesson. Therefore, plan the method(s) you will use to inform or lead your trainees to the learning you've defined in your objectives. You might use any of the following:

- Socratic method of posing questions and leading group members to reach their own conclusions.
- Straight lecture (remember that the average adult attention span is less than twenty minutes—keep it short).
- Participative lecture, wherein you create dialogue and perhaps physical activities as you go along.
- Panel discussion, using the best informed of your learners.
- Film, video, slides, or audiotapes.
- Stories, games, and exercises to vary the presentation.
- Demonstration or simulation to illustrate the practical application of concepts.

In using any of these, remember: less is more, one thing at a time, and association. Build bridges for their understanding to cross to new knowledge.

Practice

People learn by doing. All the instruction in the world will not lock in learning. Only practice makes learning happen. Consequently, to teach only content, no matter how skillfully, is to waste your time unless you also structure in practice. Hands-on experience is the best way to learn, so help them by creating chances to practice.

Every lesson must include time for practice. We are all pressured to complete training in as short a time as possible. But if you offer only content (which many public seminars do), you lessen your effectiveness, deprive your trainees of the opportunity to really learn, and fail to bring about the changes you have been hired to achieve. Without the practice stage, training becomes a pleasant and interesting way to pass the time, but nothing more.

There are many ways to challenge your group to practice. Among them are:

- Socratic reviews
- Written exams
- Oral tests
- Role playing
- Problem-solving exercises
- Case histories
- Projects and assignments
- Simulations
- Hands-on practice sessions and practice under simulated conditions

All of these methods (detailed in Chapter 5) allow learners to practice what has just been taught. Whichever method you choose, carefully relate the activity to the skills. If you demand too little, you demotivate and hinder learning. If you demand too much, you frustrate and discourage. If mastery of the skill is a requirement of the training, then more practice is needed. If, on the other hand, trainees are expected to perfect their skills in the field, then the practice phase should merely introduce the new skills and provide a chance to try them out. It should allow you to gauge whether or not they can at least perform the task before they leave your supervision.

Evaluation

Your objectives will have stated what level of learning is needed and how it will be evaluated. We will cover specific methods of evaluation in Chapter 5. Do recognize, however, that we are talking about evaluation, not grading. Evaluation is detailed feedback to the trainee to help him or her measure progress. Grading is largely an administrative and, secondly, a competitive instrument useful for

---

A Service Staff Sample Lesson Plan

Population:	Thirty-five customer service operators (interested but resistant to change)
Duration:	2½ hours
Topic:	Proper telephone response
Objectives:	Upon completion of this lesson trainees will be able to:

- Define their own need to change their telephone responses.
- Describe the four characteristics of professionalism on the telephone.
- Create a telephone log.
- Diagnose their own key problem calls from that log.
- Script a response to each of the types of calls they receive.

Preparation 9:00 9:45:	1. Ventilate resistance by explaining that the session is a chance to self-evaluate and polish personal skills. The instructor's role is merely to provide a set of critical standards for professionalism.
	2. Assign participants to list two things they hate that customers do on the phone.
	3. Debrief with volunteers and solve sample problems as they are described.
	4. Conclude with overhead projection on human relations and the need to change. Discuss.

       Give people what they want and they will give you what you want.
          But the order is crucial.
          First you must give.
          Most of us turn this around and say, *If only they would . . . then I could . . .*
       . Illustrate with examples from their problems.

(continues)

A Service Staff Sample Lesson Plan (continued)

5. Ask:
   - *Why do we do this?*
   - *What makes us want the other person to change rather than ourselves?*
   - *How many of us know someone who engages in self-destructive or harmful activity, knows it, and yet continues to do so?*

   Discuss bad habits like smoking, drinking, and overeating.

   Conclude that we fear the unknown and prefer to live and work in our personal comfort zones even when they are bad for us. We hate to change!

6. Discuss the hypothetical situation of a job where the employees hate the boss, and discuss Socratically the three changeable variables: situation, yourself, other person.

7. Ask for conclusion: The trainees must change to get the callers to change.

Presentation 9:45–10:30:

1. On flip chart (refer them to page in workbook):
   A. Introduce the four aspects that define professionalism.
      (1) Knowing what to do, when to do it, and how to do it
      (2) Remaining unflappable
      (3) Desiring to take on the challenge
      (4) Making it seem easy
   B. Draw each of the principles out through examples, stories, and Socratic questions.

2. Explain that these are the agenda for the course and that the rest of the morning will be spent on What/When/How.

3. Turn to page in workbook and project it overhead to describe a telephone log and its uses.

4. Assign the log for two weeks and describe how to use the data collected to prioritize calls and troubleshoot calls.

5. Describe steps to creating an effective telephone script using the workbook page and an overhead projection.
   A. Using the telephone log, rank in order your most frequent calls from most to least.
   B. Take one of these types of calls each week and think about it. Discuss it with friends, your supervisor, and coworkers. Talk about what to say and do differently in order to make this type of call better and easier.
   C. Decide on the best way to handle this type of call. Finalize it. Write it down and keep it in front of you when you are on the phone. Use it every time one of these types of calls comes in (or has to be made).
   D. Do this for each type of call on your list.

   Ask: *If you have ten different types of calls and you solve one each week, what will you be at the end of ten weeks?*

   Answer: *A professional on the phone!*

Practice 10:30–11:00:	Assign groups of five to discuss their problem calls and then select two problems to solve as a group. The trainees should write a script using the morning's lesson as a model.
Evaluation 11:00–11:30:	Ask each group to role-play one of its solutions. Working with the entire class, work through the solution. Everyone helps to critique and fine-tune each group's efforts.

---

screening people. Grading in the business world may be used for assessing training among fast-tracking executives or for selecting new employees. It is a legitimate function of some training; however, it is not essential to learning. Evaluation, however, is an integral part of learning. People must know how they are doing. Evaluation capitalizes on the law of effect by providing feedback, by fostering a nonthreatening climate in which error can occur, by addressing each learner individually, and by providing, in retrospect, a clear map of what has been learned. Evaluation is vital to all levels of understanding.

Evaluation is frequently not a separate step and is often integrated into the practice step. But it must be planned for, so it is included here as a separate step of lesson planning.

Some ways to create opportunities for evaluation are:

- Socratic dialogue
- Written or oral responses to projects
- Tests (written or oral)
- Problem-solving projects
- Practice in simulated circumstances
- Case histories
- Role playing and other performances
- Hands-on practice sessions
- On-the-job training
- Personal counseling

The four parts to a lesson plan are integral. Once you have broken down the material you are going to teach into individual units of instruction (using the *less is more* principle to divide your subject into topical units), each unit should have all four steps. Create a preparation session, a presentation phase, a practice session, and an outline of how you will evaluate each topical/instructional unit. If each step is complete, you will be presenting your material in the most effective manner possible. It will be harder for your trainees to not learn than to learn.

Summary

This chapter was about planning an effective lesson. We began with the single most important step in training: writing the training objectives. It was pointed out that an objective is not so much a statement of desired results as it is a map of how to achieve them. A training objective has five components:

1. It must describe what skills the trainees will be able to perform.
2. It must be specific in describing those skills and the conditions under which they are to be performed.
3. It must detail criteria to be met or specify how the trainees will be evaluated.
4. It must be realistic.
5. It must demand a specific time frame.

Two types of objectives were discussed: cognitive and affective. Though affective learning is much harder to measure, the same format for objectives applies. The measure of performance, however, becomes more subjective.

Once you have defined your objectives, structure becomes more important than content. There are several ways of structuring learning. The way you choose will depend on who you are training, what your objectives are, and what it is you are teaching.

The basic structures are: a funnel, an inverted funnel, a tunnel, and a spool. These are given life by dynamic substructures, such as: contrast, problem/solution, cause and effect, anecdotal, and logical and time sequences. The patterns of redundancy were discussed, including how to build such necessary repetition into your lessons. Timing, or when to teach your most important material, was explored within the concepts of primacy and ultimacy. We also looked at the *less is more* concept as a means of simplifying complex material.

We concluded the chapter with the four steps of a good lesson plan. You must prepare the trainees to learn, present the material, give them an opportunity to practice it, and provide evaluation (feedback) for them. With all of these elements of structure weighed and incorporated, and using the four-step method as your guide, you are ready to write your training program, which will be covered in Chapter 7.

Applications

1. Draw up a list of things that you want to teach in a lesson you are planning to give. Write them out in the form of training objectives. Use the SMART format and the formula *"Upon completion of this lesson the trainees will be able to. . . ."* Be careful to express these objectives using verbs that describe actions the trainees will have to perform. When you have completed the list, compare them with the samples beginning on page 31.

2. Select the first objective on your list. Describe in writing how you could present this material using a contrast format. Now, how could you use a problem/solution format? Alternatively, how would this material be presented as cause and effect? As a different approach, create a story that would introduce and illustrate this topic. Finally, think of a logical order for the material. Use *less is more* to condense and pattern it.

3. Using the objectives you've created in application 1, write a lesson plan. Describe how you will prepare the learners to learn, how you will present the materials, how and when they will practice what you have taught, and, finally, how you plan to evaluate the learning. Follow the format and style of the sample lesson plan on pages 49–51.

Chapter 3
The Role of the Trainer

AS we saw in Chapter 1, leadership arises naturally in any group. Because people perceive the start of a training session as a formal, institutional situation that involves some structured activity, all of their expectations demand an authority figure. That authority figure will tell them what to do, where to begin, what they will learn, and how they will proceed. People need someone onto whom they can shift responsibility for the training. In an institutional situation, people choose someone to be the leader and to assume responsibility.

Psychologists have discovered that if no one assumes the authority, the group selects someone and gives the power to that person. If you do not assume the leadership role, someone else will and your training will be undermined.

We are not talking here of autocratic leadership. The point is that trainees come expecting to be taught, that is, to be told what to do and how to do it. If you fail to fulfill that expectation, you will be alienated from the group, leaving a vacuum to be filled by someone who possibly has come to the session reluctantly or who shows great resistance. It is an invitation to mischief. I cannot stress enough how important, indeed how vital, it is to accept the mantle of leadership from the very first moment.

Leadership Roles

There are a number of ways for a trainer to assume the role of leader. This chapter is about how to accomplish that. To begin, consider the ten roles of a leader:

1. Setting the agenda and keeping track of time
2. Maintaining training objectives
3. Protecting the rights of all participants
4. Listening

5. Summarizing the material
6. Reviewing
7. Focusing the attention of the group
8. Handling challenges to your authority
9. Involving silent members
10. Providing a modus operandi

Let's examine the impact of each of these functions on your training.

Agenda

One of the responsibilities that trainees push onto the trainer is determining what will be covered and when. Time after time I've observed trainees in great discomfort while they wait for the trainer to call a break. It is your function as leader to set the agenda for learning and to conclude learning at appropriate times.

To assume leadership by setting an agenda, follow the full instructions and considerations discussed in Chapter 7. Write your training objectives, structure your lessons following the patterns described in Chapter 2, and use the four steps of preparation, presentation, practice, and evaluation. Also consider time; remember that attention spans are relatively short. Shift your methodology at least once every half hour. Whenever possible, schedule a practice session at least once an hour, more often if possible.

Make sure there are numerous, regular breaks. If you have a lengthy lecture (more than ten or fifteen minutes) or discussion session, plan on frequent short breaks. If you have a balanced presentation of discussion, lecture, practice session, and so forth, fewer breaks are necessary. You are in charge of the time and the topic.

Objectives

A good trainer keeps the course on track. Be on guard for both external and internal distractions. Outside distractions are the reason most good training rooms are windowless. Spectacular scenery can be very distracting. So can the activities of grounds personnel, animals, lovers, and passing traffic. If your training area has windows, arrange the seating so trainees face away from the action outside.

Internal distractions can be very frustrating, too. I once had to conduct a public seminar in a hotel room that remained below 40°F. Needless to say, learning was minimal. We had to take breaks every fifteen minutes just to warm up. Of course the hotel finally provided a better room, but the damage was already done.

Poor seating, inadequate lighting, uncomfortable temperature, poor visibility, noise, interruptions, and smoking are all conditions you need to protect your trainees from in order to maintain a clear focus on the subject being taught. These issues are discussed further in Chapter 11. In this context, however, review the following list of potential distractions.

- *Seating.* Is it comfortable?
- *Lighting.* Is it too dim? Is it too bright?
- *Temperature.* Is the room too warm? Is it too cold?
- *Sightlines.* Can everyone see you? Can they all see your charts and other visual aids?
- *Messages.* Is there a system for handling them without interrupting the class?
- *Smoking.* Make rules about when, where, and whether smoking is allowed.
- *Breaks.* Schedule at least one every ninety minutes.
- *Windows.* Cover them, close blinds, or arrange seating to minimize distractions.

In addition to physical distractions, there are other ways your teaching objectives can be waylaid. Many times you will have garrulous participants who try to share too many, often irrelevant, tales. These tales take the group away from the main point. Curb these asides and bring the group back on track. You might get a participant who has a hidden personal agenda—someone who tries to challenge your leadership or distract the class with humor, practical jokes, or questions. Deal effectively and quickly with such people and get back to your objective. (Handling such participants is discussed in detail later in this chapter.)

When a discussion gets going, it's often hard to stop. But if the discussion sidetracks, you need to intervene and get things back on course. This is especially so when an argument develops between participants. To handle such an event, choose the most appropriate action, as follows:

- Intervene aggressively by interrupting the discussion and preventing further debate (or comments).
- Offer to discuss or solve the problem at the break.
- Remind the participants, and everyone else, that everyone is there for the purpose of learning, not fighting.
- Point out that, in the interests of everyone, it's time to go on with the lesson. This usually allows you to proceed because most people in a confrontation are happy to stop at any excuse that saves face.

Perhaps the single most common source of sidetracking is the trainer. All instructors like to illustrate their points with stories, jokes, and examples. If a point is particularly important, some will beat it to death. Whenever anyone asks a question (often an irrelevant one), such trainers spring to answer it. These are not good practices. A trainer needs self-discipline to maintain the training objective. When you find yourself running overtime, you probably are guilty of one of these sins.

There is in itself nothing wrong with using stories to illustrate points or answering questions when they come up. In fact, it is an important teaching tool. It is only when you overdo it by telling one story too many or making an irrelevant joke or, in the interest of being perfectly clear, run a topic into the ground, that they are detrimental. When you answer every question, no matter how irrelevant, you don't maintain your own objectives. Keep a constant check on yourself. Ask yourself every day if you are guilty of straying from your objectives. Ultimately, your trainees will thank you for it.

Fairness

When groups form, as described in Chapter 1, they can reject those who don't agree with the group. Sometimes the excluded ones become scapegoats; sometimes they remain loners. Often the excluded ones are silent and go largely unnoticed. As leader of a training group, you must be fair to all. You must also remain equally accessible to all. The group has given you the power of justice; but, if you abuse it, they will take it away and undermine your authority. Don't allow others to be used as scapegoats, don't tolerate abusive language, and don't let one person dominate the group to the exclusion of others. Be aware of the political climate so you can be responsive to the needs of each member. It is not fair to let either the majority or the minority control others.

Listening

Often you hear a leader say, "My door is always open." This means people can bring the leader their problems and he or she will listen. Good leadership listens to the group. Keep yourself open and attentive. Don't interrupt participants when they speak; let them have their say. If they are wrong, explain why. If they are right, go with them.

Unfortunately, listening is a difficult skill. Our minds race ahead of the speaker and fill with our own responses. If we speak them, we interrupt the other person and are not listening anymore. Your mind is capable of processing information faster than others can speak, so you can easily be distracted from listening. To listen well you need to give your mind something to challenge it rather than let it drift off or plan retorts. Fortunately, there is a way that you can improve your listening ability (even the best listeners can improve); it is called *active listening*.

There are three steps to active listening:

1. As you listen, summarize in your mind what the other person is saying. It's like taking notes, but in your head. As the talk goes on, keep a running summary of it.
2. When you reach capacity—that is, when you begin to have difficulty remembering what the first point was—interrupt by saying something such as, "So let me see if I understand you correctly. You're saying. . . ."
3. Feed your mental summary back to the speaker so you clear your mind to listen to his or her response.

When you practice active listening, you gain several important things at the same time. First, you give your mind the necessary challenge to keep it focused. It will still want to wander, but having a specific task to perform makes it easier to keep it on track. Second, you remember what was said much better because you are experiencing it three times: You hear it, you structure it, and you repeat it. Third, you win friends. Most people are very flattered by the interruption because it tells them you are very interested in what they are saying and that you want to make sure you get it right. Fourth, the method practically eliminates all misunderstanding. It is the perfect feedback loop. If you have not understood correctly, the speaker will say so. If you have, there is no problem.

Practice active listening to hone your skills and make yourself a truly fine listener. It only happens if you practice, however. Active listening is not natural, and you may find it quite difficult at first. Persevere; it pays off when you master it.

Listening Skills

Active Listening

1. Mentally summarize what's being said.
2. At capacity (when you start to forget what's been said), interrupt by saying, "So if I understand you . . ." or "Let me see if I've got this straight. . . ."
3. Feed your summary back to the person speaking.

Advanced Active Listening

1. Mentally summarize what's being said.
2. Look for the essence, the core, of what is meant.
3. When you have the essence, interrupt and ask a single question about this item.

Once you have mastered the basic form of active listening, you can move on to my extended technique. When someone is speaking, continue to summarize what's being said but don't feed it back. Instead, look for the essence—the core—of what's being said. Most people speak around a subject, in phrases, stumbles, and spurts. They have things to say, but unless they have thought them out ahead of time, they seldom express them directly. Look for the essence, the heart, of the matter.

When you've targeted it, interrupt the speaker, or step into a pause, and ask a single question about that essential point. When you do this, the speaker will light up. It clarifies that person's thinking and makes him or her feel successful in communicating. The speaker sees you as a great listener, which indeed you will be when you've mastered this advanced active listening skill.

Summarizing

People like to perceive things in relation to other, usually larger, things. So they mark off the halfway point on a journey or for a task. They look at things as half empty (or half full), half over, and so on. At certain points in your instruction you need to stop and show how far you've come. Do this by summarizing what's been covered so far. It gives the trainees a feeling of progress. In effect, you are setting up plateaus so learners can look back and see where they've been. These summaries provide a coherence to the learning, showing how each part connects and how each is a step in the progress toward the goal.

Reviewing

Reviewing material and summarizing it are rather closely related in concept but require quite different skills. Reviewing is also looking back, but in much more depth. It is not just a *see where we've come* device, it also provides measurable feedback that says *see what we've learned*. Reviewing prepares learners for the next lesson by refreshing their understanding of prior material. You can review in several ways:

1. Quizzes and tests
2. Asking questions that invite discussion
3. Walking through the topics covered
4. Using a combination of the above methods

My favorite type of review is to ask the group, "What stands out in your memory from what we covered this morning [or yesterday, or whenever]?" This gets them to review the material in their own minds, causes each to be engaged in activity, saves my having to repeat myself, and allows me to add to or clarify any points that appear to need it.

Focusing

As leader, you must focus the attention of the group. Of course, you do so by referring to your agenda, which will highlight the topics, and by using visual aids to hold the group's attention. Group discussions, however, must be orchestrated to be effective learning devices. When you begin a discussion, remain as the moderator and control the speakers. If you have a guest speaker, gently take back control of the group when the speaker is finished by leading a question-and-answer period. For example watch a presidential news conference to see how a leader can control the focus of a discussion. As leader, you tell the group whom to listen to when you select who is to speak. This is how you facilitate group discussion without losing control.

Challenges

One of your crucial tasks as leader is to maintain yourself as such in the eyes of the group. They trust you to perform the functions we've already discussed, and they look up to you as long as you handle those functions adequately. When your leadership is challenged, whether intentionally or not, you must meet that challenge to maintain your leadership. If you fail, the group will take away your leadership and bestow it on one of its members. Once again, you have no choice. By beginning the course, you put on the mantle of leadership. It is given to you when you perform any or all of the functions of leadership. You need to have it to train successfully. But, you are also expected to defend that leadership role against all comers. You can't explain or rationalize the confrontation away. It must be responded to strongly and confidently.

The challenge may result from a participant's genuine doubt or disagreement, or it may be the need of a high-status participant to be recognized, or it can be a personal (usually irrelevant) attack. Perhaps the person feels he or she knows more about the subject than you do (or wants the group to think he or she does). Maybe the challenger is opposed to training, or is hoping to be dismissed by antagonizing all authority figures and wasting other workers' time. Whatever the reasons, you must deal with the problem.

Greet the challenge openly. Smile warmly, if possible. Walk toward the challenger. Never walk away or stand behind a desk, lectern, or projector. Your warm smile and movement toward the challenger tell the rest of the group that you are confident and in charge. It signals them to relax.

Begin to ventilate the resistance. Ask why the challenger has said whatever he or she has said to challenge you. Then ask for clarification, for details. Encourage the person to explain his or her position. If the issue is a genuine one, that quickly becomes apparent and you can use it as a learning situation, perhaps by drawing the group into the discussion or by providing a demonstration. If the challenger is a high-status participant, allow that person the floor for a moment to satisfy his or her need for recognition.

If the challenger becomes a self-proclaimed authority by questioning your agenda, when you ventilate his or her challenge through questions, it will quickly become apparent to the entire group that the person is alone, seeking some personal involvement. The group will side with you and join you in responding to the individual. If the challenger's complaint makes sense, or the person really does speak for the group, you will still command their respect by being open to the challenge. Respond to it warmly and move in while asking questions to clarify.

This is strong leadership behavior. It is also nonconfrontational. The troublemaker wins if you respond defensively or in an authoritarian manner. He or she will have succeeded in disrupting the class. You lose the group even if you win the battle. By responding openly with questions, you put the challenger on the defensive and force an explanation. And you win, no matter what explanation is given.

In rare instances when someone pushes for a confrontation, continue to smile, question, and move in. If need be, stand right next to the individual. If you must, break eye contact by walking behind the difficult participant. If the person responds by rising from the chair and turning around to face you (never in my experience, but theoretically possible), again break eye contact by turning away and walking back to the front of the room. This way you are using both your power as leader and the increased personal space that power gives you to intimidate the obstreperous individual. Of course, it is a technique to use only on someone who is trying to intimidate or confront you. One final word of caution, however. This is a culturally biased response. People of different cultures will respond differently to this kind of pressure. If you train the foreign born, don't use the technique of closing in unless you know the likely response in that culture.

As soon as you see the challenger back down—that is, start to explain and cooperate—stop moving in. Continue to smile and ask questions. When you can feel the tension ebb, move back away toward the front of the room to lessen confrontation. If the person presses, move in again. When the individual (and others in the room) begins to relax, back away, and remove the pressure.

Silent Members

There are at least two reasons for participants to remain silent: either they are shy and are afraid to speak, or are resisters who aren't going to openly disrupt the class. The first type you should encourage to participate so they will share with others and learn more. The second type may be fighting what you're teaching, influencing others behind your back. They can hurt you by undermining not only your authority but also what you've taught. Your problem is that you'll never know which type the silent ones are unless you ask. It's part of your job as leader. So be sure to engage every member of your class. Create a dialogue with each silent member particularly in order to evaluate his or her depth of participation.

Modus Operandi

We have stated that a leader must be assertive. This is not a matter of choice. People expect leaders to be decisive and authoritative. How would you respond to an indecisive, nonassertive surgeon or dentist? Would you fly with an airline pilot who was unsure about which way to go? We want to feel we are in good hands.

On two occasions I was conducting seminars when a fire broke out, once in the room below and once in the room next door. On one of these occasions I had a trained firefighter in the seminar, though I didn't know it until later. In both situations, however, the classes looked to me to decide what to do and how to do it. Afterwards, the firefighter told me that he would have spoken up had I made a mistake or ignored the alarms. Although he was in a position to know what to do, he still expected the leader to show the way.

As a trainer you must behave assertively:

- *Be decisive.* Don't stew over which way to go; just do it.

- *Never apologize.* When you are wrong, simply correct yourself and move on (as television news reporters do). People don't need or want excuses. This doesn't mean, however, that you should be rude. Common courtesy is expected. When you step on someone's toe, apologize. When you leave out part of a lesson, either ignore it or fit it in elsewhere—for example, when you review that section.

- *Avoid confrontation.* The Socratic method (described fully in Chapter 2) and the "question reflex" (discussed later in this chapter) allow you to hold firm to a point without creating extremes on the issue. Don't allow participants to become your enemies, yet be prepared to show why what you teach is true.

- *Move in and solve problems as soon as they become apparent.* Most problems only get bigger the longer they last.

Question-and-Answer Skills

Asking questions can be a means of establishing authority, fulfilling leadership functions, and ensuring effective learning. In fact, asking questions is probably the most subtle power you have for controlling people. The person who asks questions always controls the conversation.

Often we become so engrossed in our own thoughts and desires that we spend our conversation time thinking of what we want to say rather than listening to the other person. Yet if we could discipline our minds to ask questions instead, we could lead any conversation to wherever we wanted it because the other person would still be wrapped up in thinking what he or she wanted to say next. This is particularly true in training. By probing with questions, you challenge learners to think for themselves. If their answers are wrong, you can ask them why or probe further. When learners discover an answer for themselves, they really have learned it because it is their answer. If you have to tell them, it is your answer and will be theirs only if you have built a solid conceptual bridge for them to cross.

One of the rights you have as a trainer is to ask questions and expect answers. This is why question-asking is such a powerful tool. It challenges and avoids confrontation at the same time.

Types of Questions

There are six types of questions you can use in training: closed-ended, open-ended, overhead, direct, relay, and return.[1]

Closed-Ended Questions. Closed-ended questions are by far the most common in our society. A closed-ended question demands a specific, often detailed, answer. Typical questions are:

- What is your name?
- What is the next step in this procedure?
- What are the three relevant facts?
- Where can this information be used?

Sometimes the answer can be just a yes or no, but always a specific answer is demanded.

Most of us feel interrogated if asked a series of closed-ended questions. We resent being probed at and pried into, so we are reluctant to answer. Yet when I ask trainees at all levels of authority and in all types of businesses to write a series of questions they normally ask their customers, subordinates, co-workers, or bosses, 70 percent of their questions are consistently closed-ended. Most people are locked into closed-ended thinking.

Perhaps the closed-ended question is so prevalent because our system of education presents subjects in closed-ended, usually chronological arrangements. Or perhaps it is because our mass media always ask for and supply simple, direct,

immediate, closed-ended solutions to problems. Maybe it is our political structures, which forever put closed-ended Band-Aids on open-ended problems.
Whatever the reasons, we are firmly entrenched in closed-ended thinking patterns. At the end of this discussion of question types and functions are some tips
to help you break the closed-ended question habit.

The principal uses for closed-ended questions are to:

1. Review previously covered material.
2. Force a group or individual to come up with a specific solution to a problem (as in math).
3. Test for learning, understanding, or knowledge; for evaluation.
4. Control by interrogation; for example, to pin a self-proclaimed authority
   down to specifics.
5. Get back to the point when a discussion has gone astray.
6. Organize a disorganized thinker.
7. Encourage a shy participant to respond when he or she knows the answer.

Open-Ended Questions. The direct opposite of a closed-ended question is
an open-ended one. This type encourages discussion and allows a variety of responses. It is, therefore, a more low-pressure question. It still demands an answer
but with much less pushiness. People don't feel interrogated because they can
talk freely and say what they please. Open-ended questions are low-key and,
when asked warmly and with interest, are an invitation to talk. Of course, they
demand listening skills of the trainer. Later in this chapter there are tips on how
to enhance your open-ended question skills.

The principal uses of open-ended questions are to:

1. Foster discussion.
2. Draw out opinions and feelings rather than only facts.
3. Create an open climate in which trainees don't have to be right.
4. Begin and encourage the debriefing of a self-proclaimed authority.
5. Provide a strong but nonthreatening response to challenges.
6. Find out what trainees know.

Good questioning technique is a blend of these two question types. As a rule,
use closed-ended questions to speed up, narrow down, and zero in on a topic
under discussion. Use open-ended questions to explore, evaluate, widen, and
slow down a discussion.

Overhead Questions. An overhead question can be either open-ended or
closed-ended. It is a question asked of the group at large, and anyone can answer.
The value of overhead questions is that they put pressure on everyone to think

of an answer. The questions engage the group and get each member involved mentally, if not vocally.

Use overhead questions to:

1. Open a discussion.
2. Maintain a discussion.
3. Introduce a new topic or segment.
4. Open up the floor, and give each participant an opportunity to comment.
5. Draw several comments or opinions on a given topic.

Direct Questions. The opposite of an overhead question is a direct question. This is simply the same open-ended or closed-ended question with a name tacked onto it, either at the beginning or the end. It is called *direct* because you designate the answerer. The drawback is that it takes everyone else off the hook. They can all say, "Thank goodness I don't have to answer that!" Such a drawback is countered by asking a number of direct questions of several different people until everyone realizes that sooner or later you're going to get to him or her. Then each person will think and talk freely.

The advantage of direct questions is that they provide flexibility. If you ask an overhead question that no one answers, you can tag a name on it and easily turn it into a direct question. What you must never do is answer a question you have asked yourself. To do so signals to the group that they can stop thinking for the rest of the course. If you tag a name onto an overhead question and that person can't answer it, you can direct it to others until someone ventures an answer and the discussion begins.

Use direct questions to:

1. Open a discussion.
2. Call on an individual for an answer you know he or she has.
3. Involve a silent participant.
4. Avoid an overtalkative or overresponsive participant who answers every overhead question.
5. Provide recognition or status to an inner-group leader or knowledgeable participant.
6. Bring a talker or drifter back into the discussion.

The direct question is more assertive than the overhead. Use both as needed, but adjust the balance to suit the group you are instructing. A more resistant group may require more direct questions at first; a more cooperative group may open up right away with overhead questions. Become comfortable with both formats, and use either as you need it.

Relay Questions. Relay questions are like the child's game of hot potato. They are a tool for when you do not want to answer a question that is asked of you. Simply relay it to someone else by saying, "Janice, what do you think?" or "Who can answer Mike's question?" This lets you off the hook, but don't use it to cover up if you don't know the answer. Doing that will eventually trip you up, and, in any event, it undermines your authority.

Relay questions allow you to spread responsibility for answers across the entire group and give you an added opportunity to focus the learning. People expect their teachers to know the answers, but they come to rely on that to the point of not thinking for themselves and beginning to treat the trainer as an easy resource. Relaying questions is an important educational tool because it lets you step away and forces the group to think and use its own resources.

Use a relay format to:

1. Get others involved in the discussion.
2. Solicit opinions other than your own.
3. Engage a knowledgeable participant.
4. Draw in a talker or drifter.
5. Avoid committing yourself to an answer.

Return Questions. Return questions are those you re-ask of people who have asked them. They are a gentle reproof to tell those people you feel they are capable of answering them themselves and that they should rethink their questions. Of course, the return question loses gentility if you return it harshly. Then it becomes disciplinary, perceived as unfair by the rest of the group. Always return a question without rancor, either warmly or, at the very least, neutrally.

Use a return question to:

1. Encourage the questioner to think for himself or herself.
2. Avoid giving your own opinion when you feel it's important to withhold it.
3. Call the bluff of someone who is challenging you.
4. Allow someone who really only wants a platform to have one.

In this last instance, there are people who know the answers to their questions and who ask them anyway, merely to open the subject so that they may expound upon it. When you answer such a question, you put these people in control to lead the discussion wherever they want. If you return the question to them, you maintain control; they still have their say, but you can end the matter much more easily.

A balance of question types should be your goal. When originating a discussion, draw information and opinion from the group. To gain a balance of participants, use overhead, direct, and relay questions. To control the kind of information you get, use open-ended questions to ask why and get examples, then use closed-ended questions to pin down the specifics.

The Purposes of Questions

Questions can be framed to accomplish five different sorts of responses.[2] They can:

1. Gain or focus attention
2. Gain information
3. Give information
4. Direct the thoughts of others
5. Close discussions

A skilled questioner always knows the purpose of the questions asked. As a trainer, you can maintain various levels of control by intentionally framing your questions with purpose.

Gaining or Focusing Attention. We ask questions to get or focus attention and control of the conversation. "Do you have the correct time?" is as much an attention getter as it is a request for information because it changes the subject and compels the one asked to pay attention and answer. This is even more true of questions such as "Are you listening?," "Do you follow?," and "Have I made that sufficiently clear?" We have all heard the ubiquitous "May I help you?," which is designed to command our attention to the asker.

I recently watched a very skilled negotiator on television completely defuse an aggressive attack upon himself by asking a simple question. His opponent accused a colleague of the negotiator of behaving badly. The negotiator said he would need to talk to the colleague about the situation. The opponent angrily said, "I suppose you're going to tell him I said so?" To which the negotiator replied, "I don't see how I can avoid doing so. *May I have your permission to do so?*" thus maintaining complete control of the dialogue, preventing it from being sidetracked into a discussion of who was complaining. It effectively blocked the complainer and allowed the negotiator to return the focus of the discussion to the subject they were negotiating.

Gaining Information. This is the most familiar function of questions. We usually assume that all questions are asked in order to gain some form of information. To some extent this is true, but many questions have other purposes as well. Those that don't we fit into this simple, direct category. You ask because you want an answer; you need information.

Closed-ended questions are the most common form in this category because in order to frame one the asker must define the parameters of the answer before asking the question. Thus, the purpose of the question is to fill in that blank, to provide the information the asker has identified as necessary. However, open-ended formats fall into this category when they are used to ask for explanations (for example, "Why?" or "How does that work?").

Giving Information. Be very careful of this function. It implies superiority on the part of the asker and so usually sounds condescending. Its most common form is what we have come to call *leading questions* of the type, "You knew better than that, didn't you?" or "Of course you realize that you are wrong, don't you?" Unless it is very carefully worded, it makes the one who is asked look foolish or ignorant and so has little place in a training context.

The one format in which this type of question can be useful is in setting a case situation to be solved. An example of such a question would be: "Given the following conditions (x, y, z) and a circumstance in which a, b, and c have happened, how would you respond?" This type of question is suitable where the information given in the question is necessary to formulate the answer. Otherwise, it is best to simply avoid this function in training.

Directing the Thoughts of Others. This format is the most useful for trainers. It causes the trainees to think. Usually it takes an open-ended format such as "Why is that?" or "What would happen if . . . ?" or "How can you explain this?" It can be used to motivate, to prepare learners to learn, to debrief self-proclaimed authorities, or to simply examine and explore topics of interest. It is the most challenging of the formats and, at the same time, the most engaging. It can start discussion, test for judgment, challenge learners to probe further, or provide constructive feedback on previous answers or completed work. This is the teaching function of questions.

Closing Discussion. Finally, questions can serve to bring discussion to an end. "Are we all agreed, then?" or the infamous "Are there any questions?" signal that the discussion is over. Yet they do so in a way that still leaves the door open to last minute thoughts and comments. The variation "Do you feel ready to try one of these yourself?" also gains commitment from the learner to begin to try to use what has been taught and serves as a bridge to the next step in the learning process.

When you are planning the questions you want to ask and writing them out in your lesson plans, make sure that you are able to identify the function your words are performing as well as the type of question you are asking. You gain leadership skill by using questions for precise purposes in a planned and controlled manner.

Developing Your Questioning Abilities

Every trainer should become skilled—indeed be an expert—in this crucial area. Here are two techniques that will help you increase your expertise at asking questions.

Break the Closed-Ended Habit. The goal should be to become ambidextrous, so to speak, with different question types. Most of us are locked into the closed-ended format. These questions are easier for us to think of. By becoming just as skilled at forming open-ended questions, you will free yourself of that bias and comfortably choose whichever question form suits your objectives in any situation.

Bring a tape recorder to your next training session. Insert a one-hour tape and have a colleague turn it on (or do it yourself) as you begin a discussion. Record until the tape runs out. Then listen to the tape and write down every question you asked. Underline the closed-ended ones. For every closed-ended question, figure out a way to ask the same thing in an open-ended format. Write down the new question. Repeat these steps until asking open-ended questions is second nature.

Remember, there is nothing inherently better about an open-ended question. This exercise merely brings your skill in forming open-ended questions up to par with your "more natural" habit of making closed-ended questions.

Play the Question Game. The question game is not particularly fun. It is a skills practice game that is not in any way unpleasant, but enjoyment is incidental to the purpose of the game. Here's how to play:

Whenever you are with someone—anyone at all—try to see how long you can keep the person talking without having to do anything except ask questions. If you have to answer a question yourself, or respond with anything other than a question, your time has run out. You have to start over again. Play the game every chance you get. It is particularly effective (and challenging) with hotel desk clerks, waiters and waitresses, cab drivers, and people who sit next to you on an airplane. Use your advanced active listening skills (discussed earlier in this chapter) to encourage them to speak. What you'll learn from this game is what I call the *question reflex.*

You become so adept at asking questions that whenever anything happens your first reaction is to ask a question. If you are challenged, instead of rising to

---

Improving Your Question-Asking Skills

1. Record one of your training sessions for at least one hour.
2. Play back the recording and write down every question you asked.
3. Underline every closed-ended question.
4. Rephrase every closed-ended question in an open-ended format.
5. Repeat as necessary.
6. Play the question game at every opportunity.

that challenge, you will deflate it with a question. When a trainee errs, instead of becoming impatient, you'll respond with a question. When others defeat your efforts at making a change, instead of an angry outburst, you'll ask a question. This technique gives you power. Remember, the person who asks questions controls the conversation. The question game reenforces the question reflex, which in turn gives you leverage—and, therefore, control and leadership—in every situation.

You can practice the question game with anyone. They won't mind; in fact, they will appreciate it. A college professor I know is the finest question-asker I've encountered. His name is Neil, and Neil plays this game all the time. I've asked many of his students and colleagues why they like to talk to Neil. The answer is always the same, "Because he is such a great conversationalist!"

Giving Good Answers

We've been discussing how to ask questions, but do you know how to answer them? If you create a climate for the open exchange of ideas, you will be asked questions almost as often as you ask them yourself. Here are five steps to follow in responding to a question:

1. *Listen.* Use your active listening techniques to understand both what is said and what is meant.
2. *Acknowledge the question.* Show that you understand what has been asked. Use your active listening skills here, too.
3. *Ask for clarification*—but only if you need it.
4. *Answer the question.* Be brief and to the point.
5. *Verify that the question-poser is satisfied.* Check with the person to make sure that you've addressed the point to his or her satisfaction.

In following these steps be careful not to disparage in any way the person who has asked the question. Also, don't try to answer a question you can't. Say you can't, but that you will get the answer and have it by a specific time. Then do so!

It is also important that you don't change the subject or wander far afield to answer the question. If you must explain other material first, tell the questioner what you are doing and then relate that material back to your answer. Lastly, don't treat two questions as one. Answer each separately, otherwise you might confuse rather than clarify.

When listening to and acknowledging the question, as well as asking for any necessary clarification, there are several possible responses you can use. For example, you can give a neutral response while encouraging feedback such as, "I see" or "That's interesting." This response is used to great effect by psychoanalysts. It conveys your interest, yet keeps the questioner talking. Sometimes when you do this the person will answer his or her own question.

Another possible response is to probe, or gather more information. Use thought-directing questions to challenge the questioner's thinking by making him or her explore other facets of the question. Usually this response involves asking who, what, when, why, and where questions. In effect you are answering the question by asking another question that causes the person to look more closely at the original question.

A third response is to restate the question. A part of active listening technique, this is the simplest and surest way to indicate that you are listening and have understood the question. While restating the question, you can reflect on how the questioner feels. It requires you to use the advanced active listening technique to help the person clarify his or her thinking attitudes. Lastly, you can summarize the question. This is the final step in active listening. It is not necessarily either restating or reflecting on the question but rather is a consideration of, or perspective on, what was said.

Once you have listened to and clarified the question, you can move on to answering it and verifying that you have addressed it sufficiently. With practice you can develop a very smooth and professional manner of asking and responding to questions.

Nonverbal Behavior

Up until now we've been discussing various aspects of the trainer's role that involve verbal communication. But a trainer communicates in other ways as well. Now we take a look at nonverbal communication.

There are various kinds of nonverbal behaviors. For our purposes, we will define nonverbal behavior loosely to include kinesic, proxemic, vocal, and cultural behaviors, as well as habits of thought and expression. Each exerts a different degree of control and creates a different impression. Most important, each makes a strong contribution to fulfilling your leadership role. The four basic types of nonverbal behavior are:

1. Body language, or kinesics
2. The use of vertical and horizontal space, or proxemics
3. Vocal tone and implications of key words
4. Dress—you are what you wear

Kinesics

The first, and still most detailed, work on the meanings of gestures, body positions, facial expressions, and so forth was done by social scientist Ray L. Bird-

---

Projecting a Positive Image

1. Move briskly. Choreograph your opening moves, if need be. Enter the room from the rear and stride to the front.
2. Stand firm and erect. Don't hide behind lecterns or tables.
3. Smile—and mean it.
4. Maintain eye contact with the group.
5. Greet the trainees in an enthusiastic tone of voice—demand the same in response.
6. Give the group a task to perform right away.
7. Walk around the room—take possession of your space.
8. Establish credibility at the beginning.
9. Demonstrate identification with the group early on.

---

whistell, who gave these behaviors the name kinesics. His studies pointed out that we convey a great deal of unspoken information to each other by the way we stand, move, or smile. Birdwhistell tried, with little success, to formulate a complete language of gestures and their meanings.[3]

Psychiatrist Paul Watzlawick has theorized that all communication consists of two different types of messages: the content of what we are saying and the relationship we want to have with those to whom we are speaking.[4] Watzlawick believes the latter to be the more important one. In fact, if the relationship is not mutually agreed upon, no content will be exchanged. Another way of saying this is that until both parties accept their respective roles in a conversation, neither pays attention to what is being said. Instead, each jockeys for position in a relationship struggle. This is why it is so important for the trainer to respond to any leadership challenge immediately and assertively. As long as the relationship of learners and trainers is unsettled—as it is when you are challenged—no learning will take place.

Building on this concept, psychologist Albert Mehrabian has observed that there are three basic relationship messages we look for when speaking with another person.[5] We instantly measure the person for (l) the degree of general involvement (that is, what emotional state the person is in: Is he or she enthusiastic? depressed? neutral? sad?), (2) the person's degree of liking or disliking of us, and (3) the degree of dominance or submissiveness the person feels toward us.

These messages are read in the tone of voice, the rate of speech, animation in the face, expression in the eyes and mouth, body posture, and general physical animation. Mehrabian's point is that we learn to read these messages in early childhood, and continue to do so, unaware that we are responding on this level. Within the first sixty seconds of your training session, your trainees, without realizing, will measure you and respond in accordance with the kinesic messages you give them. Don't throw those sixty seconds away. Accept your role as leader, and the group will relax, and be ready to learn, because it will feel it is in good hands.

The nonverbal messages you give should all be high. Figure 3-1 shows involvement on a scale from one to ten. You should be on the upper end of the scale—enthusiastic, but not manic. Figure 3-2 illustrates the degree of liking you should project. Again, you should be on the upper end of the scale—liking, but not loving. People learn better when they feel an instructor cares about them. Lastly, Figure 3-3 gives the range for dominance over the training group. This time you should be even higher up on the scale. People must feel that you are in control—that you are a leader they can trust—not bossy, but firm and assertive.

As just noted, your group of trainees can size you up in the first sixty seconds. Here are some ways to control the initial relationship messages they receive:

- Move briskly. If need be, plan a series of movements; for example, plan to enter the room from the rear and walk to the front. Move to a chalkboard or flip chart and back, and so on.
- Stand firm and erect in front of the lectern or table. Don't hide behind furniture or objects.
- Smile—and mean it. Be warm and friendly. Remember that negative first impressions that go against you can become sources of resistance.
- Maintain eye contact with members of the group.
- Greet the class with an enthusiastic note in your voice. The way you say "good morning" can make a difference. I make certain I say it loud and strong and insist on a similar response.
- Gain a commitment from them. This is why I insist on a response to my greeting. It gives a strong message of dominance, involvement, and desire for involvement from them.

Figure 3-1. Degree of involvement.

| comatose | 1 | 2 | 3 | 4 | 5 | [6 | 7] | 8 | 9 | 10 | hysterical |

Figure 3-2. Degree of liking.

| hatred | 1 | 2 | 3 | 4 | 5 | [6 | 7] | 8 | 9 | 10 | adoration |

Figure 3-3. Degree of dominance.

| submissive | 1 | 2 | 3 | 4 | 5 | 6 | [7 | 8] | 9 | 10 | authoritarian |

- Assign a task such as filling out name tags, organizing workbooks, changing the seating arrangement, or breaking into discussion groups. This not only sends a message that you are in command, but if you are nervous, it takes attention off you and allows you to read their nonverbal behavior for the three Mehrabian relationship messages.
- Walk around the room, either while they work or as you introduce the course. Take possession of the room.
- Establish your authority and knowledge of the material.

In addition to the initial impression, you can use Mehrabian's relationship messages for several other circumstances. When you deal with a challenger, smiling, moving closer, and requesting an explanation send positive messages. It is hard to resist someone who appears to like you and is enthusiastic about your challenge, and yet who moves assertively closer and closer toward you. Likewise, when you seek to involve silent members, you are saying you care. When you handle questions well, you are reaffirming your relationship messages. When you go out of your way to protect a student's rights in the class, you are also filling your leadership role with positive messages. This is why you must be courteous but never apologize for errors.

Proxemics

Derived from the same root word as proximity, proxemics is the study of our use of space. It covers everything from positioning offices in a building to choosing the best place to sit on a crowded beach. Elements of proxemics include room arrangements, but that is covered in Chapter 11. At this point, we limit the application to a trainer's personal use of space.

In our culture, as in most others, leadership assumes and is awarded more space. According to anthropologist Edward T. Hall, we create invisible boundaries that come into play in varying circumstances.[6] North Americans regard proximities of up to about one-and-a-half feet as intimate. In normal circumstances, we allow only those we care about to be so close. On public transportation or in other crowded situations, of course, we break down this barrier but often feel intense discomfort at doing so. This is an acquired characteristic; children do not show this trait because they have not yet learned the rules.

In contrast, the space from one-and-a-half to four feet from us, we regard as casual personal space. This is our normal interaction space, and people will sit or stand to talk to each other about this distance from one another. A space of two-and-a-half feet is the normal distance for conversation, but any position within the casual space is still regarded as comfortable. When these rules aren't followed, we become uncomfortable, as we would in a crowded restaurant where tables are too close together.

The distance that concerns us most as trainers is the next one: areas of four to twelve feet. This is formal social distance, and it is the distance we sit across the desk from another person. Most important, it is the distance in the formal training seminar that we maintain between ourselves and our nearest trainees. If you move closer, you create discomfort. It is interpreted as either an invitation to greater intimacy or an authoritative encroachment on a trainee's personal space. This is also why moving in toward a challenger is assertive behavior and why moving very close to one is a powerful exertion of authority.

Edward Hall's fourth distance is what he calls public distance, which is any area over twelve feet. With large groups, a trainer uses this distance as well, in much the same way as with formal social distance.

Coupled with this sense of space distinctions is a culturally defined sense of territory. (Incidentally, I use the word *cultural* with considerable emphasis. These rules all vary from culture to culture. All cultures have unwritten, unspoken rules of behavior but the boundaries and responses to violations vary considerably. If you train non-North Americans, discover the limits of and rules for their space barriers.) In our North American culture, we stake out territories and then set up barriers within and around them. This is why trainees usually return to the same seat day after day and feel uncomfortable if someone else takes it. In setting up our own space, we leave others what we perceive as fair space for them. The front of the room usually fills up last. If the participants perceive the training as a public event to which they are not yet committed, they may distance themselves by sitting more than twelve feet from the instructor. If they perceive it as a formal, businesslike activity, some will sit closer, but no nearer than four feet. No one normally sits closer than four feet from the trainer because training is not regarded as casual social intercourse or intimate communication.

In our culture, leaders are always given more space. Use your space. If you wish to give an impression of strong leadership, walk around the room. Take it all. At the very least, use all of the space in front of you. Fill the space as the group allows, but take more if you need it. Most people are unaware of space rules, so you can use these rules to control without creating friction.

There are even gender differences in our use of space. North American males rarely stand face to face in one-on-one conversations unless they are emotionally aroused. In anger or intimacy they will talk facing each other squarely. For regular conversation, however, they stand at a 30- to 90-degree angle to each other as a rule. To shift into a direct, square, front-to-front position would be perceived as confrontational. Hence the slang expression, "In your face!"

North American women, however, apparently don't suffer from this spatial problem. They are quite comfortable having a face-to-face discussion with each other. Interestingly, women who are used to working with men will adopt the 30- to 90-degree angle when talking with them. If they didn't, the men would most likely respond with discomfort, restlessness, or dominant/submissive behavior such as raising their voices, glaring, threatening, or, conversely, refusing to make eye contact, reluctant agreement, nodding, or nervous smiling.

If a female manager approaches a male subordinate and stands face to face with him, regardless of the content of the conversation, he is likely to find her overbearing, pushy, or aggressive. He might even feel justified in thinking several other, even stronger negative terms about her.

Conversely, if a female subordinate approaches a male manager and stands face to face, he is likely either to feel a need to assert his authority over her or to think that she is interested in him in some way and is coming on to him. In this way, the seeds for sexual harassment may be planted quite innocently.

Study these nonverbal behaviors in the people you observe around you. Watch them converse in public places. You will see these unwritten rules borne out about 70 percent of the time. Use this awareness to defuse tense situations, protect trainees from each other, and assert your own authority if necessary.

In asserting your authority, don't hide behind lecterns, desks, or tables. These items are symbols of power but they are passive and far less effective than your personal use of space.

Vertical space is important, too. In our society height lends authority. Judges sit on raised benches, traditional stages are raised above eye level, and top floors are usually reserved for senior executives. No one is allowed to sit until the king or queen sits. Many seminar rooms have formal platforms at one end. Therefore, you stand while they sit. If they are standing, you can sit, and so on.

As already mentioned, moving forward while standing is a very authoritative action. In contrast, moving backward or sitting on the same plane decreases your authority. If you want to draw a shy participant into the discussion, back away while asking a question.

One final word on the use of space. As said before, space is a powerful element because most trainees are completely unaware of how you use it. But use space with care. If you are large or tall and have a strong voice, you may never need to use space to control the group. But if you are short, are younger than your trainees, or are a female in a male-dominated group, you will find space a great help in maintaining your credibility and authority.

Vocal Tone and Implications

Throughout this chapter I have used the word *control* in reference to your trainees. Has my use of that word bothered you? Does it make me sound paranoid? Would it have been better if I had used the word *influence* instead? Would you feel the same way if I had used *manipulate*?

If you are like most managers and trainers I have worked with, you'll probably say *control* is okay though a bit strong, *influence* is certainly acceptable, but *manipulate* is offensive. Yet whichever word I choose, the techniques of leadership in no way change. It is only your perception of those techniques that differs, and that perception is shaped largely by the implied meanings behind the words I choose to describe the techniques.

All words have implications, even prepositions. One of the most powerful forms of control over a group is a knowledge of the implications words have. In a recent planning session, a client was concerned that trainees might perceive the proposed training program as punitive and resent being singled out. I suggested two concurrent remedies:

1. The training should be advertised in-house as part of an ongoing program to change the customer service image of the entire organization. This seminar would be for one segment of the company population—for example, clerical workers—while other seminars would be for other workers and management.

2. The purpose of the training should be stated as a service that management was giving trainees to help them make their jobs easier for them.

Indeed, both of these statements were true. The fact that management was dissatisfied with the performance of these workers and wanted it improved was also true, but immaterial. By describing the training as a small part of a larger policy and by showing how it would benefit them, management nullified resistance. No one felt singled out. The training was perceived as a positive rather than a punitive event, and the trainees came to the sessions prepared to learn.

Understand that this is not a recommendation for lying or using underhanded tactics. You are choosing words to shape the perceptions of those who hear them. It is to your advantage (and the trainees' advantage) to select words that create positive perceptions. But do this carefully and honestly. People recognize euphemisms. Words with positive implications help you avoid resistance that might come from misinformation and incorrect interpretations. They can help motivate learners, and be an important tool in creating a positive learning environment.

The figures of speech you use also have implications. Dr. Beverly Hyman performed a fascinating study in 1980 that investigated what metaphors people use and how these metaphors control their thinking.[7] She asked a number of teachers and trainers to talk about their jobs and to describe their goals and work. She recorded the conversations, then reviewed the recordings and wrote down all the nouns, adverbs, adjectives, and verbs. She wanted to see if there were any consistent patterns. There were, and they were very clear. Slightly more than half the conversations were filled with words and phrases such as *held in, controlled, discipline, teach a lesson, hands are tied, shut up, marking time,* and *show them.* They used words quite suitable for describing life in a prison rather than a school. Fortunately, the other group—almost half the teachers surveyed—used words and phrases such as *take them, travel to, open up to, visit,* and *view.*

As the meanings behind the words illustrate, one group subconsciously saw itself as prisoners, the other as travelers. Which would you rather have teaching you? More to the point, which way would you have your trainees perceive you? When you record yourself, listen to the metaphors you use. If you find it hard to discover them, tape a lesson and write down all of the verbs, adverbs, nouns, and adjectives you use and look for patterns. If they are in any way negative, change them.

Finally, words set the tone for your training sessions. Occasionally, I have been accused of using two-dollar words. I'm glad. That's the tone I've chosen. It is challenging to my trainees, rather than boring. I've had trainers who make everything so elementary that I felt as if I were in first grade. In choosing an appropriate level of language, consider the following:

- The educational level of your trainees
- Any technical vocabulary involved with the subject
- The gender of the trainees (especially important if it is different from yours)
- The objectives of the training program
- Your personal objectives in the program
- The linguistic norms of the region and of the trainees
- The group's attitude toward profanity (mild or gross)
- The group's attitude toward sexist language

Dress

Another important nonverbal factor that helps set the tone for your training session is the way you dress. Remember, first impressions are strong determiners of how a group will respond. How you look creates a strong first impression. This is not a book about dress; there are many excellent ones, including John T. Molloy's *Dress for Success*. There are, however, some considerations that impact on trainers especially.

Always dress to suit the group you are training. An $800 suit looks out of place among bank tellers or field workers. On the other hand, a $125 polyester special will create a strong negative impression among senior managers. Dress well for the group, but not flashy. Estimate the cost for clothing in that group and wear something in its mid-to-upper range.

Be conservative. Estimate the degree of stylishness in the group and wear clothes that tend toward the quieter end. This choice gains you credibility. If you need more authority, wear a dark blue or a dark pinstriped suit. If you want credibility without extra power, wear a gray or light pinstriped two- or three-piece suit. If you want a warm reception and have no need for power, wear a brown or dark green suit. These color and style considerations currently apply to women as well as to men.

Your shoes must be comfortable, yet dressy. Avoid suede and other soft looks (such as sneakers) unless you are training in a casual environment or have trainees who expect that. High heels are very uncomfortable to wear all day.

Wear clothes that fit well. Your trainees will be looking at you for a number of hours. Don't distract them with bagginess or bulges. Also, be sure everything you wear looks neat and well cared for. If you appear sloppy (with wrinkled shirts or blouses, undone or missing buttons, or worn-down heels), you lose respect.

Suits are best; slacks, or skirts for women, and a blazer are second best. Dresses or slacks for women are not as good as skirts or suits with skirts. To some extent this standard is changing for women, but it is not yet commonly eased. Be on the safe side and adhere to the conservative norm. The jacket button should always be fastened at the beginning of each session. This applies for men but is particularly effective for women, too.

Jewelry distracts, so keep it to a minimum. This is particularly true for long necklaces or earrings. Clear all pockets of jingling change and distracting toys (for example, a pocketknife, lighter, or watch), and eliminate unsightly bulges.

Hair hides the face. Women should pin hair away from their face for training. Men should either shave off beards or mustaches or trim them back so they don't hide part of the face.

Lastly, have someone check you just before beginning class for any open zippers, showing slips, or dandruff on your shoulder.

Styles do change. Those women who broke into the boardrooms in the 1970s and 1980s are reported to be easing the strictures of feminine executive fashion. Perhaps the rules I've listed will eventually ease for all women, but in the late 1990s, high fashion has not yet filtered down to the training room. Conservatism is still the rule.

Glenn Pfau, an image consultant, has developed a simple point system for evaluating whether or not you are underdressed or overdressed.[8] To use it, assign one point each to the following articles or features:

- Shoes (one point per pair)
- Stockings (one point per pair)
- Suit
- Slacks (if they aren't part of a suit)
- Skirt
- Dress
- Shirt or blouse
- Blazer or jacket (if it is not part of a suit)
- Belt buckle
- Suspenders (if they show)
- Tie

- Tie pin
- Scarf (one point for each if more than one is worn)
- Watch
- Ring(s) (one point for each one worn)
- Bracelet(s) (one point for each one worn)
- Necklace(s) (one point for each one worn)
- Pin(s) (one point for each one worn, including men's lapel pins)
- Earrings (one point for each pair)
- Glasses (one point per pair)
- Breast pocket handkerchief
- Button(s) (one point for each one that is not an exact color match for the fabric on which it is worn, for example, brass blazer buttons, leather buttons, large white or pearl buttons)

Total all of the points you are wearing. If you have fewer than eight you are dressed too severely and can afford to lighten or brighten up. If you have more than twelve, you are overdressed to the extent that you have exceeded this norm. I find this an easy and quick system to follow in creating a "power image" or a well-dressed business look.

Establishing Your Credibility

There is one final aspect of personal training skills yet to be explored. As emphasized before, trainees will evaluate you within the first sixty seconds of your first session. If they are unsure, they'll hold off judgment for a while but those first moments will remain crucial in their ultimate decision. Leadership skills can convey a strong, most necessary message, but there are two other messages they will be looking for. Have you been where they've been? Do you know what you're talking about?

The first of these questions is referred to as *identification*. Can they identify with you? Are you one of them? The second is *credibility*. Are you knowledgeable? Can they trust you to be right? You will always be on trial in these two areas. If you can establish your credibility early, your leadership will be unquestioned and you will set the stage for learning.

You must get the relationship issue settled right off the bat. Use what they already know and what they want to know (see Chapter 1) as a starting point for your preparation stage (see Chapter 2 for details). As an alternative, begin with a case history or a critical incident from their experience. Ask them for their input, and base your course on that. I know a trainer whose courses consist solely of working through the problems that were brought out at the beginning of the seminar.

Build mental bridges for them from the known to the unknown. By starting where they are you gain credibility. Also, if you've been where they are, say so. Illustrate with examples from your experience. Cite authorities or give examples from other companies and projects. Show them you know your stuff. Be careful not to show off or be smug, though. Just state facts.

Learn and use the jargon of their field. But don't fake it. If you don't know, ask what their name is for something or how something has been done before. Answer questions promptly; don't evade them. If you can't answer, say so and get back to them with the answer as soon as possible.

Be tolerant, not picky. Once you've taught them something you can correct their performance, but until then, don't criticize. They are not ready to be corrected yet. Lastly, don't apologize, don't be condescending, and don't ridicule others. Be straightforward, honest, and open with your trainees.

Summary

This chapter was about you, the trainer. It is frequently not what is taught but who taught it that makes learning difficult or easy. You are the main message, and this chapter showed how you can become an effective and productive trainer.

We began by outlining the need for trainers to take a strong leadership stance, then went on to look at the roles of leadership and how you can fulfill them. We looked in detail at the purposes of asking questions and provided methods for improving your skill in this crucial area. We discussed how to give good answers to questions and reviewed ways of improving listening skills.

Nonverbal communication is also an important aspect of training programs. We examined ways of controlling your impact upon the group through the use of kinesics, proxemics, semantics, and dress. Finally, we concluded with procedures for establishing your credibility with the group.

Applications

1. How would you handle each of these situations? A participant says:
   a. "My boss would never go for this."
   b. "This is nice, but it's not real world."
   c. "We've tried that at the last place I worked and it doesn't work."

2. Practice active listening by:
   a. Watching television news broadcasts. During each commercial break, repeat aloud the two or three news stories that you've just listened to. This is not easy, so don't become frustrated. Stay with it and develop your skill.
   b. Try to repeat the specials when a waiter or waitress recites them for you in a restaurant.

3. Tape-record an hour of any of your regular training sessions. When you listen to the tape, write down all of the closed-ended or poorly phrased questions that you asked. Work up open-ended or clearer phrasing for each of them. Do this exercise periodically until you improve.

Part 2

Planning and Preparing for Training

Introduction to Part 2

This part of the book is about the planning and preparation that take place outside the classroom. In these eight chapters we look at the day-to-day training tasks that eventually lead to actual instruction. All too frequently trainers are appointed because of their ability to perform a task well. It is assumed that they will be able to teach others to perform that task, too. But training is a different job with its own skills to be mastered. Equally as common, new trainers are hired for their platform skills, and it is assumed that they will be capable of fully performing all the other tasks that comprise the job of training. If you find yourself in either situation, or are managing those who do, Part 2 will provide you with the means to discover and develop those other necessary skills of training.

In Chapter 4 we look at needs analysis. Changes can be planned only when you know what needs to be changed. Needs analysis establishes a base line. The discussion of needs analysis is intentionally practical and based on rule-of-thumb procedures. However, since the first and second editions, readers have requested more formal coverage of the gathering of data, including a brief outline of basic statistical analysis. I have included these in this edition.

Chapter 5 deals in a practical manner with what are often regarded as arcane procedures for evaluating the changes brought about by training. Because the ultimate evaluation of training is always the bottom line, we cover the necessary mathematics and numbers of justification. Once again, in keeping with the principle of *less is more*, I've simplified rather than formalized the evaluation process. Chapter 5 provides everyday measurements of progress and helps you measure the effectiveness of your training efforts. It is about evaluation, not statistics.

Chapters 6 and 7 take you through the vital steps of gaining expertise in a subject and planning how to communicate that expertise by shaping your material into a coherent training program. Again the approach is to simplify and demystify. The tools are practical and applicable to all training situations, useful to both the novice and the expert.

Writing a training program requires an overwhelming amount of work. Consequently, a large service industry has sprung up to address this problem, with off-the-shelf packages, outside consultants, and professional generic seminar organizations. Chapter 8 helps you decide when, where, and which of these services to use.

Chapter 9 is one of the longest in the book. It is a detailed examination of visual and electronic aids in training, including how to use each type of aid, rental versus purchase comparisons, budgeting, and availability. It is, in fact, all you need to know about audiovisual aids. In addition, there are tips on how to create your own aids, especially in regard to video equipment.

Chapter 10 examines the state of the art in training technology. We explore the evolution and the direction of technological growth, what each stage has meant to training, and the pros and cons of its use. You will be provided with a straightforward format for developing your own computer-based training and evaluation criteria for purchasing or developing CD-ROM interactive or multimedia instructional formats. We also look at distance learning and virtual reality as alternatives to classroom training.

An important part of any training effort is the physical environment in which learning is to take place. Chapter 11 provides guidelines on the environmental aspects to be considered and outlines several steps to take to ensure a positive training environment, both on-site and off-site.

Parts 1 and 2 embody the skills and background knowledge a trainer needs to function fully and effectively. In Part 3, we look at specific applications of this knowledge to three key areas of training: team building, supervisory training, and sales training. In Part 4, we explore the concerns of managing the training function, and, finally, in Part 5 we explore several key issues and trends that will shape training into and beyond the year 2000.

Chapter 4
Preparing a Needs Analysis

NEEDS analysis is an examination of the existing need for training within an organization. It is a gathering of data that enables you to make an informed estimate of the changes desired or demanded by that organization. Needs analysis performs three distinct functions:

1. It establishes what the present practices are.
2. It projects what the desired results should be.
3. It provides the basis for the cost justification of training.

To conduct a needs analysis you gather data on present performance, then compare the data to the desired performance standards projected by management, or mandated by external forces such as market conditions, and compare the costs of achieving those standards with either the cost of maintaining the status quo or the return on investment brought about by achieving the new standards. Your needs analysis should establish the overall management goals that your training will be designed to fulfill.

Be aware, however, that although needs analysis is a vital step toward establishing a training program, it is a step that is frequently overemphasized. I know of at least one company that hired a consulting firm to perform a needs analysis but had to begin its training program without it because the consultants took too long to finish their analysis. When the needs analysis finally came in, it was irrelevant to the by then flourishing training department. Needs analysis is an aid to training, not a substitute for it.

The problem arises because often needs analysis is easier to do. In effect, all that a needs analysis entails is gathering data. It can be as detailed or as general as desired. Those who like numbers and need them for making decisions tend to gather data to an infinite degree. Seldom is such a detailed study necessary. A formal needs analysis should be planned and completed in a three- to four-month period of time in order to be current and useful.

The first function of a needs analysis is to define your starting point so you can measure progress from it. By knowing the status quo you can train for change and then evaluate the results. You can measure your own progress as well as the impact your training has on the organization.

A needs analysis fills other roles as well, however. Training is usually on the wrong side of the ledger as a cost factor that seldom makes a profit. Consequently, trainers frequently encounter the attitude, especially from the accounting department, that their work is a frill. "It's nice to train employees, but it's not really what we're in business to do." When there are financial restraints, training is among the first cutbacks. A needs analysis helps develop a solid database on which to build the justification for your training program. You must always be prepared to show how money spent on training will benefit the entire organization. Whenever possible, you must show how training either saves more or earns more money than it costs. Needs analysis is the starting point for such a defense.

Finally, needs analysis establishes a database for future training. Although the attitude is beginning to change, traditionally training lies in the "soft" area of management. Management, from the senior staff down to shop foremen and women, is concerned with numbers and hard data. Hunches, theories, and communication skills are all very well, but traditionally the end result must be higher profits and more efficient production: more orders shipped, more cars unloaded, and more letters answered. Training is perceived as soft, a "like to have it" not a "got to have it" situation. Needs analysis creates a numerical justification for training. It is particularly important where the training need isn't obvious.

Anticipating Training Needs: Being Proactive, Not Reactive

Although more and more companies have begun to make training a key part of their strategic planning in recent years, most training in America is still reactive. That is, management discovers a need for training and either creates a training function to respond to that need or, if such a department already exists, informs the head of training that a new program should be developed. This should be a perfectly acceptable approach. But in reality few senior managers have the time or foresight to predict training needs. They see the need when it is nearly too late to do an effective job. Much training is a quick-fix Band-Aid slapped on with little notice and no time for careful preanalysis. Management wants results—now! So one day is given to perform two or three days' worth of training, and one or two weeks set to research, analyze, write, and test the new program. The trainer is forced to try to catch up, to perform more in less time, and to be harried into reacting on short notice to sudden demands.

A far better stance for the trainer is that of a proactive consultant. The classic reactive situation always puts time pressure on the trainer, who is continually catching up. The proactive stance allows the trainer to anticipate training needs and prepare a response ahead of time. Such a view lets a trainer anticipate peak demand rather than hustle to catch up. Needs analysis is the tool for this anticipatory approach.

As we explained earlier, needs analysis is a gathering of data. Here are the six steps to take in collecting data and drawing conclusions from it to create a formal analysis:

1. Monitor your standard sources of information to detect potential training needs before they become obvious.
2. Identify the types of problem you find in each area and determine which are training-related.
3. Gather data to establish current levels of performance.
4. Examine the feasibility of training as a solution to the problems.
5. Determine the size and scope of the program.
6. Justify the cost of the program.

Sources of Information for Needs Analysis

There are five available sources you can consult for information about the current practices in your organization and about its future direction: management, customers or end users, government, workers, and technology.

Management

A reactive training approach is totally and exclusively responsive to management as its source of information. Although a proactive stance is recommended, let's begin with a set of guidelines for gathering information in the reactive phase.

Information Gathering. Ask your management contacts the following questions:

- Who will receive the training?
- What is the nature of the population to be trained?
- What problems have created the need for training?
- What specific results would management like the training to achieve?
- What is the time frame for training?
- What is the budget for training (if appropriate)?
- What level of response does management anticipate?

Begin by establishing for whom the training will be designed. Remember, *who* is more important than *what*. What is the nature of the population to be trained? This includes both the number of people to be trained and a description of them—for example, their average age, sex, level of education, experience, and location (if facilities are scattered).

Next find out what problem(s) occasioned the request for training. In other words, you need to know management's assessment of current performance. If management has called on you to solve the problem, they ought to have the situation fairly well defined. Try also to uncover the results they would like. Again, it helps you (and them) if those requesting the training have given it some thought.

How much time are they giving you? Will they give you enough time with their people, or will you have to limit the depth of your training because of time constraints? Another important point is cost, though it may not be appropriate to all situations. Can they afford the training? Cost is a factor when there are divisional or departmental charge-back systems.

Lastly, what kind of a response do they anticipate? If, for instance, they want every member of their staff merely to be given the same basic orientation and nothing more, you won't have to worry about trainees' transfer of learning to their jobs. If, on the other hand, they expect a full change of skill from each participant, you (and they) will have to accommodate a considerably more detailed task and performance analysis, and you will have to allow more time for instruction and follow-up.

Proactive Information Gathering. To take a proactive stance you will need to find ways of anticipating management's training needs. When senior management rushes to you and says the company urgently needs *xyz* training in the next two months, you will be able to respond quickly and efficiently. You'll be prepared. Here are some ways to anticipate management's training needs:

1. Make friends with people in the purchasing department and ask them for information on orders or requests for new equipment that might mandate training.

2. Establish contacts with the real estate department, if your company has one. New plant sites will probably require training for new personnel.

3. If you work for a publicly held company read the annual report. Pay particular attention to forecasts, acquisitions, or expansion plans, and watch for other new directions.

4. Ask people in public relations to send you copies of speeches made by the president of the company or other key executives. Monitor the speeches for predictions of where executives see the company going. If your firm doesn't have a public relations section, talk to the boss's secretary.

5. Form a strategic partnership with management. Most senior executives have regular assessment meetings to take stock of the company and where it is headed. Such meetings usually include ideas for attaining planned goals, and

often they are the point at which planning decisions are made. Ask to sit in on such meetings. You are, in effect, monitoring senior management's needs. If you are not allowed to sit in, find someone who does attend and ask that person to pass on potential training information to you. Failing this, ask to be placed on the circulation list for the minutes of the meeting. If it is not against company policy to do so, try to get a copy of the minutes from a secretary, an executive, a supervisor of the typing pool, or a clerk in the copy or mail room where the minutes are duplicated. There are no better sources of information on future training needs than these meetings.

It is usually best if you make and maintain these contacts informally so the process remains free of red tape or multiple-approval levels. However, such contacts should in no way be clandestine or underhanded. Follow whatever policy is operative in your organization. Try informally if you can; if that fails, go through regular channels.

Customers or End Users

Remember that proactive analysis spots problems that will lend themselves to a training solution, thus anticipating a demand for training. Usually a company has some form of customer feedback. It may be a customer service or complaint department, market research, receptionists, or shipping and expediting. In fact, any area or department that regularly interfaces with the company's customers or end users is a way to gauge customer response to your company. Here's what you should look for:

- *Number and pattern of complaints.* If you can, document both the weekly or monthly number of complaints and what articles, services, or employees are involved. Any distinct pattern with sufficient numbers is a ready-made rationale for retraining.
- *Service records.* Too-frequent service calls imply both inferior quality and inadequate service. If your company services hardware of any kind, look for patterns in the frequency of service, both in the items serviced and among the departments or service people themselves. Retraining might be an effective solution.
- *Customer service.* One of the techniques covered later in this chapter comes from Tom Peters's phrase "management by walking around," or MBWA. There are few better sources of information for needs analyses than simply walking around observing how things are done. Look at how customers react to company personnel. Are there problems? Can you document a sufficient number of cases to justify a training thrust?

- *Customer surveys.* All of us who travel are familiar with the ubiquitous customer surveys in hotels and restaurants. These are an effective source of data on how well employees are performing and whether or not they may need training. This is especially true in the light of the old saying, "The customer is always right." No one can argue with a need for training that has been defined by an effective customer survey.

Government

Most managers are aware of the impact a change in government regulations can have on company operations. Yet such a change seldom comes as a surprise. The government debates it, the media report it, the issues are discussed. Everyone knows well in advance that the change is coming and what it will be. But time after time organizations delay planning the training needed to accommodate the new regulations and end up scurrying to create last-minute procedures.

Here's a case in point. The federal bill that will "change welfare as we know it" has been discussed and argued, rediscussed and reported for over a year as I am writing this. This week it will be signed into law by the President. Are the state welfare departments prepared to handle this change? Are there training programs in place or readily available to get their social workers up and running?

In Massachusetts in the spring of 1995, I worked closely with the Department of Transitional Assistance (Welfare), the Department of Unemployment and Training, and the Job Training and Education Corporation to perform a needs analysis and make training recommendations so that they would be better prepared for the future changes. Yet even so, we are still waiting for the necessary funding to proceed to the actual training. The bill is passed, but the people are not trained. So everyone will have to play catch-up and throw in last-minute training on an ad hoc basis. Much of it will not be as good as it could have been with greater foresight, with a proactive anticipation of upcoming events. At least in my region of Massachusetts, they have a course outline to help them cope. How many other regions or states will be caught flat-footed?

Everyone knows new regulations are coming. They all could have prepared for it and developed new programs, but most will probably fail to anticipate the change. Don't be caught napping. Monitor government's behavior whenever it impacts on your organization.

In particular, follow the state-of-the-union and your state-of-the-state addresses. Follow any court cases or lawsuits that might affect your operation. Lastly, read up on congressional hearings that relate to your industry.

Workers

Frequently the workplace can tell you when some form of training or retraining may be in order. Here are areas that can be monitored:

- *Absenteeism and turnover rates.* These are costly problems when they occur. There are many possible causes of such behavior completely outside the control of training, but frequently training or retraining becomes a part of the solution.

- *Union bargaining positions.* Even if your organization is nonunion, sooner or later it will have to offer some benefits to stay nonunion or to attract workers from union shops. The development of self-directed work teams is a case in point. Teams became a strong issue for unions during the past decade, when management began to search for more productive ways to remain competitive. Many unions saw the advantage to their members in having greater control over input and procedure on the job. Therefore, unions exerted pressure to make contractual commitments for self-direction and training that have smoothed the way for work team development and improvements in working conditions. Unions are an active force in working America. By monitoring union demands, trainers can anticipate areas for developing future training.

- *Outside seminars.* Monitor how many requests are made for or what the actual attendance is at outside professional seminars or college courses. You may be able to offer these as part of your training program. For example, if there is considerable demand for a course in business writing, perhaps the training department can create such a course in-house. If certain courses are taken regularly to qualify for key positions—for example, a supervisory course for newly appointed supervisors—the training department may have an opportunity to take a proactive stance.

- *Exit interviews.* If your company conducts interviews with departing employees, ask to review them with the personnel interviewer. Look for patterns of discontent that can be addressed by training.

- *Employee surveys.* You can arrange your own surveys in accordance with guidelines outlined later in this chapter, or you can piggyback on other sources such as an in-house publication or an employee suggestion box.

Technology

If your department does not currently offer new managers training in word processing or computer applications, you will have to provide it sooner or later. Be prepared. Monitor technological changes that affect the workplace. For example, electronic mail, the Internet, and interactive video telephones are becoming current. As these changes become widespread, prepare to offer seminars to help your company smoothly incorporate the changes.

In many organizations work-at-home programs are being tried. As they catch on, they will be enhanced immensely by on-site training that allows the company to maintain control over home-workers through procedural standardization and technical dependence.

Summing Up

Nearly all training thrusts arise from one or more of these five monitoring areas. Perhaps you cannot keep track of them all, or just one or two are applicable to your situation. Fine. Pick the two you think are most likely to reveal the future of your organization and track them. The purpose is to give you a means for taking a leadership role in planning the training for your company. Even when the training has already been mandated by management, which is by far the most common situation, you can tie your program into a demonstrated need to create a strong and efficient proactive stance to help justify the program.

These five information sources are really only problem finders. Before you can gather data to define the status quo, you must decide the extent to which the problem you've discovered is correctable by training. This takes us to the next step toward a needs analysis: identifying the problems.

Types of Problems

Not every problem you uncover is a training problem. If you take on the job of training to correct a problem that is not a training problem, you guarantee an automatic failure. Training is not a panacea. It can only accomplish changes of a certain kind; other problems demand other solutions.

In your investigations, there are four kinds of problems that can possibly turn up: (1) systemic, (2) organizational, (3) motivational, (4) skills.

Systemic Problems

Many U.S. railway systems have been in trouble for years, while in other countries many are flourishing. Our rail system was once a source of great wealth, one of the building blocks of the nation. What happened? There are many theories, but all can be summed up as systemic. Our system of government, new methods of transportation, and other factors all worked to diminish the importance and, therefore, the use of the railways. All the training in the world could not redress such a problem. A systemic problem has to do with the way the system—whatever it may be, in whatever instance—works. Training has never been able to stave off a recession.

Today, small merchants in New York City are forced to close their well-established businesses when their twenty-year leases expire and unregulated landlords raise rents by 800 percent. No training in the world could solve such problems. The change must take place in the system itself. There are many such systemic problems. If you turn up one in your monitoring, leave it alone. Training cannot solve it.

Organizational Problems

I once had a client who, despite having built his business into a multimillion-dollar concern, insisted that every decision be made by him. Procedural decisions in Europe and Australia had to wait until his New York office could track him down. The operation was grossly inefficient and created many problems, but none was even approachable through training. The problem lay in the chain of command and in my client's failure to delegate some decision-making authority.

In another organization, a major customer service operation was completely stalled because middle management stopped and held all actions on customer complaints. It was a policy decision made at a low level of management but it stymied all attempts by customer service personnel to resolve complaints. Although retraining those managers might help, as long as the policy remained in effect the problem would also remain. This is another example of an organizational problem. Unless organizational bottlenecks are removed, steer clear of the problem because training won't correct it.

Motivational Problems

Quite often training departments are called upon to motivate employees. They can succeed, but if the employees return to poor working conditions, organizational problems, dull and uninspiring jobs, long and frequent unpaid overtime, and other such situations, their morale will worsen regardless of training. Motivation is not a prime function of training. Supervisory people can be taught techniques for motivating and working with others, but unless the system backs up such efforts with rewards and changes circumstances that are demotivational, the training is wasted. Training is and should be an integral part of any motivational thrust, but it cannot alone create motivation.

Skills Problems

Skills problems are the true province of training. In my seminars I am often asked the difference between training and education. Training is the act of passing on performance. Education is the act of passing on knowledge. There is a difference. Training is responsible for achieving results, and these results always take the form of a change in trainee skill levels. Education is much broader and more conceptual. It is not responsible for results; it is up to the student to pass or fail, to use the material or not. Training can educate, but it still must produce concrete results and must, therefore, teach measurable skills.

Skills problems can be addressed by training. When a problem crops up, before launching a full needs analysis, ask yourself, "Is this a training problem?"

If not, end your analysis there. If so, go ahead to the next step—gathering data to define the present levels of performance.

Gathering Data

Without further information it is not always clear exactly what kind of problem you've uncovered. If it is a skills problem, then you need to gather data to establish the current level of performance—your baseline against which you'll measure progress. But even if it is too early to tell if it is a skills problem, gathering data is still your follow-up step once a problem is discovered. Of course, if it's obviously not a skills problem, there is no point in pursuing it. If you are in doubt, however, or if it is clearly training-related, you need to define the status quo—in other words, the need for training.

Ask yourself, "What is the information I want?" In other words, what is happening? What skills are involved? What problems are created? What is the impact, in dollars, of these problems? What is the political or organizational structure surrounding these problems?

Next, determine what you are going to use the data for. Is it as a basis for developing a program? Will you use it to justify that program to management or as a means to cover yourself politically? Perhaps you'll use it as a means of convincing those who are part of the problem that something must be done. Will you use the data to motivate your trainees? Choose which method or combination of methods will most easily and accurately supply the information you need.

You must also decide at this point how you will interpret and present your findings. Management usually responds well to numbers, and statistics generate numbers. However, effective needs analysis can be, and indeed frequently is, performed without them. Needs analysis doesn't have to be complex. In fact, it should be as simple and practical as possible.

Much of the time an informal analysis is adequate. You define both the status quo of performance and the desired change. In addition, you gather data on the population to be trained. Statistical analysis is only necessary when you need hard numbers to be convincing or when the population is sufficiently large that you can analyze only a sample, a small portion, of the total population. But, Occam's razor should apply. The best procedure is the simplest and most effective one.

Statistics

For those who have always found mathematics to be something of a struggle, the word statistics probably creates a sense of tension and worry. It needn't. Statistics is simply a system for changing direct observable facts, events, or behaviors into usable numerical data, and then transforming that data into information.

Data vs. Information

As I use the terms here, *data* is defined as a collection of facts or numbers and *information* is defined as the conclusions that can be drawn from those numbers. Although the two terms are frequently used interchangeably, they are not the same and we must make a clear distinction. Data by themselves are meaningless. They are just more or less random facts. When we detect patterns among these facts or use them to draw conclusions, we are creating information. Data are the raw materials of research; information is the finished product. Statistics is one of the principle tools for developing that information.

Descriptive Statistics

There are two types of statistics: descriptive and analytical. Essentially, descriptive statistics, as the name suggests, is a system for describing a set of facts, observations or events. Analytical statistics is a system for making predictions based on a set of documented facts, observations, or events. Historically, descriptive statistics was the first to be devised; and, because it is used to describe the status quo of any set of given observations, it is the most useful for trainers performing a needs analysis. Fortunately for us, it is also the easier of the two to perform and to work with.

Analytical statistics is probably most familiar to us through the use of political polls. If candidate so-and-so's popularity rating is only 26 percent, then he or she appears to have only about a one in three chance of winning the election. Or we are familiar with statements such as, "With only 6 percent of the voting booths heard from, we are predicting that the Republican candidate will win by a 12 percent margin over the incumbent." Trainers don't need to make such predictions. It is our job to document the current patterns of performance (descriptive statistics), describe the desired level of performance (task analysis and standards), develop solid learning objectives to reach those standards, and create sterling training to fulfill those objectives.

Frequency Distribution

The first thing that a statistical analysis allows us to do is to perform a frequency distribution. The term means, as you would expect, a graphic realization of the distribution of facts or events in a given situation. Let's say that on a production line your observations of scrap rates, production standards, and actual perform-ance identify ten different potential errors that operators make. You want to be able to document just how severe the incidence of errors is and which error oc-curs most frequently. An analysis requires you to perform a series of observations at key times over a period of days—for example, three hours each shift for eight shifts. You now have enough data to create a frequency distribution curve.

Each of the ten errors will constitute an error type, or *class*, and will be re-ferred to in our statistical formulas as x. The number of times each error occurs is called the *frequency* and is designated with an f. By comparing these two pieces of data, we can set up a frequency table for each of the hours on each of the shifts we have observed (see Figure 4-1). Depending on how detailed your analysis needs to be, you can set up a frequency table for each shift or for the total set of observations.

What can we say about the data in this distribution table? First, the most frequently documented error is number five (written by statisticians as $x = 5$), observed ten times ($f = 10$). In statistics, the number, or class, that is most fre-quently observed or documented is called the *mode*. In our example, five is the mode of distribution of the observed errors. The table also shows that the magni-tude of the frequencies diminishes unequally on either side of the mode. This means that the data is distributed *asymmetrically*. If the data had been even on either side of the mode, this would be a *symmetrical* distribution.

We can make the results clearer by representing this data on a bar graph or chart (see Figure 4-2).

Each of the columns in Figure 4-2 shows graphically the frequency with

Figure 4-1. Frequency distribution.

Types of Errors *(class)* x	Number of Occurrences *(frequency)* f
1	0
2	3
3	5
4	6
5	10
6	9
7	8
8	7
9	5
10	2

Figure 4-2. Frequency distribution graph.

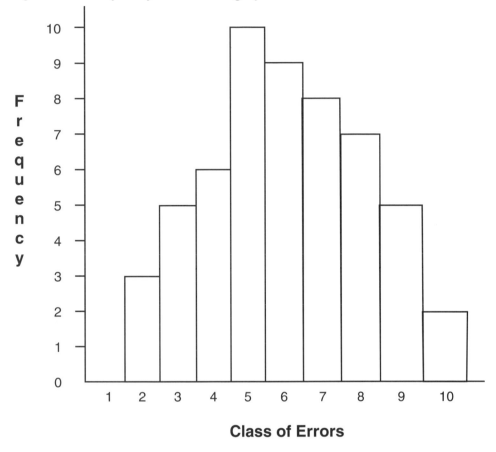

Class of Errors

which each error occurred. The mode stands out as clearly the most frequent. Note that these errors are not ranked in order of importance, only in order of frequency. If the modal error was insignificant in its impact on operations, the statistical analysis here would imply a much more serious case than actually existed on the production line. Descriptive statistics only define the range, size, and scope of observed behavior. Its impact is measured in dollars.

If we connected each of the frequency points in a flowing line instead of using a bar graph, we would have the famous "bell"-shaped curve that has become a universal symbol for statistical analysis (see Figure 4-3).

If our graph showed a symmetrical distribution, we would have a perfectly balanced bell curve with the mode at the exact midpoint of the curve. However, with an asymmetrical distribution such as we have here, our bell curve is steeper

Figure 4-3. Frequency distribution curve.

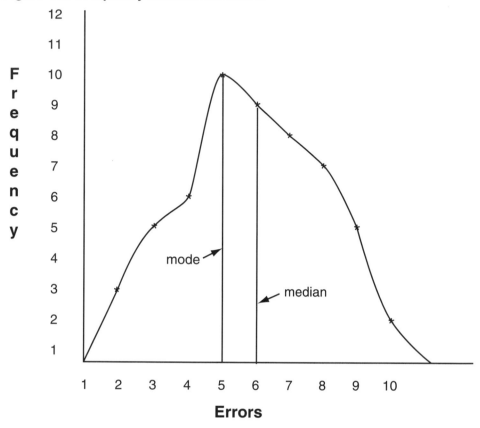

on the left side and gentler on the right. This is called a "skewed" distribution and simply means that the data didn't come out in a perfectly balanced bell curve.

Measures of Central Tendency

A measure of central tendency shows how closely the data measured cluster around a central value. In effect, this measure helps us to evaluate the distribution, or how widespread the effects of our findings are. For example, in Figure 4-1, if errors 6, 7, and 8 had occurred only three or four times, then number 5 would have been a single standout problem. However, 6, 7, and 8 also occurred with considerable frequency and so the problem is larger and covers more errors, and, therefore, probably more skills as well.

There are three important measures of central tendency:

1. The mode
2. The median
3. The arithmetic mean

The Mode. We have already seen how the mode is calculated and how we can draw conclusions from it. Remember, it is simply the variable that gets the most frequent number of observed instances. If two variables get identical numbers of occurrences, then you have a multimodal distribution, which indicates two clusters of central tendency. In our example, which is called *unimodal* because only one mode exists, if both errors 5 and 8 scored in the high frequency range, we would have a multimodal distribution.

The Median. The median is the exact middle number in the gathered data. If we arrange the data in sequence from smallest to largest, the median is the number that half of the other numbers are larger than and half are smaller than. The median in our production line example is error 6 because half of the of errors observed were less frequently observed than 6 and half were more frequent than 6. In a symmetrical curve, both the mode and the median will fall at the same spot. However, in a skewed distribution like ours, the mode is 5 and the median is 6.

Figuring the median of your data allows you to examine the distribution from a different perspective. Although errors occurred most frequently in skill 5, the median indicates that there are problems in all of the skills from 5 to 8.

The Mean. The arithmetic mean, as it is called, is simply the average score. In our example we would add the total number of observed errors and divide that sum by the ten error categories to come up with the mean. There are fifty-five observed errors in ten categories of error so the mean is 5.5. This is a different number from the mode and the median. This is because our data is skewed rather than normally distributed.

We can conclude several things from this data:

- We have a problem. On average 5.5 mistakes are made regularly in the observed time frames on the production line (the mean).
- The most frequently performed error is in skill 5 (the mode).
- However, three-fifths of the errors occur in skills 5, 6 (the median), 7, and 8.
- Skill number 1 seems to be error-free (the range).
- Skill number 10 has only two incidences of error in the observation (the range).

If we had done curves for each of the three hours on each of the three shifts for the entire week, we could further conclude which shifts, hours, time frames, and possibly even workers contributed most and least to the error totals. From those conclusions we could infer who needs to be trained and in which skills. We might also be able to conclude that some workers need to be separated from each other, that the production line is inefficient and causes certain bottlenecks of errors to occur, or that some supervisors may need training as well.

Of course, these conclusions go well beyond the statistical data presented here, but they are based on that data and can be verified by further observation.

Standard Deviation

It is usual when doing a statistical analysis to document how far from the mean each observed datum falls. This is a measure of the distribution from the norm rather than of the overall distribution. That is, it is an assessment of a subdistribution within the overall distribution. When statisticians do this, they discover that events or instances usually fall into predictable patterns, or what is called standard deviations. The mean, which you'll remember is merely the average score, is a single number. There needs to be a category of scores that falls close to the mean but is not exactly on the mean. For each analysis, these standard deviations from the mean can be calculated mathematically.

In Figure 4-4, notice that each standard deviation is labeled -1, -2, -3 or, on the positive side of the mean, $+1$, $+2$, $+3$. Any instances that fall within one standard deviation of the mean can be labeled as minus or plus one deviation. Those that fall further away are labeled minus or plus two deviations, those that fall still further away are labeled plus or minus three, and so forth. In actual practice, as most meaningful data is clustered near the mean, statisticians rarely go beyond one or two standard deviations.

How do statisticians use standard deviations? These are the measures of accuracy that allow for reasonable variations. For example, when you read in the fine print on a Gallup poll or other statistical statement in the newspapers that there is an "error factor" of plus or minus 3.5, what they mean is that 3.5 is the mathematical standard deviation and that 75 percent or more of their scores fall within the range of one standard deviation of the mean or norm, that is, 3.5 points above the mean or 3.5 points below it. So, plus or minus one standard deviation of 3.5 means that 75 percent of the scores fall in a 7-point range falling evenly on either side of the mean.

Those of you who are familiar with process quality control will recognize this as the mechanism used in a quality control chart (see Figure 4-5). Average quality is shown by the mean, represented in this case horizontally rather than vertically. Above the average are the upper control limits, and below are the lower control limits. Each represents a single standard deviation from the norm or average

Figure 4-4. Standard deviations.

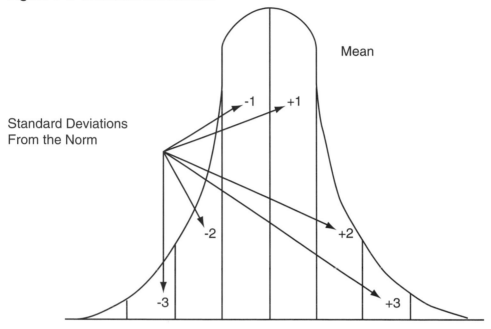

(mean). All performance must fall within that single standard deviation or it is rejected. However, variance (tolerance) is allowed within the standard deviation guides or controls.

Statistical Mathematics

All of the formulations of statistical analysis can now be done quite easily by anyone with a computer. There are dozens of software programs for statistical charting available for all types of computer formats. So what I have described so far in this section is really all a trainer needs to know about statistical procedures and terminology. However, for those who are mathematically inclined, here are the two most common and most frequently used statistical formulas:

Normal Frequency Curve

$$f(x) = \frac{1}{\sigma\sqrt{2\pi}} e^{-(x-\mu)^2 / 2\sigma^2}$$

where:

Figure 4-5. Quality control chart.

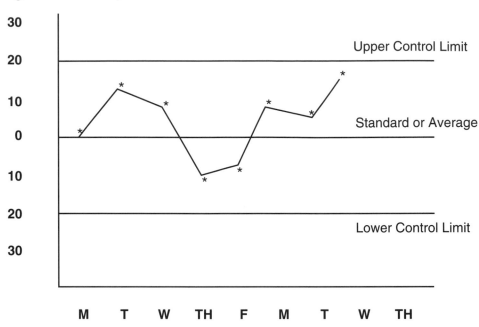

f(x) = frequency at a particular *x* value divided by the total frequency
x   = class mark (or class midmark)
μ   = population mean
σ   = population standard deviation
σ²   = population variance
π   = 3.14159 (approximately)
e   = base of the natural logarithims
       = 2.71828 (approximately)

The values of σ and μ define the frequency curve. When these two are known, the curve can be graphed.

Standard Deviation

$$s = \sqrt{\frac{\sum_{i-1}^{n} (x_i - y)^2}{n - 1}}$$

where s is the small standard deviation; x_i is an observed or measured value; y is the sample mean; n is the number of observations; and $\sum\limits_{i-1}^{n}$ denotes the operation of summing:

$$(x_i - x)^2 \text{ for } i = 1, 2, 3 \ldots n$$

Data Collection

There are seven formats for gathering data, depending on the depth and detail you need. Most of us don't have the time to be as thorough as we'd like. Choose the most feasible method for your organization that produces adequate results for you. If you have the time and want more scientific evidence, use a second method to verify the findings from the first. Remember, the simpler, the better; but, remember also that you are after *real* data, and the results of your training will depend on the accuracy of your findings.

Guidelines for Gathering Data

1. What information do I want?
   - What is happening?
   - What skills are involved?
   - What problems are created?
   - What is the dollar cost of the problems?
   - What is the political climate surrounding these problems?
2. What use will the data have?
   - Is it a basis for developing a training program?
   - Will you use it to justify that program to management?
   - Will it cover you politically?
   - Will it convince those who are part of the problem?
   - Will it motivate the eventual trainees?
3. Which method or combination of methods will most easily and accurately supply the information needed?

The standard data-gathering methods are arranged here in order of difficulty, from easiest to most difficult:

1. Field observations
2. Surveys

3. Interviews
4. Focus groups
5. Record checks
6. Task analyses
7. Assessment sessions

Let's look at each one in turn.

Field Observations

Going out and looking at the problem is one of the simplest and best ways of establishing the performance baseline. I heartily recommend all trainers do it on a regular basis whether or not they are conducting a needs analysis. If you've trained people, walk around and see how they are doing. It is one of the best ways to monitor your own effectiveness.

To perform field observations specifically for a needs analysis, consider the following:

1. *If you are likely to need it, get permission from whoever is in charge of the people you want to observe.* This usually means you will have to explain why you want to observe the people and you will have to persuade that individual to approve. To bypass such a person, however, could make him or her an enemy who could undermine any future training you might give to those subordinates.

2. *Prepare a reasonable, persuasive rationale for your observations.* I've had success when I outline my ignorance of current procedures and emphasize that, as a trainer, I'd like to learn how the department operates so I don't teach useless or wrong ways. This approach is usually persuasive because it is nonthreatening. At the same time you are being persuasive, you must open up the possibility of training to change the department in such a way that they won't feel stabbed in the back. Diplomacy is a must. An enemy can only hurt you, but a friend can be relied on. In effect, you need to balance your humility in wanting to learn with the frank knowledge that changes might result.

3. *Know what it is you are looking for.* Have your objectives clearly framed. You should be looking to discover what is happening—what the process is. You should also investigate what skills are involved and what the apparent problems are (if any). Analyze what the dollar impact of those problems is. Lastly, find out about the political climate and organizational structure involved. Be as casual and unobtrusive as possible. Try not to make a big thing of it. Simply walk around and observe, ask a few questions, but always keep your activity informal.

Surveys

Send out a written survey. Despite much socioscientific literature to the contrary, you can design and interpret an effective employee survey without outside help. You don't need a technical document that plumbs many subtleties at once. You don't need to validate your findings with statistical safeguards. You're not conducting a scientific study. Apart from the data it generates, no one will ever see your survey except your colleagues and those who respond to it. If you are concerned about accuracy, the data can be checked or verified through observations and interviews. Each of these acts as a reality check on the others.

In a survey, if you know what you want, ask for it—simply and directly. You are asking employees to evaluate some aspects of their work. In order to do that effectively you need to know in advance exactly what you are looking for. Are you assessing skill levels or attitudes? Surveys are better at assessing attitudes than they are at reflecting skills but, as you can see from the sample survey in Figure 4-6, even skills can be evaluated.

Since you don't want to survey everyone, you also need to know who and how many you will need to distribute surveys to. Once you have decided who, how many, and what you are looking for, you can set specific objectives for your survey so that you will know when you've found what you're looking for. With objectives in mind, now you can frame your questions. Figure 4-7 lists examples of each of the types of questions available to you. (Further examples are offered in Chapter 5.)

There are at least ten points to consider in using these types of questions to create a survey:

1. It is an interesting paradox that the more open-ended the questions are, the harder it will be to gather usable, statistically sound information from them. However, the more closed-ended the questions are, the less real information they reveal. You must balance between both extremes. (See Figure 4-7.)

2. The harder it is to answer a question, the harder it will be to interpret the answer.

3. Be sure to ask for only one piece of information at a time. If the question is in any way ambiguous or confusing, the answers you get will be unclear and equally confusing.

4. Keep your survey as short as possible. No one wants to slave for hours over a series of questions. The shorter the survey, the more likely it will be answered.

5. Keep it friendly. If the workers responding are forced to run a risk by, for example, revealing unkind feelings toward their supervisors, they will most likely either lie or not fill out the questionnaire. Even if you make the questionnaire anonymous, try to minimize judgmental comments that might provoke a sense of risk in those responding.

(*text continues on page 111*)

Figure 4-6. Sample survey.

___

Supervisory Skills Analysis Questionnaire

[Purpose: To determine whether there is a need to provide basic supervisory training to *current* supervisors; specifically, to get a "fix"
on planning and organization skills—including time management, delegation, and effective communication.]

A. Please respond to each of the following statements with a *yes*, meaning it is true for you, or a *no*, meaning that it does not describe your
activity or feelings correctly.

		YES	NO
1.	I feel that I fully understand the overall broad business objectives of our company for the next year.	____	____
2.	I feel that I fully understand the expectations for the next year for the unit I manage.	____	____
3.	I have developed a performance plan for my unit for the next year tied to the company objectives and expectations for my unit.	____	____
4.	I have shared this unit performance plan with my manager (superior).	____	____
5.	I have shared this performance plan with my subordinates.	____	____
6.	I have provided ideas/input to my manager to consider in the overall planning effort.	____	____
7.	I have elicited input from my subordinates for planning at the unit level and above.	____	____
8.	I don't have time to think very much about performance planning. I just need to get the job done.	____	____
9.	My subordinates would not want to participate in performance planning. They want me to be the boss.	____	____
10.	I need some further instruction in performance planning.	____	____

B. List the steps you take in creating your performance plan.

1. _____
2. _____
3. _____
4. _____
5. _____
6. _____
7. _____
8. _____
9. _____
10. _____

C. Please respond to the following by circling one of the numbers on the scale: (1) means that this statement is *never* true for you, (2) means that it is *rarely* true for you, (3) means that it is *sometimes* true for you, (4) means that it is *usually* true for you, and (5) means that it is *always* true for you.

1. I plan my day's activities in advance.
   1 2 3 4 5
2. I hardly ever accomplish all that I planned.
   1 2 3 4 5
3. My department is so busy it is virtually impossible to plan my time.
   1 2 3 4 5
4. I usually accomplish the important things I have planned.
   1 2 3 4 5
5. I feel that there is just not enough time to get all of the things done in my job that should be done.
   1 2 3 4 5
6. I find I'm the only one who knows how to get a project accomplished.
   1 2 3 4 5
7. I work the longest hours of anyone in my unit.
   1 2 3 4 5
8. I suffer burnout from the heavy demands of being a supervisor.
   1 2 3 4 5

(continues)

Figure 4-6. *(continued)*

D. Circle the response that most accurately describes your approach to supervision.
   1. I meet with my subordinates
      (a) on a regular basis.
      (b) as needed for new assignments and follow-up.
      (c) when they ask me to.
   2. I generally give feedback
      (a) when work needs to be improved.
      (b) when work is well done.
      (c) when asked to.
   3. I wish this company would
      (a) offer more skills training for my subordinates.
      (b) provide better talent for me to hire.
      (c) relate training to real needs.

E. Please provide a written response to each of the following:
   1. What do you see as your major challenge as a supervisor this year?

   2. What do you feel are your personal strengths as a supervisor?

   3. In what areas do you feel you could improve your supervisory skills?

Thank you.

          Name: (optional) _____

Figure 4-7. Question formats (arranged from most closed to most open).

Type of Question	*Example*
Yes/no	Would you use "Option/Command/M" to select an entire document?*
	Would you favor a ten-minute coffee break in the morning?*
Multiple choice	Which of the following procedures for selecting a paragraph is incorrect?
	(a) Place the cursor at the beginning of the paragraph/scroll to the end of the paragraph/place pointer after the last word of the paragraph/press "shift"/while holding "shift" down, click mouse
	(b) Place pointer at beginning of paragraph/click and hold mouse down/drag diagonally through the paragraph/release mouse
	(c) Use extreme left margin selection area/double click on mouse
	(d) All of the above
Menu selection	Of the following procedures, check the ones you do *not* normally follow.
	_____1. Use the "window" menu to change from one opened document to another
	_____2. Use a menu command to underline copy
	_____3. Use the "format" menu to copy a style for a new document
	_____4. Set up and use a personal glossary to save time
	_____5. Close manually each document and window on the desktop before shutting down
	_____6. Use "Command" "Q" to change point size to a smaller size
	The following are steps that might be used in formatting a document. Check the ones you would use.
	_____1. "Tab," "space," and "return" to indent and create columns

(continues)

Figure 4-7. *(continued)*

Type of Question	Example
	_____2. Select "Set Styles" menu/select "open" to copy a style
	_____3. Select "Set Styles" menu/create individual styles
	_____4. Select "Template" from desktop/copy template to new document
	_____5. Create document "Workbox" of the style commands to be used as needed
	_____6. Select "Page Setup" as part of your format to link documents in sequence for printing
	_____7. Use "Page Preview" to number pages or change margins
Menu response	Of the following procedures, circle whether you perform them (a) regularly, (b) occasionally, (c) rarely, or (d) never.
	1. Linking printing sequences (a) (b) (c) (d)
	2. Using two or more columns on a page (a) (b) (c) (d)
	3. Multiple fonts in one application (a) (b) (c) (d)
	4. Immediately back up work completed (a) (b) (c) (d)
Semantic differential	Evaluate how you feel about the following by marking (a) excellent, (b) good, (c) fair, or (d) poor.
	1. Microsoft Excel (a) (b) (c) (d)
	2. Microsoft Word (a) (b) (c) (d)
	3. Aldus Pagemaker (a) (b) (c) (d)
	4. Graphic Works (a) (b) (c) (d)
Descriptive lists	List and number in sequence the steps you follow when you insert a chart or graph into the body copy.
	1. _____
	2. _____
	3. _____

Type of Question	Example
	4. _____
	5. _____
Case history	Describe what you would do in the following situation: You have just finished working up a large spreadsheet and have administered a "Print" command. The printer has begun to print the copy. Suddenly your assistant hands you a fax that has just arrived which will change some of the figures on the spreadsheet. What should you do?
Essay	Describe how you would perform each of the following tasks: (a) Create a bar chart in Excel (b) Design a page layout in Microsoft Word for a newsletter (c) Incorporate a chart in Microsoft Word and have the body copy conform to it

*All of the computer operation examples used here reflect Microsoft Word or Microsoft Excel on a MacIntosh computer.

6. Remember, each question must perform two tasks: It must gather the desired information, and it must do so in a usable form.

7. Key the survey to the educational and work levels of the group you plan to survey.

8. If you have a previous survey that was successful, why reinvent the wheel? Use that format.

9. Test the survey beforehand. Try it out on friends and relatives, coworkers, and, if possible, on several members of the client population itself to be sure that you are neither ambiguous nor threatening and that you will get the information you seek.

10. Be sure to gain whatever approvals you will need before you distribute your survey.

Decide how you will distribute the survey. It could be given to employees as they leave work, mailed to their homes, included with their paychecks, inserted in the in-house publication, or placed in the cafeteria to be picked up at will. Including the survey with the paycheck carries authority, so it may get a higher response, but that response is less likely to be critical and honest. Distributing them to employees as they leave work gets a response that is usually balanced. Mailing them to the home will most likely give you the most honest results, but also sometimes gets a low response. Surveys inserted in in-house publications or left in convenient places tend to produce honest responses but have the lowest return rate.

When you compile the results, don't force the data. If you draw too many conclusions, you could end up training to solve the wrong problems. If there are job descriptions, company goals, or personal objectives involved, measure your

---

Creating Surveys

1. Decide what population will be surveyed.
2. Decide on the size of the survey population.
3. Decide how deeply you will probe (procedural, political, personal).
4. Isolate skills involved (job descriptions, task analyses, etc.).
5. Define a set of attitudes you want to examine.
6. Set your objectives. (What exactly are you looking for and how will you know when you find it?)
7. Create questions to examine each skill and attitude in each category.
   - Ask for only one idea or piece of information at a time.
   - The harder it is to answer a question, the harder it will be to interpret that answer.
   - Make the questions easy to understand and respond to.
   - Try to find a previously successful survey and adapt it.
   - Keep it as short as possible.
   - Keep it as friendly as possible.
8. Test the questions on friends and relatives, associates, potential trainees, and on your *clients*!
9. Adjust and refine as needed.
10. Gain final approval (if necessary).
11. Let the survey population know that they will be surveyed (advertise).
12. Survey.
13. Evaluate according to your objectives.
14. Don't try to interpret too much from limited data.
15. Let the respondents know what the results were.

---

results against them. Then publicize your survey. Try to tie it in with some major company thrust or activity. Let management know what it is, why it is, and what should happen because of the results. Let everyone know the general results (overall response, percentage breakdowns for each answer, and so on). Use the in-house publication to call attention to it and to thank the respondents.

Interviews

There are two problems with interviews: They are very time-consuming, and much of what is discussed may be irrelevant. The first problem can be solved by limiting your interviews to checking the accuracy of data you've collected in other ways. Simply select individuals at random from the group you've observed or surveyed. Alternatively, interview only management or supervisory personnel to clarify the data you've gathered. This approach has the added benefit of establishing connections with these managers or supervisors. It also introduces the risk that they will distort or falsify to cover poor performance. If that is a problem, combine the interviews for a valid cross section.

The second problem, too much irrelevant data, can be avoided by carefully planning your interviews. The interview generates the fullest and most complete data. It is an integral part of both task analysis and assessment. It can be an important part of field observation and, as just seen, it also can be an effective check on survey data. If you plan your interviews, they can give you very effective results with a minimum investment of time.

Here are some steps for planning and using the interview format for needs analysis data gathering:

1. *Select key people.* Unless you want first impressions, new employees probably won't give you meaningful data. When interviewing supervisors, select those who will tell you what you need to know.

2. *Keep your interviews short.* Not only don't employees have time to spare, but the longer the interview is, the more time it will take you to sort the data.

3. *Establish your goals before you set up the interviews.* Know what you want to accomplish in each case. Don't think it, write it down. Keep that goal in mind as you interview so you stay on the topic and the interview is short.

4. *Know to whom you are talking.* Do your homework and find out where they stand in the political and organizational network.

5. *Plan the questions and the sequence you are going to use.* Then use them. Remember, you need to know what is happening (how they do what they do), what skills are involved, what problems there are, what these problems cost, what the political and organizational structure is surrounding these tasks, and what their attitudes are toward the work and the problems. If there are delicate or emotional

issues, you may have to think through your choice of words and phrases. Use open-ended questions and practice active listening. (See Chapter 3.)

6. *Keep the interview brief.* Ten minutes should be all you need unless you're using only one key individual for all your data. Even then, don't waste time.

7. *Clear the results with the interviewees.* Let them know what you're doing with the data and give them a chance to approve or suggest changes in your proposal to change their procedures.

8. *Use your questions as a guideline.* Don't hesitate to probe further and to ask for clarification.

There are several important differences between interviews and surveys that must be considered in deciding which format to use when. Interviews take much longer than surveys to complete. The planning is the same, but the gathering of data takes much longer and so does the interpretation of that data. On the other hand, surveys are necessarily much more impersonal than interviews and provide a much greater opportunity for falsification.

Because they are personally involving, interviews are much more subjective and therefore more open to interpretation. As a result, they are much more difficult to evaluate and draw data from, but they do yield very quotable comments that can be noted and used persuasively in proposals and justifications. Surveys lend themselves to more closed-ended questions, while interviews are often more open-ended. However, the interview allows for the flexible use of each format.

Each format can be used to verify the other, but survey data are much easier to record and quantify so that form lends itself better to cross-checking during interviews. Recording data in interviews is a problem in itself. Ideally, if the interviewee doesn't mind, I prefer to tape-record the interview. Failing that, I like someone else present to take notes so I can concentrate on asking questions and on the answers as they are given.

Differences Between Interviews and Surveys

- Time consumed
- Personal impact
- Opportunity for falsification
- Role of subjective interpretation and personality
- Use of closed-ended versus open-ended questions
- Ability to use survey data to clarify interview issues
- Ability to use interviews to verify survey data (and vice versa)
- Means for recording data

One final word on planning interviews. It is easy to get off track in the give and take of interesting discussion. One way to make sure that interviews gather data on the same issues, and so produce comparable data, is to create a core list of eight or nine questions that are always asked of each interviewee. This way you ensure that, when you look at the data, you will be able to compare apples to apples.

Focus Groups

A special form of interview is the focus group. It has several advantages over individual interviews, among which is that it is much less time-consuming. A focus group is a gathering, a meeting of a group of managers or workers for a question-and-answer discussion of the problems about which the training department needs information. It is, in effect, group interviewing, and the best ones are conducted very much like a regular training class with objectives, methods, group activities, and much Socratic discussion.

To plan a focus group you must first decide whom you will invite. The optimum number is usually twelve to fifteen persons. More than this becomes cumbersome; fewer runs the risk of not getting broad enough input. Invite parties that represent all sides of a controversial issue. A focus group of friends is merely self-affirming. You want all of the sides represented in order to get a full and accurate picture.

It is inadvisable to have reporting relationships in the same focus groups together. Subordinates tend to want to try to please management and management tends to need to demonstrate its superior position. Both of these behaviors are counter to getting an accurate picture and so should be avoided. This means that, because people often have different regional standards of conduct, it is sometimes necessary to hold several focus groups on the same subjects at different locations and with different populations.

Once you know your population, set clear objectives for what you want to achieve. Because this is a meeting format, they do not have to be training objectives. They can be simply a list of key pieces of information that you must acquire. Then all of the activities in your focus group will be focused on the target.

The third step in planning a focus group session is to create activities for the participants to work on in the session. One of the extra benefits of focus groups over other forms of needs-analysis data gathering is the synergy that comes from groups of people interacting over the problems you bring up. Information on attitudes and skills is revealed as the participants work through case histories, simulations, or group projects. I usually assign participants to groups of three or four and then give each group either a case history or a set of problems (defined by an earlier survey or set of interviews) with perhaps tentative answers. Then I ask them to evaluate the answers and come up with better ones if they can.

Planning and Conducting Focus Groups

1. Decide on population.
2. Set objectives.
3. Design group activities:
   - Case situations
   - Simulations
   - Group projects
4. Design tentative solutions to anticipated problems so that they become the subjects for discussion and/or negotiation.
5. Design a series of questions to lead participants into discussion of the issues involved.
6. Set time limits.
7. Book space and notify attendees.
8. Thank them for helping you.

In order to make the focus group more effective, you should always have a set of solutions that they can evaluate and challenge. Such solutions spur discussion and allow you to demand that they create better ones and, in the process, reveal the status quo of affairs surrounding those problems. In addition, as you would in an interview, design a set of core questions to be discussed.

Be sure to book an adequate space plenty of time in advance. Two hours should be enough for a focus group. One hour usually feels rushed and leaves out some questions, while more than two hours leaves participants exhausted and sometimes disgruntled. Notify participants with enough lead time for them to arrange to attend, and be sure, before they leave, to thank them for their help and active participation.

Record Checks

Several types of records can be checked to investigate the problem phase of a needs analysis. These records can also be used to establish the present level of performance. Here are some of the records that produce useful data:

- Absenteeism records
- Complaint records
- Sales call reports
- Scrap and reject figures
- Shipping figures
- Training evaluations

- Turnover figures
- Workers' compensation claims
- Reports of safety-related accidents
- Customer service call records
- Employee evaluations
- Exit interviews
- Infirmary reports
- Inspection reports and figures
- Production figures
- Quality control figures

Remember, the purpose of a needs analysis is not to establish blame or even to solve problems, but merely to gather data that provide a picture of what skills can be changed to improve the situation.

Task Analyses

A task analysis serves two main functions: It can be a diagnostic tool in needs analysis and a prescriptive or regulating guide in preparing training programs. When used for a needs analysis, it becomes a detailed observation of what exactly is being done. In connection with the training program, it is a detailed description of what should be done. The prescriptive use—the formal task analysis— must be perfect because it is the model for performance. We cover it in detail in Chapter 6.

The diagnostic use, however, need not be as detailed. You are simply documenting how the job is currently being carried out. For the most part, this entails making close observations and writing them down. When detailed technical skills are involved, for example, in a lathe operation, you must study each move minutely and interview the operator on what is being done and why. The study then sets the baseline of performance.

The task analysis defines the top and bottom ends of the gap in performance between the existing level and the desired level. In fact, needs analysis is often referred to as *gap analysis* for this reason. However, it is the task analysis, technically, that defines the parameters of the gap. This relationship can be expressed as a formula.[*]

Required Performance − Actual Performance = Potential Training Need

or

$$RP - AP = PTN$$

*This formula is taken from an American Management Association seminar entitled "Developing Effective Training Needs Analysis," created by Dr. Elaine Ré.

In conducting informal descriptive task analyses, here are a few guidelines:

1. Get permission of both supervisors and the people you will be observing.

2. Make several observations of the same people. The first time they may feel self-conscious or perhaps obliged to perform the task better than they normally would.

3. Assure the people that your purpose is not punitive and that only good can come from helping you. Make them feel special, that the job of being observed is an honored one.

4. Since standards will be set later, remember that what you are recording is strictly what is being done, not what should be done or what you or others would like to be done.

5. Once you have recorded the activities, review them step by step with the person you observed to be certain you have captured the actual performance.

6. If you can (and it is appropriate), videotape the operation, with permission. You can study it in slow motion and the tape will stand as inarguable documentation. Do make a written, step-by-step analysis of the videotape, which will be much more useful in writing your program.

Your results should resemble a computer program in its step-by-step detailing of procedures. A task analysis is exactly that—a detailed record of how a task is performed. We'll document how to perform the much more detailed prescriptive task analysis in Chapter 6.

Assessment Sessions

Some occupations have regular assessment requirements, usually mandatory performance tests that key employees take to maintain their standing. For example, airline pilots must undergo simulator tests every six months. In a similar way, but without the pressure of being tested, volunteer fire departments compete with each other to maintain their skills. Rodeos originated in the West for much the same reason. They are both for fun and for an assessment of skills. Assessment sessions of many types can be excellent opportunities for trainers to evaluate performance levels. If your company has such activities, use them.

A more widely used form of assessment is the personal interviews that supervisors or managers use to evaluate an employee's performance. Different companies use different names and formats for such interviews, but they all are, in effect, assessment sessions usually recorded in the employee's personnel file. Gather data from these sessions by interviewing the supervisors or managers. If you have access, look over the personnel reports. This can be a touchy area because the employees being examined don't usually know you are doing so. If you have qualms about it or your company is not comfortable with it, don't use this approach.

Determining the Level of Performance

Most of the time, the information gathered will reveal the level of current performance. This is certainly so for task analyses and assessment sessions. In surveys or interviews, however, the level of performance isn't always apparent. In these cases, you will have to follow up with an informal task analysis to establish the performance baseline. It need be no more detailed than necessary to (l) indicate what functions need training, and (2) convince management that the training is necessary.

If you are taking a proactive stance and are anticipating a need for training in a task that isn't being done now, you must go outside your company to establish performance parameters. (For example, your company has ordered a new piece of computer-automated high speed production equipment for the plant. While it is being installed and tested, you are developing the necessary training for the future operators.) This can be done by networking with trainers in other organizations, shopping for vendors or service agencies that already have courses to train in the area of concern, and comparing your proposed requirements to existing practices in similar or related tasks.

Examining Feasibility

Once you have discovered a problem and have probed to find its exact nature and cause, you must ask once again, "Is this a training problem?" If not, there is no point in proceeding further. If so, go ahead. Your next step is to evaluate the political climate for change in the organization.

Rarely do we achieve what we want without opposition. Others have their own agendas and goals, which are seldom completely parallel to ours. This means that some managers are almost sure to oppose your proactive training thrust. Before spending time and effort working out the details of what you propose, look into the political feasibility of your plans. The first step is to analyze the climate for change that currently exists in the company.

Analyzing the Climate for Change

To analyze the current situation, you need to define your organizational culture and determine how it responds to change. There are five dimensions for measuring change in an organization:

1. Rate
2. Bias
3. Magnitude
4. Structure
5. Power

Let's explore each.

Rate. How fast has change taken place in the past and how long do you think it will take to make the changes you propose? Ask yourself these questions:

- What changes in management are imminent? What happens when management personnel are replaced?
- When was the last senior-level reorganization? What management changes resulted? How did those changes impact on the rest of the organization?
- Which new ideas have been accepted into the organization during the past eighteen months?
- What current ideas have yet to take effect? How long have they been in the offing?

Then choose an innovation, such as a new procedure begun by a new manager, and track it until it is in universal use. These findings will help you to draw conclusions about the rate of change.

Bias. Changes in operation are shaped considerably by the biases of those who are in power. In fact, any change you plan will have to be modified to flow in the direction of bias in your organization. To discover such leanings, you will need to ask yourself these questions:

- How do things get done in the organization? You are not asking what is being done but rather how. (This is a question of style, and it therefore indicates bias.)
- How does management style differ among the most powerful people?
- Within the last two years, have any middle- or upper-level managers left the organization because of differences in style? (This is another question of style—how things get done, not what gets done.)
- What past training programs have failed despite initial management support and enthusiasm?

Then compare the educational, ethnic, familial, social, and professional backgrounds of three or four of the most powerful middle managers. Do the same for a few people in the top management team. Compare the results to predict potential friction or compatibility. This information will give you an idea of the underlying management biases and whether they will continue into the future.

Magnitude. What kind of change has succeeded or failed historically in the organization? If only major changes succeed, you will have to build a major change very carefully. Otherwise it may be wiser to subtly ease in the smaller changes you want. To determine which approach to use, you will need to know the answers to these questions:

- What apparently sound ideas have failed to take hold in the past five years?
- Which pet projects of top management have been sidetracked by middle management's failure to implement them effectively?
- Which past training programs succeeded in bringing about change?
- Have any proposed changes been dropped or simply forgotten because of resistance from the rank and file?
- What is the largest major change that has taken place under the present management? How was it managed?

These answers will give you an idea of how receptive management will be to either large or small changes in operations.

Structure. How a proposed change is packaged usually becomes a major fac tor in its ultimate success. Advertising agencies, for example, spend much creative time determining how to present a new product to make it as appealing as possible. New ideas in the corporate culture are no different. There are two forces that come into play when presenting a new idea: formal corporate channels of communication and informal routes such as the grapevine or friends in key positions. Anyone familiar with the military or government agencies knows the difference between the two, as well as the powers and limits of each. Corporate cultures are the same, and the channel you choose to bring about a change impacts heavily on how well the change succeeds. To map your corporate structure you will need to answer the following questions:

- What are the formal channels of communication in your organization?
- What are the informal channels of communication and how are they approached?
- Who, regardless of position, are the people most effective at packaging ideas and selling them to top and middle management? How do they package what they want done?
- Who, regardless of position, are the people with reputations for getting things done? And what channels do they use to do so?
- What new procedures or ideas have been extremely successful in recent months? Who originated them? Who sponsored them? Who packaged them? How were they eased through the organization?

These answers should provide some ideas for packaging your proposals so they are accepted and, ultimately, are successful.

Power. Who holds the real power in the company? That is, who will the rank and file follow? That person is not always the designated leader, as you saw in Chapter 3. The real power is in the hands of the person on whom the group bestows its trust. In fact, power is often the most important of the five factors mentioned here. Certainly, a powerful person is a great ally in making changes, and you are doomed to almost certain failure if that person openly opposes you. In identifying where the power lies, you must find the answers to these questions:

- How has top or middle management used the company grapevine? Do they fight it or do they promote it? Does the grapevine ignore them?
- Who in the company, regardless of position, defers to the senior secretary?
- Who does the organization's senior secretary report to?
- Who has inordinate power for the position he or she holds?
- Who gets things done? Who are the people always powerless to achieve their goals?

These answers will point you in the direction of where the power is that can help you achieve your goals. The answers to all these questions should provide you with an effective map of your corporate culture. Use the map to plot the route for reaching your goals as an agent of change in the company.

One of the cardinal rules of office politics is *never call a meeting unless you know the outcome in advance.* This means that you must know who your sources of resistance will be. If they could succeed in blocking you, don't proceed. Hold your data in readiness for changes in climate or personnel or wait until the problem itself changes. When the time is ripe, proceed. But always assess your likelihood of succeeding before you put a lot of work into the project.

One final question must be asked when examining feasibility. Are there any other solutions to the problem? Ask this of yourself and of those you try to win over to your side. It will position you as a reasonable person. You won't appear to be building an empire for yourself if you ask others for their solutions. Also, you will find out if there really *are* other solutions. You will broaden the responsibility for correcting the problem so that the solution doesn't rest entirely on you. Lastly, you allow those who oppose you to solve the problem their way. This step alone may turn an enemy into an ally. In effect, asking others for solutions makes you a team player, which is an excellent stance for a service function on the wrong side of the ledger.

Determining the Size of the Training Thrust

If the political air is relatively clear, it's time to shift from gathering data to projecting a response to that data. You must decide on the scope, length, format, location, cost, frequency, and population that will be involved:

- *Scope.* What will the program cover? How much information needs to be taught? What is the management goal of such new training? What will the training accomplish for the company?

- *Length.* How much time will you need to effect the change you want? What are the costs of having workers or managers away from their jobs for considerable time, for example, ten hours, thirty hours, or eighty hours?

- *Format.* Does this subject lend itself to a format already familiar to the participants? For example, three hours per morning for six mornings, one day per week for six consecutive weeks. Is the workforce already comfortable with one particular format? Have other formats worked for this organization in the past? For other organizations?

- *Location.* Where is it best to hold this training? See Chapter 11 for more information on this. What are the cost factors involved in different locations?

- *Cost.* What are the outright costs of creating this training package? What are the costs of buying an off-the-shelf package? See Chapter 9 for more on this. Which of these alternatives best meets your need? What is the cost of new visual aids or equipment?

- *Frequency.* How often will the training program be offered? What are the cost amortization figures for each of several different possible frequencies?

- *Population.* Who will be trained? What will be the cost per person of the training?

When you have answered these questions and have decided which way best brings about the needed change that earlier research uncovered, then move to the final phase of your needs analysis: justifying the expense to the company.

Justifying the Cost

Management at all levels is concerned with the bottom line—what is the training going to cost? The formula for determining cost is really very simple. Total the costs for the program as you'd like to do it, then as inexpensively as you can possibly conceive of doing it. If you are preparing the program yourself, include the cost of your time. Also include any preparation costs (duplicating, typing, supplies) and the costs of outside services such as off-the-shelf packages or consultants. Tally the results, presented in two ways: (1) the total cost to the company, and (2) the cost per person to the company.

Now figure what the results of improved performance will be in terms of dollars and cents. In order to perform both these calculations you will need the following information and data:

Performance Goal. Your task analysis will provide you with a performance goal. (We'll cover creating a formal task analysis in Chapter 5). Such a task analysis defines the specific skills needed to perform the job. It is the top end of the gap that the full needs analysis defines. Once you have discovered the gap, you need to define training objectives before you can create a course to address it. These are your performance goals. These goals define the new skills to be acquired during the proposed training.

Units to Be Measured in Evaluation. How will you know if your training is working? What do you look at to evaluate the impact of the training on the day-to-day job performance of those trained? The answer is to monitor those sources of data that you used to develop your needs analysis. If you checked customer service records, then monitor them. If you surveyed supervisors, then survey them again. If you documented the need for performance improvement by using focus groups, invite the same people back to discuss and document the improvement training has provided. Use the gaps you have discovered to isolate observable activities that you can monitor as cost variables.

Dollar Value for Each Unit. This is sometimes a difficult task. It entails putting a dollar figure on each skill you teach, on each hour of training you conduct. When you teach improved quality control measurement skills, you can easily document the increased efficiency your trainees gain. But when you teach interpersonal communication skills to managers, the dollar impact may be much harder to pin down. One of the most effective ways is to compare efficiency (that is, time saved) before and after training. Then, using the manager's salary as a base, break down what the company is spending for each minute of that person's time. Now the minutes saved have a direct dollar impact.

If your organization uses job descriptions that outline the percentage of work time each of the individual's responsibilities should be consuming, by increasing or shaping a manager's control over any of these, you can easily bring the dollars in line with the improved performance your training has developed. Use the total salary again but break it into percentages this time. Thus, training allows the manager to spend 65 percent of his or her work time performing those tasks that are defined as most important to that job function (that is, 65 percent of it).

You can put a dollar value on almost anything, but it carries more weight when it can be documented directly. I had a client whose company slashed its safety training budget by $800,000 during an economic downturn. After monitoring the safety-related downtime and the time lost because of accidents during the following twelve months, the training department was able to show that the cut in safety training cost the company $7.5 million in the first year alone. Needless to say, management quickly restored the training budget.

Even something as hard to pin down as the attitude of those who answer the telephone can be given a dollar value. For example, you could figure the average dollar value of a customer, and then cite the results of a March 1979 *U.S. News and World Report* survey, which indicated that 68 percent of the customers who switched vendors did so because of the attitude of a single employee. If you documented (or estimated) the number of customers your organization lost in a given period, took 68 percent of them, and multiplied that figure by the average dollars in business from each customer, you would have a dollars-lost figure that related to employee attitude. Multiply that figure times the number of employees you'd train, and you have a rather convincing argument.

To assign a dollar value to such intangibles, therefore, estimate a dollar amount per instance (per item, per customer, per hour or day or whatever), then devise or use another source (salary figures, the cost of training a new hire, a survey, industrial averages, or Dun & Bradstreet reports) to demonstrate the value of preventing a loss or improving performance to the company. Relate the average cost per instance, or per unit to be measured, to the average loss or improvement based on the statistics. Then express this difference as a ratio. For example, for every dollar spent on training, two and a half dollars will be saved (or earned). This is a 2:5 ratio.

An alternative method is to cite a single massive instance in which the company lost out because employees lacked training. For example, suppose a company won a $10 million contract but lost money on it because of poor budgeting skills. You could easily justify offering managers with bidding authority a course in budgeting.

Time Needed for Training. Time is an important cost factor in training. It impacts in two areas: first in the dollars spent paying employees to spend time in training and not in the field, and second in the speed with which newly trained employees are able to perform the money-saving skills you've taught them. If training takes months, the cost can become prohibitive. But even the most expensive training is justifiable if the improved performance is immediate and can be demonstrated efficiently.

Current Level of Performance. This is the data that you have collected during your needs analysis. You use it, of course, to figure out a dollar value both for maintaining the status quo and for improving it.

Number to Be Trained. It is particularly important to factor in this figure when you are justifying a large initial expense to introduce a unit of training. As you will see in Chapter 10, interactive instruction on CD-ROM can be quite expensive to create. Entry-level programs start at about $50,000. To train only ten or twelve people at such a cost would be expensive. But if you train a thousand people over a period of time, then the same program costs only $50 per person.

Costs of Training. There are a number of costs that impact on the training budget. We will talk about them in Chapter 15 when we discuss budgeting methods. However, the cost of each training program can be (and for cost justification should be) broken down into its own budget. The usual factors are:

- *Preparation time.* The rule of thumb for course development is that each hour of instruction or class time will take three to five hours to plan and prepare. Developing training is a time-consuming affair. And time is money in terms of departmental salaries or the cost of hiring outsiders. Multiply the hourly wage of each person who works on development by the total number of hours he or she has devoted to the development of the course. Add the total of all persons involved (including secretarial help) to come up with this cost figure.

- *Training space.* If you use facilities off-site, they will cost money to rent. So will the visual aids or equipment you rent there. Meals and coffee breaks have to be figured in, too. Even when you use in-house facilities, unless they are dedicated training facilities, there will be a cost in that others cannot use the rooms or equipment while you are using it. Estimate a fraction of overhead for such facilities. (Accounting can give you detailed overhead figures.)

- *Visual aids.* Production or acquisition of aids can be a significant cost. Before you can justify the benefits of training, you must know such costs in detail (see Chapter 9).

- *Outside help.* If you are going to use consultants, temporaries, off-the-shelf packages, or other help (see Chapter 8), you will need to figure in these costs, too.

- *Supplies.* This category covers a general list of such things as the production of trainee workbooks and manuals, bindings, papers, pencils, flip charts, markers, and transparencies. Knowing that most of these are bulk purchases, the easiest way to estimate their cost is to take the total annual cost of such materials and divide it by the number of days or hours of instruction for the year. Then the materials for any course will be this daily or hourly cost times the length of the program.

Cost Justification Data

1. Desired performance goal
2. Units to be measured in evaluating success
3. Dollar value for each unit
4. Time needed for training to achieve the goal
5. Current level of performance
6. Number of people to be trained
7. Costs of training

- *Travel.* If the training is to be offered off-site, costs must include the expense of sending the trainer and/or trainees to the location.

- *Training staff time.* This figure is simply the number of trainers and other staff in attendance during the training, multiplied by the cost of their salaries for this time.

- *Participant time.* This can be a major cost. It is usually not a part of the training budget per se, but it must be looked at by management considering funding training. It must never be hidden; it should be figured into the cost justification. Again, the figure is arrived at by multiplying the number of participants by the number of days they will be absent from their regular work and by the per diem dollar figure of their salaries or wages.

- *Evaluation.* Most people overlook the cost of performing evaluation of training. As we have seen earlier in this chapter, there is no way to know how effective your training is without careful scrutiny and follow-up. This takes time and materials and therefore entails costs that need to be figured into your cost analyses.

- *Contribution.* It costs the company money to supply the training department with space, desks, electricity, computers, and telephones. All of these together constitute the overhead of the department. In justifying training, it is often good policy to charge a percentage of these costs back to each program offered by the department so that, when it comes time to evaluate and justify existing training, the contribution of each course can be documented.

The Process of Justification

If we put all of the information we have gathered up to this point together, we can create a balance sheet of costs versus return on investment—a cost justifica-

---

Steps for Justifying Cost

1. Decide or create a dollar factor unit of comparison.
2. Set a dollar value on each unit or on the total of all units (production).
3. Describe the difference in dollars between performance prior to proposed training (current performance) and after proposed training (estimated improved performance).
4. Work out the cost of each option you are mentioning in your proposal: status quo, training option one, option two, option three, etc.
5. Compare the difference between status quo and posttraining dollars.
6. Multiply by the number of people to be trained.
7. Compare total cost of training to total dollar benefit for each option.

---

tion. The steps are relatively simple. Multiply the dollar value you have set for each unit of measurement by all of the units. Do this twice: once for the status quo and once for the posttraining estimated performance. Now add up the costs of producing this training. You will have the cost of present practice, the cost of changing that practice, and the dollar benefit of making the change. Describe these difference in dollars: a before and after comparison. Work out such a comparison for each of several training or budgetary options, if you have more than one. This will produce a before and after comparison for each trainee's performance (or for each offering of the course), the cost of changing that performance, and the anticipated benefit of doing so. Now multiply the cost savings by the total number of people to be trained (or by the total number of times the course is to be offered) and compare the total cost with the total benefit.

Summary

In this chapter we discussed the various stages of compiling a needs analysis. We examined the primary and auxiliary uses for the needs analysis, and made a distinction between the proactive and reactive approaches to meeting needs for training. It was pointed out that the needs analysis is a data-gathering operation that ultimately provides you with the basis for determining the size and scope of a proposed training program, as well as helping you justify the cost of that program.

We also looked at the need for some political analysis skills, as it is necessary for the trainer to be aware of the impact that any proposed training will have on the organization.

Applications

1. Write a survey to assess the level of performance in a given area in your organization and the workers' attitude toward that work. Use all of the question styles we've discussed in this chapter.

2. Plan and schedule a focus group for managers to assess the information you've gathered from your survey. Prepare an agenda, a set of questions and cases for the managers to work on in their small groups, and a set of recommendations for training based on your findings that they can discuss and approve (or reject).

3. Assess and justify the costs of your proposed training. Prepare a persuasive rationale to convince management that the expenditure is worthwhile.

4. Create a political assessment of the climate for change in your organization.

Chapter 5
Evaluating Your Effectiveness

TRAINING is the business of bringing about change. To know whether you have achieved change, you must be able to evaluate the effects of your instruction. You've defined your objectives and determined what the change should be. You've assessed the present status and have a program for changing it to meet those objectives. Now you need a means of measuring the success you've achieved. This last step is evaluation.

There are three levels of change in performance that must be monitored and evaluated. Level one is the measurement of how well the trainees can perform the skills you have been communicating to them. It takes place during and upon completion of training.

Level two is the observation of the trainees' performance when they return to the job. It is a measure of what theorists call the "transfer" of learning to the workplace. You know from level one evaluation how well each of the trainees is able to perform the skills you've taught. Now you must follow up and observe whether or not they are actually transferring those skills to their jobs. If they are not doing so, you will need to perform a narrow-focused needs analysis in order to troubleshoot the problem, diagnose it, and propose a solution.

Level three is a measurement of the impact of the training on the operations of the department for which you have performed the training or, indeed, on the entire organization. It is a measurement of the dollar return on the money investment by management in training. Level three is the bottom-line evaluation. It answers the question "Are we getting our money's worth out of training?"

As you can see, evaluation is an important ongoing function for the trainer. It is also a vital function for the trainees. If you remember, one of Thorndike's principles of learning is the law of effect: nothing succeeds like success. Trainees must get constant feedback to develop the motivation to continue. Constant evaluation not only lets you know where you are, but it also does the same for your trainees. For convenience, the evaluation function has been divided into several operations, but there is considerable overlap and much mixing of technique. It is likely that you will be using several methods at the same time.

Level One: Short-Term Evaluations

Level one evaluation consists mainly of short-term projects with which we are most familiar. Homework assignments, class projects, term papers, and tests are the forms of evaluation we all remember from school. This level of evaluation usually consists of some challenging task set by the instructor and performed by the student. How well the student performs the task is the measure of his or her success at learning it. The task provides the learner with necessary feedback on how well he or she is learning. At the same time, it provides the instructor with feedback on how well the learner is mastering the skills being taught and what coaching, if any, will be required. Incidentally, it also provides feedback on the instructor's success at teaching the material.

Exams and Tests

Many people dread exams because, when they were in school, the results were associated with passing or failing. Since exams were the basis for vital judgments affecting our future, it isn't surprising that exams are thought of as almost punitive to some of us. You will have to reposition the purpose and function of exams to show your trainees how tests let them know how they are doing. Let exams be a service to them, a diagnostic tool to point out strengths and weaknesses. The fact that you can also use them to evaluate yourself is really immaterial. Tests exist solely for them, to provide important feedback. We'll talk about how to structure those tests later in this chapter.

Alternative Types of Evaluation

There are, however, several other types of short-term evaluations. They range from observational techniques, such as eye contact, to various types of projects and reviews. Let's take a quick look at them, then discuss in detail how to create and use each one as an evaluation tool.

- *Socratic questioning.* In Chapter 2, we established the power and teaching value of asking questions. But one of the other major benefits of asking questions is that it lets you monitor the state of mind of the learners and assess the degree of learning taking place. To develop your questioning technique, see Chapter 3.

Methods for Short-Term Evaluations

1. Examinations
2. Socratic questioning
3. Eye contact and observations
4. Spot quizzes and reviews
5. Project sessions
6. Case histories
7. Practice sessions
8. Formal and informal assessment sessions

▪ *Eye contact.* Also in Chapter 3, we mentioned the importance of eye contact as positive nonverbal communication between instructor and learner. As with most communication, eye contact is a two-way exchange. Contact is initiated and maintained by the instructor, but the learner sends back a message as well. What do your trainees' eyes tell you? Eyes that stare or glare at you are challenging you or disagree with what you say. Eyes that frown are expressing challenge and doubt. Eyes that are glassy and expressionless have had enough. It's time to change the subject. Eyes that shine are challenged and interested, while eyes that droop are sleepy. Ask questions or change the topic. Eyes that blink rapidly or wander about are nervous; the person may be holding something back.

Interpreting Eye Contact

- Glare or stare—challenge or disagreement
- Frown—doubt or deep thought
- Glassy or blank—had enough
- Shining eyes—challenged and interested
- Droopy or sleepy—tuned out or bored
- Blinking or wandering—nervousness or hiding something

▪ *Spot quizzes and reviews.* By reviewing a topic using a question format, in either a written or oral quiz, you can take the pulse of the group and find out how well they understand the material. Formal testing and how to structure questions for tests are discussed later in this chapter.

▪ *Project sessions.* Assigning work to be done in class allows you to circulate and check their understanding as they work. In a project session, you are looking for how well the trainees can use what you've taught them. You also have the opportunity later on to respond in writing to their projects, expressing your evaluation of them. I usually follow up by discussing the project with the group, using several of their efforts as examples.

▪ *Case histories.* The case history is a more involved, practical project. It challenges the learners to use what they've learned. while it allows you to see how well they are doing. Case histories are discussed in greater detail in Chapter 7.

▪ *Practice sessions.* Hands-on practice serves to lock in learning. It also provides you with an excellent opportunity for evaluation and correction.

▪ *Assessment sessions.* Assessments usually take place at the end of a program. When technical training has been involved, it might be a troubleshooting session in which equipment has been intentionally maladjusted. Trainees are evaluated on their speed and accuracy in correcting the situation. In "soft" skill areas, you can create hypothetical crises and assign members of the class to respond appropriately. Role plays are useful simulations.

Creating and Using Short-Term Evaluation Tools

Let's look more closely at the evaluative tools just cited. Asking questions and using eye contact have been covered in Chapters 3 and 6, so let's begin with quizzes and reviews.

Oral Reviews and Spot Quizzes. Oral reviews are a series of well-framed questions. You want to get the trainees talking about what they've just learned. Don't recite what you've covered—ask them to. I like to ask my classes to highlight what they remember from the previous session. This forces them to review the material and allows me to expand upon key areas, correct misunderstandings, and include material that was inadvertently missed.

Structure the review questions around your objectives. This creates strong redundant patterns. Also, never answer your own questions because that allows the class to stop thinking, and it defeats the purpose of the review.

Don't review large blocks of work at once. Break them down into segments and review each shortly after you finish it. You can always test overall knowledge later. Likewise, keep your reviews short. If you find, however, that the group doesn't know the material, you may have to cover it again by prompting Socratically. Look at it as an effective redundant loop. Lastly, be consistent. Review regularly, and don't miss a chance to review. Reviews not only provide feedback and evaluation of what trainees have learned but give them a perspective on what they will be learning. One way to ensure regular reviews is to make reviewing previously covered material a part of the preparation step of each new unit of instruction. I find that this keeps me in the habit of reviewing regularly.

Written quizzes are similar to oral reviews, but remember that the level of understanding you are testing is simple recall. The quiz should (1) discover what the trainees have grasped, and (2) provide a redundant loop to help lock in learning. Questions should be straightforward, not tricky.

Keep the quiz short. Ten questions are more than enough. Fill-in-the-blank questions or questions calling for one- or two-word answers usually work best. Avoid true-false, multiple-choice, and essay questions; save them for full exams.

Since the real value of a quiz is to let the learners see how they're doing, have them self-score the quiz. Do ask, however, to look over those with more than a couple of wrong answers. You may be able to correct a problem before it escalates.

Alternate quizzes with oral reviews, but be sure to cover each segment of your course with one or the other. In addition, consider using a pretest-posttest format to measure growth and mastery. Administer a quiz at the beginning of the class; most will do poorly. Upon completion of training, give them the identical test; their responses will show a marked improvement.

Project Sessions. As mentioned earlier, project sessions are in-class assignments. For them to work, make the tasks real. There are several ways to do this, but my favorite is to ask participants to bring a critical incident to the training seminar. (A critical incident is an event they recently experienced that was crucial to or had a significant effect on the performance of their job.) If the group is with you for several days, collect the incidents and choose the most germane. Assign them to be worked on the following day, then discuss them.

Developing and Evaluating Project Sessions

1. Make them real.
   - Critical incident
   - Worst-case scenario
   - Actual case
   - Routine problem
2. Fit the project to the group and the content of the course.
3. Have correct answers ready, based on the material taught.
4. Make the difficulty level realistic for the time allowed. Allow seminar time for at least part of the project. Be available to help and explain.
5. Alternate assignments between individual and group projects.
6. Give each project a written evaluation, with both positive and constructive feedback.
7. Set clear objectives for critiquing and remain consistent.
8. Take up the project with the whole group. Give them feedback.

Project sessions could be based on a real-life situation with which you are familiar or the worst situation you can imagine. A third way is to simply provide routine problems the trainees would handle every day. But whatever project you use, make your sessions fit the group. If they are not training in crisis management, don't give them a crisis to manage. If they are learning routines, give them routines to perform. Have correct answers ready if there is a chance there may be some doubt about the outcome. Use the material you've taught to verify their answers. (This repetition also locks in learning.)

Assign a project that can be completed in the time you allow. The projects should be challenging (nothing is more boring than an easy project), but not unreasonably so. Allow seminar time for at least part of the project to be completed. Homework is good, but practice time at the learning site (with the trainer available) is better.

Projects can be either individual or group; in fact, give them both. An individual project ensures that everyone participates and gets a chance for feedback and evaluation. A group project builds teamwork, and reflects the more realistic working environment. Group activities set up the personal interactions that all of us must cope with every day.

Evaluate each project individually. This is usually done most easily in the evening after the day's training session is over. Give each individual attention and indicate that you have seen the work by making marginal notes, corrections, and responses. Give both positive and negative feedback. If you allow only the negative, you will discourage the learners. If you give only the positive, they will not correct bad habits. I prefer to begin with the positive specifics of what I like about their work and then address the problem areas. (See Figure 5-1.)

Remember also that you are not grading! Make no comparisons. You are providing feedback on how each trainee or group has done. Set in your mind the specific things you will look for, and remain consistent. Usually these things relate directly back to your objectives, which will help you target your criticism. Don't hesitate to correct the work if it appears they don't understand, but be wary of doing it for them. If you feel they should be able to respond, challenge them with your critique. Make them rethink their work and correct the errors. After all, they will be expected to do that in their jobs.

Discuss the projects with the whole group. Explain what you were looking for and show examples of those who did it correctly (use different people each time if possible). Select one or two that weren't up to par and ask the group to explain how they could have been done better (again, not always the same people). This is not as hard on them as it may seem. It provides them with shared constructive feedback, helps to create a climate that allows for errors (see Chapter 1), and reenforces a strong leadership message (see Chapter 3).

Case Histories. A case history is an enlarged project session. Rather than addressing an isolated incident, it encompasses many separate events in realistic

Figure 5-1. Sample feedback from one of my training the trainer sessions.

[Trainee project]

Objectives

Affective
At the end of the one-week course, the trainee will be able to present a cost analysis based on actual test results.

Cognitive
After one day, the trainee will be able to describe gas-metal arc welding.

[My comments]
Both of these sound cognitive, Lydia. Both are excellent, as such, but the one labeled affective describes a skill performance, not an attitude. To be affective it would have to be written more like *be able to describe the need for cost analysis* or *present a cost analysis enthusiastically* or *confidently prepare and present a cost analysis.*

---

complexity. It is usually structured around a single large problem or event that must be solved by using techniques covered in your training.

Case histories can bring the subject alive for your group. They are a way of approaching real-life problems. In writing a case history for the group, remember to define the basic situation (company, division, and so forth) and then describe the problem and the events that led up to it. Also mention any complications, barriers, political drawbacks, or missing data. Provide all necessary and relevant data, then ask specific questions that will help the group solve the case.

Make the case history real. Use the same sources and approaches as for project sessions, but develop a rich context for them. People love stories. The more realistic texture you can provide, the more you'll motivate and involve the group.

The cases should be realistically complex; they need to be challenging. Therefore, save them until trainees have mastered enough material to solve them, or use the case histories as a topic around which to structure each step or phase of your lesson. Have answers to most of the questions but leave some unanswered as would be the case in real life. Use the group's answers whenever possible as correct or acceptable ones.

Case histories can be assigned to individuals or to groups. If given to individuals, they can challenge and motivate learners who are ahead of the others. They can also be used to involve shy participants who wouldn't get much input in group work. On the other hand, it is more work for you to evaluate. If you are not prepared to give them individual attention, don't assign cases to individuals. When groups handle a case history, the work simulates the real world in that it forces the members of the group to cooperate. It also builds team spirit in class and encourages sharing of knowledge—the most experienced help the least experienced. Group work also encourages division of labor, as more complex tasks are divided up. Lastly, the group activity can be evaluated in more detail because you'll have fewer case histories to review and critique.

Practice Sessions. As with the project sessions, make these hands-on practices as real as possible. Again, material should come from real-life situations. In the case of technical training, use the actual equipment that would be in the field. If that's not feasible, use as close to the real thing as possible. The purpose here is to simulate reality. Use real forms, real computer programs, or real job templates.

However, when they are not available, alternatives to actual situations include computer-generated simulations (such as interactive videodisc or CD-ROM); computer-generated data (which involves either writing or buying a program—see Chapters 7, 9, and 10 for more information on both of these computer options); buying or building a working model of the equipment; acquiring a similar piece of equipment; using old equipment that approximates the operation; working with real equipment that is not on-line (after hours, back-up equipment, or equipment being serviced).

But regardless of what you have to work on, create clearly defined, structured tasks that involve the skills you have taught. Make sure each objective is covered, but nothing more. Be certain your trainees know what it is they are to solve or do. If possible, have checkpoints at which everyone can stop and evaluate the work in progress. These checkpoints give you more control and give the trainees an early chance to correct errors. Lastly, have a correct method or model to refer to.

Whereas hands-on practice is most appropriate in situations involving equipment or procedures, role-playing is a good way to practice interaction skills. If there is reluctance to participate in role-playing, assign teams, with each team responsible for one role. Have the teams prepare a strategy for their side and select who will play the role. This takes each player off the hook. Individuals can blame the team's strategy, if need be. Also, using teams allows the "hams" to go first and break the ice, but it keeps them under control too, because they don't want to let the team down.

Team role-playing allows everyone to participate. If you don't have enough time for everyone to role-play, the team approach lets you begin it in an organized way, yet stop when you need to without cutting anyone off. If you have time, it ensures that everyone role-plays without your having to force them. Lastly, the team activity builds the competition that makes the team a group.

As an alternative to the team approach, you can encourage greater realism by breaking the class into groups of three. Each one then takes a turn playing a role while the third critiques the other two. This frees you to wander and critique other trios. Make sure, though, that the feedback given follows a clear model, that the ones giving that feedback have carefully structured formats for providing it. Otherwise this variation of role-playing has a tendency to become a case of the blind leading the blind. It doesn't work.

If understanding is lacking, interrupt the role-play and have participants switch roles. If the situations aren't public and your trainees are self-conscious, consider videotaping the role-play in private. Then allow the group to view and critique the tape. If possible, videotape all role-plays in any event to let participants see themselves in action. See Chapter 10 for how to use video.

Always schedule time to discuss and analyze the performances. The evaluations are as important as the sessions themselves. Also, structure your evaluations. Don't critique off the top of your head, but rather set objectives for yourself and the trainees, then cover all bases. Avoid information overload. If an individual is very poor, pick the most readily correctable problem, forget the rest of the performance, and concentrate on bringing that one skill up to par. Once you succeed, work on each of the other problems in turn. Lastly, praise in equal measure, but praise only what is truly good. False praise demotivates almost as fast as too much criticism.

Examinations. Exams test for "book" learning. They cannot really test practical experience. In fact, because most colleges rely very heavily on exams as a means of evaluation, a common criticism of recent college graduates is that they have a good academic, but no hands-on, background. In a business environment, case histories and projects, assessment sessions, and, of course, on-the-job training are much better means of evaluating actual performance.

What exams can tell you is the extent to which the trainees have learned and can recall what they have been taught; used for this level one purpose, exams are effective measuring tools. Where content, vocabulary, formats, formulas, and the like need to be mastered, the exam is a vital evaluation mechanism for both trainer and trainee.

Reliability and Validity of Exams. It is important to consider two defining factors about exams: reliability and validity.

Reliability means that the test you've created gets consistent results over a period of time, with similar groups of trainees. It means the results are probably quite accurate. The more times a good test is given, the more reliable it becomes because each administration increases the database against which an individual's or group's performance is measured. Reliability is a statistical function.

To test for reliability, record all of the raw (actual) scores for each group of trainees who take the examination. Figure 5-2 is a graph showing the scores on a

Figure 5-2. Trainee test results.

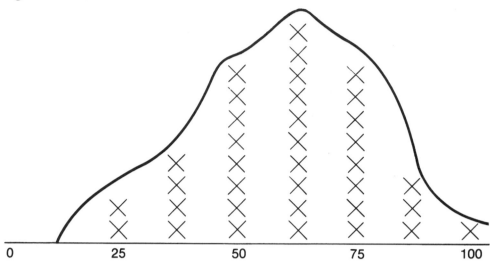

scale from 1 to 100. Each × represents a trainee's score. That is, for each trainee who scores a 99 on the test, make an × above 99 on the graph. For each score of 98, place an × above 98, and so on. Stack each × for a particular score on top of the previous ×. When the tops of columns of ×'s are connected, you have what statisticians call a standard distribution, or bell curve. In any large population, a small percentage of the people will score very high, a slightly larger percentage will score quite high, still more will score high; most will score in the middle range; and fewer will score below average, still fewer well below average, even fewer yet will be poor; a small percentage (about equal to the group that scored highest) will score very poorly.

Remember, you are not being graded yourself. No one will see these results but you. You need only use a rule-of-thumb measurement to keep on track and establish consistency. It is possible, even desirable if you are a statistician, to make a detailed analysis incorporating a standard deviation and correction for possible errors and with means, norms, and so forth. (See Chapter 4 for a detailed description of how to do this analysis.) But it is not necessary. I have informally tracked hundreds of exams over the years and found them as reliable as those tested by sophisticated analyses. If you like statistics and work for a boss who thrives on them, compile the information. If you don't, and your boss cares only that the results be accurate, you will find my simple system more than adequate.

Record the results each time you give the test. Once you have a dozen or so instances, chart them on a master bell curve. Each time you give the exam, compare the results with your master curve. The same test should get approximately the same spread of scores, forming the same basic curve. If so, you have a sufficiently reliable test.

If you fail to get consistent results, either adjust your teaching or change the exam. A single aberrant score for an otherwise reliable test indicates either an exceptional group or a change in content emphasis. Such a score can act as a signal to you that you are changing your emphasis in the training and need to get back to basics in order to maintain your consistency. If you have a number of trainers teaching the same class material, such a score can indicate the need for one or more of your trainers to get back on track. On the other hand, if the new emphasis is desired and intentional, you will need to change the test to accommodate the new thrust. To fine-tune a test that scores outside the normal range you expect, make the questions more difficult if you want to lower the scores and easier if you want to raise them.

Reliability refers to whether you can depend on test results to accurately reflect performance. *Validity,* on the other hand, indicates whether what you are testing is directly related to the material you have taught. For example, standard intelligence quotient (IQ) tests are among the most reliable ever devised. Thousands upon thousands of people have scored in classic distribution curves, and each score is ranked in relation to other scores. However, no one has yet proved that an IQ test is a valid indication of intelligence. There is only marginal proof that a high IQ score indicates a tendency to earn high grades in middle-class American schools. This is why the U.S. Equal Employment Opportunity Commission has long regarded them with suspicion, and requires prospective employees to be tested directly and legitimately for the job for which they are applying.

Validity establishes what is being tested. The process of validating a test can be complex and time-consuming, or relatively easy. All you really need is what is called *surface validity,* meaning that the questions you ask are directly related to the material you have taught.

To establish acceptable validity for a test, make each question relate to one of your written objectives. The best way I know to accomplish this is to write the test before you create the lesson plan. Set your objectives, create a test that challenges learning for each of them, then flesh out the lesson plan so that you are teaching to pass the test. Academics have always frowned on this practice, but their goals are different. An academic test is designed, among other things, to separate the best from the less than best, to grade responses on a scale. On the contrary, the purpose of training tests is to let learners and instructors know how well they are doing. In training, ideally everyone should get 100 percent. That is your goal, so teach to fulfill the rigors of the test.

If you are teaching from a manual, write the questions to relate to specific statements in that manual when planning tests. If you are working with a particularly detailed manual, include the page number where the answer can be found at the end of each question. This learning and study aid facilitates self-correction.

Be prepared to accept discussion from trainees (in fact, you might want to solicit it) on how fair or difficult your test was. Another approach is to run the test by several area experts or other trainers for their feedback.

Maintaining both reliability and validity records will provide you with (1) hard data on the effectiveness of your training, and (2) documented evidence of your fairness in evaluating trainees, should a dispute or EEO lawsuit arise.

Types of Exam Questions. Various specific types of questions are used in tests. See Figure 4-7 in Chapter 4 for further examples.

Most of us are so familiar with *multiple-choice questions* that we turn automatically to this format.

Sample: Which of the following is a demonstrated principle of learning:

   a. Trainees learn best what they hear.
   b. Trainees learn best by making and correcting mistakes.
   c. Trainees learn best by watching role models perform.
   d. All of the above*

It is effective for evaluating straight recall of facts and for testing recognition of principles, but otherwise this question type is rather limited. If you do use it, offer at least four choices. If you wish to test the ability to discriminate among alternatives, make several choices correct but only one perfect. Use *all of the above* and *none of the above* sparingly. They encourage guessing.

The multiple-choice format allows humor. Lighten the pressure from time to time by making one choice absurd. This can be particularly effective if the humor comes from some event or situation shared by the group. Try to vary the format with other types of questions, too. Use only twenty multiple-choice questions in a set (several sets are possible in a longer test). This gives a built-in break.

If you give regular exams and worry about having different questions for different groups, write and store about one hundred questions in a computer and then program it to select at random and print the quantity of questions you need. This is a great time-saver.

Fill-in-the-blank questions serve much the same purpose as multiple-choice but are not as easy to guess right. Include enough information in the sentences so they can be understood. Few questions are more frustrating than ambiguous fill-in-the-blank questions.

*The answer is b. We learn best by making and correcting mistakes. a. is wrong because we forget 50 percent of what we hear within twenty-four hours. c. is wrong because, although we may get ideas by observing others, we will learn little from watching without actual practice. If you doubt this, try letting someone learn to drive a car by merely watching you do it!

Sample: The first step in planning a training lesson is to formulate

your _____.*

Minimize your use of *true-false questions*. These are temptingly easy to write, but psychologically they reenforce the false statements as strongly as the true ones. Frequently, trainees come away remembering the negative statement rather than the true one.

Sample: The trainer must always be the most assertive person in the room.

True   False†

Matching questions are excellent for evaluating recall and discriminating between choices. *Labeling diagrams* are perfect for subjects in which trainees must recall the names of parts.

Sample: Match the following methods with the learning principle they utilize:

1. role-play
2. project session
3. demonstration
4. lecture
5. anecdotal case history

a. multisensory input
b. readiness versus resistance
c. active versus passive
d. trial and error
e. understanding what is to be learned‡

Tests also include *short* and *long essays*. If you are evaluating judgment—that is, a trainee's ability to use the material taught—then the essay question is hands-on problem solving. It forces thought and involves the test-taker far more than any other question format. The essay question is the type from which the Harvard Business School developed the concept of case histories. Short essays (a sentence or two) draw specific responses; long essays probe thinking processes. Also, the essay format exposes those who don't understand and need extra help.

Sample: Describe how you would respond to a participant who openly challenged something you have said to the group.§

When making essay questions, keep your objectives in mind. Be sure the question asks for a specific response. This makes the question easier to evaluate and more valid. Mini-case histories work nicely, too.

*"Learning objectives," because what is learned is much more important that what is taught.
†True. It is part of the mantle of leadership that is given to us to wear.
‡1, d; 2, c; 3, a; 4, e; 5, b. If you get any of these wrong, think them through again carefully.
§The answer would need to include: smile, move toward the difficult participant, and ask open-ended questions to debrief him or her.

Assessment Sessions. If your training programs are used to assess employee performance, for legal reasons you must keep accurate testing records. Convert performance to numbers, and chart both reliability and validity, as we described earlier. Informal assessment sessions, however, can also be effective forms of evaluation. Here are some common types:

- *In-basket exercise.* Each participant is given an envelope of materials that are imagined to be from his or her in-basket that morning. Each participant must deal with all of the items during a limited time. Some tasks are hard, some impossible, some frivolous—even fun. You then evaluate them in terms of creativity, use of time, correct procedures followed, and so on.

- *Presentations.* These are particularly effective for training sales representatives, platform speakers, or anyone who regularly makes presentations. Videotape the talks if possible, so trainees can see themselves; few critiques are as powerful as your own when you see yourself as others see you. In addition, give the participants time to prepare. Provide specific instructions for what you want them to do. Evaluate immediately, and praise as well as critique their presentations.

- *Role playing.* As mentioned earlier, role-playing is excellent for improving communication. Role playing as a practice session has already been discussed. For an assessment session, make sure that the assignment demands participants use the material you've taught. If the role-play wanders off the subject, interrupt it and make the participants replay it, then discuss the difference. If you are comfortable doing so, you can role play with them, but don't be too hard on them. The purpose is not to show them how hard it is to do it your way, but rather that doing it the correct way works.

Self-Evaluation. So far, we've talked about the evaluation of trainees. You, too, need to know how you are doing. Bring a video camera to your classes and record an hour here and there at random. Do it several times, then watch the tapes and ask yourself if you could learn from that trainer. If so, why? If not, why not? If you don't have a video camera, bring in an audiotape recorder. The trainees won't mind, and the experience is invaluable. Invite someone whose judgment you respect to observe and critique you. Give that person a list of attributes to evaluate.

Ask your trainees to fill out evaluation forms during or at the completion of their training. Follow their advice. You can't please all of them, so don't try, but look for patterns in negative comments and change in response to them. Enjoy the positive comments, but seriously weigh the negative ones. Ask questions like, "Was the material too theoretical? Just right? Too practical or too elementary?" "What did you feel you learned?" Have them rate you or the seminar on a scale of 1 to 5, where 1 is poor and 5 is excellent, or just use categories of excellent, very good, good, fair, and poor.

One of the problems with standardized evaluation forms is that they are expected to be ideal for all occasions. They cannot be. Consider designing the evaluation form for the specific class it is to be used in. Such forms are also a good opportunity to gather data on other areas that may require training. Ask trainees what else they feel a need for on their jobs. Finally, be sure to stick to the topic and keep the form simple. Allow enough time at the end of the session for the trainees to fill out the form if you expect them to give it some serious thought.

When you want to change your own pattern of teaching, set goals for yourself with set time limits. Don't be locked into certain methods. Try different things and see how the group responds. Go with a good response. If you have to break a bad habit, like saying "okay" at the end of each thought, try these:

1. Create a mnemonic device to remind yourself you are breaking a habit. It can be putting something unusual in your pocket (my favorite is a pegboard hook), wearing a watch upside down, tying a string on your finger, putting a sign in the back of the room. Use anything that will remind you not to do the habit.

2. Invent a new behavior to replace the old one.

3. Every time you notice your mnemonic device, immediately stop doing the old habit for five minutes and do the new habit. Increase to ten minutes, then twenty, then forty-five minutes, and so on.

4. If all else fails, ask your trainees to help. Explain that you are trying to break a bad habit and show them what it is. Ask them to make a loud noise whenever you do it. I have used this with great success to break several bad habits. (I ask them to give me a Bronx cheer.)

Evaluation of Affective Learning. So far the discussion has focused on evaluating cognitive learning. It is relatively easy to tell when people improve their performance of a job. It is more difficult to ascertain whether you have influenced someone's attitude. The key, again, is finding a variable that changes with attitude change. By monitoring this variable you can gauge the change in attitude as well. Here are some variables that indicate attitude change:

- *Facial expressions.* The face is so obvious we tend to forget how much it is a barometer of attitude. A smiling, alert, animated face has an "up" attitude. A stiff or drooping face indicates the reverse. Maintaining eye contact, using the Socratic method, and moving closer to the group cause changes in facial expressions that reveal true attitude. Monitor these to determine immediate moods.

- *Instructor evaluations.* Receiving an "excellent" rating on evaluations not only means that your training skills are good but that the group has a positive attitude toward both you and the material. The two are directly related. Exciting material makes the instructor look good, and a good instructor can make even poor material exciting. Of course, if you receive a "poor" rating, you can assume the trainees have learned little and feel "down" about the session. Ask questions such as, "Did you achieve your personal objectives in coming here?" and "What do you feel you've learned?" You can garner feedback that reveals the trainees' attitudes.

Level Two: Immediate Application on the Job

What happens to your trainees when they leave your course and return to their jobs? Your task was to change their behavior. You can document that you've given them new skills by asking them to perform those skills during the training. When they leave you, they have the skills to do the new work required of them. But what happens to those skills when they return to their jobs?

All too frequently their supervisor says, "Forget all that stuff you learned in training. Here's how you're gonna do the job. . . ." and all of your careful training is wasted. If you find yourself in this predicament, remember that you are a service function, not a judicial system. It doesn't matter if your way is "right." Your job is to see that the training is consistent with the on-the-job demands that are put upon the workers once they have completed your training.

It is on the job that most of your trainees will actually master the skills you've taught them, and so a formal On-the-Job Training (OJT) program becomes the prime means of level-two evaluation. Chapter 13 covers in detail how to go about setting up an OJT function. Because you are turning your trainees over to them, supervisors will be your major source of on-the-job evaluation. This is why it is vital to seek out supervisors in the needs analysis process and gather their input. They are the ones who can make your training work—or fail to work—for the organization. You must provide special training classes for the supervisors. Show them how to evaluate the trainees and coach them on the job. This will standardize the approach for you, the supervisors, the trainees, and the company.

If possible, change your course to match the supervisor's procedures. Talk with the supervisor and get his or her input. Explain your position as one of serving, and nail down what should be taught. If the supervisor is a maverick, try to persuade him or her to go with your way. See if the other supervisors can bring the maverick in line. Failing that, teach both ways so trainees won't be confused.

Of course, if the supervisor wants to do it one way and your manager wants it done another way, you have an organizational problem, not a training problem. I had a client who planned to train all of the workers in his company's very large plant. He didn't want to train managers or supervisors, only the frontline workers. I had to point out to him that if the supervisory staff didn't know what the workers learned, they would look foolish in their charges' eyes. Rather than appear foolish, they would denigrate the training and see to it that the workers couldn't use what they would be taught. In order to save face they would completely sabotage the efforts of training. You must always train from the top down. Bottom-up training doesn't work.

If you run into supervisory resistance, you'll need strong management support to retrain or bring the supervisor in line. Bring the supervisor to the training and let him or her coach your trainees in class. This will help you gain respect and cooperation. You can also retrain the supervisor to the standard way. Supervisors will be more cooperative if they decide which way will become the company standard.

In any case, work closely with the supervisors to define the need for training, to develop the course materials, and to create the training itself, and then train them to coach and reenforce what has been learned in the workplace and your training will be very successful. This is the answer to the problem of the transfer of learning to the job.

You still must evaluate performance on the job and document that transfer of learning. The process is simply one of repeating your needs analysis. Whatever data you studied in the first place to define the training need must now to be monitored to discover what impact your training has had on the job. However, there are a few problems you will probably encounter in doing so. People grow and change constantly. Many things in our daily lives impact on our behavior. In the work environment, training is only one cause of change. Consequently, posttraining evaluations are difficult to compile. How can we know:

1. If any changes that have taken place are a result of our training?
2. Whether other powerful influences have counteracted our training somewhere along the line?

The task is complicated further by a gradually diminishing population. True, we may train more people, but over the years each group grows smaller as people retire, move, or change jobs.

Yet it is obvious that some form of posttraining evaluations is needed. If you are happily training hundreds of employees and have no idea whether they perform to the standards they've been taught—or even if they use the skills you've given them—you are failing in your mandate. Remember, the purpose of training is to bring about change. If you don't measure the change that has taken place, you can't know if you are performing the task. There are, fortunately, several ways of overcoming such difficulties:

1. *Mandate posttraining action plans.* Sun Life of Canada currently practices one of the best evaluation techniques I've run across. At the completion of each lesson, trainees are given five minutes to create an action plan for how and when they will use what they've just learned when they return to the job. Upon completion of the entire course, they are required to spend about thirty minutes consolidating these plans into a final action plan for integrating the course into their

daily work. Trainees are paired up to exchange their action plans with their partners for discussion, commitment, and a reality check. Finally, two to three weeks
after the training, participants are required to make an appointment with their
individual immediate supervisor or manager to go over the action plan to assess
which elements of it they have already accomplished and where they may be
having problems. This system guarantees transfer of learning, but it requires full
management support and training as well as commitment.

2. *Set key variables.* Plant a method or a word in the midst of your program—
some particularly clear example or acronym. Even years later, as you talk to those
you've trained, listen for those key terms, techniques, or descriptions. They may
have forgotten how they learned them, but you'll know. Of course, this technique
assumes that you'll keep in touch with at least some of those you trained.

3. *Take posttraining surveys.* Let your trainees know that at some future date
they will be asked to respond to a survey. Send out a simple survey no sooner
than three to six weeks after training, asking which skills they are using and which
have benefited them. Have them describe an instance in which they feel their new
skills helped them do a better job. Ask for comments on the validity of the training
now that they have had a chance to put it into practice. While they are still in
training explain that the future survey is an aid to *your* performance rather than
an evaluation of theirs and that you need their feedback. You should then get a
reasonable response when you send out the survey. Do the survey three months
to a year after the training, if you can.

4. *Hold follow-up sessions.* Structure your training in well-spaced intervals. If
you get the same group every six months or even once a year, evaluate how well
they have used what they were taught last time. Use pretests and posttests as well
as assessment sessions, projects, case histories, and role-playing. I've had particular success with this technique in sales training. Often in unsupervised work such
as sales, the trainees enjoy the session but fail to put into practice much of what

---

Methods for Long-Term Evaluations

1. Mandate posttraining action plans.
2. Set key variables to follow.
3. Send posttraining surveys.
4. Offer segmented training over months or years.
5. Prepare a follow-up needs assessment.
6. Check data on performance impacted by training—scrap, sales, and so
   on.
7. Convert data to percentages whenever possible.

---

they are taught. One or two of them do, however, and their sales performance soars. At follow-up sessions, I use those who've succeeded as examples to motivate the others.

5. *Perform another (or a continuous) needs analysis.* Six months after training, collect data in whatever way you used to establish the need for the training (see Chapter 4). Then compare that data to your earlier results. Don't forget that walking around is one the best and most available tools for gathering data both before and after training. As long as your learning objectives are clear, you will be able to easily gauge how effective your training has been.

6. *Monitor company records.* If your training impacts directly on measurable data like scrap rates, sales, or customer complaints, track these data over the years and see what the accumulated information reveals.

7. *Convert your data to percentages.* As the population shrinks, fewer and fewer trainees can respond. Straight data would erroneously imply a decline in training effectiveness. By converting the results to percentages, you can report such facts as 98 percent of those responding to a recent survey felt that training significantly impacted on their work—even though only six or seven former trainees were left to respond.

Long-Term Evaluation of Affective Learning

- *Word of mouth.* It is possible to gauge how employees feel about a subject, a type of work, an impending or recent change, their training, and other trainees by tapping the company grapevine. Find someone who always knows what's going on. You won't get hard data, but you'll find out how well you've achieved your affective training objectives.

- *Surveys.* The in-house magazine or newsletter is a good place to run a survey. Surveys are usually anonymous so that they invite honest answers. If you are not perceived in a hostile light, you might circulate among workers and ask for their responses to key attitude questions. This technique was used in the famous Mayo-Hawthorne studies,[1] which discovered that people work harder and better when they know others are watching them. Dr. Mayo and his team interviewed employees and asked them to tell how they felt.

- *Participation.* If you have been doing motivational training, monitor the figures on voluntary participation in such things as blood drives, the United Way, or toy collections for needy children. In a similar vein, watch for employee activity in company-sponsored events such as Little League or the annual picnic. Participation in such activities usually reflects a positive attitude.

- *Confrontations.* Look at the company records on confrontations. A reduction in the number or types of arguments in the workplace reflects shifts in attitude.

- *Absenteeism and turnover rates.* High absenteeism is related to employee attitude, as are turnover rates. Employees who stay with the company usually like something about it.

- *Safety-related accidents.* The number of accidents tends to decrease with increasingly positive attitudes toward safety, safety training, and the company as a whole.

- *Scrap (reject) and error rates.* Happy workers make fewer errors. People who care about quality take the time to do a job right. On the other hand, excessive errors and wasted materials point to poor work attitudes.

Level Three: Bottom-Line Evaluation

In order to move from a reactive to a proactive status, training must become an integral part of strategic planning in the organization. Indeed, as we shall see in Chapter 19, U.S. industry is moving in the direction of increasing the importance of training in its operations. However, in order to become incorporated in strategic planning, training must be able to demonstrate its impact on organizational operations in a tangible way. This means training must be evaluated in terms of the bottom line. If training is to create a positive change in work-related behavior, then that change must be examined and demonstrated. It must be evaluated as a return on investment.

We looked at the basic procedures for creating a relationship between costs of training and the results of that training in Chapter 4. But it must be emphasized here that the key element in the process is creating a dollar value unit that can be related back to improved skill performance upon completion of training. Obviously, if you have justified the costs of providing the training against promised improved performance, you are obligated to monitor the posttraining performance in order to assess the bottom-line impact your training has had.

Two issues need to be addressed. The first one is what an executive in one of my courses called "Jell-O on [her] desk." If you are going to make cost comparisons, they must be as substantial as possible, not just shimmering, insubstantial numbers that look nice but have no solidity to them. Jell-O has no place in strategic planning and so cannot contribute to either cost justification or evaluation. Make your cost estimates and justifications as solid and tight as possible. To the extent that you succeed, you will find them easy to evaluate. To the extent that your cost/benefit relationships are ephemeral, you will find it difficult to evaluate the bottom line.

The second issue arises in those situations where there is no dollar-oriented return on investment. This is a particularly common situation in the civil service and in nonprofit organizations. It is still vital, though, to define a relationship between the costs of operations and the results obtained. In such organizations the bottom line is usually the volume of work to be done, the distribution of the budget, or a combination of both.

The volume of work is a function of staffing and hours; therefore, relationship between training and the number of necessary staff or a reduction in the time needed to complete a task will both constitute the bottom line. For example, many companies in the U.S. have undergone reengineering and downsizing. This invariably means maintaining a staff of fewer workers to perform the same amount of work. Training these workers to become more efficient, better organized, or more skilled at their tasks will impact on how well or how poorly the organization maintains its vital services. Thus, dollars spent on training can be directly related to specific improvements in performance. This improved performance can be measured and evaluated as a bottom-line improvement, a better distribution of limited budget moneys.

Finally, in order to establish a non–Jell-O, factual relationship between improved performance and training, whether by dollars or efficiency, it is often necessary to set up a pilot program in order to verify and document that money spent on training does affect the bottom line. In the face of limited budgets and management unfamiliar with the benefits of training, it is advisable to propose such a pilot study be done first. This is, after all, how contractors sell large programs to the government. Pilot first to prove that training works, then roll out a full program using the data collected from the pilot study as parameters for evaluation.

Level three evaluation is a measure of the impact of training on the organization at large. It can relate to a mission statement, a budget, departmental goals, or training objectives, but its purpose is to assess how well training has succeeded in creating changed performance in the organization.

Summary

Evaluation is the feedback that keeps training programs on track. It is how you can measure the changes you are bringing about. Evaluations are also vital for trainees to see how they are progressing. Evaluation engages the law of effect by forming the base against which performance can be measured.

There are three levels of evaluation: short-term during the training; long-term evaluations on the job; and bottom-line, return-on-investment, corporate-impact evaluations. There are also two areas in which to evaluate: cognitive learning and affective learning. Of these, the short-term impact of cognitive training is the easiest to evaluate, using traditional tools such as exams, quizzes, questions, or projects. Affective learning is harder to evaluate because it is more subjective. However, by observing mood and effort, you often have enough information for a short-term evaluation.

By far the most difficult are long-term evaluations of affective learning. Measuring long-term cognitive skills is only marginally less troublesome. For both, the essential tasks are (1) to monitor key variables, (2) to remain in touch with those you've trained, and (3) to convert all long-term data to percentages so as to counter the problem of a shrinking population.

Third level, bottom-line evaluation fits the training function into the overall activity of the organization and provides training with perspective on the impact it has throughout the organization.

Finally, remember that the purpose of evaluation is not just to see how well you've done, though that is important, but to diagnose those areas in which you can do better. We don't evaluate just to prove we did something, but rather to improve how we do it in the future.

Applications

1. Select a course of study either from existing training in your organization or from an off-the-shelf package or a college curriculum. List the tools for evaluation of learning that are apparent from this course. Create three more means for evaluating short-term learning.

2. Select a lesson. Create a short test to assess learning. Be sure to include at least three different types of questions to assess three different levels of learning. Try the test out on trainees and record the data in a distribution curve.

3. Take a critical incident from your workplace and write up a detailed case history that could be used in class to teach principles and skills.

4. Think of the worst training you have ever received. Write down what made it poor. Now create new methods and evaluation tools to change it into dynamic and effective training.

Chapter 6
Researching the Subject Matter

THIS chapter could have been called "How to Become an Expert in any Field." Of course you won't really become an expert in complex fields, since that would take years of study, but you can easily gain enough expertise to train others in most subjects. Let me explain.

One of the principal errors new trainers make is to confuse content with method. As a trainer, you are an expert in method. Content, while obviously important, is subordinate to method. It is not what you teach, but how you teach it that makes you an expert. I realized this years ago when, as a high school English teacher, I was approached by students to help them with their math. I didn't know the math, having struggled with the subject myself, but I was able to teach them a great deal by using the Socratic method, challenging them to deduce for themselves the principles behind the formulas. Their grades improved, and I learned math from them. When I taught college, the same pattern reconfirmed my discovery. I was able to teach subjects I knew little about because I could recognize a learning difficulty and devise a method that would help the learner around it and stimulate him or her to become excited about it.

Many years ago I was driving with my ten-year-old daughter and one of her friends. The friend asked what I did for a living and I answered, "I teach teachers to teach."

"To teach what?" she said.

"To teach whatever it is that they teach," I replied.

"Yes, but what?" she insisted, puzzled.

"To teach better," I said.

"To teach *what* better?" She was becoming angry, thinking I was playing a game with her.

"Just how to teach better," I said gently. She had simply never considered teaching as a thing in itself—a science or art, a discrete activity. Yet this entire book is about the art, science, and activity of teaching. It is said that a good salesperson call sell anything; a good teacher can teach anything.

Understand, I do not hold this view out of arrogance. I am not making a boast that I can teach anything better than the experts or without expertise. I am not saying that I can become an expert in the sense of being vastly knowledgeable about a subject in a short period of time. I *am* saying that any of us can gain sufficient understanding in most subject areas to be able to apply sound teaching methods to motivate learners and help them to master those subjects.

There is no charlatanism, no hype here, just good, solid, analytic, methodical, problem-solving techniques. We are expert teachers who can use subject experts to train others. This chapter is about how to do so.

Let us say you train customer service personnel for a manufacturing company. Business has been off lately, and senior management asks if some form of training would help. You offer to perform a needs analysis, and they agree. Your needs analysis uncovers the fact that there is no one in the company who knows about marketing. Products have been sold off the shelf in the same way since the company was founded 150 years ago. No one knows a different way.

You recommend that the senior staff be trained in creative marketing. Management likes the idea and says, "How soon can you teach a course like that?"

"Well, I really don't know anything about marketing either," you say, having been a schoolteacher before you moved into training.

"We certainly can't wait for everybody to learn it on their own, and I don't have the budget to bring in an outside expert. Take whatever resources you need and put together a course in three weeks," says management.

How do you begin? You look for information on the subject. There are three basic sources of information on any subject: printed matter, electronically stored information (including the Internet), and people.

Information From Printed Sources

You can obtain a great deal of information by reading what others have said on your particular topic. Begin your search by going to your local public library, nearby college library, or perhaps a private library in your area. Also check general and business bookstores as well as college bookstores.

These sources should have two or three books or articles on whatever subject interests you. To become reasonably well informed on the topic, read three books and at least three articles. Cross-check topics in each, then tentatively decide which topics are most applicable and what methods you'd use to best teach them.

Public Libraries

Know what information you need before you begin your search. For instance, if you ask for books on marketing, a librarian will have too many to refer you to.

Narrow down your topic to, for example, creative marketing techniques in your industry. Also, don't wander the aisles aimlessly. Ask the reference librarian for assistance, because he or she knows the library from top to bottom. If there is an appropriate book, the librarian will locate it for you. Ask for exactly what you want, and chances are it will be there.

The *Subject Guide to Books in Print* is a useful set of volumes available in all libraries. It lists every book in print, arranged by subject. Find your topic in the guide and you'll have a list of current books that you can borrow from the library or have a bookstore order.

The *Business Periodicals Index* is another set of volumes found in all libraries. It lists articles that have appeared in the most important business journals and magazines. Arranged by subject, the listings give title, author, name of the periodical or magazine, volume number, and date of issue. The index also categorizes book reviews, which might prove useful.

College Libraries

Colleges and universities that offer business courses, especially at the graduate level, usually have excellent libraries with good selections of current and classic business books. Even if your topic is not related to business (advanced physics, for instance), college libraries are often better resources for specialized information. You may have to be a student to use the library, however, but simply enroll in an evening class and you'll receive an ID card. (You may be able to hire a graduate student to do your research for you; check with the college librarian or appropriate graduate department.)

Private Libraries

Many professional organizations, even some private companies, have excellent libraries, which can be a good source of information, particularly for technical subjects. Most public libraries have a copy of the *Directory of Special Libraries and Information Centers;* check it for names, addresses, and phone numbers for nearly all of the private libraries in the United States. An alternative route is to contact the appropriate professional association. In the case of training, you could call the local chapter or national office of the American Society for Training and Development. In the marketing area, you would try marketing associations, which are listed in the *Encyclopedia of Associations* or the *National Trade and Professional Associations of the United States.*

Bookstores

Most large independent bookstores have a section devoted to business books. The bookstore chains, like Waldenbooks, usually don't stock many business books, but specialized business bookstores have a very wide selection of current titles. If a book is in print but the store doesn't have it, ask the store to order it for you.

College bookstores are excellent resources because their books are always arranged by subject and are usually very current and first rate. Furthermore, the books are sometimes discounted, and you rarely need to prove you are a student. To return to our example of marketing, you would find a first-year text to be the fastest way to learn about the field. You could then follow up with specialized books on creative marketing.

Direct Mail Promotions—Catalogues

Every day your company receives literature promoting seminars, books, audio-cassettes, and videocassettes on topics of interest to people in the field. These brochures contain lists of topics that experts see as relevant to the field. Essentially, they give you outlines and summaries that you can use to research a training session.

Electronically Stored Information

There are currently three available sources of information available electronically: the Internet, including the World Wide Web; CD-ROM storage disks; and private networks, including both LANs (Limited Area Networks) and WANs (Wide Area Networks). If you are on a LAN or WAN, ask your systems administrator what information is stored and accessible on the network. You may have to request a specific level of security clearance to gain access. However, the Internet and World Wide Web are available to everyone.

Internet

The Internet is the largest public library in the world. It allows you to search out any imaginable topic and access whatever data or information has been stored electronically about that subject anywhere in the world. And it allows you to do so from the comfort and convenience of your personal computer at home, in the office, or from your laptop computer when you travel.

You need only to have a computer, a modem, a telephone line (you can even access the Internet from a cellular phone), an access server (a telephone number to which you subscribe for a small monthly fee that, when dialed, will give you access to the Internet), and some sort of software to help you get to where you want to go once you are on the Internet. If you don't have one or more of these required elements, you can easily rent them from local computer service and rental stores or through public libraries or business associations such as airline traveler clubs and lounges, hotel business centers, or service organizations.

The Internet is not an organized place, so it takes a little practice and skill to navigate around it. However, each location you access usually has some system of organization to its databases, which you can work with in much the same way you might work with a card catalogue in a library. Information is usually cross-referenced, so you should be able to compile a list of possible topics of interest stored in the particular database you are searching by using a key word search command.

There are many databases that specialize in linking multiple databases. These act as central clearinghouses or card catalogues and can greatly simplify the process of searching through virtually endless cyberspace to find a topic. These service databases generally are freely available and have distinct names and addresses. They have names such as Yahoo!, a justifiably popular one, and Lycos. Many are specialized and act as specialized libraries you can search for key subjects.

The Internet is available solely in an electronic print medium. That is, whatever you find will be available to you only as simple text. You may read this text on-line (an expensive proposition when you are accessing it by long distance) or copy it into your computer (a process called downloading) to be read or even printed out later at your leisure. However, if you also have some version of navigator software, you can access the World Wide Web on the Internet. WWW, as it is called, is really just the Internet with color, photographs, graphics, video, film clips, and full stereo sound.

There are several full-service organizations that charge fees to provide you with access to both the Internet and the World Wide Web and, for their fees, organize the information into categories for you as well as providing such services as electronic mail, interest groups, and chat groups where subscribers can converse with each other in real time. The three principal ones, as of this writing, are America Online, CompuServe, and Prodigy. These companies offer services that are often attractive, but membership in such service organizations is not necessary for researching the Internet.

Information From Experts in the Field

The second major source of information is people. Interviews with experts can make you knowledgeable very quickly. Television reporters and talk show hosts seem very well informed, even when the topic is new to them. They get that way by reading up on the subject first, then perhaps talking to an expert to discuss finer points before they do their interviews. You can do the same.

Experts are all around you, but look especially for in-house people at your company, nearby colleges and universities, those involved in service or professional associations, the regional chamber of commerce, and a local speakers' bureau or Toastmaster's club. Direct mail catalogues are also a useful source of names.

In-House Experts

By far the most accessible and credible source is the expert who works for your company. To find such an expert, go to personnel and review your needs with them. Check their files for resumes to uncover work experience, education, and hobbies. Also go to the department in question and ask the supervisor for the name of the best worker, sales rep, clerk, machine operator, secretary, researcher, scientist, or whomever.

Colleges and Universities

Go to the chairperson of the appropriate department and explain your purpose. Most professors are more than happy to help local businesses. Make your visit official, and you should be received warmly.

Professional Organizations

The professional organizations know who their stars are. The stars have written books on the subject and are leading speakers in their field. Several associations, like the American Society for Training and Development, publish directories of their members, and some organizations rate their speakers, courses, and off-the-shelf packages. A phone call to one of these groups can get you advice, a proposal, or a schedule of when and where one of its experts will be giving public seminars. You can be certain that nearly every speaker or seminar leader is terrific. However, some organizations and associations maintain a rating service for their members to evaluate speakers, courses, and off-the-shelf packages. For a reasonable fee and a few days or hours of time, you get immersion in the subject with an expert. There are few better ways of learning something.

Chambers of Commerce

These are organizations that service the community and promote local business. They often compile lists of member experts or consultants, and can be very helpful.

Speakers' Bureaus and Toastmaster's Clubs

These clubs are starting places for people building their consulting businesses. The yellow pages of your phone book will list a nearby bureau or chapter. Ask if it has speakers in the subject area you are researching. There may be a small fee, but you will have an expert who is more than willing to help.

Direct Mail Promotions—Catalogues

We've already discussed how brochures and catalogues that come in the mail can give you information on a subject. Most of these brochures also describe the background and expertise of the speaker or author. These people are reachable at the addresses or phone numbers given in the brochures, but remember that they make a living selling their time. Don't expect free advice.

Interviewing the Experts

You will have to polish your interviewing skills, either to obtain information from experts or, later on, to identify the tasks involved in particular job skills. In Chapter 4, we discussed interviewing skills in relation to needs analysis. The same techniques can be used to draw information from your experts. For example:

1. *Know what you want to accomplish.* Plan the interview to be thorough and efficient. Plan your questions to meet your objectives.

2. *Know to whom you are talking.* Experts will relax and be more open with you if you can establish credibility right away.

3. *Use active listening.* Probe for full information and ask questions to clarify information. Ask, don't tell. You are there to learn, even if you disagree.

4. *Keep the interview short.* Key people are usually busy, and they don't have much time to spare. Furthermore, the closer you stick to the point, the easier it will be to analyze your results. Set a time limit and stick to it, unless your expert wants to run over.

If you are using the interview to identify the tasks involved in a particular job, structure your questions so you obtain a title and a complete job description, full delineation of constituent activities for which the individual is responsible, and a complete list of the tasks involved with each constituent job. Clear your conclusions with the expert. Let the person know you will come back to verify the information, so he or she can give you that extra time.

Preparing a Task Analysis

Training must be focused on clearly defined learning objectives. These objectives must spell out exactly the skills that trainees will acquire during training. They define the desired performance, the new improved manner in which the targeted job gets done. The needs analysis defines the gap between status quo performance, which training must change, and the target performance, which training must achieve. The task analysis defines this top range of behavior. It delineates the standards to be specified in training objectives, and so creates the standards against which training must be evaluated.

Therefore, making yourself a subject expert requires a formal task analysis in order to transfer the information you have gathered from your expert sources into a precise and complete description of the skills involved in a particular job. However, this is a time-consuming task in itself. It is a lot of work, and as a result, some trainers try to skip this step. They ask, why should we perform a task analysis? What benefits do we gain? Here are some of the benefits of a task analysis.

Standardization

Sometimes, on-the-job training can lead to problems of standardization. The training department teaches one way; supervisors demand a different way. They may agree initially, but over time the concept shifts until they are at odds again. Task analysis becomes the standard against which all performance can be measured.

Training Content

A task analysis describes what a job is. Consequently, it specifies what needs to be taught. It sets the content for your training program. It provides you with the skills list that allows you to frame meaningful training objectives.

Performance Requirements

One of the essentials of training is some form of evaluation. Task analysis provides measurable, goal-oriented performance objectives. You can determine how well or how poorly your trainees are learning because the task analysis defines performance standards that allow you to observe and evaluate level-two performance on the job.

Trainee Objectives

A formal task analysis provides trainees with criteria by which they can gauge their own performance. Remember, one of the principles of learning (see Chapter 1) is that people learn better when they have a perspective on what they will be learning. Also, they are motivated by seeing how far they've come. The task analysis gives them this learning aid. It also provides the trainer with the basic building blocks of training.

Training Evaluation

Task analyses are a crucial way trainers can demonstrate their effectiveness to management. If those whom you train can perform their tasks to the set standard, you will have trained them well. Of course this can come about without a task analysis, but the analysis gives you a written standard. This is particularly important when you must justify a budget, an expansion, or your own survival in the organization.

Basic Performance Data

Any improvement in employee performance is likely to go unnoticed without basic performance data. Those who excel at their jobs will show up clearly when measured against company standards based on observed data.

Planning Aid

During budget crunches, many large organizations look to eliminate duplication of effort. Frequently these duplications become apparent through task analyses. Task analysis also resolves misunderstandings about what various jobs actually entail by defining the limits of each.

Performing a Task Analysis

Although the process of creating a task analysis can be very time-consuming, it is not an especially difficult task. It consists essentially of creating a tree chart to lay

---

The Purposes of Task Analysis

1. Define performance standards.
2. Frame and direct training.
3. Evaluate training.
4. Assist in planning and controlling work flow.
5. Clarify the job, training, and communications for both employees and management.
6. Provide basic performance data.
7. Act as a strategic planning aid.

---

out the skills involved in a job in detail and arranging those skills into a usable and accurate pattern. Let's look at each step in turn.

Locate Your Information or Expert

The sources of information have been mentioned, but remember not to become bogged down with this phase. The nearest, most accessible, and easiest-to-work-with expert is the best one. If yours is a leader in the field, so much the better. But someone closest to home is usually easiest to get to, talk to, and work with. Keep it simple; this should be an easy step, not a complex one.

Define a Preliminary Task List

The best ones are simple job descriptions. If you have them in your organization, so much the better. If not, you will have to create one. First let's look at how to work with an existing job description.

With a Job Description. Make a list of all areas of responsibility for this job title. If we were performing our analysis on the job of executive secretary, we might have a list like the one shown in Figure 6-1.

There could be other areas, but these are generally the job responsibilities of an executive secretary. Notice that I have connected them to make the beginnings of a tree chart with a branch for each skill area. Now we continue the process for each of these listed skills. That is, ask yourself, "What skills will this secretary need in order to fulfill this area of responsibility?" Continue to make branches for each component. The area of, for example, letter writing would look like the list shown in Figure 6-2.

Figure 6-1. Executive secretary's job analysis.

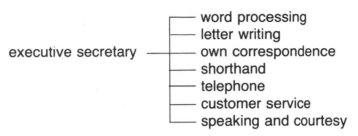

Again, the list might be longer. At this point, you would continue to take each one of these skills and draw a further detailed branch to describe what component subskills or tasks would be needed to perform it. Ask yourself again, "What other skills are needed here?" Keep asking this question branch after branch until the answer is "None." Then move on to the next area of responsibility.

Figure 6-2. Letter-writing skills needed by executive secretary.

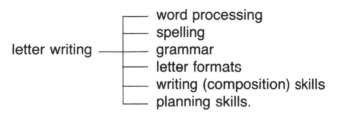

Finally, eliminate and prioritize the skills in related clusters. That is, word processing, typing, spelling, grammar, proper formats, and written composition are all sufficiently related that they could be taught as a single course or unit. They are related and so can be clustered. Prioritization is a matter of which of the skills are most important to the job or which ones are most in need of improvement. If your job descriptions list the percentage of time each task should occupy, this can be a big help in prioritizing. You can even eliminate some skill areas as being better taken care of by some other process than training. For example, the hiring process could screen for typing and shorthand, which would remove them from training needs.

Without a Job Description. If you do not have a formal job description, you will need to go to the supervisors and workers in each job category and ask them what their responsibilities are. It helps to draw up a chart that lists possible responsibilities and allows the respondent to make judgments on the task's importance, whether it is usually performed well, and so forth.

Procedure for Performing a Task Analysis

1. Locate information or an expert on the subject.
2. Prepare a list of the skills involved.
    A. If you have an existing job description,
        - Chart the job description components on a tree chart.
        - Create a branch for each of the requisite skills involved in handling each job responsibility.
        - Continue to branch until the answer to "What other skills are needed here?" is "None."
        - Using the percentage of time to be spent based on job descriptions and/or hiring guidelines: prioritize the skills; eliminate the lowest priorities and/or those that should be taken care of during selection; select those that can be improved by training.
        - Cluster skills into related areas.
    B. If you do not have an existing job description,
        - Distribute and collect responsibility charts for each job category.
        - Follow up with interviews of managers and workers to establish job parameters using a job analysis form.
        - Draw a tree chart, as with a job description.
3. Establish and verify skill levels with both a skill expert and management.
4. Correct as necessary
5. Gain management approval
6. Finalize the format

Using this data, formalize each job category, listing each responsibility, the tools needed to perform it, its relative importance to the job, and its frequency. Work with managers and supervisors to refine this job analysis into a formal listing. At this point you can draw a tree chart like the one you would do with a job description.

Observe the Expert Performing the Job

Before proceeding, it is wise to verify the skills you've selected with your subject expert or at least with management. If you are already your own subject expert, then you'll need to check only with management.

Most people who are very good at something find it hard to describe precisely what they do. They seem to just have a knack—an instinct or talent that guides them. Putting your finger on that element can be difficult. It is often impossible for those with the talent to tell you what it is that works for them. You need to observe very closely how they perform their tasks. Videotaping can prove useful in allowing you to study the expert's performance. You are looking for the components of each task. For example, you might have to list the ways a salesperson talks to secretaries and receptionists. What are the smallest units of performance you can observe? These are the steps to mastery. Perhaps one of them needs to be broken down still further to yet another sublevel of activity. Ask yourself again with each step or skill, "Can anything else happen at this point?" If not, you've reached the essential task. If more can happen, break it down to still smaller tasks.

Refine the Task List

The best way to put it all together is by creating a tree chart. Figure 6-3 is an example of such a tree chart. With the flowchart you have laid out at least four distinct layers of work: the job description for that particular function, the constituent jobs within that function, the specific tasks involved in each constituent job, and the steps (and substeps) necessary to complete each task. You can finalize your task analysis in any of three formats. I find the tree chart we've already created is usually more than adequate, but you can rewrite your analysis into a job description to make it more useful to the personnel staff. Finally, if it is for internal use, simple lists of skills are fine.

Check the Refined Task List With the Expert

Ask your expert to go over the steps with you to verify the information. This is an iterative task. It is not only a check but also a negotiation. Use the videotape, if you have one, to clarify perceptions and validate your observations.

Verify the Task Analysis With Management

If you have full autonomy, this step is unnecessary. On the other hand, if you have been given this assignment by someone higher up, now is the time to get that person's okay. Make sure that management fully understands the discrepancies between present and ideal performance of the task. Show how your training program will correct the situation. If possible, get approval in writing.

Validate the List With Others

Give the list a dry run with other experts. Find out how close your observations come to the defined performance level. Check the analysis with the supervisors

Figure 6-3. Task analysis tree chart.

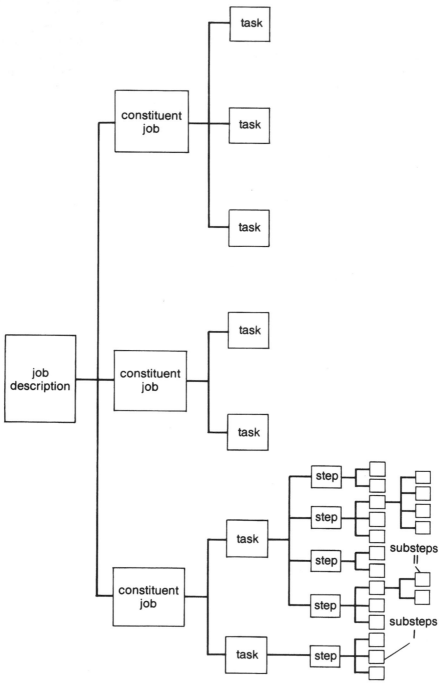

Task Analysis Formats

- Tree charts
- Detailed job descriptions
- Task lists

---

to be sure it is accurate and meets the demands of those for whom you'll be doing the training.

Develop Specific Criteria for Training

Break the steps into training sequences. Group similar sequences and arrange the material to make it easy to learn. Remember, the sequence seldom *has* to be chronological: there may be better ways.

At this point you should also establish your standards of performance. Must the trainees match the performance of the expert? What margins are you allowing for individual differences? How will you measure trainee ability? Under what special conditions will each task be performed, and how will this affect your training?

Refine the List After Each Training Session

This is how you validate your course. Use the task analysis to fine-tune the course; then use the course to fine-tune the task analysis. When your trainees are learn-

---

Specific Criteria for Training

1. Which tasks or steps are similar and can be grouped together?
2. Which steps can the trainees already perform?
3. How can these tasks be broken into learning sequences?
4. What is the sequence easiest to learn?
5. At what level of mastery should I aim?
6. What margins should I allow for individual differences?
7. How will I measure trainee performance?
8. What special conditions must be met before I can assume they have mastered the subject?

---

ing each step without difficulty, you can feel you've completed the task analysis. Even then, check back about once a year to make sure you are still on track.

When you don't have an expert to guide you in compiling the task analysis, written information becomes your only source and your ability to verify steps is seriously impaired. In such cases you have to depend even more on management review, on checks by supervisors, and on refining the analysis during and after each session.

It is obvious that there is a great deal of work involved in creating a formal task analysis. Remember, the purpose of training is to bring about a change in performance. Your needs analysis should be only as formal as you need it to be. When you compare the status quo with the first three levels of the task analysis, you are likely to find similarities, even identical behaviors. In such instances, you don't have to analyze those steps. Do a formal analysis only on those tasks that must be changed. Of course, if the purpose of your task analysis is to create a detailed job analysis for company records, you can't skip any steps. In addition, the nature of the trainee group also dictates the detail of the analysis. A group of experienced systems engineers might not need the detail that a group of new employees might. Such considerations depend upon the group, the degree of change desired, the standards set with supervisors, the demands of management, and the subject to be studied.

Be careful. Although spending grueling hours perfecting a task analysis may sometimes be unnecessary, taking shortcuts may mean detailed reevaluations later. And those usually are more grueling. One tip I've found useful: college and high school interns and graduate students can perform a considerable part of task analyses for you and save both your time and sanity. In fact, this is an ideal job for them. The students learn in detail what goes into the jobs that they are assigned to tabulate, and you are saved the routine of collecting the steps. It's an excellent solution.

Summary

In this short chapter we have concentrated on the preparation phase of a training program. The need for such preparation and how much time you spend are determined by the degree of expertise you feel you need to have to plan and deliver a training program. We looked at ways to become sufficiently expert in any field, either through research or by working with an expert. Lastly, we covered the steps for performing a task analysis and the benefits that such an analysis can bring.

Applications

1. Select a training topic about which you know very little. Go to the library and research this topic. Use at least three separate sources for your research. Test your degree of mastery with an expert.

2. Select another topic but use the Internet this time. If need be, take a course on how to use the Internet for research. Again, check your mastery with an expert.

3. Review the guidelines for interviewing an expert. Then select an expert in a field with which you are unfamiliar and arrange to interview that expert. Get him or her to explain, or even teach you, key skills.

4. Prepare a task analysis for a job with which you are familiar. Now create a task analysis for one of the newly acquired skill areas you have researched in applications 1, 2, or 3.

Chapter 7
Writing the Training Program

IN Chapter 2, we looked at how to structure effective lesson plans. Now we look at the overall training program. Many of the same principles apply, but the perspective must expand beyond a single lesson to encompass a series of lessons. The series must show the relationship of one lesson to another and to the program as a whole. I usually look at the program as a necklace where each planned lesson is a bead. It is a useful metaphor.

Remember that you are creating an environment to make learning easy and attractive. Environments are more a result of structure than of content. Put differently, it is what you do with the material that enhances learning, not the material itself. At this point you have already set the content of your program. You've completed your needs analysis (see Chapter 4) and your task analysis (see Chapter 6). You are now sufficiently expert in the subject to consider how you should best present it.

Documentation for a training program consists of:

1. A detailed thirteen-step proposal, as outlined in this chapter
2. Lesson plans for each sequence, as outlined in Chapter 2
3. A detailed trainer's manual, as described later in this chapter
4. A trainee's manual (workbook), also described in this chapter

Full documentation on a training program should also contain, in the same file, all visuals and support materials (discussed further in Chapters 8 and 9); any needs or task analyses done earlier; any publicity or advertising; plus all evaluation materials (or summaries of them) and their results.

Writing the Program

When asked to prepare a training program, many beginners start by writing the trainee's manual or workbook. If you do that, you create several problems. You lock in the content too early. Your course can't reflect the needs of the trainees because it has been planned without them. Frequently, the course later shapes itself to the trainees' and the company's needs and is completely different from the workbook you have written, so you need to write a new, more meaningful book.

Problems like this can be prevented by following thirteen logical steps. When you finally get to writing the manual, you will know your audience, your needs, your structure, your content, and your methods. To create a training program that embodies what is to be taught, to whom, and why, you need to address these thirteen elements:

1. A budget
2. Supervisory and management support
3. A tie-in to a larger company effort
4. A system for advertising the program
5. A rationale expressing the company's need for the program
6. A set of management goals
7. A plan for recruiting participants
8. A demographic statement outlining the population the program addresses
9. Training objectives
10. A decision regarding who will deliver the program
11. A set of evaluation tools
12. A step-by-step agenda that outlines when each element will be covered and how much time is allowed for it
13. Training manuals and handouts

Many of these elements are examined in specific detail elsewhere in this book. But we need to draw them together at this point, so let's consider each of them a little more closely.

Budget

If you do not yet have a budget for your course, you may be putting in a lot of work for nothing. Know how much money you can spend before you plan the course. On the other hand, you may have to do some preliminary work to acquire a budget for the program. In any event, you need to know what costs will be accrued. Budgeting procedures are covered in Chapter 15. The discussion of cost justification in Chapter 4 will also prove useful.

Supervisory and Management Support

If you have been following the procedures in this book up to this point, you will have already partnered with and gained support from managers and supervisors during your needs analysis and evaluation work. If you are starting at this point, however, make sure you get that support now. To proceed without managerial or supervisory support is a waste of time. See Chapters 1, 4, and 16 for ways to build that support.

A Tie-In to a Larger Company Effort

One of the surest ways to sink a new training program is to promote it in competition with a major management project. By the same token, if you tie your training to a companywide thrust that has already galvanized the staff, you'll guarantee its success. During your needs analysis, find out what key management people consider important or what the major thrust of the company will be, then align your training program with it. Chapters 1, 4, and 18 will again prove helpful in this task.

A System for Advertising the Program

Unless you already have a system in place for getting out the word on training, don't proceed any further until you've built a public relations network. We discuss ways of publicizing your training opportunities in Chapters 4 and 18. Let's list them here briefly:

- Use in-house publications as much as possible to call attention to upcoming programs as well as to report on successes.
- Develop a word-of-mouth program with graduate trainees.
- Send memos to all appropriate managers extolling the virtues of your training programs.
- Post flyers and handbills on company bulletin boards and in cafeterias.
- Ask for time at key meetings to promote your training programs.

A Rationale for the Program

Use the results of your needs analysis to explain why the company needs the training program. This is a vital element if you are preparing the program as a proposal, but it is important even if you have approval and a budget in place. The rationale summarizes the findings of your needs analysis and expresses them in management's terms, outlines the desired results, and lays out a format for achieving them. Two or three pages of justified rationale should always head the document that defines and outlines the program. Chapter 15 will provide you with several effective approaches to take in creating such a rationale.

Management Goals

With the rationale your training program will be on target. Frequently, training programs are given simply because someone feels they should be or because they've always been given. I've been hired on several occasions to hold in-house seminars merely so "the employees will feel better . . . feel management is doing something for them." Such reasons are fragile justification for training programs. Instead, spell out exactly what management will gain from the training program. Remember, these are not training objectives; they come later. For the difference between training objectives and management goals, see Chapter 2. Partnering with management to help it achieve its goals is discussed in Chapter 16.

Recruitment Plan

An important part of any program is the method of selecting candidates for the training. You must consider the qualifications trainees will need for the program, and who will select the participants. Also consider which areas or divisions of the company the training will address and which will be excluded. Should there be a minimum or maximum number of participants? How do you arrive at these figures? What happens when these numbers are exceeded or not met? All of these questions should be addressed in your planning stage.

Trainee Population

Using your needs analysis and the answers to the questions just asked about recruitment and the management goals, describe the training group. Remember that whom you train is far more important in shaping your program than what you are teaching. Describe the trainee population you will reach, covering areas such as:

- Age
- Sex
- Years of experience
- Years with company
- Specific jobs or tasks
- Levels of aspiration
- Performance levels
- Common problems
- Elements from your recruitment plan, if needed

Make your description of the trainees real. It will shape the environment you create for learning. Obviously, all the items I've listed are not always applicable, and you may need to consider other specific questions for your application. The end result is a profile of your trainees. The more detailed it is, the more help it will be when you structure your lessons (see Chapter 2).

Include also in this section a brief mention of the overall size of the group (that is, all entry-level employees, 10,000 clerical workers, assembly line personnel, and so on) and the anticipated length of the program (that is, how long you think it will take to train such a group). Decide and say how long each session should be and what patterns the sessions should follow (for example, Monday mornings, 8 A.M. to 12 noon, for three months; three consecutive weekends, from 7 P.M. Friday to 6 P.M. Sunday; or one week, from 9 A.M. to 5 P.M., in the spring, followed by one week, from 9 A.M. to 5 P.M., in the fall of the same year; and so on). The pattern and hours you choose will depend upon these factors:

- Your training population
- Your objectives
- Management's goals
- Your budget
- Your available time and resources
- Management support for the program

Training Objectives

Using your needs analysis and task analyses, write your specific training objectives. We've covered these objectives in Chapter 2; here you are pulling together all the thinking you've done and all the material you've collected to set down exactly what this group of trainees will achieve so as to fulfill management's goals and bring about the changes mandated by the needs analysis. All of this, of course, should be accomplished within the usual constraints of time, budget, and facilities.

Program Delivery

Once you know exactly what must be covered (your objectives), give some thought to who the best person is to conduct the training. You may want to do it yourself, in which case proceed with the remaining steps and the rest of this part of the book. On the other hand, you might want to use an outside public seminar organization like the American Management Association or a private consultant. You might also want to consider commercial off-the-shelf training packages. Choosing among these alternatives is covered in Chapter 8; however, you will need to justify that choice in your program. The reasons you might choose another source to present the program could be cost, expertise, flexibility, suitability, and applicability to the trainee population, as well as the corporate needs, the outside source's availability, and ownership of the program or its materials for repeat offerings.

Evaluation Tools

Specify the means of evaluation before you write the program. This helps you ensure that what you test will be what you taught. We tend to think "teach first, then test," but by deciding on and writing the tests, projects, case histories, and role-playing assignments first, you know that you will be teaching to pass the tests—that is, the short-term mastery of skills.

All this material does not necessarily belong in the description of your programs, however. Keep a file on each program, and put the evaluation material there. In your program description, spell out the elements of the course, and include a paragraph describing the evaluation tools you will use. Write another paragraph specifying the long-term evaluation plans, too. But *do* create these materials before you write the program agenda. They will keep you on track and make the program easier to assemble.

Program Agenda

This is the agenda that will be the heart of your program. There are several important aspects to drawing up such an agenda.

Overall Structure. Begin by dividing up your total time into separate blocks. For instance, you may have decided after your needs analysis that the trainees need twelve hours of instruction to master the skills to a level at which they can work independently. You have also decided which are the most flexible or available time frames—for example, two six-hour days. Now further divide these into smaller blocks of time (for example, two mornings and two afternoons). Break each block into yet-smaller units, such as the morning session before break, morning session after break, afternoon session before break, afternoon session after break. Depending on your needs, common practices in the organization, the needs of the trainees, or nature of the subject, you may want different chunks of time—for example, one-hour periods (as are common in high school). Use whatever elements are relevant to your situation to set up the basic time chunks for instruction.

Six Steps in Writing an Agenda

1. Divide your training time into smaller blocks of time.
2. Using needs analysis, task analysis, and training objectives, select the learning pattern (funnel, spool, or whatever).
3. Match each unit of time with one or more objectives, then select appropriate substructures (problem/solution and the like) for each unit (module).
4. Select the best methods for each module.
5. Fine-tune the program by checking for variety and proper timing.
6. Write a lesson plan for each module.

Content Learning Pattern. Using the needs analysis (see Chapter 4), set your training objectives. Using the task analysis (Chapter 6), break the content into individual topics that correspond with the steps in the analysis. Then match the steps with your training objectives. If you have more tasks than objectives, either eliminate those tasks not relevant to your objectives or cluster related tasks so that each cluster supports a training objective. Once you know the trainees to be taught and the material to be covered, as well as the objectives to be met, you can decide on the overall pattern for your course: funnel, inverted funnel, tunnel, or spool (see Chapter 2). Arrange your topics to follow that pattern.

Module Substructures. Once you have your overall pattern, match each unit of time with an objective or series of objectives. The content of the program will now be broken down into separate time slots—modules—in a logical sequence of steps. Decide which substructure (Chapter 2) is most engaging for each module (for example, problem/solution or cause and effect). At this point, your program should look something like what is shown in Figure 7-1. (See also Figure 7-4 later in this chapter.)

Methodology. Decide which method (discussed later in this chapter) is most appropriate for your trainees, your objectives, and the substructures you've chosen. You are already engaged in structuring each lesson plan at this point; however, consider the overall pattern of the program as well.

Fine-Tuning. Now fine-tune your program by considering some of the other factors that influence learning. For example, most participants are best able to respond to lectures in the morning. Schedule passive activities (if you need them at all) before lunch. In addition, lunch makes people sleepy, so schedule a project or stimulating activity closely after lunch. Most trainees fade after 4 P.M. Either

Figure 7-1. Sample training module.

Day 1	Objective	Task
9:00 A.M. to 10:30 A.M.	Objective 1 Objective 2 Objective 3	Substructure 1 Substructure 2 Substructure 3
Break		
10:45 A.M. to 12:00 noon	Objective 1 Objective 2 Objective 3	Substructure 1 Substructure 2 Substructure 3
Lunch		
1:00 P.M. to 2:30 P.M.	Objective 1 Objective 2 Objective 3	Substructure 1 Substructure 2 Substructure 3
Break		
2:45 P.M. to 5:00 P.M.	Objective 1 Objective 2 Objective 3	Substructure 1 Substructure 2 Substructure 3

end the session at four o'clock, or schedule your most stimulating or challenging work for this last hour of the day.

The average adult attention span is no longer than twenty to thirty minutes. Keep *all* presentations shorter than thirty minutes. Remember also that even great techniques grow dull if they are used constantly. Vary your methods. In the presentation, practice, and evaluation stages, use variety in your techniques. Adjust your material, if necessary, to accommodate these changes—it will be worth it. Vary your audiovisual aids as well (see Chapter 9).

Make the final adjustments to your program. Figure 7-2 shows the fine-tuning that was done on Figure 7-1.

Writing the Plan. You are now ready to write the lesson plan for each module. Use the four-step method (see Chapter 2). Log in each substructure by time

Figure 7-2. Sample training module after fine-tuning.

Day 1	Objective	Task	Method
9:00 A.M. to 10:30 A.M.	Objective 1 Objective 2 Objective 3	Substructure 1 Substructure 2 Substructure 3	Method 1 Method 2 Method 2: key activity
Break			
10:45 A.M. to 12:00 noon	Objective 1 Objective 2 Objective 3	Substructure 1 Substructure 2 Substructure 3	Method 4 Method 6 Method 3: key activity
Lunch			
1:00 P.M. to 2:30 P.M.	Objective 1 Objective 2 Objective 3	Substructure 1 Substructure 2 Substructure 3	Method 2 Method 5 Method 4: key activity
Break			
2:45 P.M. to 5:00 P.M.	Objective 1 Objective 2 Objective 3	Substructure 1 Substructure 2 Substructure 3	Method 1 Method 6 Method 5: peak activity

unit. I find it useful to use blank sheets of standard planning paper with time frames marked off in ten- or fifteen-minute intervals.

Figure 7-3 shows part of the final program plan begun in Figure 7-1.

Manuals and Handouts

Once you have completed the preparation steps, chosen an appropriate blend of teaching methods, and prepared your methods of evaluation, you can finally write the training manual. Later in the chapter I discuss formats for two basic types of manuals: the trainer's and the trainee's. The trainer's manual is a detailed step-by-step outline of what you will do, when you will do it, what responses you can anticipate or work for, and what tools you need. It is your reference for

Figure 7-3. Sample customer service course (final version of program plan, in funnel pattern).

Day 1	Objective	Task	Method
9:00 A.M. to 10:00 A.M.	• Define need to change self.	• Handle erratic callers. • Handle irate callers. • Handle confused callers.	• Individual project and Socratic discussion
	• Define professional.	• Describe four characteristics of a professional.	• Socratic lecture
	• Create a log.	• List all calls. • Type all calls.	• Socratic definitions
	• Diagnose problems from log.	• Weigh each one.	• Lecture • Socratic discussion • Project
10:00 A.M. to 10:30 A.M.	• Prioritize problems.	• Compare each. • Adjust each.	• Group project
	• Write script for each.	• Brainstorm. • Write script. • Refine.	• Lecture • Group project • Socratic discussion
Break			

the course. In contrast, the trainee's manual is a workbook containing exercises and other activities, background materials, supporting charts and graphs, and room for notes. When you write these manuals, begin with the trainer's version because it will help you define and structure the trainee's manual.

One of the saddest experiences is to start a new training job and find all the office shelves empty. Often the former trainer took everything or never had any materials in the first place. Almost as bad is finding reams of disorganized notes and random inserts. A professional program prevents these situations. In the file for each program should be at least the following:

1. A document detailing the elements of the program
2. A trainer's manual
3. A trainee's workbook or manual

In addition, it is helpful for future reference if there are needs analyses, task analyses, visual aids such as overhead projections or slides, classroom handouts, and evaluation materials. A good reference file facilitates the training of new instructors and the reevaluation of older program materials. It is also a source of information when you want to refresh yourself on a course not often offered. And if you move on to another position, that file of past programs will help your replacement. Don't take it with you. You owe the company the materials you developed on their time. By all means take a copy, but leave the information there, too.

Determining the Methods of Training

The section on preparing the program agenda made reference to one of your most important considerations—methodology. Let's look at some of your options.

There are three broad philosophical approaches to methods of instruction. Some teachers, college professors, and even trainers are purists and espouse one or the other of these approaches to the exclusion of the rest. I am convinced that a much more productive approach is a synthesis of all three, using elements from each to their best advantage.

The three approaches are:

1. Cognivitism, which is an updating of the blank-slate method
2. Humanism, which constitutes the modern Socratic approach
3. Behaviorism, which is exemplified by a training version of psychologist B. F. Skinner's behavior modification technique called *behavior modeling*[1]

We are already familiar with blank-slate and Socratic environments from Chapter 5. Behavior modification is a technique for directing learning that was developed by B. F. Skinner from the 1930s through the 1950s. It is still used in scientific research on rats, pigeons, monkeys, and other animals. You are probably familiar with examples of rats learning to run mazes or pigeons learning to type short messages. The basic principle is that of reenforcement of desired behavior by rewarding that behavior and/or punishing undesirable behavior.

We gain learning insights from each of these philosophical approaches.[2] Humanism draws on the learner's experiences, treats trainees as adults, is adaptable to a broad range of applications, and develops critical thinking, creativity, judgment, and self-directed learning. We use it in questioning techniques, class projects, constructive feedback, and discussions.

Behaviorism, on the other hand, provides us with the concept of setting clearly defined *behavioral* objectives that focus training on skills development. It ensures that training must be mostly practice and not theory. It keeps training highly specific and creates observable results that can be evaluated. We use it in simulations, role-plays, coaching sessions, on-the-job training, and throughout all of our reenforcement and feedback procedures.

Cognitivism provides us with a sense of organization, structure, and efficiency. It allows us to practice *less is more* and ensure that the learners can follow the flow of the content we are teaching. It too treats trainees as adults and builds up a base of information and concepts. We use it when we show films and videos, use diagrams and maps, assign readings, give lectures, perform presentations, and solve case studies and projects.

Many of the methods we are about to examine draw more heavily from one of these philosophies than from the others. I recommend using a variety of methods; the method chosen should reflect the trainees, the material, the training objectives you have set, and the material to be learned. All methods can be overused or used poorly. All of them can also be used appropriately and well. Careful planning and the development of your own skill in using each of them is vital. To help, let us now look at each of the specific methods available to you.

Lectures

Sometimes the best way to convey information is to lecture. The lecture method can save time by coming directly to the point. It is probably the most frequently used teaching method and the most familiar to your trainees, but, as we have seen in Chapter 2, it demands attentiveness from the learners, and so can make learning more difficult rather than easier.

Effective lectures are short. Know the group. If you have college graduates, you can lecture for thirty minutes, but no longer. If your trainees are high school graduates, don't go over fifteen or twenty minutes. If you train high school dropouts, keep your lectures under ten minutes.

Making the most of your available time takes careful planning. Here are some tips:

- Select among your substructure formats (Chapter 2) and create problem/solutions, cause-and-effect relationships, or other ways to illustrate your points quickly and dynamically.
- Make one or, at most, three points in a lecture. Remember, *less is more*.
- Make your points directly and clearly. Don't wander around the point—come to it head-on. Avoid extraneous material.
- Follow the lecture immediately with a practical application of the concept.
- Create Socratic interaction. Ask questions of the group to keep their attention focused on the topic.

Record your lectures or ask others you can trust to provide honest feedback to sit in. Check yourself to be sure you are saying what you want to say in as simple a way as possible, in the least amount of time.

Handouts and Other Written Materials

Supplementary materials are a speedy and efficient way to communicate factual information. They enhance your oral explanations by providing carefully worded examples and illustrations. They are also a means for bringing in outside sources

---

Training Methods

- Lectures
- Written materials and handouts
- Demonstrations
- Panel discussions
- Class discussions
- Team teaching
- Role playing
- Case histories
- On-the-job training
- Project sessions
- Simulations
- Games
- Programmed instruction
- Computer-based training and interactive videodisc

---

such as quotes and charts. They can serve as notes of lessons and checklists of steps trainees can study. Here are some tips for using written materials:

- If you pass out materials in class, give trainees time to read them. Don't talk until they've finished.
- Discuss the material or relate it immediately to the topic at hand.
- Explain the materials before you hand them out—or after—but never explain *while* you are distributing them. People aren't listening. They're too busy examining the handout.

If you are writing the materials yourself, remember that *less is more*. Make them simple and direct. Use handouts only to make a point or get across information that you can't explain better another way. Be sparing in your use of supplementary written materials. If you assign the material as homework, it becomes a redundant loop (see Chapter 2). Be sure, however, to discuss it the following day or trainees will learn that they don't have to do such assignments.

Demonstrations

A demonstration is an opportunity for you to convert a concept into a practical application. The biggest problem, however, is that not everyone sees exactly the same thing. This is particularly true when you show a group how to handle a piece of equipment. Those close to you see everything while those in the back see next to nothing. Using videotapes is the best answer to this problem. The camera shows actions at close range, so every participant sees everything the camera sees.

Here are some tips for using demonstrations to instruct:

1. *Streamline the demonstration.* Showing involved and intricate tasks will overwhelm the trainees with too much detail.

2. *Structure the demonstration around key points or steps.* Create such keys by setting precise objectives. Unless you are asked a question, ignore areas not part of your key objectives.

3. *Let the demonstration show the basic processes or principles.* If you must teach skills by demonstration, break the skills down into small steps that show the process and the principles involved.

4. *Practice ahead of time.* Demonstrations that don't work usually are detrimental. If something goes wrong, use the old sales dodge "I'm glad that happened because it allows me to show you what to do if it happens to you." Of course, be sure you know what to do.

Build redundancy into your lesson by referring to the demonstration later on. Ask questions about it, and use the demonstration to start discussions. Also, don't expect the demonstration to train for you. You must engage their minds in the activity. The demonstration can't have its full impact until they get their hands on equipment or perform the skills. Lock in the process with practice; do this as early as possible after the demonstration.

Panel Discussions

A panel is, in effect, a debate in front of an audience. Each person presents a point of view, then argues it with other members of the panel or answers questions from the audience. Panels are useful for examining ideas and for sharing experiences. You can explore the different sides of important issues and can engage the group in controversy, but you can't really teach skills. For example, I use panels most often to discuss equal employment opportunity (EEO) issues, but the panel always needs to be followed or preceded by EEO content, regulations, and guidelines. There must also be hands-on practice for trainees to apply those concepts debated by the panel.

Panels are particularly effective for capitalizing on available expertise. Use the knowledgeable trainees in your group or get people from other areas of the company (or outside of it, but that can be expensive) to address the class. They engage the group, vary the presentation, and open up controversial or ambiguous issues to discussion. Panels can also be used to culminate activities, such as when you have groups present their work projects to the entire class.

To make panel discussions work, follow these tips:

1. *Focus on your objectives.* Know exactly what you want to accomplish and keep those objectives in mind. Don't let the discussion degenerate into a free-for-all.

2. *Draw up specific guidelines for what is to be presented.* If you bring in experts, make your purpose clear. This not only keeps your objectives in focus but also lets you maintain leadership.

3. *Be the moderator.* Lead the discussion. If you use a panel as a culmination, let the members present their materials, then moderate the questions or discussion from the group. This allows you to control and direct the discussion.

4. *Prepare good questions in advance in case no one in the audience has any.* These questions will get the discussion going and relieve tension among the panel members. As an alternative, plant key questions with knowledgeable trainees to enhance the group's image and to prime the audience for greater participation.

5. *Set time limits and stick to them.* Attention spans are short, so don't exhaust the panelist trainees before you've had a chance to pull the ideas together and draw out the essentials from them.

6. *If you use outside experts, prepare both accurate introductions and concluding thanks for their presentations.*

Class Discussions

Discussions can serve many purposes. By using the Socratic method you can pose overhead questions (see Chapter 3) to the class and thus start discussions, which you moderate and control. This approach seems (and often, indeed, is) spontaneous. People get involved and voice their views. The discussion lets you quickly and pleasantly cover subjects they know, creating strong motivation for learning new subjects. It also allows you to discover what they know and how they feel. New material (theory or practical information) can be interjected by you as part of the discussion so that it can be used as a teaching tool.

If you begin discussions with an overhead question, here are some tips:

1. Unless the discussions happen spontaneously, practice your Socratic skills ahead of time.

2. Don't dominate the discussion. Loosen the reins to open up the group and pull back only to summarize and draw out key points.

3. Maintain order at all times. Protect the rights of all participants and be prepared to deal with challengers to your authority (see Chapter 3).

4. End the discussion when it has gone on as long as time allows or when it threatens to take time away from other areas of your course. Also, end it if the discussion begins to wander off the topic or the arguments degenerate into factionalism.

Another way to start discussion is to break the trainees into groups of four or more and assign a topic to each group. The groups discuss their topics, then share the results of their discussions with the rest of the class. At this point, of course, you can also add your input. This is an excellent method when you have a series of points to cover about which the participants are likely to have opinions. I often use this approach to show how theoretical principles relate to the trainees' everyday experiences.

If you assign groups to initiate discussions, here are some tips:

1. Have your objectives in mind and specify what you want each group to discuss.

2. Wander about the room while the groups discuss their topics. This underlines your authority and allows you to learn more about them. It also makes you available for questions.

3. When the groups present the results of their discussions, pull those results together by adding to or correcting their impressions. Draw out the basic principles you want them to remember.

Team Teaching

Team teaching can be an effective approach or an expensive frill. The concept is simple. More than one instructor trains the group at one time. The advantage of team teaching is that there is a stimulating variety of voices, training styles, expertise, and personalities. As with most joint efforts, there can be a synergy that stimulates instructors to perform more effectively. Trainees gain several perspectives on the material, which in turn promotes deeper insights.

The problem most frequently encountered in team teaching is that variety and synergy do not take place. Sometimes the instructors do not have clearly defined roles, and much time is wasted dividing up tasks or repeating work. Also, instructors may openly disagree with one another, causing confusion among the trainees. Consequently, the trainees gain nothing, but the instructor costs are doubled.

To avoid these problems, select instructors carefully for their contrasting styles and personalities, which galvanize one another. Also, balance the teaching load. Divide content by area of specialty; to create variety, divide structure by skill level. For example, one instructor can give the lectures and lead the discussions while a second carries out demonstrations and coaches group projects. A third can lead role-playing exercises and manage case history projects. Together they can participate in a panel discussion.

Have all instructors reach an agreement on any controversial topics before beginning to teach. Devise a system for airing disagreements outside the training class. For example, allow each instructor one or two preemptory challenges. If he or she feels strongly on an issue, that instructor may claim a preemptory privilege, which forbids other instructors from arguing or even discussing the point. If the number of such preemptory bids is limited (only once in a given week, for example), and is distributed equally, you'll keep peace in the training room and reserve disagreements for planning sessions.

Team teaching can be effective as on-the-job training for instructors. Experienced people can observe and coach the less experienced. Everyone has a chance to work with the best trainers, too. In short, team teaching can be a fabulous method, but, as with anything in training, it requires careful planning around precise objectives.

Role Playing

We discussed role-playing as an evaluation tool in Chapter 5. It is also a hands-on teaching method that allows trainees to practice what they've learned. Role playing can be used very effectively in the preparation stage, too (see Chapter 2). Allow participants to show how they would normally handle a situation, then use this performance as a reference point from which to teach principles and techniques. In fact, you can even use role-playing in the presentation stage by coaching the players much as in master classes in music, where the maestro interrupts and fine-tunes the performances of the learners, using their errors as a springboard for instruction. But vary the role-playing format occasionally. Even an exciting practice like role-playing gets dull if it is always the same.

In using role-playing, here are some tips:

1. Carefully set up your characters to prove your point. Provide two characters who are going to clash in exactly the way you want. For example, use one player to force another either to use the skills you've taught or to illustrate what happens when those skills aren't used. Don't write a script (unless you are teaching rote responses), but provide detailed background on characters' habits, attitudes, goals, personalities, and mood, as well as business restrictions that motivate or restrain them.

2. Use role-playing to illustrate one key problem. Don't try for more than one topic or you'll diffuse the impact and distract the learners with too much information.

3. Take the time to introduce the situation. Give them enough background to understand what's at stake. Then assign the roles.

4. Both the role-plays and the discussions can tend to get off the topic. To prevent this, make sure participants understand your instructions. For example, tell them, "The customer service representative must: (1) use the customer's name three times; (2) organize, clarify, and confirm the nature of the customer's problem; (3) empathize with the customer; and (4) offer to do something for the customer." If you plan to use observers to provide feedback, have each of them use an observation sheet to look for key behavior and to respond to key aspects of the performance.

5. If the role-play gets off the topic, stop the performance and ask, "What are the problems here? Why isn't the conversation moving in the right direction?" Be assertive. Demand that they stay in character and on the topic.

6. After the performance, always discuss what happened. This is when learning takes place. Ask questions of each player, and have the group advise the players. Encourage discussion. Challenge them with alternatives—"What would have happened if . . . ?"

Case Histories

As described in Chapter 5, case histories can be a means of evaluation. There are two other ways to use a case history:

1. As the practice stage of a lesson or series of lessons
2. As the structure for the skills you teach

The use of case histories as a form of practice is perhaps the more common. A case history challenges people to apply what they have learned to solve a real problem. It is used in military training, in the sport of orienteering, for management simulation training, and throughout the academic world as a final step to a graduate degree—in fact, it appears in most situations in which showing performance is the final step of training.

Case histories are also used in teaching situations in which assembly or disassembly of parts is mandated. For example, it is found in auto mechanic courses, aeronautical construction courses, computer training, medical school cadaver labs, law school mock trials, and biology lab classes. Use case histories in either or both ways. Their value is in challenging the learner in real situations.

Here are some tips for using case histories:

1. Let your objectives govern the level of difficulty.

2. A case can be used to practice and evaluate one skill or twenty. Therefore, it can be used as a single practice step, as a progressive series of steps, or as a final test of all that has been learned.

3. Have a correct solution, but leave some areas open. In the real world, there are usually several effective approaches to solving problems.

On-the-Job Training

Details of on-the-job training (OJT) are discussed in Chapter 13. However, briefly, on-the-job training is a classic and still popular method. It was the basis for the medieval guilds, and every civilization has used it to pass on information. Every primitive community perpetuates itself by it.

The principal problems of OJT are standardization and control. Each supervisor in the field has idiosyncrasies and individual approaches to the job. Each will do it his or her own way, often completely differently from others handling the same work. To be effective, OJT training must be standardized. Likewise, if you have a mandate to train, yet field supervisors actually do most of the training, you must set standards and maintain supervision over that training.

To establish OJT methods, talk to those involved in the training. Get their input to design a course of instruction that meets *their* demands. When their demands conflict with your objectives, negotiate to set agreeable standards. Agree first on the objectives, then use these to set the performance standards.

Next, draw up an outline of the program and check it with the field supervisors and with management. (The written program will add authority to your training.) Include in your program the need for and intention to supervise the supervisors. An excellent way to do this is to organize your training in stages so that you train the supervisors first. Then give the trainees their first session. They then go for a period of on-the-job training, followed by a return to you for additional training before their final OJT session. Such an approach gives you much more control and monitoring ability.

If you find serious variances from the standard, meet with the supervisors involved and negotiate a solution as quickly as possible. This, too, gives you an added degree of control.

Project Sessions

In Chapters 1, 2, and 3 we discussed how learning must come from the learner, how the trainee must connect the known with the new. Project sessions are, perhaps, the most effective way to bring these two educational principles together. They ask the learner to use new skills. But because they offer hands-on experience, they also draw on the learner's established abilities and help build both skill and knowledge bridges to new learning.

To create effective project sessions, follow these tips:

1. *Make the project a task the learner will have to perform on the job.* If this isn't possible, develop one that is as close to the real situation as possible.

2. *Set up the project so that the trainees can practice as many new skills or processes as possible.* If necessary, include skills or processes you haven't taught yet, but only if they are closely related to those you have taught. In other words, the project can challenge them to do more than practice what you've taught if such steps are a logical outgrowth of what they have already learned.

3. *Make the project challenging, but not impossible.* Projects that are too easy are boring; ones that are too difficult are disheartening and demotivating.

4. *Allow time for work on the project during your seminar session, if only for initial planning.*

Project sessions are excellent vehicles for group activity. They can be effective as individual assignments as well, so alternate the two for best results.

Be prepared to give considerable feedback. It is direct evaluation and correction when needed that provides the core of your instruction. Pick key principles or skills and concentrate on those.

Simulations

As mentioned in Chapter 5 and discussed later in Chapter 10, simulations are excellent for evaluation. Additionally, they are fine practice exercises. They also can be used as an instructional format in much the same way that a case history would be used. In fact, case histories, role-plays, and many group projects are all forms of simulation. Any critical incident or culminating activity that demands that the learners use what they have been taught in a realistic, lifelike setting would classify as a simulation. A typical example is an in-basket exercise, which is a set of familiar tasks likely to be faced on the job. It is usually given without warning. Trainees are confronted with a series of tasks or problems and given a time limit in which to respond correctly. The tasks can encompass anything trainees might reasonably face.

The value of the in-basket exercise is that it is completely flexible, realistic, and challenging. Use it as a pretest or posttest, or as an assessment session. You can scale it to the work and skills levels of any group, and because the content is so flexible, you can use it several times with the same group without risking boredom. Finally, it is fun. The in-basket exercise is rather like a scavenger hunt; participants enjoy the sense of competition that grows among those struggling to solve the same problems.

To use an in-basket exercise, follow these tips:

1. *Don't make all your simulations paperwork tasks.* The most common example of its use is in sports training. Batting practice, pattern running (football), tennis practice, and trapshooting all follow this basic idea: Trainees (players) handle whatever is tossed their way. Be creative if you train in areas other than desk work.

2. *Gather as many exercises from real situations as you can.* If necessary, get ideas and solutions from several people who handle these tasks frequently.

3. *Use several tasks (at least five and no more than fifteen to twenty).* Base them on what you've taught or want to teach, the skills level of the group, your training objectives, and the time available.

4. *Set a realistic time limit for completion.* The time limit adds challenge and lends a sense of completion.

5. *Prepare detailed, step-by-step instructions, both written and oral.* State the goals (objectives) they should achieve.

6. *After the exercise evaluate the performance.* Use a discussion of the exercise to crystallize the learning experience.

Games

People love to play games, and games can be fabulous teaching tools. The problem is that games can be so much fun that trainees forget to learn. Games can also get stale. Most are fun only for the first or second time; after that, they demotivate learners.

Use games to test for recall, recognition, and skills; challenge participants under pressure to use the material taught; and introduce topics or areas for discussions. Games can encourage behavior that increases a trainee's depth of understanding or sensitivity to problems. They also provide a common experience upon which future lessons can be based. Lastly, you can develop essential principles from the interaction of the game, which can then be redefined in terms of the tasks you are teaching.

To use games, follow these tips:

1. *Be creative.* You can buy books on training games, but it's often more fun to invent your own. Or adapt popular television game shows and table games.

2. *Relate the games to your training objectives.* If the games don't address your objectives, don't use them.

3. *Schedule your games at the end of the day, when trainees need a lift.* Or let the game mark a change of pace. Games are best for starting seminars off on a challenging note, or for ending a hard day (but do allow time for full debriefing).

4. *Don't overdo the use of games.* One game in a day is enough; never use more than two. When you play too many games, their impact lessens. Participants have a wonderful time and love your training, but either don't remember or confuse what they have been taught.

5. *Debrief the players at the end of the game, so as to make your points clear.* Let the trainees have fun, but always pull the experience together so they realize the principles involved.

Computer-Based Training

Computer-based training (CBT) is an outgrowth of the work begun several years ago on artificial intelligence and the development of expert systems. The incredible technical advances in electronics and software design in the last few years has added tremendous impetus so that computers and computer-assisted instruction have been thrust into the forefront of training issues. They are the state-of-the-art, high-tech, hot number of the training world. And they may well be one of the major modes of training in the next few decades. They are sufficiently important that I have devoted an entire chapter to discussing their full role and implications for training (see Chapter 10). But a few caveats here are still in order.

Most computer instruction is still only a high-tech form of programmed instruction. Programmed instruction was a series of written questions, with the answer to each hidden but immediately verifiable by the learner. The main drawback of programmed instruction was that it proved to be extremely dull. There is little inherent motivation, and the minimal interaction involved (answering questions, checking answers, and moving on) is extremely repetitive.

In the late 1950s, when the concept was introduced in conjunction with "teaching machines," it was lauded as the teaching method of the twenty-first century. But programmed instruction failed to catch on except among educators. Unless the learner was already highly motivated, he or she was never able to overcome the tedium of the format.

Most computerized instructional programs, even the flashy ones on CD-ROM, are still beset with nearly all of the problems that weaken any programmed instruction approach. Many programs are much more exciting, but only when they are programmed to be as dynamic as videoarcade games, and even then, learners tire of too much intense interaction. Basically, working with a computer is still a nonsocial, repetitive, and intrinsically unrewarding activity. It can be made somewhat richer by tailoring it to offer a wider range of possible answers (see Chapter 10). But learning still occurs exclusively through repetition and trial and error. Trial and error is fun, but repetition is not.

When it is well written and programmed, interactive CD-ROM is exciting, even very effective. Certainly it will also improve. But learning is still largely an oral and kinesthetic experience, and it is unlikely that even artificially intelligent, sophisticated, Socratically programmed computers will satisfy the need for human interaction in the learning process. Despite the claims of multimedia gurus to the contrary, face-to-face training is—and appears destined to be—the most effective means of bringing about change through learning.

If you now use or are considering using CD-ROM or other computer simulations, here are some tips:

1. *Make them specific.* Consider writing your own programs (see Chapter 10). Even if you are not computer literate, this is a viable route.

2. *Be wary of generic programs.* Unless they teach exactly what you want and teach it well, they are unlikely to be worth what they cost. Be a careful consumer here (see Chapter 8).

3. *Assign specific, short units and vary assignments with other types of work (projects, case histories, and so on).* This prevents learner burnout (which happens quickly with any form of programmed instruction, even CD-ROM). Computer interactions and simulations are best when integrated into an overall lesson sequence.

4. *Schedule frequent sessions to discuss what has been learned.* In cases where learners are remote, consider conference telephone calls or distance learning (see Chapter 10), but live is best.

Videotape

Every athlete today in any sport uses videotape to evaluate his or her performance. There is no finer feedback than watching yourself do well or make mistakes.

As a learning tool, video is perhaps the most powerful method of instruction to come along in this half-century of technological wonders.

It is powerful because it taps into so many of the principles of learning. It provides powerful inarguable feedback, allows us to see and so profit from our errors, and provides multisensory stimulation and overwhelming association. Use it whenever possible to create feedback for your learners. We will discuss in detail the best ways to use it in Chapter 8.

Here are some tips for using videotape:

1. *Remember that video watching is a very passive activity, and a poor method of instruction.* Showing commercial videos is the least effective use of video available to you. Its value is limited to creating associations, providing sensory variety, and helping with simulated role-plays or techniques.

2. *Always prepare a framework of questions for the learners to answer as they watch the videos.* The questions help keep the trainees focused on what is to be learned.

3. *Make your own videos wherever possible.* Videos that you make, or better still, that the learners make, are far more exciting and effective learning tools than commercially constructed ones.

The Trainer's Manual

The final step in developing a training program is to write a trainer's manual and a trainee's workbook. There are several possible formats for trainer's manuals but perhaps the simplest is used by Beverly Hyman, in her Institute for Training and Communication "Training the Trainer" course.[3] The first column of each page shows the units of time. Next to each time is an entry stating what the trainer will do at that point. To the right of each entry is a description of the trainee's activity. Finally, on the far right is a notation of visual or other aids to be used during that segment. See Figure 7-4. In our example, OH Proj #1 is an overhead projection of the questions each participant would ask his or her neighbor. It would remain on the screen as long as the trainer felt it was needed. The agenda would be listed on a flip chart.

This description of events would continue, step-by-step in timed sequences, until the course was completely outlined. The manual then becomes a record of the course. It would brief anyone with knowledge of the subject on how to teach the course. This document should stay on the shelf if you leave. It is your legacy for those who come after you, because it has several strong features:

▪ *Standardization.* No matter who teaches it, the course covers the same material in the same way.

Figure 7-4. Model of a trainer's manual.

Time	Trainer Activity	Trainee Activity	Audiovisual
9:00 A.M.	Introduce self and group by having each participant introduce his or her neighbor.	Each person interviews the person on his or her right for 5 minutes. Each asks: (1) who the other is, (2) what he or she does, (3) the reason for being there, (4) other pertinent or pleasant information. Upon instruction from trainer, trainees take turns introducing their neighbors, starting from the trainer's right, front of the room.	OH Proj #1
9:20 A.M.	Review agenda for the day and spell out ground rules (breaks, smoking, and so on).	Refer to handout.	Flip chart
9:30 A.M.	Ask group to list two behaviors that customers perform that upset them.	Each participant lists two.	
9:35 A.M.	Divide class into groups of five and instruct each group to share problems and select the two toughest ones.	Groups share and discuss problems.	
9:45 A.M.	Ask each group for its problems and lead discussion of possible solutions for each one.	Groups provide problems, and individuals offer solutions.	

- *Consistency.* No matter how often you or others give the course, it remains essentially the same.

- *Quality control.* By detailing the procedures and events you set a standard for regular evaluation of both your own training and that of others who teach the course.

■ *Documentation*. When questioned by management or challenged by an unhappy employee, you have documentation of the content and methodology of your course, as well as the normal response patterns of the participants.

The trainer's manual is not the same as the lesson plan, although the manual contains the four steps of the lesson plan. In the manual, you simply outline the steps as you use them. For example, in the preparation step, list what the trainer and trainees will be doing. If your preparation step is Socratic questions, list your questions under *Trainer Activity* and the anticipated responses under *Trainee Activity*. If, instead, you are using a game, say so. Tell what the trainer does to explain the game (but you need not give all the descriptive material or rules; these belong in the trainee's manual) and what the trainees are expected to do.

In the presentation step, list the activities of both trainer and trainees (taking notes, answering questions, and discussion) and also list any visual aids you may be using. You also might want to list page references for similar material in the trainee's workbook. This helps coordinate your lesson with the trainee's workbook.

For the practice step, detail the activity of the trainees and describe what the trainer will say to introduce and monitor the practice.

Finally, in the evaluation step (which may be combined with the practice step), state what the evaluation is. Describe how the trainer will introduce it, but relegate the actual evaluation to the trainee's workbook, especially if it is a test, performance, or similar exercise. If, however, the trainer is expected to evaluate a project at home, say so under the *Trainer Activity* column.

What is *not* needed in the trainer's manual is a list of management goals, needs or task analyses, philosophical discussions (although you might want to briefly describe your approach to the subject both as an orientation for other trainers and as a disclaimer for yourself), cost factors, budgets, or learning patterns. What you *must* include are a list of objectives, a timed agenda, application of the four-step method for each topic, the teaching methods you will be using, necessary visual aids and other equipment, patterns of redundancy (through the use of reviews, aids, or tests), means for evaluation, what-to-do descriptions of the trainer's performance, and anticipated reactions and behaviors of the trainees.

The format shown in Figure 7-4 is too detailed for a trainer to teach from, however. I work from a simple topical agenda, supplemented by notes when needed (lists of points, examples, or acronyms). But I use the manual to brief myself and as a foundation for my topical agenda.

The Trainee's Workbook

As the last part of writing a program, you'll need to put together the handouts and other materials for the trainees. Think of it as a workbook, not a textbook.

The trainee's workbook should contain an agenda (not timed) for the course; space for work on exercises and for notes; instructions for all planned activities and projects, plus tools for such activities (facts, figures, tables, descriptions, and letters); charts, graphs, and other data used in the course; case histories and role-playing situations; and any descriptive or background material not fully covered in the training sessions.

The workbook may optionally contain the objectives for each lesson; descriptive or textbook essays on the subject; supplementary materials (for example, magazine article reprints); a bibliography for further reading; biographies of any guest speakers; speaker evaluation sheets; and title pages, company logo, and so forth.

Figure 7-5 contains sample pages from a trainee's workbook I use for supervisory training. Note that there is a wide margin on the left to leave ample space for the learners to take notes. Each section illustrates a different format. The first is an exercise with learning points included. The second is a list of steps to perform a task with a brief description of each step. The third is an acronym that is to be filled in by the participant as the material is covered in class. Finally, the last one is a detailed set of instructions for a small project session.

Summary

Writing a training program can be a prodigious task. We reviewed the thirteen elements of a training program, including establishing budgets and support networks within the company as well as developing a rationale for your program in terms of solving management's problems. We also explored the need to know the potential training group, how you'll reach them, and how they will be selected. The chapter further explained when, based on your findings and your rationale, you should set specific training objectives. It also showed how to describe to management how best to meet those objectives; looked at whether to write the program yourself, hire a consultant, or buy a generic package; and how to determine whether or not you did meet your objectives.

We also considered the six steps in writing an agenda, including decisions on structure, methods, and lesson plans. To help you, we covered the most popular teaching methods, from Socratic lectures to computer-based training and interactive CD-ROM programs. Finally, with all elements in place, we explored the actual writing of the program. As noted, a training program has two manuals. We described the purpose and content of the trainer's manual, with its lists of what to do, where to do it, which aids and tools to use, and what to expect from the trainees. The characteristics of the trainee's manual were described complete with the necessary agenda assignments, charts and graphs, case histories, and work space.

Figure 7-5. Sample pages from trainee's workbook.

Brainstorming

In your groups of four create a list of all of the possible uses for a paper clip that you can come up with. The only rules are:

1. No critical judgment is allowed. Every idea, no matter how ridiculous it may seem, is as good as every other idea.
2. Quantity, not quality, is the purpose. Quantity is the only thing that counts here, not cost or reason.
3. The wilder the better! Have fun. Be creative.
4. It is good to build on to or use somebody else's idea. Run with it, add to it, take it to the next level if you can. Hitchhiking is allowed and encouraged.

These are the four rules of brainstorming. Brainstorming is a way of breaking out of a rut. If what you have been doing to solve a problem isn't working, then you must change what you are doing in order to solve it. Brainstorming is the way teams do just that.

Problem Solving

Define the problem.

This is not always as easy as it sounds. Be sure that you are defining the whole problem, not just the symptoms. Solutions for symptoms never solve the real problem. Ask yourself what the causes of the problem are and which ones can be addressed (there are always more than one).

Brainstorm possible (and impossible) solutions.

Use the techniques we've just learned. Remember not to prejudge any answers. This stifles creativity and causes you to lose out on sometimes brilliant solutions.

(continues)

Figure 7-5. *(continued)*

Define the conditions that must be satisfied in order for a solution to be satisfactory.

What has to be working and/or completed before you can say, "This problem is solved"?

Assess each option against these conditions you have just defined.

Think not only in terms of immediate effects but long-range ones, too. Look beyond the specific problem to the bigger picture. Who else (what other departments) is affected by the ideal solution? How? The point here is to eliminate most of the solutions you (or your team) came up with by brainstorming. Normally only a few will come close to the conditions that will satisfy or solve the problem.

Assess the impact of each of the surviving solutions on the operation and on the company.

Now each solution should be assessed as to what it will cost; how difficult it will be to get the necessary cooperation of others; what the long range effects of the solution will be; what new problems, if any, it may create, etc. Usually only one or perhaps two solutions are left now. If there are none, go to the next step.

Can you combine any of the solutions or adapt them?

Be creative again. Go back over the best of the possible solutions you have, even the ones you've eliminated. Perhaps you can come up with new alternatives. Repeat this process until you have the best possible solution to the problem.

Clear Objectives

S _____

M _____

A _____

R _____

T _____

Project Session

In your groups of four, please use the brainstorming and problem-solving techniques we've just discussed to come up with the best possible solution your group can develop for the following problem:

Safety has not been a really hot issue in your plant for some time. As a result, employees are very lax on some safety practices.

Two areas in particular are very dangerous practices:

- Many workers are ignoring proper lockout and tagging procedures when working on machines.
- Many are not wearing hearing protection while working on the floor.

The problem is made worse by the fact that you have a number of older workers, supervisors, and managers who've simply gotten careless over the years. Many of

(continues)

Figure 7-5. *(continued)*

them already have serious hearing loss and say they hate to wear ear plugs. The younger workers see this careless attitude from the senior people and naturally do the same.

The company owners have recently realized how vulnerable they are to very heavy OSHA fines and lawsuits and so have charged you with a safety crackdown. This comes at a time when business is booming and the plant is running full bore.

Your team must solve this problem so as to gain the support of all employees and so that the problem doesn't repeat again in three months, as it did the last time there was a push for improved safety. Your solution must also cause the least possible disruption in the production schedule and should not demoralize the workers or other supervisors.

Applications

1. Using the material covered in the first half of this chapter, prepare a plan to develop a full training program. Create a budget, gain support, plan how you will market your program, align it with a company thrust, etc. Make it a real training program based on the needs analysis you performed after Chapter 5.

2. Write a trainer's manual and a trainee's workbook for this program.

3. Think of the worst training you have ever had to experience as a learner. Write down in detail the poor methods and instruction. Now, using the list in the latter half of this chapter, create dynamic and exciting methods to bring this training alive, to turn it around and make it exciting.

Chapter 8

Alternatives to Writing Programs

AS we saw in Chapter 7, it takes considerable time and effort to write a training program. In the end, however, you have a specific training course that can bring about dynamic changes in your organization. The program has been tailored to meet the needs you have identified. For your purposes, there is probably no finer program available anywhere. There are alternatives to this lengthy process, however, and they are the subject of this chapter.

Because of time constraints, many trainers look for outside sources when they need a new program. Outside sources are quick, frequently cost-effective, and often quite successful at meeting both demands and expectations. Their drawback is their inability to be specific. They are, by nature, generic programs. To be successful in the marketplace, they must aim at the majority's needs, with a general content and structure that appeals to widely diverse groups. As a rule, assume that the more general such programs are, the less useful they will be for you, unless your need is equally general. To some extent they can be adapted to your needs, but almost never can they be as effective as a program you have built to solve a problem in your organization. With this limitation in mind, let's look at some of these alternatives.

Off-the-Shelf Programs

An off-the-shelf program is a complete package, ready for your trainees. These programs are mass-produced like books, hence the name *off-the-shelf*. They can take several forms:

- Textbooks of all kinds and on any subject
- Textbooks with study questions at the end of each chapter

- Study questions and/or tests arranged by topic, available in limited subjects (such as math, health care, or psychology)
- Self-study programs that combine explanatory material with study questions and projects
- Standardized instruction materials such as games and exercises
- Audiocassette (or disk) learning packages
- Audio and slide presentations
- Videocassettes on specific topics and generic subjects
- Films, usually on key generic topics (for example, time management)
- Computer-based instructional materials
- Interactive CD-ROM instruction

These packages are available from many different sources. Frequently, elements are combined to form a series of generic lessons for self-study or group study that might include a combination of expository materials, study questions, projects, and programmed instruction. There are some companies that even offer films or video- and audiocassettes matched to self-study programmed instruction. There are programs like these for most subjects with a sufficiently wide base of occurrence in industry to make them commercially viable. For example, they can be found in such areas as time management, negotiation skills, sales, business writing, basic supervision, telephone techniques, banking skills, health care techniques, presentation skills, or basic finance. In fact, most general business skills are covered by one or more such off-the-shelf packages.

The Benefits

Without exception, the prime benefit of off-the-shelf programs is that they are ready to use. Just give them to your trainees and turn them loose—at least that is the impression we are given by the advertisements that sell them. The off-the-shelf programs are at least convenient. Although such programs seldom train to the extent promised, they are easy for trainers to apply. And sometimes they actually work well, particularly the packages computer manufacturers sell to teach basic software. By their very nature, these packages require trainees to put in much hands-on practice, so they learn despite sometimes poorly written (occasionally, even incomprehensible) manuals.

Off-the-shelf programs are not, however, maintenance-free. They can be worthwhile supplements to your tailor-made programs. This is, in essence, how textbooks are used in schools and colleges. A text is seldom the entire course itself; instead, readings and exercises are selected from it and used to illustrate or add greater depth to classroom topics. Used this way, off-the-shelf packages can be an asset.

Another benefit of off-the-shelf programs is that they provide standardized training in scattered or remote locations. Many times it is not feasible to bring workers to a central location for training. Sometimes, too, there are not enough people needing training to justify a centralized program. More and more today, however, companies are turning to another alternative to solve these problems—distance learning. We'll talk more about this high-tech solution in Chapter 10.

I hesitate to mention a frequently touted benefit: price. Off-the-shelf packages can be economical, certainly when at the level of a textbook. But at the other end of the spectrum, there are many companies that waste a great deal of money purchasing off-the-shelf programs that cannot solve their problems. I know of more than one company that spent $150,000 to $250,000 for a set of videotapes that ultimately proved of little value. Such expenditures are hardly a savings.

The Limitations

Off-the-shelf programs fall into two categories of limitations: management and educational. We've already mentioned management limitations, but we would like to stress that such programs can be very expensive and yet not achieve the results you want. Also, there is a tendency to use off-the-shelf packages as a way for people to train themselves. They cannot do this well. Even the best packages are far better when used by an instructor. Off-the-shelf programs simply do not self-start, self-teach, or self-evaluate as human interaction can.

Off-the-shelf packages are designed to be sold. Consequently, there is always puffery in the advertisements and accompanying literature. Be a careful and thorough consumer. There can be hidden costs. Many standard self-instruction and programmed instruction packages come with only one set of workbooks. Since it is a violation of copyright law to photocopy them, you will have to order new workbooks each time you use the program.

In addition, you need to schedule your uses of these packages. One of the benefits of programmed instruction is that everyone can work at his or her own speed. But because these programs demotivate, you must set deadlines by which time everyone must finish the program. If you are training a disparate group (one of the best uses for off-the-shelf programs), you'll need a fairly complex scheduling and monitoring system to remain aware of their progress. Lastly, if you must add your specific applications onto the package, you will have to work out and write up those parts of the program.

The educational limitations, likewise, are many. Foremost is the fact that the off-the-shelf programs are generic; and, because they are generic, they can only achieve generic results. Unless your training objectives are also generic, off-the-shelf packages may be of no help—they may even be counterproductive.

Moreover, in nearly every case, these off-the-shelf packages tend to demotivate learners. Textbooks are frequently dull to all but the most highly motivated; test packages tend to create anxiety; self-study programs are usually as monotonous as an assembly line. Many people have trouble concentrating on audiotapes since they are accustomed to the primarily background sound of radio. This is somewhat less true in an age of talk radio, but by far the highest percentage of radio listeners still tune in to music-format stations, which are mainly for providing them with background company. Because of movies and television, darkened rooms signal to us that we are going to be entertained, so we relax and stop thinking. Even computer programs become tiresome and demotivational when they follow a linear progression of instruction.

These are serious problems. As we've pointed out throughout this book, good training—effective training—consists of creating environments that make it easy for trainees to learn. All the off-the-shelf packages have some sort of learning demotivator inherent in their format, which is counter to good training and for which you must compensate.

Finally, while most textbooks and tests are written by educators, most audio, video, film, and many computer-aided instruction packages are not. They are mainly written and produced by those promoting the technology in which the training is delivered. Furthermore, while many such companies hire academic advisors, many of these academics are not familiar with the demands of industrial training, thus their teaching objectives may not be to produce action-oriented, measurable skills. As a result, many off-the-shelf packages lack industry-oriented objectives and do not aim at creating change that can be evaluated.

Evaluating the Programs

I am not saying that there are no good off-the-shelf packages. What I am stressing is that a great number of them are not very good and a few are really bad. If you need a purchased program, be a careful consumer. To ensure that you get what is best, always measure the package against your training objectives. For each aspect of learning in the program, ask yourself which measurable, specific, action-oriented objectives this will satisfy. If the answer is few or none, don't buy the program. If you feel satisfied that it will address a sufficient number of your objectives (at least two-thirds), then buy it.

Always try the program before you buy it. The sales literature is not enough to judge how effective or flexible the program may be. Remember that the literature is intended to sell first and inform second. It is usually written by marketing or advertising people and almost never by trainers or even by those who designed the package. Ask for a free evaluation copy of the program. If the supplier can't or won't give one, offer to rent a copy. If they can't or won't do that either, don't buy the package.

Frequently, the supplier will give you a list of previous purchasers whom you can call. This is useful, but remember that the supplier is only going to provide you with clients who are pleased. In addition, you have no way of knowing how reliable that reference is. Even large corporations with significant training departments often train poorly, and their trainers sometimes know very little about effective training. A recommendation from such a person is insufficient reason for purchasing a generic package. Instead, check the promises of salespeople or advertisements with your own network of trainers.

If time is a problem and the package you are considering costs more than $5,000, hire a training consultant to evaluate the choices and make specific recommendations. It will add to the total cost but could limit the possibility of buying a useless or ineffective program. As the cost of these packages increases, the expense of a consultant becomes more and more reasonable. Any package above $20,000 demands an independent evaluation as a safeguard.

When comparing packages estimate their shelf life. Ask yourself how susceptible the material is to becoming dated. This is particularly important in high-tech fields and for technical training packages. Also consider these questions:

- What will be the cost of updating it?
- Does it lend itself to easy updating?
- Who owns the rights to this material?
- What rights do you acquire with the purchase?

For example, there may be hidden costs involved in duplicating or adapting the material to your operation. Or there might be unanticipated costs in repeat orders of supplies. Know what is included in the initial cost.

Ask the suppliers of the off-the-shelf packages you are considering these questions: What is their philosophy of learning? What theory of learning is the basis of their instruction? This book, for instance, is based on the theories of British contemporary philosopher Sir Karl R. Popper, who believes that all learning is:

1. Tentative
2. Iterative (that is, by repetition in ever-expanding contexts)
3. The result of the interaction between what a learner brings to an event and the environment in which he or she interacts during the event[1]

Consequently, teaching is the creation of semantic, emotional, psychological, and physical environments that engage the learner's mind. If your supplier cannot answer such a question, have the person find out who at the company can answer it. If their philosophy is not in accord with yours, don't buy the product. If you are not familiar with the theory, research it at your local library or college to find out whether or not it will work for you.

Here's a final tip on off-the-shelf programs: Justify the cost *before* you buy. There are always two dimensions by which to measure effectiveness—results and cost. As a trainer, you are responsible for results; as a manager, you are responsible for costs. Effective training management reflects a balance between the two. To justify costs, follow these steps:

1. Divide the cost of the training by the number to be trained.
2. Factor in all costs, including hidden ones such as administrative time, lost work time, space requirements, and incidental supplies. Do this for each of several ways in which you might obtain the program (for example, with a consultant, off-the-shelf, or developed in-house).
3. Tally the costs of maintaining the status quo (no training at all).
4. Project the savings from training or other economic impacts your proposed program will have on future operations of the company.

In preparing your justification, remember that all off-the-shelf packages, no matter how disparate, can be compared to each other on a cost-per-person basis. In essence, you are measuring the effectiveness of each option for its economic impact on future operations. Diagnose the strengths and weaknesses in your justification in terms of cost-effectiveness, and compensate for shortcomings or play down the problem areas. (See Chapter 14.)

External Consultants

A consultant is a specialist who has developed a reputation for being good at something. For the trainer, there are two types of consultants: internal and external. An internal consultant is usually a subject-matter expert who is only incidentally likely to have training skills. An external consultant, on the other hand, should have both subject-matter and training expertise. Frequently, a training department functions as a consultant itself. Consultants are resources for advice, analysis, skills development, and information. They perform specialized tasks at which they excel or for which the regular staff has either insufficient time or no ability to perform.

There are three general areas in which consulting is done:

1. *The consultant may act as a subject-area resource—someone you seek out to gain special knowledge or information on a procedure.* You might seek a subject-matter expert when preparing a task analysis, for example.

2. *A consultant could research and prepare documentation for you.* You might hire a consultant to perform a needs analysis or write a training program or a trainer's manual. Perhaps you need a feasibility study done or a powerful proposal written. You might want a consultant to prepare a series of evaluation tools. Or a consultant might be engaged as a ghostwriter, in which case he or she would work closely with you to get an understanding of the material and your style and then work independently to prepare the documents.

3. *A consultant most commonly becomes a resource for supplying live training quickly and efficiently.* The training consultant tailors his or her expertise to a company's requirements and writes or adapts a program for it. Starting with a list of the company's needs (with or without a formal needs analysis), the consultant works with the company to create training objectives and then writes and delivers a program to meet them. In many cases the program becomes an ongoing feature for employees and managers. It can be given each time by the consultant or taken over by a company trainer.

In effect, then, you may seek out a consultant as either an information resource, a documentation resource, or a performance resource.

The Benefits

There are at least ten reasons why you might want to hire a consultant:

1. *Consultants are (or, at least, are supposed to be) experts.* You may be able to write a good program for yourself, but a consultant has written literally hundreds of successful programs. He or she will be able to do so more efficiently, in less time.

2. *You may find yourself frequently too busy to develop a new training program, or you may not know the field.* You could hire and train someone to do it, but that would take time, too. Consultants are a ready-made talent pool from which to draw on short notice.

3. *Consultants have verifiable credibility.* By being experts and working with many organizations, they gain credence from vast experience. This is particularly important if you are training senior management. Division heads usually are not very comfortable being trained by their subordinates, but they relax and learn from an outside expert.

4. *Consultants are politically neutral.* An interoffice squabble often can be resolved by hiring an outside person to research or perform the training.

5. *Consultants represent the state of the art in their field.* To stay in business, consultants must remain fully current.

6. *To stay in business, consultants must be able to produce results.* If you hire a consultant, you'll get the job done quickly and well.

7. *Frequently, a consultant is the most cost-effective way to achieve your results.* On a cost-per-person basis, hiring a consultant is nearly always less expensive than preparing the program yourself. Because a consultant tailors and delivers the program, it is also more effective than an off-the-shelf package.

8. *Working with a consultant usually is an excellent opportunity to learn new skills and gain new competencies.*

9. *Your degree of input and advice to the consultant is completely flexible.* You have whatever level of control and involvement you want.

10. *Your commitment is to the contracted service only.* If you are not satisfied with a consultant's performance, you need not rehire that person. Get another, better consultant. You have not committed large resources to a useless program that you are stuck with. Hiring consultants on contract allows you to shop around until you find exactly what you need.

The Limitations

There are some drawbacks to hiring consultants. First, as in any field, there is a great range of competence. Someone who was excellent for the ABC Company may not fit your organization at all. Merely talking a good game doesn't make one a good consultant. Evaluate a consultant's current work to assess his or her competence before you draw up your contract. (In fairness, remember that, like all of us, consultants have great days and not-so-good days; a poor performance is unacceptable, but a fair one deserves at least another observation.)

A second limitation to hiring consultants is time. You are hiring expertise, but the consultant is selling time. For a consultant to devote full time to you, he or she must charge the maximum. To remain competitive, most consultants practice "streaming" clients (working on more than one project at a time) or they "boilerplate" (patch courses together from already existing programs), "modularize" (plug in standard learning modules whenever needed), and use other shortcuts. The more generic the subject, the more efficient they can be. If you need completely new material, with exercises created just for your application, you will have to pay considerably more because it will involve exclusive use of the consultant's time and creative talents.

A final limitation to hiring consultants is that, as in many fields, you pay for glamour as well as quality. Consultants range from newcomers (who can be excellent) to the world famous (almost pop culture figures). Expertise can be found at all levels, but you pay more for it from big-name stars.

At present, the range stretches from $500 per day to $25,000 or $30,000 for a single one-hour presentation. As with most other things, you get what you pay for. As a rule, $500 to $900 a day gives you the relatively untried or unskilled; from $900 to $1,500 per day you get solid performance with limited experience; from $1,500 to $2,500 per day you get the greatest expertise, seasoned with solid experience. Beyond $2,000, you begin to pay for a consultant's overhead or for the organization that is brokering his or her services. Beyond $2,500, you enter the world of glamour and pay for star quality. Consultants sell their time to whoever will pay the most for it. They are truly free-marketeers.

To hire a Peter Drucker, a Tom Peters, or a Thomas Covey at his peak is to hire someone at the cutting edge of what's happening in management. You are getting instant credibility and guaranteed impact. A Rolls-Royce is indeed different from a Honda, and a major part of that difference is intangible—image, reputation, and exclusivity. Are these intangibles important to your objectives? Sometimes they can be important, and this is one of the considerations in hiring a consultant.

How to Evaluate Consultants

With so wide a variation in price and considering how many of them there are, it is essential that you be able to evaluate the performance and quality of a consultant. Here are twelve guidelines:[2]

1. Try before you buy. Most consultants give public seminars as audition pieces in which to "strut their stuff." If you like what you see, talk to them on the spot. If you don't, leave quietly and no one will be the wiser.

2. As with off-the-shelf package salespeople, ask the consultant what theories or rationale justifies his or her approach to training. Someone who can answer that question at least has given thought to the matter.

3. Ask what the training objectives are for the program you've just observed.

4. Ask for a list of present clients, particularly those with on-going relationships. A one-time seminar may or may not have been good, whereas a series is likely to be done well.

5. Find out what the consultant knows about your company and, even more important, about your industry. If it's little or nothing, you will have to spend time and money supplying background if you want the work to be customized.

6. Once you've described your problem, ask the consultant to describe how he or she would address it from a training point of view. Look for answers that lead to positive changes, not just information.

7. Ask the consultant how he or she would tailor the work to meet your specific requirements.

8. Get the consultant to explain how the results of the training program would be evaluated.

9. After discussing a potential program, ask the consultant for a written proposal that specifies the rationale for the program, the training objectives, the agenda (content), the methods to be used, the materials needed and who is to provide them, and the cost of the program.

10. Request biographies of all key people who will be working with the consultant to deliver the work you require.

11. Check out the key people with organizations that rate speakers, for example, Seminar Clearing House International (see the Appendix for their address). Such organizations usually require membership. If you aren't a member, network with other trainers at organizations similar to your own.

12. Ask for samples of the consultant's written work, then gauge whether it meets your standards.

Of course, many of these guidelines apply only to seminar services. If you are hiring a consultant as an information source or to research, write, or advise, you need only those guidelines that apply to your purpose.

Negotiating With Consultants

Principles of good negotiation are covered in Chapter 18. However, there are a few additional points to consider when negotiating with consultants. The most important element in any negotiation is knowing how badly the other side wants what you have. Coupled with that is a correct estimate of what they value most and, therefore, would be willing to bargain.

Consultants, for the most part, are stars. What they do makes them special, and they like to be treated accordingly. Second, what they are selling is their time. It is most precious to them, and they cannot give it away. Third, most consultants are self-employed or work for rather small organizations. They constantly must seek new business. Most consultants have about a six-month operating horizon; beyond that there is no business—yet. They forgo the sense of security that most company trainers enjoy. Fourth, most consultants travel a great deal, which makes travel in itself unrewarding, even undesirable.

These four aspects of consulting are probably the most effective tools you have in negotiating with consultants. For example, time is the consultant's pressure point. You become more attractive when you save him or her personal time. You can do this by being very well organized yourself. Offer to gather and supply data and handle duplicating or typing arrangements, and make effective use of time during consulting sessions. However, to pressure the consultant during the negotiations, negotiate for more time to be included or set a package price that includes extra hours or longer days at the regular per diem. If you hold a hard line and then give in on it, you should gain concessions in exchange. Use this strategy carefully, however, because a hard line makes you a less desirable client.

One of the most attractive things you can offer is future work in a sizable volume. If you schedule a year in advance and have more programs in mind, you make yourself an important client, and the consultant is more willing to make compromises for you.

Finally, if you can offer special attention, a travel-weary consultant will want to work for you. Supply luxury transportation to and from the airport, flights in a company plane, first-class travel and lodging at a hotel, a fancy rental car, and dinner at home or in a favorite restaurant. Most of these are not brought up openly as negotiating chips, but let the consultant know of them. Perhaps a little less money will be a favorable exchange for being treated royally. In addition, a married consultant usually leaves a spouse behind. The chance to bring that spouse (and even the children) along on a trip, especially to an interesting location, doesn't come often. If you can include the family in the travel expenses, you make a very attractive offer. Many consultants trade in first-class air tickets in order to take their spouses along; others work for much lower rates in order to have an expense-paid vacation with their families.

All consultants' fees are negotiable. Your task is to find something the consultant wants enough to concede a portion of the fees to you. Use these elements to negotiate that concession.

Public Seminar Organizations

Public seminars are a multimillion-dollar business. It is a high-risk operation but potentially an extremely profitable one. This profit potential has motivated many organizations to compete with each other in holding public seminars on different business topics. The oldest and largest such organization is the American Management Association, a nonprofit member operation serving management through its public seminars, business library, publishing arm, private in-house seminars, and conferences. Many others are also legally nonprofit operations, while some are profit-making private companies. In every case, however, all of them derive at least a portion of their income from seminars and conferences and so are intensely involved in marketing.

There are three types of organizations. Some, like Gerard Nierenberg's Art of Negotiation seminars or Dale Carnegie's seminars, are straightforward and designed to promote a particular approach. A second type capitalizes on a name and puts on seminars under that banner. For instance, the Dun & Bradstreet seminars are run as a separate division of that leading financial organization. The third type is different only in that the named or sponsoring organization is not responsible for the seminar. Seminars are mounted by a seminar-packaging organization for a client through a conference center or as a part of a conference, or to follow a particular theme, such as genetic engineering or the care of the aging. The client, conference center, or sponsoring organization has no responsibility for the seminar.

The pattern for the seminars, however, is much the same for all three types. The organization engages consultants in various fields to deliver seminars. Consultants agree to do so for less than their normal rates because of the exposure and the guarantee of steady employment for a period of time. The organization handles the advertising (nearly always direct mail), coordination, and administration, as well as arranges the details of the seminar itself. The consultant simply shows up and delivers it.

These organizations also book in-house seminars, in which a consultant tailors a public course to a client's individual needs. The client is billed by the organization who, in turn, pays the consultant's fee. In effect, the seminar organization acts as a broker for its consultants. Thus, the organization takes on the responsibility for the consultant. Ineffective consultants are simply dropped from the roster, which guarantees that those who continue to present for the organization are top experts on the cutting edge of their subjects.

Consider these seminars as an alternative to an in-house training program. Seminars are an excellent way for people to become acquainted with generic skills and requirements. If you have fewer than six or eight people to train, there is no less expensive way to do it. Once you have more than six or eight people, it becomes more cost-effective to hire the consultant to tailor an in-house course. It should also prove educationally more sound, because you can incorporate much more practice and evaluation into a tailor-made course.

These seminars can be evaluated in many of the same ways as off-the-shelf packages and consultants. In addition, it is usually easiest to evaluate a program simply by going to it. All organizations I've seen or worked for give excellent seminars. From time to time, each must have a dud. Don't judge the entire organization by one seminar; see a few and then decide.

The Benefits

These seminar organizations could not survive unless they continued to provide worthwhile services. Because of the competition among these organizations, you have a tremendous selection from which to choose. It is a buyer's market. Also, because of this stiff competition, the seminars are usually quite reasonable.

Constant evaluation following the seminars means that you are being offered the topics that are in most demand. It also ensures that what is being taught is up-to-date—indeed, the latest in its field. This is especially true for technological areas. In addition, most organizations stand behind their seminars and will refund or give you free admission to another seminar if you are not pleased with the one you've attended. Lastly, as mentioned in Chapter 7, the promotional materials for these seminars are a quick and easy way to keep up with what's going on in a given field.

The Limitations

Nothing is perfect, and of course these seminars have their limitations. For example, by their very nature they must be generic. The seminars are most profitable when large numbers attend, so they are intentionally geared to as broad an audience as possible. The most popular format is a one- or two-day program. This is almost never enough time to do more than provide an information meeting. The meeting will be informative, but little will be learned unless you develop practice exercises that will provide practical follow-up and reenforcement for the seminar.

Some seminar leaders tend to be better performers than trainers. They are highly entertaining—great to listen to—but they only put on a show. Unless your trainees will learn something, don't send them to a public seminar.

Unprofitable topics get dropped, while profitable ones attract more competitors. Consequently, for all of the plethora of courses offered there is frequently little choice of topics. Coupled with that problem is the tendency of seminar organizations to follow fads. It's hard to find a course today in transactional analysis, or management by objectives, both still excellent management tools but out of fashion for public seminars right now.

The least expensive programs are usually attended by the largest groups. This is the way the organization makes a profit. The larger the group, however, the less interaction there can be and the more it becomes a blank-slate, information meeting. As a rule, the more expensive the seminar, the fewer the attendees and the greater the opportunity for real learning.

Employees away from home and in a new town have been known to play harder than they work. I've even had people approach me, the seminar leader, to ask if it would be okay for them to sightsee rather than attend the seminar. Protect your investment by giving them an assignment based on the seminar.

A final word on seminar organizations. All the organizations I've done work for have been very conscientious and honest. However, if you should ever feel the need to sue a seminar organization, don't be misled by the name. The legal entity may be a very small corporation, a partnership, or a sole proprietorship even though the seminars are given under the banner of a well-known name. You can be sure the famous name has protected itself. On the other hand, it is sometimes very difficult to enforce a suit and collect from a small entity.

Summary

In this chapter we explored the various alternatives to the lengthy process of writing a training program. One of the major alternatives is off-the-shelf programs, which are available in a wide variety of topics. The benefits and limitations of these programs were discussed, along with some tips on evaluating individual programs. Also given were some suggestions for incorporating these programs into an in-house training program.

The chapter discussion then proceeded to uncover the benefits and limitations of working with an outside consultant, either as a subject-matter resource or to research or actually develop and teach in-house training programs. Consultants' fees were explained in connection with the different ways they approach their work. There were tips given for evaluating the work of consultants, as well as suggestions for successful negotiations with them.

The final part of the chapter was devoted to professional seminars, including a discussion of the types of seminars that are held and the organizations that offer them, plus some guidelines on how to use these seminars as an alternative to or as part of your training program. We also commented on the benefits and limitations of these seminars.

Applications

1. Using an area of expertise in which you are not currently training, explore the benefits of off-the-shelf programs, outside consultants, and professional seminars.

2. Pick a subject area, as you did for Application 1 above. Call Seminar Clearing House International to get a rating on all of the public seminars offered in the subject. Select the best three. Call up the organizations presenting the seminars and request the name and telephone number of the consultant(s) giving each seminar. Call each consultant and assess whether he or she is best suited to fulfill your training objectives.

3. For Application 2, prepare a qualifying list of questions to ask the seminar leaders you call.

4. Prepare a similar list of questions (see Application 3) for off-the-shelf providers in your chosen subject area. Check catalogues for suppliers and Seminar Clearing House International for the best-ranked names. Call the suppliers and ask their program directors the list of questions you've prepared.

Chapter 9
Aids to Training

THE key to the term *audiovisual aids* is the word *aids*. American managers have a history of throwing money at problems in the hope that the money will solve the problems. However, it isn't the money that solves a problem, but rather how that money is spent.

Why then is pouring money into visual aids such a common practice? Purchasing videotapes, films, slides, off-the-shelf packages, or slide and audio extravaganzas benefits the manager because it provides visible evidence that something is being done about the problem. And because the aids are tangible things, they are manageable. Furthermore, when the aids fail to solve the problem, the blame for their inadequacies can be put on the suppliers of the aids. From a political standpoint these are sound reasons for purchasing visual aids. But from a training standpoint they are not.

Audiovisual aids are just that—aids. They cannot and should never be acquired to train people. They are effective and powerful helpers to learning, but they are no substitute for teaching. To use them as a way to solve a training problem is a waste of both money and good audiovisual aids.

Audiovisual Aids as Learning Tools

In Chapter 1, we examined the ten key principles of adult learning. One of them, the multisensory principle, is based on the premise that what we perceive with more than one sense has a greater impact on us than what we perceive with just one sense. Furthermore, out of habit each of us depends more heavily on one of the senses to provide our information. Some like to read and understand written material best. Others find it easier to learn by listening or talking. Still others learn best by doing something physical. Audiovisual aids provide the opportunity to address and capitalize on these aspects of learning.

In addition, audiovisual aids provide for another of the principles of learning: They create a built-in form of redundancy. In Chapter 2, we discussed the need for building patterns of redundancy into your lessons. One of the easiest and most effective ways of doing this is to use audiovisual aids for the presentation of key concepts, clarification of points, and review of topics concerned. In short, an audiovisual aid can accomplish one or more of the following six functions. If it fails to do these, it should be discarded. It must:

1. *Simplify.* One of the most important uses of an aid is to simplify complex or obscure material. A picture, graph, diagram, or model is worth a thousand words. The reverse is not true, however; a thousand pictures are not a substitute for words. Often a concept or process is comprehensible only when diagrammed or illustrated. This is certainly true with blueprints and schematics in the building and mechanical trades. Furthermore, complex relationships are often immensely simplified by spatial diagrams. If your visual aid simplifies what you are teaching, keep it. If not, create a new one or do without.

2. *Focus attention.* A second key function is to focus attention on the essence of a topic. Frequently, discussions get sidetracked. Use a good visual aid to keep what's important in front of the trainees at all times, so everyone stays on the topic.

3. *Make points memorable.* Audiovisual aids should be hooks on which to hang the memory. A striking slide, model, film, diagram, sign, poster, or sound event can be retained far longer than words. From a simple acronym built up on a flip chart to a two-hour documentary film, visual aids create an impact; they can make what you are teaching unforgettable. Anyone who ever watched the high school chemistry teacher make rotten-egg gas, demonstrate the effects of laughing gas, or drop phosphorus into water will never forget the experience. Devising memorable graphics or producing audiovisual effects is a challenge, but it's also fun— and it pays off handsomely when you succeed.

4. *Take you where you cannot otherwise go.* Of course, this use of visual aids isn't essential, but visual aids that can do it are invaluable. Movies and videotapes are best, but slides also can be very effective. Sounds are wonderful for setting atmosphere and mood. You can tour the plant without leaving the room, hear the company president welcome trainees, enter into minute spaces, and watch processes that cannot be brought into the room. But when using aids in this way, remember that your purpose is to get trainees to learn. If you lose sight of this, your visual aids become merely entertainment. This happens all too often with commercial films and tapes. They try so hard to entertain that they have a negative impact and there is no learning at all.

5. *Create variety.* Too much of anything becomes boring. A film, tape, or unit of slides, a story, or other change of medium can help concentration by creating a refreshing change of pace, a feeling of newness. The danger again is overuse.

Audiovisual Aids

- Slides
- Charts and posters
- Boards (chalk, white, and flannel)
- Overhead projectors
- Films and videos
- Audiotapes
- Models and simulations
- Videotaping
- Computers
- Handouts
- Pointers
- You—the trainer

Too much variety becomes just as dull as too little, and variety for its own sake wears thin after a while. Your visual aids should have challenging learning content as well as variety. For example, I frequently use two flip charts instead of one, with a variety of colors. That allows me to hold trainees' attention for a longer period, while enhancing the impact of new material by changing the colors and switching from one chart to the other across the room.

6. *Save time.* Finally, a visual aid can save a great deal of time. Having a model to handle or a diagram to refer to not only simplifies presentation but makes working with the item modeled or diagrammed much easier and, therefore, saves time.

There are many types of audiovisual aids. In the pages that follow we discuss each in terms of its uses and problems (see Figure 9-1).

Slides

Slides are a ubiquitous, easy-to-use medium that makes things memorable through color and variety. They are effective in simplifying material with graphs and charts and in focusing attention on key data in an organized sequence. They take us where we cannot go, and they provide considerable variety.

Slides are relatively inexpensive, particularly if you shoot your own. They can be changed and updated easily, too. If you travel to your training sessions, they are easily transported and projectors are readily available.

Figure 9-1. Advantages, disadvantages, and primary purpose of audiovisual aids.

	Advantages	Disadvantages	Primary Purpose
Slides	Colorful, varied, easily transported; give uniform presentation.	Require darkened room; no personal contact; possible mechanical problems; overused; passive, not active.	Take us where we cannot otherwise go (close-ups, enlargements, other locations).
Charts and Posters	Flexible, simple, readily available, colorful; show organization of material; enhance interaction in the group; can be referred to several times.	Limited sightlines, limited viewing distance; replacement costs; markers dry out; awkward to transport.	Can develop material interactively with the group; can refer back to earlier material.
Boards (Chalk, White, Flannel)	Can be colorful, flexible; familiar; universally available.	Limited sightlines; messy, smelly; must be erased; associated with school.	Best when you need to add or remove things in a diagram. Excellent for chart development; good scratch pad; useful when reinforcing school atmosphere is desirable.
Overhead Projectors	Universal, readily available; simple to use; flexible, colorful; great with large groups; easy reference to past materials; enhance interaction.	Limited sightlines; distracting if used sloppily; keystoning of projection.	Overlap of transparencies to show layers of complexity in a simple form; good for systems presentation, flowcharting, and developmental materials.
Films	Colorful; show action; readily available; give uniform presentation; lend credibility and professionalism.	Require darkened room; cover generic principles only; easily dated; not always focused on training.	Take us where we cannot otherwise go, *with action* (other locations, fantasies, dangerous or noisy sites, and so on).
Audiotapes	Effective for sound-oriented training; portable; create mood.	Limited aural attention span; talk at trainees, not with them; no interaction; limited sensory input.	Let you hear yourself as others hear you; let you listen and learn while traveling.

(continues)

Figure 9-1. *(continued)*

	Advantages	Disadvantages	Primary Purpose
Models, Cutaways, and Actual Items	Real thing, larger than (or as large as) life; help visualization of the abstract; take you where you cannot otherwise go; some easily made.	Limited sightlines; initial cost; unavailability; storage and breakage problems; maintenance; distracting if used sloppily; tendency for information overload.	Demonstrate how things work, look, or will look; show complex relationship of parts in context; show internal movements; allow close inspection and hands-on practice.
Video	Dynamic; takes us where we cannot otherwise go; easily updated; easily transported.	Incompatible formats can be a problem; fairly high initial cost.	Lets us see and evaluate our own performances; action-oriented like film but can be homemade and is easier to update.
Computers	Self-paced instruction; interactive; exciting future.	Mechanical process with no human contact; high initial expense; time-consuming to program; tied to commercial software; monotonous to use; tendency for information overload.	Hands-on practice; can be used to give trainees practice on equipment they will actually use; excellent for simulations.
Handouts	Can be referred back to after the course; no sightline problems.	Distracting if distributed while you are talking.	Useful for hands-on practice and for giving assignments.
Pointers	Can be used to enhance several other aids (slides, boards, posters, and so on).	Distracting if played with.	Excellent for focusing trainees' attention on one specific detail at a time.
You— the Trainer	You can adapt any training method to suit the exact needs of your trainees.	None!	To train: for everything, you are the main message. You can motivate trainees as nothing else can.

Uses of Slides. Slides are at their best when they take us where we cannot go. We can see other locations, people, or equipment that would otherwise be unavailable. Close-ups and enlargements present detailed views of material, particularly when it is microscopic or enclosed.

Using Slides

1. Preset projector and screen. Mark their positions with tape if you intend to move them during the lesson.
2. Load slides into projector.
3. Check that all slides are right side up and all slides are in right order.
4. Focus projector. Check that there is a spare bulb.
5. Check that all mechanical equipment is working properly.
6. Check your control of room lights.
7. If you are using audiotape, check that it is cued up correctly and synchronized with the slides.
8. If you use a microphone, check that it is working, is set at the right volume, is where you can find it, and has a place where it can be put down.

Working With Slides. Synchronized audiotapes and slides enhance your presentation by adding music to create an environment. They can also help standardize your material. However, you sacrifice flexibility in updating and changing the program, and you eliminate your interaction with the group, leaving them passively viewing a mechanical show. Weigh this trade-off and choose which alternative corresponds to your training objectives.

In assembling your presentation, make sure each slide is top quality, that each is inserted properly in the tray, and that all are in the proper sequence.

When making your presentation, preset the projector and screen and focus the projector before your session. Test the room lights. Check the operation of the projector. Have a spare bulb and know how to install it.

If you will be speaking along with the slides, practice ahead of time to be sure your slides have maximum impact in context. If you are using an audiotape with your slides, run through it before your session to ensure that it works properly.

Problems With Slides. The major problem with slides is that the room has to be at least partially darkened for them to be exciting. The darker the room, the more striking the slide, but as soon as you turn down the lights you trigger an "It's show time!" response. Your trainees become prepared to be passively shown something, not to actively learn something. Remember the time your neighbors invited you over to watch slides of their recent vacation? Training slides usually draw the same response, even more so when the voice is recorded and therefore impersonal.

To correct this problem, don't dim the lights all the way. Leave the room lighter than it would be in a "show." Keep the slide sessions very short—stay under ten minutes. Five minutes is good and three minutes even better. Provide the trainees with work to do during the presentation. Ideally, give them map lights so they can see to take notes. List key points they should look for and respond to during the presentation.

A second problem with slides is that they have been seriously overused. Slides are everywhere, and trainers have come to rely on them too much. Weigh your use of slides against your training objectives and against the six things visual aids should do. If your slides aren't accomplishing at least two of them, drop the slides.

Currently with graphics software, you can produce a multiple slide show, called multimedia, that incorporates motion—animation and video—on your computer. Although multimedia is regarded as state of the art, it is still just a slide show and is necessarily subject to the same guidelines as any other slide presentation. We'll talk more about multimedia in Chapter 10.

Always remember to keep your slide presentation short. Avoid using a montage of slides to try to depict motion. They are a static medium, and even multiple-screen razzamatazz fails to create the impression of motion. If motion is important (for example, to show how a machine works), don't use slides. Lastly, avoid being sold a bill of goods by an off-the-shelf package salesperson or by someone who makes a living selling slides. Always ask, What are my training objectives? Does this aid help to meet them?

Charts and Posters

Charts are wonderful visual aids. They are ubiquitous, flexible, and uncomplicated and serve five of the six functions of audiovisual aids. If you are not using charts, find a way to do so. They will enhance your training.

Actually, there are three types of charts: the standard flip chart, sometimes called newsprint (a pad of blank paper suspended on an easel); prepared charts, which may be in a flip format or in separate sheets; and posters, which are displayed in the training room or workplace.

Uses of Charts. Charts simplify, focus, and make material memorable. They also provide variety and save time. They can be used to prepare the trainees for training, to present material, to document practice activities, to organize evaluations, and to provide redundancy in the form of summaries and reminders. Indeed, charts are the most universal and versatile of audiovisual aids.

Flip charts can be prepared ahead of time and then used to forecast a series of points you will cover in the session. They can provide a simple framework of notes to keep you on track, and they can form the basis for trainees' personal notes. They are very effective in posting elicited responses from the group and building each point with trainees' input. They are also useful in illustrating con-

---

Using Charts and Posters

1. Check sightlines. Walk around the room and be sure you can always see the charts.
2. Make sure you have enough paper on each pad you'll use for flip charts and that each pad is firmly attached to a solid easel.
3. Make sure you have enough markers in correct colors. Check that each marker is neither dried out nor smashed.
4. For prepared charts, check to see if they are in the correct order, if they are all right side up, and where you will place each one when you are finished with it.
5. For posters, check that they are firmly in place and unlikely to fall down during your presentation.
6. If you will tear sheets off a flip chart to hang up as posters, be sure you have tape, tacks, magnets, or other adhesive materials.

---

cepts that are getting bogged down in language. One of their greatest advantages is that you can refer back to them from time to time simply by flipping the pages. Or tear several key pages from the pad and attach them around the room as posters.

Perhaps the best use of charts, however, is in developing both your own and the participants' materials. Charts can function as a giant scratch pad on which you and the class figure out processes. This lends an immediacy, a freshness, that no other medium can give you. Such charts reflect the group's responses, which become principles they have *built* rather than things they have been told. This approach demands Socratic interaction with the group and so enhances your training effectiveness by creating effective participatory learning.

The value of prepared charts is that they can be done professionally to produce striking visual impact. Colored base stock can be used to heighten the effect, too. However, they are awkward to transport, and eventually they show wear and tear and have to be replaced. If the charts are separate cardboard sheets, you must have a place to stack them neatly as you finish with them.

Posters are not used as often as they deserve to be. They can be placed around the room and referred to from time to time. For example, I once observed a trainer who posted a series of quotes from related literature around the training room like an eye-level ribbon or band. Then he systematically referred to each quote as he covered the material. Posters can serve as review tools or as reminders of key concepts. One of the most effective uses of a poster is as a reminder in the workplace after training is completed. These reminders can range from epigrams to steps for performing tasks. This reenforcement is, oddly enough, not common though most workers could benefit from it.

Working With Charts. In general, rules for using charts, especially flip charts, apply as well to prepared charts and posters. To begin, plan the content and layout for the charts in advance. In planning, list the key ideas and then ask whether a visual aid will help convey those ideas. (This is a good question to ask of *all* aids.) If so, develop the chart always keeping in mind that *less is more*. Don't overcrowd the page. Limit yourself to seven points per page. Omit *all* unnecessary details, particularly in diagrams and pictures. Being a technical expert, you may want to ensure that the diagrams are correct, but equally important, they must be simple. Caption or title every page except poster slogans. (They can stand alone.)

Write large enough for everyone to see. This usually means using uppercase letters; however, if your lowercase lettering is neater and easier to read, use lowercase or mix the two. Only if your penmanship is exquisite should you even consider script. Print larger for larger groups. If what you've written can't be read from fifty feet away, print larger still. Also, avoid abbreviations, if possible, or use only standard ones. Use numerals rather than spelling out numbers.

Make your drawings large, too. Use flowcharts to illustrate processes, procedures, or organization of elements. Use bar graphs to show comparisons or to weigh advantages or disadvantages. Try to avoid line graphs unless they are exceptionally clear. These tend to be harder to read and interpret.

Use color to identify main parts or movements in diagrams and in general to emphasize key points. Color also provides simple variety. When I use two flip charts I use black on one and blue or green on the other. After lunch break, I swap colors, solely for visual variety. With black lettering I use red, blue, or green to highlight. (Some theorists argue that red should never be used because it is inflammatory—I have no problem with it.) With green lettering, I use black, blue, or dark brown to highlight. Purple is possible, too. With blue lettering, red, black, or brown make the best highlighters, although dark orange is possible. Avoid light colors; they are hard to see from a distance.

Practice with the aids before using them. If you are developing the charts with the class, practice writing (printing) from the side of the chart so you don't cover it as you write. This both enhances your professional style and allows the group to read as you write. If you have prepared charts, keep them covered until you need them. If you use two flip charts, place them on opposite sides in the front of the room so your trainees make a physical shift when you move from one to the other. Or place them side by side (with room for you to stand between them to write) if you want to compare or contrast the two. Put them alongside one another (or use a special double-width chart and easel) for a horizontal diagram. Needless to say, if you are using two charts in this manner, the charts and easels must be of the same height and design. With two charts you can use them apart or together for even more visual variety.

Avoid talking to the chart. Look at it briefly in silence if you need to, but then face the group and talk to the trainees. This maintains your leadership role and keeps alive the personal involvement. Lastly, give the group time to read and absorb the information on the chart. Don't dispose of an aid too quickly.

Problems With Charts. The main problems with charts are sightlines and distance. A visual aid is useless if it cannot be seen. Check all sightlines before you begin by standing in front of each chart and looking at all the seats in the room, particularly those to your extreme left and extreme right. In addition, walk around the room and check whether each participant will be able to see the charts clearly.

Avoid wall-hung flip charts. They may look good but usually are inflexible and can't be adjusted to accommodate the group. Furthermore, they force you to turn your back to use them, hiding what you are writing and breaking eye contact with the group. In fact, *never* stand in front of your charts.

The maximum reading distance for flip charts is fifty to sixty feet. If, because of numbers of participants or room configurations, people are sitting farther away than that, don't use flip charts except as posters with one- or two-word slogans. Switch to an overhead projector, slides, or computer-generated graphics instead.

In addition to the problems of sight, there are a few things to watch for when using flip charts. If you are using charts developmentally, be sure you have enough paper on each pad. Delays to change pads are a waste of time. If you tear off a sheet (or use prepared cardboard charts), have a place nearby to stow each one neatly as you finish with it. Remember that your trainees will react to how you treat the sheet. If you crumple it or drop it on the floor, they will mentally do the same.

There are physical problems with charts as well. Frequently, when you turn a sheet over, the top edge won't fold down neatly and will crinkle or bulge in an unsightly manner. Take the time to smooth it out. Your respect for the material will be transmitted to and reflected by your trainees. If you talk while holding an open felt-tipped marker, sooner or later you will go to print and the pen will have dried up. Prevent this unprofessionalism by checking all pens before you begin, having backup markers on hand, and *always* replacing the cap immediately after making an entry on the flip chart. Never leave the cap off a marker for longer than it takes to write on the chart.

Boards (Chalk, White, and Flannel)

Blackboards, or chalkboards, are the precursors to charts. Although "black" boards are still found today, most are now green or brown, but all use chalk as the writing medium and so are called *chalkboards*. Whiteboards are a much newer invention. These are smooth white boards with a surface that you can write on with erasable alcohol-based markers. Flannel (or felt) boards are just that: wooden boards wrapped in flannel. Cutouts of felt in brilliant colors can be pressed onto the flannel surface. Anyone who has attended a Protestant Sunday school is familiar with flannel boards, but they are not often used in training programs. Their possibilities in training, however, are still exciting despite their lack of frequent use.

Uses of Boards. Chalkboards were borrowed years ago from education, where they had evolved from the personal slates pupils used in nineteenth-century schools. Chalkboards have the advantage of being very familiar to all trainees and the disadvantage for some of a negative association with school. With chalkboards you can do most everything you can do with a flip chart except refer back to earlier material. Chalkboards also provide a larger format for your diagrams and notes. Usually chalkboards are mounted on a wall, but are also made on reversible, rolling frames.

Chalkboards are best when you want to reenforce the school-like aspects of your training. They are also useful in planning or developing materials not meant to be saved. They make excellent scratch pads.

A major limitation of chalkboards is that any attempt to use color turns out pallid pastels. Another drawback is that chalk creates dust, which pervades the room. This is why whiteboards were invented. They are used in the same ways as chalkboards, but the surfaces accept brilliant color markers. In fact, whiteboards

---

Using Boards

1. Check sightlines.
2. Be sure all boards are clean.
3. Check for ample chalk or markers in the colors you want. Check markers to see they are not dried out or crushed.
4. Check that there is a clean eraser and other tools you'll need (compass, ruler, and so on).
5. If you have a scrolling whiteboard, make sure it is in working order.
6. If you have a flannel board, brush it against the nap to ensure a fuzzy surface for gripping.
7. Be sure all your cutouts are in their proper order and are where you can reach them.
8. Check to be sure you have your lab coat or chalk holder, if you use them.

---

are most effective with brilliant colors. They are excellent for diagrams, flow-charts, and graphs. Because they don't have wide use in schools, whiteboards are useful when you want to show a difference between your training and most people's schooling. Whiteboards are usually wall-mounted, but can be acquired on wheeled frames as well. In fact, state-of-the-art whiteboards allow several "pages" of board that can be accessed at any time by scrolling forward or backward. Furthermore, a "page" of whiteboard can be photocopied with the push of a button. Almost instantly, a hard copy in black and white emerges in the copy tray. To my mind, the scrolling device to some extent solves, albeit clumsily, the problem of referring back to earlier work, but the hard copy capability, although amazing, seems to have little practical application for training. It appears excellent, however, for preserving work in progress, such as new design ideas or mathematical formulas.

Using flannel boards or magnetic boards is a bit different in that you must prepare cutouts in advance and rehearse your presentation to be effective. They might be used for variety, for color, or for fun. Their application is limited to presentation, however, and would probably be best for a change-of-pace illustration of a logical progression or a spatial relationship.

Working With Boards. Here you can refer back to the section on working with charts. The major difference with boards is the size of the surface. Give some thought ahead of time to your use of this increased space. Remember also that, with more space filled, you must allow trainees more time to copy or absorb the material before erasing it. Obviously, you will need to stand in front of the board to write, so take extra care with sightlines.

Problems With Boards. I prefer not to use chalkboards or whiteboards (and I confess I've never used a flannel or magnetic board) because I feel the problems they create outweigh their advantages. For the most part, anything you can do on a board you can do more easily on a flip chart. However, you may prefer to use a chalkboard or whiteboard, or may have inherited them and have no choice. If so, remember that chalkboards are messy. If you don't want your clothes full of dust, wear a lab coat or duster and keep a dust rag handy for wiping your hands. In addition, you might want to use a chalk holder, which is a handle that holds the chalk. In theory, it keeps your hands clean. Likewise, don't let chalk dust build up on the erasers or on the ledge at the bottom of the board. Clean both daily and wash the board with a damp cloth at least once a day.

Always have spare chalk with you; you will surely need it. Break a new piece of chalk into fairly small pieces. Large chalk causes a high-pitched shriek that upsets many people.

With whiteboards, there is a tendency for the colors to imprint permanently if left on too long. Always erase the whiteboard within thirty minutes of writing on it. Clean the whiteboard erasers regularly. A dirty eraser smears color. Be careful how you use the markers, too. You can get "high" from sniffing them. Again, these are felt-tip markers and they dry out very rapidly if the cap is left off. Replace the caps instantly after use.

If you use flannel boards, keep track of the various cutouts after you use them. They are easily lost and a bother to remake.

One of the worst problems in teaching with boards is talking to the board. Often it takes time to fill that large space with notes and diagrams. Few things break your contact with the group more quickly than talking with your back to the group. Instead, write on the board and then turn to face the trainees to discuss what you have just written.

As mentioned earlier, be aware that it takes time for trainees to copy the material. Don't be in a hurry to erase the boards. Finally, take special care always to start with a clean board each day. A clean slate creates a strong positive impression; a smeared or partly filled one gives a negative impression.

Overhead Projectors

Overhead projectors shine a beam of light through a transparent sheet to a mirror above or below the sheet, which reflects the image on the transparency through a lens onto a large screen. They are almost as common as flip charts and are used in much the same way. Overhead projectors have a built-in problem, however. Usually the projector must be placed between the screen and at least one of your learners, seriously affecting sightlines. In addition, they tend to be used carelessly and distract attention from a presentation as much as they focus it. With such problems and the fact that overhead projections usually duplicate what can be done more easily on a flip chart, why would anyone want to use

---

Using Overhead Projectors

1. Preset projector and screen.
2. Focus projector and adjust screen for keystoning.
3. Mark floor with tape if you are going to move either.
4. Check transparencies for correct order and positioning.
5. Check that you have a spot to stack transparencies to be used and those which have been used.
6. Check that you have a pointer, pencil, or marker if you plan to use one.
7. Make sure electrical cord is taped down to floor.
8. Make sure you have a spare bulb.
9. Check sightlines.

---

them? The first answer is size. When people in the back can't see your flip chart, the overhead projector is ideal. The second reason is that an overhead provides visual variety, particularly if you use color on the transparency. An added plus is that you get a large-screen projection with little or no dimming of room lights.

Uses of Overhead Projectors. Overheads can be used to project a ready-made visual onto the screen and as a large tablet on which to develop your points. In effect, you have a giant chart, and you can use it as you would cardboard or the flip charts discussed earlier. The transparencies can be professionally produced or your own, although better artwork conveys greater professionalism. You can combine the two very effectively by developing new ready-made material on transparencies. For example, this method would be particularly useful if you wanted to show how to fill in a form. You project the blank form, which is identical to handouts each participant has. As you describe what is to be done, you fill in the form while the trainees follow suit. Upon completion, you can erase your entries with a damp sponge or cloth (assuming the form itself is printed in indelible ink). As an alternative, you could use a scrolled transparency over the top of the permanent one. (Most projectors will take a scrolling attachment, which is simply a rack that holds a roll of transparent acetate, stretches it across the glass projection tray, and allows you to scroll it from one side to the other.) You can then write, correct, and rewrite on the top sheet without ever writing on the form itself.

By far the best—and almost unique—use for overheads is with multiple overlays. With a series of acetate sheets placed one on top of the other, you can show the development of a process or operation or the complex interrelationships in a system. Each overlay can exhibit one step, phase, or system. For example, in a diagram of the human body one sheet shows the skeleton, the next has the vital organs, then the circulatory system, after that the nervous system, followed by the muscular structure, and finally the skin. No audiovisual aid except a computer can show this kind of layering as well as an overhead projector can.

If you use transparencies in this fashion, you will need to create accurate registration. That is, each sheet must fit in place exactly over the prior one. You can ensure this by binding the acetate sheets together with tape or by using a projector with registration pins at the side or bottom of the glass projection tray. These half-inch-long pins hold the sheets in proper alignment. Such an arrangement allows you to use a dozen or more layers and still get good projection. The diagrams are more comprehensible if you use color codes—for example, a different color for each new system or process you are showing.

Working With Overhead Projectors. Always set up the screen and focus the projector before the seminar. If there are participants present and you don't want them to see the first projection, use any relatively flat object to focus the unit. I use a coin, paper clip, or even a comb. When preparing the projector, also be sure you have a spare bulb. Most modern machines have a built-in spare you can engage by simply moving a lever or twisting a knob. Familiarize yourself with the projector ahead of time. Check the room for sightlines. Be sure everyone can see.

Make sure you have space near the projector to stack the acetates to be used as well as those you will have used. Arrange the transparencies in the order in which you will use them. They are easier to handle in cardboard frames, but if you don't have frames, slip a sheet of paper between each transparency so they don't stick together.

When you finish with each transparency, turn off the projector, then remove the transparency to the used stack and place the next one on the projection tray. Do this even if the next one won't be needed for hours. It makes you seem prepared when you have the correct projection already in place when you switch the unit on. There is an exception to this method, however. When you are using two or more transparencies in immediate succession, leave the light on, remove one transparency with one hand while at the same time replacing it with the next transparency in your other hand. Make this a smooth motion—practice until you can do it easily from either side of the projector. Few things are more distracting than a bright blank screen or a sloppy shift from one visual to the next.

A relatively new aid in the transfer process, available for some projectors, is a time-delay dimmer switch. When you want to change a projection, push the button. The projector fades to black, allowing you to change your visual and walk away from the unit. In the desired number of seconds (preset by you), the projector comes back on again automatically. It is a frill, but a nice one that adds a professional touch to your presentation.

In developing the transparencies, remember that *less is more*. Don't put more than seven points on an overhead projection unless you are showing a form or data sheet identical to one each participant has. Then walk them through it and explain how it is used.

Use a pencil, pointer, or pen to point at the transparency on the projector tray rather than at the projection on the screen. When you point at the screen, you turn away from the group, sometimes touching the screen itself and making the projection wobble. Also, you might walk into the projected image with at least your hand, which never fails to look ridiculous. Remember, though, that sightlines are vital. Whenever you stand beside the projector, someone can't see the projection. Instead, leave the pen or pencil on the tray pointing to what you are stressing and walk out of the sightline to discuss your point.

Problems With Overhead Projectors. We have touched on most problems already, but the main one is sightlines. Pay careful attention to where you set up the screen and where you place the projector. Sometimes it helps to set them up on a diagonal or to one side of the room. In any event, be very careful not to stand between the screen and participants when the projector is on.

Another problem is keystoning; that is, since the projector is lower than the top of the screen, it throws a broader beam of light at the top than at the bottom. The effect is a keystone shape, but because this distortion is so common with overheads most participants will ignore it. You can correct it two ways, however: Tilt the screen forward so the bottom is farther from the projector than the top (many portable screens have an extension hook on the top for just this purpose), or tilt the projector until it throws an even picture on the screen. A combination of both techniques often makes a perfect picture. If you tilt the projector, though, be careful that your transparencies and pointer don't fall off the tray.

Avoid walking through a projection on the screen. If you must cross from one side of the room to the other, either walk behind the projector (that is, the end that is not projecting) or turn it off, step through, and turn it back on again. Either of these is far less distracting than walking through the lighted projection.

Projectors are usually in your way when not in use. Wherever possible, use a rolling table for the projector so you can move it to one side when you don't need it. If you do this, mark its position on the floor with tape so that the projector will be in focus when you use it again.

Lastly, you will look clumsy if you trip over the cord. Tape it to the floor with wide duct tape. If you are going to move the projector, use an outlet to one side so the cord is not in your way. Of course, all of these cautions also apply to the use of LCD panels or projectors to display computer screens.

Films and Videos

Above all else, film and video take us where we cannot go. They can be used to show how something operates or to take us into the inner workings of the boardroom. Film shows action and interaction. Films are usually professionally produced, so they lend an aura of professionalism to your training. In some cases, when they use big-name performers or spokespeople, they also lend considerable credibility. By crystallizing certain key actions, films and videotapes can clarify concepts and make ideas memorable. Finally, they are a wonderful change of pace. Used well, they can be an effective break from a single speaker—even an amusing bit of fun in the middle of the seminar.

Uses of Films and Videos. As mentioned, these media are excellent for taking you outside the classroom or into other environments. Hollywood was built on this simple yet powerful attribute of film. From the beginning of the film era, we have seen romance, history, fantasy, science fiction, and mystery. Video can take us to dangerous sites or show us infrequent events, such as the aftermath of real accidents (for safety training), or operations in which noise level would normally hamper training, or situations where training groups would interfere with production.

Both are usually much more action-oriented than slides. Apart from this aspect, however, films and video suffer many of the same problems and enjoy many of the same benefits as slides. They are readily available. Projectors and VCRs are simple to operate and always available to rent.

Films and videotapes usually cost far less than writing a program would and can be rented for even less money. As we've said, they can be glamorous, amusing, and provide a change of pace. Sixteen-millimeter is the preferred format for film, VHS for videotape.

Films and videotapes are best for the presentation step of a lesson. They can be used for the preparation stage, but have very limited potential for practice or evaluation, except perhaps to test ability to spot or identify key behaviors.

Working With Films and Videos. Always preview a film or videotape before you buy it. Many distributors will allow a free trial. If they don't, rent the film or videotape for a single showing to determine if it meets your needs. If you order a film or videotape from a distributor or rent one from the local library (often an excellent source, by the way), arrange for timely delivery and return.

With film, preset the projector and screen and focus the picture and adjust sound levels before your session. Have a spare bulb handy, and know how to change it. Run the film before the meeting to ensure it is in working order, that it is the film you ordered, and that you can run the projector. With videotape, check to see that it is rewound and properly cued up. Check the sound and sight-lines.

As with slides, leave enough light on in the room to allow viewers to work while the film or videotape is on. Assign key concepts for them to look for during the film, and then discuss the film afterwards.

Problems With Films and Videos. We've already discussed the problem of a darkened room. This is further compounded by the fact that training films and

---

Using Films and Videos

1. Preset projector, screen, or playback monitor. If you will be moving them during the lesson, mark their positions with tape.
2. For film, thread film. Make sure you have the right film loaded.
3. For film, focus projector.
4. For both media, check and adjust sound levels.
5. Check your control of room lights; be sure they dim.
6. For film, check for a spare bulb, and know how to change it.
7. Rewind film or videotape after use.

---

videotapes are usually less entertaining than their commercial counterparts, so there is a built-in disappointment factor.

In addition, material shot in these media becomes dated very quickly. If styles change, your film or videotape appears to be out of date. This may not seem serious, but look at most films made before EEO regulations or before we became sensitive to sexist treatments. If you use one of these today, you will step on toes, and a discussion of biases will ensue. Equally important is that if your procedures change, so must your film or videotape, and that is expensive.

This brings us to the problem of cost. To make your own film is prohibitive. Even renting the equipment costs $50,000 to $100,000 to produce a ten-minute film. And, of course, the film would soon become dated. Video is less costly, but still can be expensive (see the section later in this chapter for how to create videos). The alternative is to use generic films or videotapes, but this brings up another problem. Are they really applicable to your situation? Some industries, such as insurance, banking, and health care, are large enough for filmmakers to profit from films and videotapes that address their specific problems. (And even these are not completely specific.) Commercial films and videotapes are fine for generic topics, but to make them specific to your application, you must build a lesson around them.

Moving beyond these problems, when you consider buying a film or videotape, don't let yourself be sold a bill of goods. Remember, salespeople are in the business of selling, not training. Don't be sold a pig in a poke. Always preview before you buy, and measure the film or videotape against your training objectives and the six functions of an audiovisual aid.

Once you've selected your film or videotape, avoid depending on it to teach for you or to entertain your trainees. You *must* integrate it into your lessons by discussing it, assigning material from it, bringing it into future lessons as part of your redundant patterns, and, if possible, using materials from it for role-playing or projects. Often you can use the same characters, but suggest alternative scenarios that customize the material to your company's application.

Audiotape

If you are training people who will work primarily with sound (radio operators, telecommunication engineers, telephone operators, or safety inspectors who use sounds for diagnostic tests), audiotapes are vital; otherwise, these tapes have limited application to training. As pointed out in Chapter 1, ours is no longer an oral culture. Radio in the 1920s and 1930s was one of the last vestiges of purely oral experience, and it has been supplanted by visual television. Radio today is largely background. We no longer attend well to what we only hear. Consequently, it is difficult for people to learn just by listening.

Uses of Audiotapes. There are still, however, several legitimate uses for audiotapes in training. If trainees are being taught to listen, then audiotapes can be valuable. (In addition, many people swear by audiotapes as a way of learning while driving or flying.) For those in jobs where the voice is important, the tapes can be both a model for and a reflector of personal performance. In addition, audiotapes frequently are coupled with slides for a multimedia format that grabs and holds attention.

By far the most powerful use of audiotapes is as a reflection of the trainees' own voices. People learn when they can hear themselves. Use audiotapes to allow trainees to hear themselves as others will.

Working With Audiotapes. Use good-quality equipment. Cheap equipment distorts sound, so if you want your trainees to hear themselves as others do, you have to use equipment that can do the job. This doesn't necessarily mean a top-of-the-line sound system; usually, these systems have features you won't need, like multiple mixing and editing. However, you do need good microphones and recorders.

Keep taped material short, and follow it with immediate coaching. Play a sequence, then analyze and critique it. One-on-one development with a trainee is best when feasible. People can and do learn to listen. As you progress with the audiotapes, increase the demands on your trainees by lengthening the content. If you use audiotape to present examples, direct the trainees to listen for specifics. Play the tape, then discuss with them what they heard. If need be, play the tape again. If you use audiotape to instruct individuals while they travel, encourage them to listen by assigning homework based on the tape. Brief them on what specifically to listen for and provide for interaction on what they have heard.

If you are dealing with telephone fear (a frequent problem when training telephone solicitors), it may help to play examples of supervisors doing a less-than-perfect job. Hearing the mistakes supervisors have made helps get trainees past their initial fears to the realization that even role models make mistakes. If you are training in areas in which recognition of key sounds will help trainees perform, record several instances of the sound. If you can't do this because of

---

Using Audiotapes

1. Make sure tapes are rewound and cued up.
2. Make sure machine is in working order.
3. If your player uses batteries, make sure they are fresh. Have a spare set with you.
4. Check sound levels.

---

technical or safety reasons, ask a sound recording expert to reproduce the sounds with parabolic microphones, stethoscopes, and multiple tracking with filters, or even special effects.

Problems With Audiotapes. There is one big problem: inattentiveness. Everything you can do to heighten and maintain interest will help. For example, avoid segments longer than two or three minutes. Anything longer runs the risk of boring your learners.

There are some other things you should be careful to avoid. For example, few things are more annoying than turning on a tape and finding it not cued up. Always rewind tape after use and check it before you use it again.

If you use a portable cassette player, make sure before your lesson that the batteries are good. Keep a spare set handy, especially if you plan to record, because weak batteries record at a slower speed, producing playback that sounds like a cartoon character.

Models and Simulations

When you are training people to operate a tool or a vehicle, or to use certain hardware, it helps greatly to have the actual thing on which trainees can practice. The problem, however, is that it is often prohibitive to supply each trainee with a real unit. The situation is compounded when the units are likely to be damaged easily by beginners. The answer is to build or buy models or simulations that let novices make harmless errors, yet show in some depth the operation of the real unit. Thus, full models, cutaway models, simulations, and actual practice models are an important aid to training.

Cutaways are models that show a cross-sectional view, as if you had sliced away the outer part to reveal the inner workings. Cutaways are used frequently in fields like medicine, mechanics, architecture, and mechanical design.

Uses of Models and Simulations. Often the major use of models and simulations is to show what the real thing looks like, how it works, and what the parts

---

Using Models and Simulations

1. Check sightlines for all demonstrations.
2. Make sure all parts are labeled correctly.
3. Make sure all moving parts work properly.
4. Test actual equipment to see that it is in working order.

---

are. Better than any other aid, models show the often complex relationships of parts to each other. In areas in which conceptual work is done, like mechanical design, computer modeling, or architecture, a model shows what something will look like as well as allows trainees to troubleshoot problems before they appear.

Cutaways are best for showing movement, location, and function of internal parts. Both full models and cutaways are used often to enlarge or shrink elements to a size that allows for easier viewing. Thus, doctors are trained on larger-than-life cutaway models of the eye or the ear. Aircraft technicians fly model airplanes in wind tunnels to diagnose airfoil problems. Of course, the actual item provides the best opportunity for close inspection, hands-on practice, and real adjustments of parts. A special case is the working model, which combines the cost and safety advantages of a model with the hands-on practice and adjustment advantages of the real thing.

Working With Models and Simulations. Give careful thought to the model you use. Ask yourself whether it is the best visual aid for the lesson and whether you really need a model. Consider whether there is a less expensive alternative that would work almost as well.

If the model is the best way to go, consider making your own model. If you are illustrating an operating principle or the relationship of parts, any reasonable facsimile can be used. We are all familiar with the stereotype of the retired military officer retelling glorious exploits by manipulating knives and forks, saltcellars, and glasses to represent the model battlefield. Often it is the concept you need to teach, so you don't need the real thing, only objects to simulate it.

Before class, check that your model is in working order. Practice your performance until it is smooth. Make sure the model will illustrate exactly what you want it to.

Often the best way to use a model in class is to have an assistant (perhaps one of the trainees) demonstrate it while you explain what is happening. In presenting the model take special care of sightlines. Be sure everyone can see it, and don't allow the trainees to crowd in close, excluding others.

Don't pass the model around while you explain it. You'll split the trainees' concentration. Talk about the model while you show it, then allow free time for it to be passed around. Provide time for the model to be handled or used by each learner until you are sure all are familiar with it.

Lastly, beware of information overload. If you have set your objectives and know what you want your trainees to learn, you can pare your demonstration down to the essentials. When possible, use models to show processes and relationships rather than technical details and nice-to-know information.

Problems With Models and Simulations. We've already touched on the two major problems with models: limited visibility and nonfunctioning equipment. These are easy to avoid if you plan ahead. In addition, try not to let your model upstage you. You can make it the centerpiece of your lesson, but always remember that it is what the trainees *learn* that counts, not what they see or enjoy.

Videotaping

Video is probably the most dynamic and exciting invention for training since the overhead projector. It solves nearly all of the problems inherent with slides and film and creates completely new opportunities for training. It is relatively inexpensive, easily updated, portable, action-oriented, flexible, easy to use, instantly replayed, reusable, and doesn't require darkening the room to see it. Furthermore, both films and slides can be transferred to videotape at nominal cost. Add to this how videotape gives the ability to tape and review a trainee's performance, and you can see why I hold videotape in such high regard. There is no more flexible or useful training tool.

Uses of Videotaping. Once again video takes us where we cannot otherwise go. As with slides and films, video presents views or interactions of absent characters. It can be used to professionally produce programs; special effects can be produced with multiple screen projectors.

More important, it can present very precise up close views. This is probably demonstrated most clearly in the field of medicine. There was a time when interns hunched over viewing windows in a gallery high above the operating table to catch glimpses of a skilled surgeon performing an intricate operation. Today

---

Using Video

1. Run tape to check for operation of unit, that tape is properly cued up, that sound is working, and that color looks natural.
2. If recording, test recording process to be sure everything is properly hooked up and working.
3. Check sound levels to be sure microphone is working and that you are recording sound.
4. Check that you have enough tape.
5. If trainees are to operate equipment, make sure they know how.
6. If trainees are to view themselves in another room, have a set of instructions on how to run the viewing equipment. Include how to load and start the tape, adjust the sound levels, and rewind the tape.
7. Upon completion, rewind tape, cover camera lens or point it down to a neutral color, and turn off all power to camera, tape, and monitors.

---

every nuance and gesture of the surgeon can be caught in close-up detail, with three or four cameras creating a demonstration tape of superb quality and usefulness.

In addition, thanks to fiber-optic technology, the video camera lens can enter the body to show students and diagnosticians internal conditions that once would only have been revealed by a full-scale operation. Coupled with the microscope, video takes us into the world of molecular science. Used with X rays, it allows us to watch our own hearts, lungs, brains, or circulatory system in operation. I use medicine as an example only because it is an area in which the full potential of video has been used. With imagination these uses may be applicable to your training.

The third boon of videotaping is that it allows us to review and evaluate our own performance. It gives us the gift "to see oursel's as ithers see us!"—a wish expressed by Scottish poet Robert Burns more than a hundred years ago.

It is hard to decide which use of video is best, but if pressed I'd opt for its reflective capacity. Videotaping is used by every professional athlete in every sport to troubleshoot and analyze technique or play. Watching ourselves make a mistake increases learning many times over. You can tell me I'm doing something wrong and show me a better way, but nothing drives the point home as powerfully as seeing myself do it wrong! Find a way to tap this use of video and the effectiveness of your training will increase.

Because cost is low and many photo and video shops have the capability, use a professional service to convert your slides or film to videotape. With slides, give careful thought to sequencing and the sound track. The video professional will help you match these with your training objectives.

Working With Videotaping. Set up and test the camera, microphone, tape player(s), and monitor(s) well in advance of use. Be sure you are familiar with the operation of all pieces of equipment.

If you are using videotaping to have the trainees view themselves, you have several options. First, you can tape the performance prior to your seminar. For example, you could tape your trainee salesclerks, operators, or customer service personnel at work. In the seminar, you would show them the tapes and critique their performances either individually or with the group.

A second approach is to tape role-playing. For example, you could set up a realistic "office" outside the training room (a Candid Camera–like arrangement), tape the performances, and then show the tape in the seminar for critiquing. This helps to solve the problem of role playing's sometimes being unrealistic when done in front of a group.

Third, you can tape a performance in class, critique the performance, and then let the performer view the tape privately later on. In this instance, while the last performer is viewing his or her performance, the group is taping the next individual. This is an efficient way to tape large numbers of participants, but it requires two tape players and monitors (but only one camera and mike), two rooms (seminar and viewing), and three tapes (one in use, one being viewed, and a backup tape in case a viewer takes longer than the next performer).

A fourth option is to tape all participants in sequence, critique their live performances, and then schedule times during breaks or before and after the seminar for them to see themselves. Alternatively, you could play the tape back immediately and use the playback as the basis for a group session.

When you have more than ten participants, are taping role playing, or are at a distance from the participants, use a separate microphone. Most cameras have microphones built in, but these are effective only at moderately close range. Since you will be watching the performance, have one participant operate the equipment and another keep track of time.

Taping itself is not enough. Critical feedback must accompany the taping, either before, during, or after viewing. Most effective, but time-consuming, is critiquing while viewing—stopping the tape to discuss a problem. Critiquing before viewing is the next most effective.

Plan your time carefully, and assign time limits for each sequence. As a rule, follow-up feedback takes twice as long as a performance. To calculate time frames, take the total available time and subtract the time for breaks. Divide the result by the number of people to be taped. Then divide the time for each person by three (one-third for the performance, two-thirds for the feedback). Don't be too concerned if the first few take longer to critique and you get off schedule. Usually, there are general principles to establish in the beginning that take extra time. As you go along, you'll pick up time by concentrating on individual performances rather than general principles.

When you are giving feedback on the trainee's performance, follow these five simple rules:

1. *Don't overload.* Limit critical comments to no more than three things (skills), and indicate the order to follow in improving them. Remember, *less is more*.

2. *Balance negative feedback with positive.* When people's feelings are hurt, they stop learning. Be supportive.

3. *When work is excellent, say so.* Don't feel you always must be critical. As a learning exercise, however, ask the group (or the individual) how it might be done differently. This way even the best work presents a challenge and forces them to think creatively.

4. *As the group becomes more expert, let them critique more while you do less.* This breaks monotony, keeps them involved, and makes them more observant.

5. *Center your critique around a few (about five) key skills or variables.* This creates redundancy and uniformity. It also allows you to establish at the beginning what the standards are.

Purchasing Video Equipment. You will have to give some thought to format and equipment. For example, you have to decide between a Beta format and VHS. By far the most popular and widely accepted is VHS; however, Beta produces superior quality recordings with its Super 8 format and is backed by Sony. Because of Sony's size, market clout, and steady innovations (especially the now very popular minicam format), Beta will be around for the indefinite future. There will also be less costly Beta equipment manufacturers because Sony keeps the market alive. The one drawback to Beta is that the recording process is more complex than VHS, and so is much more difficult to service. Half-inch VHS format is certainly adequate for the uses we've mentioned, but regardless of which you choose, avoid mixed-format equipment. All video equipment is not compatible. When you decide what to use, stay with the half-inch format (unless you plan to produce training tapes, in which case go with three-quarter-inch to ensure across-the-board compatibility).

There is no point in throwing money away on top-of-the-line equipment with capabilities you won't need or use. However, you will need:

- Two monitors (perhaps a third for backup, if you use them a lot)
- Two videocassette recorders (perhaps a third for backup)
- One camera (one-color tube is adequate; a zoom lens is useful; a second camera for backup, if needed)
- One tripod, preferably with a floating head or other smooth action
- One power transformer for camera
- One microphone (two for choice and backup), either lavaliere or standard table type; omnidirectional, not unidirectional; and at least one cordless microphone
- Two wheeled racks or dollies for equipment
- Necessary cables and hookup cords, including at least twenty feet of microphone cable

In purchasing these, look for brand names of products that can be serviced locally. There is usually no need to go for the most expensive, but don't buy the cheapest, either. Consider what size and price range rental car your company allows you, then go for the same bracket in video equipment. Take the advice of knowledgeable salespeople, however. You will have fewer problems and be more likely to get good service.

Remember that the simpler the equipment, the less there is to go wrong with it. You probably do not need a tripod with wheels; a Neuman or Telefunken microphone; three-tube color cameras; character generators, automatic focus, or electronic zoom in the camera; edit features on the tape player; extra lighting; or other frills. A wheeled rack or stand in which to carry all this equipment and to hold the players and monitors would be a plus, though.

Be wary of sharing your precious equipment with other departments. Scheduling becomes a major problem, and when others use it, equipment may not be functioning when you need it again. If you must share, set up guidelines for scheduled use, maintenance, and repair.

Problems With Videotaping. Videotaping is so useful that there are few problems associated with it. There are a few things you should avoid, however. For example, an all-too-frequent situation arises when people want to save the tapes and you've been rotating them, erasing each performance to record the next one. To avoid this, make your procedures clear in the beginning, or record all the participants on one tape and have them scramble to find time to see themselves. As an alternative, let each person have his or her own tape on which *all* their training performances are recorded. This is costly but of great educational value because each participant has a record of his or her progressive improvement.

One frequent mechanical problem is sound. Few things are more annoying than recording a performance only to find that the sound wasn't turned on. When you set up and test your equipment, pay attention to the sound, too. In addition, I usually check sound when recording my first participant.

Incidentally, I have deliberately avoided the mechanics of setting up equipment because each brand is different. The person who sells or installs the hardware will be happy to explain everything. If you are unsure of your requirements, rent before you buy to become familiar with what you are getting before you are stuck with it.

Computers

I include computers as a training aid because in recent years with LCD panels and animated graphics software we've come into the age of multimedia presentations. These are briefly discussed in the section on slides and more thoroughly in Chapter 10. In addition, educators have made much of computer-based training in recent years. See Chapter 10 for full coverage on computer-based instruction. The sole function of many training departments is to train in the use of computers or in new software applications. In this case, computers are "actualities" in that they are not simply aids but rather the real thing themselves. For these reasons computers today are a rather special and important training aid.

When coupled with laser disk storage and fiber-optic linkage, computers may become an even more dynamic training tool than video. Laser disks allow video to be programmed into the computer so that learners can watch the effects of their mistakes carried through to the ultimate resulting failure. People learn best by making mistakes. Through laser technology, the computer can supply an array of animated or acted-out options, *each* of which can be played to its logical conclusion. Errors can be made, the consequences demonstrated, and corrections learned and practiced, all through interaction with the computer. Such devices are currently in operation in many large organizations. Fiber optics and satellites make this technology linkable with PCs and mainframes so that training is possible simultaneously in several locations—a phenomenon that has become known as distance learning. This, too, will be discussed in much greater detail in Chapter 10.

Uses of Computers. In training, the computer is most effective when used to respond to and/or manipulate data to produce answers to hypothetical questions. These are usually part of case histories or simulated training exercises. It is in these hypothetical situations that computers are best used. They become a problem-solving tool producing results based on the data fed into them. This gives you the opportunity to devise exercises involving decisions structured around realistic data. Simulations or in-basket exercises become much more realistic.

The second-best application of computers to training is as the actual equipment trainees learn how to operate. They learn from the machine while also learning to operate it for consistency. This is one form of computer-based training (CBT). Standard programmed instruction (covered in Chapter 10) is a series of questions put to the learner in a carefully organized sequence, each building on information contained in the answers to previous questions. A correct answer moves the learner to the next question; a wrong answer stalls the learner at that question or moves him or her to some remedial material. Self-tutoring software programs follow this same pattern, but when the programming is very interactive the CBT format works exceptionally well because the errors are real and the results are immediately measurable. In fact, the immediacy of results is one of the best features of computers. It is this immediate responsiveness to user activity that makes virtual reality so exciting (see Chapter 10).

What computers do *least* well is CBT in the form of linear progressive tutori-

---

Using Computers

1. Turn on all units; check that all are working.
2. Check that correct disks are loaded (unless this is a trainee task; if so, check if correct disks are in place).
3. Test the command sequence (for example, log on and off) to be sure equipment is working correctly.
4. Have a manual handy in case you need it to troubleshoot a problem.
5. Upon completion of class, be sure all disks are unloaded and computers are shut down.

---

als—a sort of electronic page turning. As programs become more realistic with the growth of laser storage capability and the responses to questions more dynamic and less artificial, this situation will change. For the present, a few CBT programs do a commendable job training basic processes and relationships to already motivated trainees. They also succeed with theory and in bringing operational skills to acceptable levels of understanding (such as recognition, recall, and discrimination). If a simulation program can then be added to test for judgment, you may be able to create an excellent package, but only to the degree of reality you can achieve in the simulation. Except for simulating computer operations, computers themselves provide artificial environments, and that is one of their drawbacks.

Working With Computers. In Chapter 10 we examine how to construct a basic CBT program. For now, let's assume you have purchased one and are about to use it. Promoters of CBT sell the programs on the idea that they are completely self-paced. Trainees learn at their own rate. This is true, assuming the trainees want to learn. For unmotivated trainees, their "own rate" is not at all. This is one of the major problems of CBT. Therefore, to use CBT effectively, follow these five guidelines:

1. *Work in groups.* Find ways to share answers and problems. Use E-mail and Internet chat groups. Try the buddy system. The more human you make the environment, the more dynamic the training becomes.

2. *Use those trainees with aptitude to help those who are slower or demotivated.* Keep their interest alive with coaching assignments or other projects.

3. *If you need to work with separate individuals in remote locations, keep in frequent contact by telephone and, where possible, by computer.* This way you can monitor progress and personalize the instruction.*

4. *Use computers as an aid to training, not as a substitute for your instruction.*

5. *Mix technologies.* I've always found it advisable to use a large-screen projector to display your own or one of the trainees' screens for the whole class to see. This allows you to solve the problem together.

Problems With Computers. The principal problem with computers, in addition to their lack of interpersonal skills, is their cost and availability. For most of

---

*I sound like a Luddite crying out against computers in the world of training. It is not that I don't admire computers; I have great hopes for them in the future. It is just that human beings are social animals. We can learn to use tools and come to depend upon them without human interaction, but it is harder. All learning is faster, more thorough, and easier when human interaction is involved. The problem with computers is inherent: They are mechanical. Research into artificial intelligence has come a long way toward alleviating the problem, but it hasn't solved it—yet! Until that time keep your computer training as interactive and supportive as you can make it.

us, even the cost of individual personal computers prohibits classes larger than five or six, which is great for individualized instruction and more effective coaching. If you are going to acquire computers, check if you can train on less expensive hardware. Much available hardware costs far less and runs many IBM-compatible programs. The transfer to IBM configurations becomes relatively simple once the program capabilities and operations have been mastered. Regardless of what you purchase, don't share the equipment. Make sure any hardware you buy is reserved for your training use only. This will save you much trouble down the road.

If you are buying generic CBT programs, remember they have all the problems of other off-the-shelf packages. They are generic and can only teach the basics, so you will have to teach any in-house applications. Furthermore, many are little more than fancy page turners. If you buy one, be very careful of copyright. Software manufacturers are becoming increasingly vigilant about any pirating of their material. It is unethical. Write your own CBT programs, or buy ones you can't write—even adapt the ones you've paid for—but don't copy, use, or sell anyone else's program without permission.

Here's a final note on computers. They have wonderful training advantages. Whatever you do on the computer gets an immediate result, and this enhances learning. However, they also have disadvantages. Computer programs are rather dull—long strings of command sequences in not easily comprehensible language. Information overload and monitoring are constant dangers. Concentrate instead on working your computer instruction around the principle of *less is more* and on changing the pace as often as possible. Both will help make your computer training easier.

Handouts

Handouts are too commonplace and familiar to warrant more than a note or two here (they are also discussed in Chapter 7). Self-study materials, workbooks, textbooks, or illustrations can be used as teaching aids. Here are five pointers on their use:

1. *Distribute your materials before you refer to them or after you have covered the topic—never while you are covering it.* Allow time for people to look over the materials.

2. *Make the handouts more important by assigning homework based on them.* At the very least, walk the group through the handouts so they will be familiar with them.

3. *Keep the material relevant.* Many people feel frustrated when given more material than will be covered or needed. If you give out material that will not be covered, explain its applicability to the course.

Using Handouts

1. Count to be sure you have the correct number.
2. Make sure they are in the correct order.
3. Check to be sure you've planned when and how to distribute them.

---

4. *Less is more.* If they have to read a book, they don't need you. Keep your handouts to a minimum.

5. *Prepare neat and attractive materials.* It helps make the learning easier.

Pointers

A pointer is an extension of your arm. Its main purpose is to focus attention on a particular detail. The problem with pointers is that trainers use them idly. They lean on them, play with them, and wave them about. In doing so, they distract attention from the matter at hand. All eyes are on the pointer, not on the topic. This is particularly true of laser pointers used with slides. A wobbly pinpoint of light can flutter about like a firefly.

Using a pointer well takes self-discipline. Point *once* to the object, words, or visual, and then either hold that point or put the pointer down until needed again. Used with this discipline, a pointer is excellent. Used without it, it is a disastrous distracter that does more harm than good. If you can't control your use of a pointer, don't use it at all.

The easiest kind of pointer to use is the collapsible type, but be very careful not to open and close it too frequently or it, too, will become distracting.

Using Pointers

1. Be sure your pointer is where you want it.
2. If it is collapsible, check to be sure it collapses and opens properly.
3. Remind yourself not to play with it.

You—the Trainer

You may not be used to thinking of yourself as a visual aid. But you are the main message, and it is your attitude toward the material that the trainees will buy.

Make it good. This is why I stressed personal appearance, dress, and manner in Chapter 3. If you have been reading this chapter separately for audiovisual ideas, please spend some time with Chapter 3. It will pay off for you.

Remember that because you are the message, you should enjoy yourself. Have fun; get psyched up about what you teach. You have set affective training objectives as well as cognitive ones, and trainees won't feel good about the material if you feel poorly toward it. They'll love the subject if you are excited about it, too. So work at smiling, gesturing, and using other forms of animation and generating personal enthusiasm, especially late in the day. You'll become the best audiovisual aid you can use.

You—The Trainer

1. Make sure you have a clock or watch, not on your wrist, that you can see easily. It is best if the trainees can't see it.
2. For women, check to see that your makeup is correct and that you are not wearing jewelry that would distract trainees.
3. For men, be sure all zippers and buttons are done. Button your coat jacket.
4. Go over your opening remarks to be sure you are comfortable with them.
5. Check your agenda to be sure you are on track for the day.
6. Check *all* your audiovisuals.

Acquiring Audiovisual Aids

Having discussed the uses of audiovisual aids, we need now to spend a little time looking at how to acquire them. Remember, the measure of an audiovisual aid is its usefulness to you. Does it help you to produce the results you want? To answer that question, first you must weigh any audiovisual aid choice against your training objectives. Then ask yourself:

- Does this aid simplify material for my trainees?
- Does this aid help me to maintain focus?
- Does this aid make material memorable?
- Does it take us where we could not otherwise go?
- Can it be used to create a change of pace?
- Does it save time in presentation or learning?

It must do at least two of these; otherwise, as mentioned earlier, it is a waste of training time and money.

Is the visual you want more complex or fancier than it needs to be? Is there a simpler way to explain the idea? Also consider how quickly the material will date itself. When will you have to replace it? Give thought to the level of quality you need. What levels are unacceptable? Do you really need the top-of-the-line product?

What are the costs involved? Are there extra costs this new aid will incur? I once worked for an organization that accepted an offer of two free broadcast-quality television cameras from a local station that was upgrading its equipment. With great excitement we laid plans for using them—that is, until we realized we also needed control room equipment, cables, lights, dollies, and other equipment that would drain our training budget for the next eight years. As far as I know, the organization still has not used the cameras.

Consider what usefulness the equipment will have beyond the course for which you are considering it. How can you adapt it for other functions? Can it be used for more than one course? In more than one department?

Answering these questions will prepare you to negotiate for the best audiovisual aids. They should protect you from purchasing a disaster. There is one other tactic, too. If you are in doubt, rent before you buy. I have never found hardware that couldn't be rented. Most commercial packages, films, slides, video- and audiotapes, and the like can be rented easily. If you are not permitted to rent, insist on a thirty-day free trial. If that's not permitted either, there may be something wrong with the product. It is amazing to me how many trainers have been stuck with materials they don't use or don't like. Always try it out before you buy it.

If you use an aid only once or twice a year, you may find it is more reasonable to rent than buy. If renting, avoid the audiovisual groups that serve the large hotels and conference centers. They usually have excellent equipment and fine service, but they charge exorbitant prices. Instead, go to a good electronics or camera shop—one that provides full repair and customizing service—and ask where you can get rentals. It may well be one of the hotel service facilities, but at least you'll know they are the most reasonable available.

For prepared visuals such as films or slides, membership in the American Society for Training and Development will put you on the mailing lists of everyone in the country who sells these aids. Actually, you'll be put on the mailing lists of everyone who sells *anything* to trainers. Excellent! There is no better way to keep abreast of the marketplace. In addition, your membership brings you a subscription to *Training and Development Journal*, the professional magazine of the American Society for Training and Development, which is filled with ads for every imaginable audiovisual aid. Another magazine is *Training*, which does not require membership and which provides much the same service. (See the Appendix for more information.)

Finally, an excellent, highly recommended source is your company purchasing agent. A good purchasing agent is expert at ferreting out sources and pursuing the best possible prices, delivery, and service.

In most large organizations, purchases have to go through the purchasing department anyway, and because their job is to get the most for the least, they may override your order and purchase something of lesser quality than you want. Don't fight them; befriend them so they can help you acquire the best aids at the best price. By working with them, you'll ensure that you get what you want.

An excellent source of rental films is your public or college library. Most libraries participate in a statewide central lending agency that gives them access to almost every film available. Using the libraries is inexpensive and efficient; you need only institutional membership to participate.

When planning audiovisual purchases, consider what you'll use. If you dislike overhead projectors or never train more than five or six people, you certainly wouldn't want to buy one. On the other hand, every trainer needs some kind of board or chart to write on. I recommend flip charts on portable easels as the most versatile and easiest to use. The pads, of course, are a constant supply cost. Using a chalkboard or portable whiteboard eliminates this, but neither is as flexible. A good compromise is oilcloth- or acetate-covered sheets for the flip chart easels; they can be erased and reused many times. These materials are more costly than newsprint, but are less than whiteboards.

Video equipment is so useful that I recommend highly that you consider purchasing a unit. Even if you don't use it at present, weigh how you might be able to use it in the future. Unless you train only on actual equipment, like computers, you will find video a tremendous help. There is more information on purchasing video equipment in the section on video earlier in this chapter, and instructions for making your own training tapes later in the chapter.

Other visual aids are strictly a matter of preference or need. Computers are vital for computer training. A slide projector is necessary if you want to use slides. Models are a great help if you train in subjects for which they can be used. Give some thought to what you are now doing, and ask yourself if an audiovisual aid might not simplify or enhance your training.

In fact, at least once a year, probably approaching budget time, evaluate where you are and where you want to be in one year, in five years, and in ten years down the road. Weigh your needs analyses against your present capabilities and future projections. If your department is going to be growing (and it will be; see Chapter 20), you will need to give thought to expanding your audiovisual and equipment needs. Plan your acquisitions in one-, three-, five-, and ten-year cycles. Let management know well in advance what your budget requests will be (see Chapter 15).

If you have a large capital expenditure coming up—for example, buying a number of personal computers—go to the accounting and purchasing departments and explore with them the possibility of leasing rather than purchasing the equipment. Leasing will increase your operating budget, but it completely avoids a large capital outlay, which might have both tax and operational advantages for your department. Alternatives might include a rental with payments toward purchase; a limited-time lease with a buyout upon completion (many car leases are of this sort); or a phased purchase system whereby new items are added each year—purchased by setting aside a fixed amount in your annual budgets. Discuss the pros and cons of these options with the accounting and purchasing people, and seek out the best alternative that provides what you need, has a realistic acquisition schedule, and is the most painless option for the company.

Creating Audiovisual Materials

An alternative to purchase or rental is to create your own aids. Of course, I'm not referring to hardware; I wouldn't want to try to build an overhead projector, let alone a video camera. But you can prepare much of what we use the hardware for.

There are three important advantages to doing it yourself. First, your materials are totally customized, hand-tailored to your needs and to suit your company. Second, while the cost of your time and effort is high, making the aids yourself often saves money, freeing it for acquisition of hardware. Third, you gain a wonderful feeling of accomplishment and pride when you can create something and then use it successfully.

There are, of course, drawbacks and limitations. Paramount is the cost of your time and effort. Unless you are prepared to spend a good deal of your work time and most probably a lot of your personal time, this isn't the route for you. A second large liability can be an amateur result if you aren't used to this kind of work. A third drawback is that once you've done one and it has been successful, you can get hooked on it and want to do more. Furthermore, as the word spreads around the company, other divisions will approach you to do media for them. You can get far busier than you ever intended to be.

A good response to the first two problems is to seek professional or semiprofessional help. You can keep your time commitment down and the professional level up with someone else's expertise. I have a client who wrote a great script for a twenty-minute training tape on employee assessment and goal setting. He hired a local producer to shoot it; the producer hired local professional actors, used in-house sets, and came up with an excellent training tape for under $20,000. Even more money could have been saved by engaging the local college filmmaking or television instructors. They love to work with business, are reasonable, have considerable expertise, and produce work with maximum quality in mind. So these options help solve the time and quality problems. As to the third drawback mentioned—becoming too busy making other aids—you'll have to deal with that problem when and if it happens to you, but Chapters 15, 16, and 17 will help.

We've already discussed elements involved in preparing charts and posters. It is unlikely you will make your own boards, so let's move on to making models.

How to Create Models

Often you can hire a retired artist or model maker who will be thrilled to create a professional model for you. Today computers have taken over many of the functions of models, and model makers are either forcibly retired or working at something else. These people were trained artists who could use any suitable medium to create desired models. The models were used by companies involved in mechanical or structural design, automobile design, engineering, construction, architecture, aircraft design, shipping, and furniture design. To find an expert model maker, check with a local mechanical engineering society or association, ask an architect, call up a theatrical designer or set maker, or contact schools of mechanical engineering or architecture. For a reasonable fee you can get any model you can imagine built professionally.

If you cannot find a professional model maker, remember the retired military man refighting his triumphs. You can make a model using anything you have on hand. First plan the model in your head, then on paper. Gather the best (that is, the least costly, the most adequate) materials for your project. Keep the model simple. Only show relationships or basic processes; don't get stuck in details. Use color-coding to highlight parts.

If your model is fairly easy to construct, consider assigning it to one of your children or young relatives (eleven to seventeen years old) or offer it to a class in design, business, art, or science (grades six through twelve). They'll have fun, you'll have a selection of models to pick from, and the school can apply the money to a cause, such as a scholarship, new band uniforms, or dance decorations.

If your model has working parts, it is probably best to seek a design expert. Alternatively, convert the real thing to a working model. Take an old piece of equipment and restore it to the point at which you can use it to illustrate basic principles or operations. This is frequently done with engines, presses, and guns. You can also make a cutaway model by slicing an old unit in half and then color-coding its parts.

How to Create Simulations

The simulations to which I refer here are participatory ones such as management games, role-playing, case histories, and so on. Here are some guidelines when setting up simulations:

1. *Whenever possible, base your simulations on real events.* I recommend the critical-incident method, in which you select a situation either you or the trainees

have just experienced. Alternatively, select an incident that is ongoing or about to happen. I use this frequently in courses on negotiation techniques.

2. *Have desired answers and approaches, but don't cover all the bases.* Leave some questions unanswered. Challenge the group by letting their work exceed the standards you've set.

3. *Provide all the background information in detail.* If part of the training is selecting data, provide the trainees with irrelevant and excess data to challenge their ability to discriminate. Give them choices.

4. *If possible, let the choices play to their natural or logical conclusions.* Let the group err; they'll learn from their mistakes.

5. *Use games.* Games work well. Simulate popular television game shows by paralleling their steps or events. I've used *Let's Make a Deal, Jeopardy,* and *Family Feud* very successfully.

6. *As an alternative to real situations, set up artificial ones to illustrate a point.* And keep them short. An example of this is an exercise designed to demonstrate the teamwork involved in listening. Each participant, paired with another, is instructed to do anything and everything but listen while his or her partner talks. After two minutes the roles are reversed and the exercise is repeated. In the ensuing discussion it becomes apparent that both sides of a conversation need to share the listening responsibility. For further considerations, see Chapters 5 and 7.

How to Create Videos

Video is fabulous in taking you where you cannot otherwise go. But the commercial films and videotapes are so generic that they lack specifics. An answer to this problem is to make your own movies. You can use film, but that's much more complicated and expensive. Videotaping is feasible, however, and can be very cost-effective.

Your first concern is your training objectives. Will videotaping help bring about the changes you desire? Why videotaping? Are there other media you could use? Create a rationale for the videotaping and relate it to your training objectives.

Establish what equipment you will need.[1] It will vary with your applications, budgets, and needs. If you need to have copies to distribute to various locations, do everything in three-quarter-inch tape. Home videotape is half-inch; it's good, but doesn't hold up to copying. Each copy loses quality until, after four or five copies, the picture is poor, colors fade, and sound becomes muffled. The best is one-inch broadcast quality, used by television stations. You can shoot in three-quarter-inch or even half-inch, transfer to one-inch, and then edit and make copies in one-inch. But one-inch equipment is very costly. Sony has a relatively inexpensive Super 8 Beta half-inch format it claims is as good as three-quarter-inch; the disadvantage is that it is not compatible with any other system. I recommend shooting in half-inch, transferring a single copy to a three-quarter-inch tape, editing in three-quarter, and making all the half-inch copies you need from that three-quarter-inch master.

Equipment. To make your own videos, you will need the following equipment:

- One camera (at least)
- One tape editor (simple is fine)
- One character generator (simple is fine)
- Two tape recorders
- Three monitors
- One to three microphones, depending on your application
- One fluid-head tripod
- One four-piece lighting unit
- Cables, batteries, cassettes (as needed)
- Several rolls of seamless paper in various widths and colors

You also will find a commercial music library useful.

- *Camera.* As of this writing, costs for industrial-quality equipment range from $2,000 to $10,000, depending on the quality and the number of picture-generating tubes in the camera. One tube is least expensive; three tubes (which produce much better color and pictures) are more expensive. Cameras are made by Sony, JVC, Panasonic, Ikegami, and Hitachi. The Hitachi, at about $8,000, is very near broadcast quality. The JVC at half that price is not as good. There is one saving grace: Secondhand cameras can be excellent and are far less costly. Buy a used Hitachi for $5,000 (in good condition, of course) and it will pay off.

- *Tape editor.* An editor is used to link together electronically all the pieces of tape you've shot. Each scene or still photo can be shot in any convenient order and edited into its proper sequence. Tapes can be changed and updated by editing or material can be deleted. Having the power to fade to black means you can fade out on one scene and fade in on the other. It makes for smoother transitions. Mix these fade-outs with straight jump-cuts from one scene to the next. Incidentally, an inexpensive way to include slides or still photos (these normally require a special camera to be edited onto a tape) is to project them on a wall in a darkened room and then tape the projection. This tape can now be edited normally.

Editors need not be fancy. A simple cut-and-paste unit that will fade to black is fine. Buy good-quality equipment, but don't go for fancy capabilities such as a special effects generator or a switching unit. Industrial-quality editors are made largely by the same manufacturers as the cameras and range from $7,000 to

---

Minimum Video Equipment

Minimum Requirements for See-Yourself Taping (half-inch format)

- One camera (one-color tube)
- Two videocassette recorders (VCRs)
- Two monitors
- One microphone
- One power transformer for camera
- One tripod
- Two wheeled racks or dollies for equipment
- Connecting cables, extension cords, tapes, and so forth
  Cost: $3,000 to $12,000

Minimum Requirements for Do-It-Yourself Production (three-quarter-inch format)

- One camera (three color tubes)
- One tape editor
- One character generator
- Two tape recorders
- One fluid-head tripod
- One four-piece lighting unit
- Three monitors
- One to three microphones
- Cables, batteries, cassettes, tapes, and so on, as needed
- Commercial music library
- Several rolls of seamless paper in various colors and widths
  Cost: $30,000 +

$15,000. Again, you can save some money by buying a secondhand unit in good working order.

    ■ *Character generator.* This unit lets you write captions and titles, either on a choice of colored backgrounds or superimposed on the picture. Your equipment need not be fancy. A simple character generator will have one or two fonts (particular style and size of type), a possible mix of up to 250 color combinations, and the power to superimpose and justify (that is, to move the print around on the screen). You won't need more than this. These run about $3,000 and secondhand ones are usually fine. A computer can do this as well but it requires special software and it must be compatible with your system. Telecomp 1000 is a $400 computer-video combiner available from Universal Video Catalog (an excellent source book).

■ *Tape recorders*. Do *not* buy these secondhand. Of all of the equipment mentioned, tape recorders are the easiest to break, require the most service (full service every 1,000 hours of use), and suffer most from neglect. The three-quarter-inch tape recorders work like the smaller ones you have at home. They don't need to be fancy. They must have a separate audio-in port to allow you to dub sound. I recommend two tape recorders because when you are editing, one must play your tape while the other (your master copy) receives and records the new edits. With three machines, you can alternately feed material from either tape, through the editor, onto your master tape. Costs are $1,500 to $ 4,000 per machine.

■ *Monitors*. Monitors are plain television sets. You will probably want more than one, although you could get by with only one. I recommend two: one for what's being put into the editor and one for what's being recorded. You can get a small audioboard and tape recorder or cassette recorder. This allows you to mix in voice-overs, or outside sounds such as music or special effects. (In this regard, I would recommend buying a standard musical background library for about $400. This is a set of records or tapes of mood, effect, and background music. It adds a very professional touch to your tapes.)

■ *Microphones*. One microphone is enough but can get cumbersome when you have more than one person talking. Ideally, have one cordless lavaliere mike (small ones that clip onto clothing), one shotgun-type mike (which is very directional and allows you to control background noise; it only picks up sound in front of it), and one omnidirectional table mike for use on a desk or on the floor with several people around it. Again, these don't have to be first-quality. Expect to pay about $200 each, although the shotgun type may be more. And remember that you'll need cables and extension cords, too.

■ *Tripods*. These are used to hold your cameras. Don't stint on them. Buy one with a fluid head, which allows you to pan the camera back and forth, to tilt it up and down, and to raise and lower it for special angle shots—all without jiggling the picture. Spring-mounted or plain tripods are simply not smooth enough to ensure good quality. If you plan on doing tracking shots (in which the camera moves horizontally along with people who are walking or moves around those standing still), you'll need wheels for the tripod. Tripods cost $1,000 to $2,000 new, but a secondhand one in good working order is fine.

■ *Four-piece lighting unit*. Even though most cameras will shoot in natural light, colors are dropped and details are lost under these lighting conditions. You should have a four-piece kit consisting of two lights and two stands and the cables for connecting them. A company called Lowell, Inc., makes such a production kit; it is available in photo shops and video stores, as well as in catalogues. These cost around $1,200. Set the lights up on each side of your subject, one higher than the other to control shadows. To create shadows, hang a venetian blind in front of one of the lights or use a branch with leaves, or whatever. You can create silhouettes by lighting the background rather than the subject, or backlighting by setting one light to shine from behind the subject but off camera. A soft-light effect can be created by shining the light on foil or a sheet of bright white paper and bouncing it indirectly onto the subject. Use your imagination.

■ *Paper rolls.* One of the handiest supplies you can buy are rolls of seamless paper in various colors and widths. These allow you to change your background simply by hanging a different color or texture from the wall and shooting in front of it. You can cover windows and doors, create rooms, or make neutral areas. One very effective, prize-winning industrial training tape I've seen uses black paper to create a multitude of scenes in a limited space. The furniture becomes the setting, the background is totally neutral.

A final few words about hardware. For example, the facility at Uniforce Temporaries in New Hyde Park, New York, has all the equipment I recommend here. It has a full studio operation (but not a studio facility, in that they work out of an office and a conference room) to produce one or two thirty-minute tapes per month for distribution to all its offices. These tapes are done in a news program format and contain company news, current events, motivational materials, and training how-to's. The entire Uniforce facility cost the company under $40,000. However, to produce the volume of quality material they put out, they have a full-time production and operations person to run the studio. Using half-inch minimal industrial equipment, you could produce a worthwhile videotape with $15,000 worth of hardware. Uniforce's facility is excellent at $40,000. If you want to set up your own studio, you can get superb quality work of professional caliber but may have to go as high as $180,000 for top-of-the-line hardware. In video, cost impacts directly on quality.

A word of caution. You will need an expert! Manuals on video equipment are written by engineers and are very confusing to the nontechnical person. Furthermore, there is a plethora of hardware available, much of it useless. Hire a consultant to help you design, purchase, and learn to operate your facility. It will be money well spent. I know of a major American company that sidestepped the consultant and spent $400,000 on video equipment which is gathering cobwebs today. Know what you want (your training objectives), and get expert help in acquiring it and learning to use it.

Writing and Shooting. Consider your staffing capabilities, too. Do you have time to produce a tape yourself? Determine the distribution and number of copies you'll need as well as the production style you want. Do you want a dramatic script? A documentary? A series of involved graphics? Simple head shots? A news format? I had a client who limited his time to writing the script and then hired professionals to do the rest. He brought in an excellent twenty-minute training film for under $10,000. And he had no equipment overhead.

Draw up a budget for equipment purchases or rentals and extra staffing costs (such as overtime). If you don't yet have the money, justify the cost. Show how what you're asking will be repaid many times over by the use of your tape.

Draw up a script. In film or video it is less effective to tell something than it is to show something. The worst videos are "talking heads," in which one person stands or sits and talks to the camera. Video is an action medium. When doing the script, visualize how it will look. Whenever possible show something happening or create a dialogue. Talking heads are acceptable occasionally and for short periods, but keep them to a minimum. The entire video should really be no longer than ten minutes maximum.

Once you have the rough script, ask yourself whether it will meet your training objectives. How will it fit into the lesson? Can it be used for more than one subject area? If your answers are satisfactory, break your script down into specific camera shots. This is called a *storyboard*, and it is often done in cartoon fashion. The storyboard is a step-by-step portrayal of what will be on the screen. The average length of a shot (a single camera view or a take) on commercial television is three seconds. The more shots, takes, or camera moves you have, the faster paced the final product will look; the fewer shots or takes, the slower it will be.

Making Your Own Videos

1. Review your training objectives and create a rationale for the project based on those objectives. Justify your costs in terms of company goals.
2. Determine what equipment and how much staff you have and what you'll need.
3. Establish the end use of the tape: distribution, number of copies to be made. Decide on the best approach: drama, documentary, news format, and so on.
4. Write the script. Keep it active; don't tell, show through action. Use dialogue and very little monologue.
5. Draw up the budget for equipment, staff, and so forth.
6. Storyboard the script. Break sequences down into specific shots. Keep shots varied and short.
7. Scout for or create sets and locations. Be creative; have fun.
8. Schedule your shooting, people, use of sets, and the like.
9. Shoot your video.
10. Edit to a finished copy, adding sound and graphics.

When you have lots of action, this alone will hold the trainees' attention. When you have only one or two people talking, add the appearance of action by breaking the dialogue into many shots. Try close-ups, full master shots (the whole physical scene or set in one shot), and medium-range shots. Vary them and mix them up. Make each a different length. Professionals create dramatic rhythms this way and so can you. One word of caution, though. Don't overdo it! If you jump around too much it will put your audience on edge and make them uncomfortable. Work on achieving variety with a smooth blending of angles, types of shots, or different lengths of shot.

Plan and, if need be, scout or create your sets and locations. Schedule your shoots, actors, equipment use, and crew. One time- and money-saver that Hollywood uses is to shoot all the scenes that take place in one location at that location regardless of when they occur in the script. For example, say you're using your company president's office. There is one scene in the beginning of your film, two midway through, and one at the end that take place in that office. Don't schedule four separate visits; that would drive the president crazy. Schedule one visit and shoot all four scenes, out of sequence. This sometimes means having different actors or having frequent changes of costume, but it saves time and bother in the long run.

A logistics problem needs to be addressed here, though. Keep careful track of what scene is shot where, and on which tape. Keep a log of your takes to avoid the frustration of not being able to find footage you know you shot or failing to shoot footage you meant to shoot but simply lost track of. Movie companies have a person whose only job is keeping track of footage.

Finally shoot your video. Be flexible and creative. Sometimes the shot called for simply doesn't work, so try others. Maybe a better idea will occur to you while you are shooting. Try it. Shooting is the best part of moviemaking. It's work, but try to enjoy it. It can be exciting. When you've finished shooting, edit the tape and add sound and graphics to the edited version. Now you have your own training tape. And every one you make will get better than the one before.

Summary

In this chapter we have taken a close look at audiovisual aids and their application to training. A trainer must consider each aid in connection with training objectives. Effective visual aids perform at least two of six possible functions: to simplify material, to focus attention, to enhance memory, to take us somewhere we cannot otherwise go, to save time, and to provide variety. We examined the audiovisual aids available, discovered their best uses, how to work with them, and what problems might be anticipated.

As cost is a factor in any business, we discussed the question of rental versus purchase. Too often trainers buy unsatisfactory media, so we established some criteria for evaluating aids. We looked at sources of audiovisual materials, and we considered some ideas on budgeting for media acquisition.

The final section of this chapter dealt with alternatives to ready-made, mass-produced materials. We described how to get help in building models, and gave guidelines on creating meaningful simulations. Finally, we examined the costs and considerations of setting up a video production unit, plus how to script and shoot your own training films.

Applications

1. Select a unit of training you are currently presenting or are planning to present. Review the visual aids you are planning to use. Assess the aids using the six functions of a visual aid and eliminate any that are marginal or are performing only one or two functions.

2. Use your local photo shop and purchasing department to draw up a cost list for fully equipping your training facility with video capability. Do the same for minimal videotaping facility.

3. Evaluate your proposed or current training to assess where you might add additional hands-on computer-driven simulations. Draw up a plan for building or acquiring these simulations and cost out your plan.

4. Repeat the exercise from Application 3, but this time look for opportunities to create video scenes. Script the scenes you'd like to use. Research and find local help to shoot and produce the work, and get quotations on costs.

Chapter 10
Technology and Training

WITH innovations such as virtual reality, distance learning, interactive CD-ROM, and multimedia, what's a trainer to do? We are inundated with technology and special interest groups who promote their preferred technology as the state of the art and the pathway to the future. Many groups claim their technology will become the "default mode" of training. Furthermore, at the rate technology is changing, we will soon have even more choices—and even more experts to help us to decide in favor of their technology. Indeed, what are we to do?

I'd like to first establish some perspective on the growth of technology in training and then describe each of the four main technologies affecting training today. Finally, I'll provide a set of guidelines to help you stay current with these technologies.

Where Are We?

Training technology has been growing for years. Tools such as overhead projectors, whiteboards, slide projectors, videotape recorders and players, and laser pointers were completely unheard of only a few years ago. Techniques such as small group interaction, Socratic questions, games, simulations, and case histories were quite rare until the post–Vietnam War era. But all of these shaped the face of live training. Truly high-tech training, however, began with the concept of desktop publishing in the late 1980s.[1] Growth since that time has been increasingly toward user-driven training; training that the learner initiates and controls.

There are six levels or steps in this evolution of technology:

1. Desktop publishing
2. Speaker aids
3. Information tools

4. Computer-based training
5. Performance Support Systems[2]
6. Knowledge Support Systems

Desktop Publishing

This type of software first put dynamic graphic design into the hands of individual trainers and program developers. Trainee workbooks no longer needed to be simple text but could now be filled with fun graphics and saturated with bright and colorful shapes and patterns. At first, the learner's activity was limited to turning pages, albeit with enthusiasm.

Speaker Aids

While most training workbooks were still largely print, desktop publishing fueled the rise of colorful graphic overhead projections and led to the next technological evolution—multimedia speaker aids. In this mode, now considered state of the art in many presentation areas, the trainer shows the presentation on a computer and the image is projected onto a standard reflective screen. These visuals are usually animated and accompanied by stereophonic sound, hence the name *multimedia*, which is usually used to refer to such presentations. If a computer has CD-ROM capacity, it is possible to run full action video clips in these projections as well. It is training with bells and whistles, and engages more of the learner's senses, but it is still a passive activity, not an active one.

Information Tools

Information delivery tools evolved somewhat independently from the speaker-aids technology. This type of viewer-driven software is used in public kiosks to provide passers-by with information. You will frequently see such kiosks in malls and large department stores, airports, major hotels, theme parks, and tourist information centers. They can provide graphic pictures, video clips, exciting colorful designs, sound, and even hard copy, but the learner's interaction is limited to the simple selection of options to be viewed.

Computer-Based Training

This technology is ideally suited to self-paced, self-motivated learners who can work alone with computers that train using text, sound, pictures, video, and animation. While the earlier models were largely passive experiences, with the learner's main interaction limited to selecting a page to work on or opting to correctly resolve the problem posed by the computer, current models can become quite interactive. CD-ROM technology allows for vastly greater memory storage than earlier hard-disk technology. Memory-hungry applications, such as animation and video, can be incorporated, and outcomes can have realistic consequences (see the section later in this chapter on conditional branching).

Virtual reality (VR) is currently considered to be the *state of the art*. It involves full immersion of the learner into a three-dimensional world of simulation in order to learn how to act correctly (perform the requisite skills for the task). As it is defined by columnist Maureen Minehan in *HR Magazine*:

> VR is a computer-based technology that enables users to learn in a three-dimensional environment. The student can move through a simulated world and interact in real time with its components by viewing a virtual model on a computer screen or through a head-mounted display.[3]

Since the 1930s trainee pilots have used Link-type trainers to safely learn to fly in simulated comfort. Today's full-scale simulators are quite remarkable (see the section later in this chapter on their uses). But the current trend is toward miniaturization and so most virtual reality programs require the user to wear a helmet or a set of heavy, complex goggles—and in some full simulations an electronically wired glove—that remove him or her from the real world in order to project the computerized "virtual reality" of the program. The learner's activity is to freely respond to the programmed environment that, within the limits of its program, will respond in turn to the learner's actions.

Performance Support Systems

One might think that computer-based training is about as far as technology can go. Indeed, as the "reality" level of the simulations increases, this is so. But they are still only simulations. From a training perspective, there is still the need to transfer the learning from the simulator to the real job. Therefore, experts are experimenting with a still higher but somewhat different level of technology. Performance Support Systems are intended to provide training "just-in-time." In this operation, the computer becomes a resource at the workstation. Workers don't undergo formal training, but, rather, are put in the real job with the computer as a sort of performance coach or guide to teach them how to perform each step or task as it comes up. The person will learn by repeatedly doing the real task.

The focus of Performance Support Systems is on producing, not on learning—on actual results in the workplace, not on tests. This makes it a very attractive technology in those job situations where it is practicable. In situations that require split-second decisions and interactions with live customers or finely honed motor skills or judgments, this system would necessarily function too slowly. However, when it can function as an expert system, advising a worker on procedures or choices, it can be very effective. Currently, it is being used by Microsoft to train staff in its *Wizards* program, American Express to support its customer service representatives, Prime Computer in direct sales, Intel on the manufacturing floor, and Dow Chemical in its total quality management program.

The focus here is on production. Learning is incidental. As a result, the learner's action is to simply perform the real task. This is why the system works.

Knowledge Support Systems

This technology is still in the future. Its seedlings are in the Internet and the World Wide Web, but, as yet, these are merely the seminal germ of the ideal system. The concept is to have a universally accessible knowledge (perhaps skill as well?) base that is accessible at any time by anyone, much as the Internet is now. The difference is that this system would provide virtual reality instruction, Performance Support Systems expert advice and instruction, or merely multimedia instruction upon request. It is envisioned as being "a giant hard disk in the sky" or, perhaps, HAL from the movie *2001*. In this film, the computer, named HAL, acts as an adviser, controller, trainer, playmate, and friend to astronauts in space. It interacts as if it were a person, conversing with the astronauts, joking with them, and, in the end, trying to take over completely.

The Four Main Technologies

Three of the major technologies have already been introduced: virtual reality, computer interaction through CD-ROM, and multimedia production. The fourth one, which has grown out of a different set of technologies, is distance learning. Let us examine each of them.

Virtual Reality

In the summer of 1990 I had an extraordinary experience. I was privileged to sit in and operate a fully functional level II flight simulator. These are the training simulators that professional commercial and private pilots must "fly" at least once a year to maintain their current license. Each is an exact replica of the working cockpit of an aircraft. Every dial, button, lever, light, and seat belt functions, through computer simulation, exactly as it does in the real airplane. The view through the cockpit windows, entirely computer generated, is complete. There is moving traffic on the roadways surrounding the airstrip. Buildings, trees, mountains, and whatever else surrounds the airport in the real world are visible. The sun sets in real-time simulation and lights come on in recognizable buildings. Neon trade names and logos glow in their familiar locations and colors.

As the craft "taxis" down the runway to take off or land, even the bumps in the paved landing strip are simulated, so accurately that La Guardia, in New York City, is much rougher and bumpier than DFW in Dallas, just as it is in the real world. If the pilot or copilot takes his or her foot off the brake with the engines running, the craft creeps ahead, as it would in the real world. Everything is so real that it comes as an uncomfortable shock when one realizes that there is no G-force on turns and no compression to make one's ears pop.

Pilots learn to fly in such simulators. Perhaps more important, they also use them to improve their skills or to practice new or unfamiliar maneuvers. When a major crash occurs, the black box information from the downed aircraft is programmed into the simulators so that pilots can practice avoidance maneuvers in the situation that brought down that plane. Wind sheer is simulated. Cargo doors can be blown off, engines fail, fuel lines break, flaps fail to function, and landing gear refuse to operate. In addition, pilots use these simulators to familiarize themselves with new equipment or to practice take-offs and landings on unfamiliar airstrips.

These are the state of the art in computer simulation. Each costs $8 to $10 million for corporate jets and $20 million or more for the larger commercial jet liners. They are a magnificent and thrilling experience for a trainer. However, even these ultimate simulations require live one-on-one instruction, classroom sessions, and inexpensive (comparatively) noninteractive simulations and visual aids in order to be fully effective as teaching/learning tools. They provide a wonderful application and evaluation loop for learning, but they do not prepare the learner to learn, nor do they present material in a sequence designed to instruct. In fact, because they operate on real-time chronological simulation in actual level flight, they can be rather boring and demotivational. They are only exciting when they present challenges that test what has been learned or existing skills. The excitement is due to the immediate consequences of the "flier's" behavior. The operator learns by making mistakes that cost nothing in a simulator but which would be disastrous in the real world. I have the distinction of having flown harmlessly right *through* the Empire State Building.

Technically speaking, of course, flight simulators are not a complete virtual reality system. The user sits in a real cockpit, unlike the computer-simulated full virtual reality where even the environment is a simulation. But the effect is the same. Because the cost of creating such virtual realities is coming down due to improved microchip performance (currently $30,000 to $100,000), CD-ROM storage, and hard-disk memory, virtual reality simulation training is available for personal computers and uses merely a headset or goggles, rather than a multimillion dollar cubicle. Currently, Motorola is testing VR as a means for training operators on its assembly lines. It has re-created a virtual reality assembly line, complete with sights, sounds, and operations. The results are that the learners want to practice longer, learn faster, and remember better than those in conventional training situations.

CD-ROM Computer-Based Training

One of the best ways of combining instruction with simulated response that I have ever seen is used by another client of mine, one of the originators of computer-simulated learning environments and one of the very few companies today engaged in creating effective CD-ROM programs for training. Thousands of U.S. armed service personnel have been trained to use high-tech weapons systems that use this design. They are trained on a unit that is an exact duplicate of the control system they will use in the field, except that all of the responses are computer-controlled simulations. As in the aircraft simulators, each switch, light, indicator, or screen behaves as if it were real. It responds to whatever commands are given and all of the indicators indicate whatever status changes those commands effect. However, there is one additional monitor included, usually located on top of the control unit the service personnel are learning to use. It is an instructional screen. It provides the preparation and presentation steps to guide the learner when he or she is using the simulated console. Following the instructions from the top screen, the trainee performs the learned sequences of commands. If it is correct, he or she can move on to the next instruction. If it is not, the computer carries out the wrong commands. The errors are acted upon as they would be on the real piece of equipment in the field, so that the learner gets to see what happens when he or she makes a mistake. Then the effects are evaluated and remedial instruction is given before the learner tries again.

This simulated response pattern is not limited only to formats that involve learning to operate systems or pieces of equipment. Using CD-ROM for the action sequences, interactive communication skills can be taught as long as the responses of the learner trigger a playing-out of what happens when that response is given so that both errors and positive reenforcement can be perceived and reacted to in turn by the learner.

In fact, one of the best uses of interactive video I've come across is one used for training salespeople. After instruction and typical "correct response" sequences, the learner is asked whether he or she is confident and ready to use the newly taught response. If the sales trainee chooses no, the unit provides remedial instruction until he or she chooses yes. When the trainee chooses yes, the video shows a full-face view of a "customer" behaving in a way that will set up a situation calling for the newly learned response. For example, the customer objects to purchasing what the salesperson is selling. When the customer is finished objecting, he or she freezes and a video recording camera pointed at the learning salesperson comes on to record the salesperson's live response. Upon completion, the sales trainee can review his or her responses on tape and refine the answer to each of the objections or other problems presented. Ideally, such a system should be reviewed with a coach, trainer, or sales manager, but it can work well with self-review when the salesperson is motivated.

As with all good training, computer-based instruction works best when it is invisible. The computer acts as an aid to instruction when it becomes a tool that the learner can use and control to achieve desired results. Working a flight simulator seems like flying, not learning. Solving a simulated problem is a challenge, not a lesson. Responding skillfully to predictable (and sometimes unpredictable) behavior from others becomes a game, not a test. Those young people who congregate in video arcade parlors would never show up there if they thought they were being given lessons or were learning a skill. Yet they learn lightning-fast reflexes, strategic planning, creative thinking, and possibly several other important skills while believing that they are only having fun. Skilled artisans are frequently completely unaware of the tools they are using, as are most musicians. If a pianist had to worry about the mechanics of how he or she was playing, the music would sound stilted and lose its vitality. Anyone who has ever given his or her child piano lessons knows this. But once the technique becomes invisible, unconscious, internalized, and automatic, real music can be learned and played.

To accomplish this transparency in training, the computer must become a resource for the learner, not an instructional manual. The problem/solution format lends itself powerfully to computer interactive CD-ROM instruction. Perhaps the best model of the kind of learning suited to it is the inexpensive computer game *Where in the World is Carmen Sandiego?*[4] In this game the player, who becomes an international detective, is given a crime to solve, a series of possible procedures to follow, and options to take. The player then uses the computer and the *World Almanac* as data resources in tracking down and apprehending the criminal. The player asks the computer for directions and clues and uses the computer and almanac databases to piece together the criminal activity. The computer provides feedback and further challenges on the correctness of the player's deductions. Instructions are minimal. But the learning of both analytical skills and world facts is tremendous—and fun!

Limitations of Computer-Based Training

In the training/learning universe, computers have both wonderful power and major limitations. They can bring much involvement and interaction into the learning experience. On the other hand, they can easily become demotivational and counterproductive experiences. This is particularly true when they are forced into the uncomfortable role of linear progressive tutorial instruction. Computers, even with interactive CD-ROM simulations, are rather limited when it comes to presenting material to be learned.

The problem stems from the degree and type of interaction the computerized instruction can provide. Reading instructional content and then being asked to choose which of three or four answers is correct based on that material is very tedious for the learner. Indeed, such "page turning" programs are probably even less effective as a training method than straight lectures. These sorts of programs, and the packaged authoring systems available to create them, unfortunately still make up the vast majority of what passes for computer-assisted instruction and interactive videodisk instruction in the marketplace today.

Companies that vend such programs cite research that indeed demonstrates that learners learn more thoroughly, more quickly, and retain their learning longer using the programs. The examples usually cited are drawn from test programs done by the U.S. Army, IBM, Xerox, United Technologies, and Federal Express.[5] They claim to have experienced:

- Learning gains of 56 percent or more as measured by content tests between CBT and classroom training materials.
- Consistency of learning, 50 percent to 60 percent better as based on the learners' understanding of what had been learned on CBT.
- Delivery variance of 20 percent to 40 percent less. All individuals vary in their presentations. The computer never does.
- Compression of 38 percent to 70 percent of learning time. Learners learned the material faster and thus spent less time away from the job.
- Mastery of the material up to 60 percent faster with CBT than in classroom instruction.
- Retention of the material learned with CBT programs 25 percent to 50 percent greater twenty-five to thirty days after training than it was for classroom training.

Although these numbers are impressive, they hide as much or more than they tell. For instance, they give no inkling of what sort of classroom instruction was given. I would agree that almost any form of training would be an improvement over simple lectures.

Furthermore, the workers involved in the CBT training were volunteers who knew they were being studied, wanted to find out how well they could learn using this method, and were generally highly motivated to take part in such a study. We don't even know what it was they were learning—facts? history? skills? Even in Motorola's VR experiment, some credit for its success is because this is a "fun" and exciting technology and, until the user gets used to it, it has a mystical, space-age aura that is highly motivational. When and if it becomes commonplace, it will most likely lose this magical aura and, I suspect, a considerable degree of its effectiveness.

In the field, many clients have told me that they spent a lot of time, money, and effort on interactive CD-ROM programs only to have their employees ignore them or, if forced to use them, fail to learn anything useful from the experience. Many fail to even complete the programs they start. One client, a very large financial firm, held a training fair for its customers, management, and workforce for a full week to demonstrate the resources of the training department to "show off" what these programs could do. For one exhibit, they set up a typical interactive video kiosk and invited participants to experiment with it. In a whole week, only three people (out of hundreds) stopped to play with it and none of them finished a whole fifteen-minute learning segment. There wasn't enough "happening" to hold their interest.

Of course, commercial vendors of such programs jazz them up with color, animation, and sound effects. However, in order to be effective, interactive video must provide at the very minimum some sort of simulated response to the learner's input to the machine. Choosing a true-false or multiple-choice response is inadequate. Choosing to push or touch a button to merely go to the next screen is only marginally better. Only when the response chosen causes a simulated response, even a wrong one (perhaps most especially a wrong one), do you have real interaction. It is the power of the computer to provide such a simulation that allows learning to take place, that intrigues and motivates the learner so that he or she can (and will) desire to learn and retain what has been learned. It is only this kind of simulated practice that makes interactive videodisk instruction an exciting and worthwhile technology. To the extent that such simulated response is limited or missing, the computerization of instruction is largely a waste.

The Three Vital Elements of Effective CBT

According to Gloria Gery, a well-known consultant on computer-based training, "Sustained interest lies in experiencing challenging and complex tasks, having curiosity incited and being able to fulfill that curiosity, being able to see oneself 'learn' and gaining feedback about the skill increases, competition, and 'fantasy' (e.g. role-plays, simulators, etc.). Color, animation, noises and other cute things don't hold attention for very long."[6] She sees the power of the computer made interactive by technology as threefold:

1. Ability to make data and images available randomly
2. Conditional branching of logic
3. Ability to manipulate variables

Let's look at each of these in turn.

Random Accessibility. For training purposes, this means that the computer needs to be programmed to work as our minds work. Data is accessible randomly as needed, not in a linear progressive regimented format, but conceptually. If I need information on the state of training in America today, I go to a database to access it. You access that same database to find out who the five most influential figures in training have been in the past twenty years. The database contains both sets of information at all times, ready for access by any interested seeker at random. This is exactly how our memories work. When I am training trainers I don't think of all that I know about automobiles. But if a memory triggers it, or I need (desire) to know it, my mind instantly jumps to automobiles.

Programmed to act as such a database, the computer becomes the all-knowing servant of the learner. It presents information to the learner *on demand* rather than by imposing a sequential order on the learner. It begins to operate as a very accurate and commodious adjunct to the learner's mind, accessible for instruction as easily and naturally as memory. Anyone who has ever used the "help" menu in learning a new software package is familiar with how natural random accessibility can be (however, how effective it can be is usually not well demonstrated by most sketchily or poorly written "help" instructions). The computer moves forward and backward as the learner needs, jumping from one subject to another connected by no other link than that in the mind of the learner.

Conditional Branching. This is the learning-by-making-mistakes facet of the computer. Its logic is conditional. If you do such and such, the following will occur. Most of us who use computers are familiar with it in the spreadsheet command "If . . . then," which merely means that the machine is programmed to perform a conditional branch—If I do this, then that will happen. It makes the learner responsible for his or her actions, able to see the results of both errors and successes. It allows the learner to experiment, to try other ways of addressing the problem, and to discover, and therefore to *learn*, the best way. It provides the sense of accomplishment that motivates the learner.

Variable Manipulation. The learner can use any tool or instruction available to the computer to address the problem. All variables are under his or her command, including the level of difficulty of the problem if so desired. The flight simulator is the finest example of this. Given the universe of controls, all are accessible to the learner at any time. In addition, various other elements may be chosen, such as weather conditions, type of aircraft, or position from which one views the craft. For those less familiar with computer simulations, it is close to the range of flexibility you have when driving your car. You can control the speed, temperature, seat adjustments, and sound. Given that universe, you have control of the variables to combine them in a way that pleases or benefits you.

It is the presence of these three elements that makes virtual reality such a major improvement over other forms of CBT. To the extent that the computer-based training you are evaluating or creating has these three elements and uses them, it will also have the potential to be an effective learning tool. To the extent that it lacks them, it will be potentially demotivational. Although self-motivated people may be able to learn well using it, it will also be difficult to integrate successfully into your other training efforts.

Multimedia

Multimedia are really glorified slides and/or overhead projections. As a means of instruction, multimedia provides and enhances the same benefits and incorporates the same drawbacks. Plus it is quite a bit more expensive.

The main educational benefit derived from multimedia is that it involves several senses of the learner rather than just one. For example, I have prepared a set of multimedia screens that contain a cockatoo that flies onto the projection accompanied by a flurry of music and then flies off again. It wakes up learners, startles them with delight, and so helps to hold their interest and attention. But it has absolutely nothing to do with the lesson I use it in. In fact, I would be hard-pressed to find a lesson topic in which I could use such a thing as a flying cockatoo. I use it only to illustrate the potential and the pitfalls of bells and whistles in training.

We are in the business of creating learning environments. Therefore, a multimedia format unquestionably creates a professional, well-prepared, and state-of-the-art environment. It is useful at this level. But apart from this public relations window-dressing function, albeit it is a valuable one, I don't see it particularly enhancing what is learned. This is particularly true when, in order to project the computer screen successfully onto a screen, the room must be darkened in order to bring out the full impact of the colors. Ask yourself, "Why is this material best presented in a darkened room?" If there is a good answer, then this is a good medium to use. If there isn't, then rethink the validity of using multimedia this way.

Of course, there are now on the market projectors that will throw your laptop screen up on a giant screen directly without the use of an overhead projector. These work much the same way that a slide projector does, and the colors that they project are much purer, brighter, and more attractive than those shown with a conventional overhead projector and LCD panel combination. The room doesn't even have to be dimmed. The problem is that these projectors currently cost $4,000 each and, therefore, are somewhat prohibitive. This is especially true when you consider that the minimal level of sophistication required in a computer to do multimedia is a $3,000 machine. There is some relief if you train in fairly small groups. There is an adapter for around $100 that will allow you to display your computer output on any video screen. This allows full video color in any light. It does, however, limit you to the size of your television monitor.

Distance Learning

One of my clients, the United Nations Development Fund (UNDP), operates in 147 countries. Training has been traditionally performed at world headquarters in New York City. The costs of bringing people from all over the world to New York are prohibitive. The UNDP is currently exploring distance learning as an alternative. Distance learning is not really a new technology. It grew out of efforts in the late 1950s and early 1960s in Canada to bring education and medical services to remote areas in the far north. Using satellite technology, a television signal can be beamed to any receiver anywhere in the world. When each station sends and receives, we have teleconferencing. When the content of the conference is training (or teaching), it is called distance learning. This technique has been used by the U.S. Army since the 1970s. What makes it exciting today is that the technology has grown to such a level that it is easily affordable, and with the help of the Internet, it is fast becoming ubiquitous.

More than 200 colleges in the United States now offer degree studies through distance learning. An unknown number of high schools offer such programs. School systems throughout the nation (and perhaps the world) have distance learning facilities for uplinking and downlinking lessons. Diverse organizations such as the Smithsonian Institute, Walt Disney, Public Broadcasting Systems, and a host of private concerns all offer distance-learning classes for a fee. For a mere fraction of the cost of traveling to a location for a seminar, anyone can enroll and, using their local community college or even high school facility, participate in a class being conducted on the other side of the continent. With this much interest in the public sector, more and more private training departments are considering the cost savings and exploring distance learning.

Pros and Cons of Distance Learning. Although there is considerable expense in equipment and satellite-time leasing as well as complex administration, distance learning can be a great savings over travel costs for an entire class of learners attending training at a single location. The principal limitation of distance learning is equally obvious. Talking heads on a video screen are extremely dull and constitute long-distance lecturing, a notoriously poor way to facilitate learning. Cost savings are not effective if the quality of the learning deteriorates because of the medium of instruction.

Distance learning, however, doesn't have to be just talking heads. If the video image and sound are two-way for both the instructors and the learners, a sense of community and Socratic discussion is possible. Add personal computer terminals for each participant, all linked through the satellite or Internet in a private chat room, and you have the makings of quite a dynamic interaction. If the video screens are split to carry both the live, real-time, full-animation image and the computer input/output simultaneously, it is possible to carry on small group discussions, full class discussions and individual instruction as needed. Finally, if you add coordinated case studies, perhaps as simulations or even in virtual reality for each learner to work with between central distance-learning sessions, you have a full spectrum of viable training. To the extent any of these elements is missing, of course, the quality of training will suffer.

The technology is currently available and will only become more accessible at increasingly less cost. The key to the effectiveness of distance learning lies in ensuring that the training that gets done still follows the rules and guidelines of effective learning that are outlined in the first three chapters of this book. Obviously, considerable planning and coordination need to precede any instruction in distance-learning format. Materials have to be prepared for this medium and distributed. People, space, equipment, and time need to be scheduled. To maintain efficiency, distance learning needs to be set up to take advantage of short, less expensive video-interactive sessions with longer Internet-interactive sessions and still longer assigned project work on personal computers.

The Social Nature of Learning

Some detractors say, "Why bother with the video at all? If people network by computer, isn't that enough?" To some extent they are right. After all, we've had the option of learning by correspondence courses since the beginning of the twentieth century. Many people have taken and continue to take advantage of learning this way; but more do not. The answer lies in the social nature of learning.

This is the core problem with all technology as training media. Each technology inserts itself as one more remove between the learner and the trainer. Learning, as we've seen, does not take place effectively in isolation. It is a group, a social process, and people must interact with each other in order to fully and correctly master material that is learned. We must all join the great dialogue. This is even more true if you train people from highly discursive cultures like France, the Mediterranean, or Latin America. Time to talk and interact is essential. It is frequently when we learn most through the sharing and interaction with others.

Therefore, to the extent that a medium or technology removes a piece of this interaction, it risks producing a lesser level of learning. Results may still look good, as in all of the studies on computer-based training we alluded to earlier, but part of what makes these successful is the sharing of the results; the discussing and exploring of the programs among the learners. Even the best virtual reality programs include, where appropriate, human speech when it would most likely be encountered. The social facilitation theory of group dynamics still holds true; people perform better with others around than they do alone.[7]

Guidelines for Using Training Technology

The danger in incorporating the latest technologies into your training is that, in order to cut training costs and take advantage of quicker learning curves, the personal sense of learning and interaction will be lost and the overall quality of your training will decline. There are two safeguards:

1. Remember that we learn what we *do*, what we perform.
2. We learn best with others in a social context.

If your technology enhances these two prime factors, keep it. It is good. If it hinders or diminishes them in any way, either compensate by adding these dimensions to some part of the training or eliminate the technology. If the technology takes these two principles away or makes them very hard to achieve, eliminate the technology.

There are several things you can do to restore and integrate hands-on activity and social process into new technologies. First, realize that the more generic a computer-based training program or distance-learning package you wish to use is, the more difficult it will be to apply to the job and fit into the rest of your training thrust. This is a cost trade-off. The generic programs are much less expensive because they can take advantage of economies of scale to lower their price. However, as in most areas, you get what you pay for. The trade-off is in the effectiveness of the training, the amount of hands-on activity, and the amount and quality of interaction allowed.

At the minimal level, as a second option, you can create discussion groups among those who are taking the computer-based or distance-learning course. If they are at one physical location, these sessions could be an open forum for sharing techniques and insights and discussing specific job applications for the material learned. If the trainees are located in many areas, use the Internet and private chat groups to facilitate such meetings. By holding these sessions at least once or twice a week you create an incentive for learners to keep up in much the same way that college classes do. Such groups might even be modeled on the common personal computer user groups that share information informally through E-mail or the Internet. Specific topics or skills could be assigned and shared and even discussed using electronic mail. The point here is to provide feedback and a forum outside of the computer-based program or distance format that allows learners to make the content specific for themselves.

Perhaps the simplest approach is a combination of generic with tailored portions or supplements. This is your third option. The least costly and easiest level of supplement would be to create a series of job-specific exercises or live simulations, which would correspond to key content and instructional levels in the generic computer program. Then, as the trainees complete each such unit, they can be given an additional simulation or test that requires them to apply what they've learned to their real-world jobs. In fact, this step could be combined with the second option of discussion groups and made into group projects to further facilitate the learning process and counter the demotivational aspects of the generic computer-based program.

If you have the time, staff, or expertise, the fourth option is a logical outgrowth of the third. You can create and program (or hire a consultant to do so) a series of job-specific application simulations to replace or supplement the ones in the generic package. Because of their job specificity, you would invariably also be improving on them—particularly if you incorporate Gloria Gery's three crucial elements: randomly accessible data, conditional branching formats, and a set of variables controlled by the learner.

The final option is to take the fourth one all the way and write the full computer-based training program yourself. I don't necessarily mean that you should become a computer programmer, however. One of the problems that makes the vast majority of commercially available CBT or distance-learning programs less effective than most of us would like is that they have been created by experts in computer programming, marketing, artificial intelligence, distance-learning technology, or virtual reality with experts in education sometimes used as consultants. Their work shows their orientation. The programs look great but train less than effectively. In the few instances where vending organizations are driven, not even by educators, but by *trainers*, the difference is striking.

When trainers run the creation of such programs, the programs become results-oriented, skills-oriented, learner-friendly, and much, much more effective. The technology is subservient to the training objectives. Anything less than this, to the extent that it is so, is inadequate. A training consultant can do this for you, but an even surer bet is to do it yourself if you can. You don't have to be a computer programmer or satellite expert, but you will need to plan your program in precise detail so the internal or external computer programmers and distance-learning purveyors you use will give you exactly what you want.

Writing Your Own Program

Unless you are a designer of computer languages or a highly skilled computer programmer, don't tackle the programming phase of CBT design. Follow the outline given here to create the instructional modules and computer guidelines; then seek a computer pro to create the program for you. The same planning format will apply even to virtual reality programs if you choose to do them.

CBT and Distance-Learning Options

- Select the least generic program you can find.
- Create discussion groups or personal interaction sessions to foster the exchange of techniques and approaches. These could be modeled along the line of computer user groups.
- Supplement company-specific exercises and/or simulations at the end of key instructional units in order to facilitate the transfer of learning to the job.
- Create CBT units that combine the generic material with your organization-specific content in order to help learners translate what they have learned to their job concerns.
- Develop your own computer-based programs.

There are two types of computer-based instruction. The first is computer-aided instruction, in which the computer actually instructs and the learner interacts with the computer. The second is computer-managed instruction, in which the computer directs the learner to perform specific tasks, such as to read a chapter of a book, perform several steps on a machine, or solve a set of problems. Upon completion of the task, the computer tests the learner as to what has been learned. If the CBT is in interactive format, the test will be a simulation. Otherwise, the test will be in some type of question-and-answer format. Depending on the answers, the computer either directs the learner to remedial work or moves on to the next level.

The latter format, computer-managed instruction, requires a resource library of structured tasks to which the learner can be directed (which doesn't really have to be assigned by the computer but can also be included in the program as one or more databases), a series of tests or activities that demand the learner use that material, and one or more remediation programs.

Computer-Managed Instruction

To create such a program, you need three items:

1. *An organized, progressive set of reference materials and/or tasks to be assigned to the trainee.* These tasks should be structured from least to most difficult in an inverted funnel pattern (see Chapter 2), in much the same way mathematics is taught in school: simple arithmetic to algebra and up through advanced calculus. These can be programmed into the computer as databases or can be separate

from your program to be assigned to the learner to access on his or her own in order to complete the computer-assigned tasks.

2. *A series of tests (see Chapter 5) administered by the computer.* It asks a question; the trainee answers. The computer asks the next question, and so forth. Upon completion, the computer gives the learner the score and offers advice on remedial work to improve it. Interactive programming improves on this format by presenting the learner with a series of events he or she must respond to appropriately.

3. *A remedial program that can be planned by following the response analysis format covered later in this chapter.* Such a program, relatively easy to build, is most useful where you have only one or two trainees at a time and when you have the necessary resource materials available to them.

Computer-Aided Instruction

This program involves four principles of good lesson design (see Chapter 2):

1. It requires clear-cut objectives.
2. It requires trainees to be active.
3. It allows trainees to check themselves for corrections and relevance (they can make errors).
4. It allows trainees to develop mastery of the subject.

To create a program, begin with a very detailed task analysis (see Chapter 6). To review, there are four basic steps:

1. Acquire or write an accurate job description.
2. Break the job down into separate tasks. That is, what are the various things someone with this job would do? A task is defined as having a clear beginning, a discernible end, and a product or result.
3. Break each of these tasks down into the steps that must be performed to accomplish that part of the job.
4. Break each step down into all the substeps or individual actions that go into completing the task.

Using the task analysis and your training objectives, plan a series of learning modules or lesson plans following these six steps:

1. *Select tests for each topic (task) module.* That is, write a simulated task or test by which you will measure whether the trainee has learned a particular task (not the substeps, yet).

2. *Outline the steps to mastery for the task.* For each step, create an activity or test that demands the learner use the material covered in that step. This activity frame or test is the climax of a learning unit. Each unit instructs and then tests the mastery of each substep leading to the performance of the task. Each such unit consists of a set of instructions (how-to's or explanations) called an *instructional frame;* a series of problems to solve based on the instructions with coaching or prompting from the computer, called a *practice frame*; and a minitest question or problem activity, which is not prompted by the computer.

3. *Each unit is a miniature lesson plan.* It follows the four-step method (see Chapter 1) by preparing the trainee to learn, presenting the material to be learned, providing skills-building practice, and evaluating how well the trainee has learned the material.

4. *Enlarge the unit patterns by writing out the instruction steps.* Write them out in full and verify (with others) that they are clear and comprehensible. Then, based on this *instructional frame*, devise one, two, or more problems (depending on complexity), with hints or prompts and directions to help the trainee solve the problem. Each problem is a *practice frame*. Here, you might also write in praise for correct answers. These problems can be dialogues performed by your actors, animated sequences, or activities simulated on the screen.

5. *Set up a series of units like beads on a string (subtask units).* That is, write a brief statement of what will be learned. Then plug in Unit 1, which, as we've seen, consists of an instruction frame, practice frames, and one test frame. Next come Units 2, 3, and so on, up to Unit 6 (or until the complete subtask is learned). More than six units usually requires more strings of learning units. At this point, write a culminating simulation or posttest drawn from materials covered in all units. What you have at this point is each task broken into subtasks or steps, and each step broken into learning units (see Figure 10-1). Upon completion of each unit, the trainee is tested for mastery, is challenged to use what he or she has learned. Upon completion of each step (string of subtask units), the trainee is again tested for mastery. Upon completion of instruction for each task (all the subtasks making up the task), the trainee is tested with the original test devised in the first step above. It is passing this simulation or test that your lesson unit has been written to achieve.

6. *Go back over the entire string.* For each test frame, create a series of remedial instruction frames and practice frames leading back to the test frame again. This is, of course, only for those who got the test frame wrong and need extra practice or instruction. Until they get the test frame right, they cannot progress to the next unit.

You now have a self-paced instruction program, but you still must get it into the computer. To ensure that the programmer produces your instructional package in a workable form, he or she will need the following documents: mainline

Figure 10-1. A learning module in computer-based instruction.

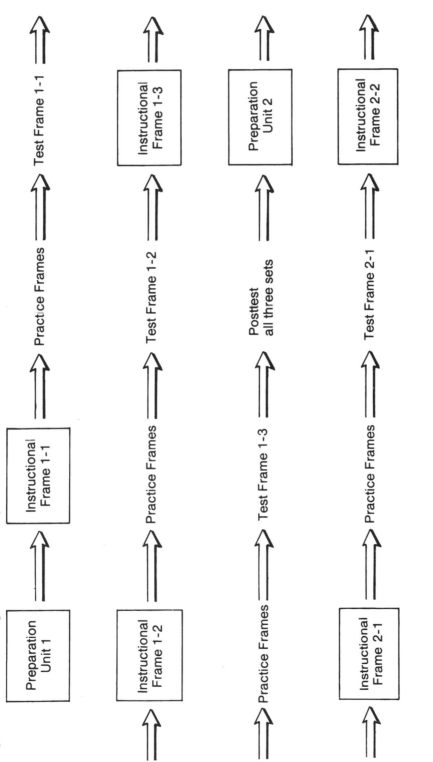

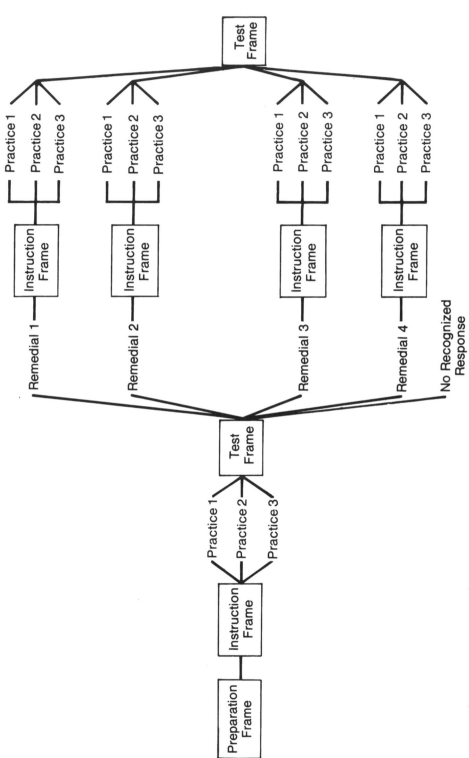

Figure 10-2. Flowchart for computer-based instruction.

chart, flowchart, response analysis form, and screen layout form. Let's look at each in turn:

- *Mainline chart.* Essentially this is the same as the string of units you've just created. Add to it reference material (so you will have it documented for future use) if applicable, and give tentative suggestions for where screen changes should come.

- *Flowchart.* This lays out the program. It allows both you and the programmer to keep track of the remedial units (which will stack; see Figure 10-2). This should be kept as simple as possible.

- *Response analysis form.* This is a breakdown of each frame and all of the allowable (predictable) responses, plus what the programmer must program the computer to do (see Figure 10-3). The response analysis form must do this for every practice frame and every test frame.

- *Screen layout form.* To ensure that the program does what you want it to, use the discussion from your tentative screen requests in the mainline chart and type out an exact copy of what you want each screen to look like. Use one separate page for each screen layout. If you are shooting video action or animation, this step is called a storyboard. Every screen, every event should be sketched in this manner so the professionals who actually shoot or draw your material will know how you want it to look.

Armed with these four forms, your programmer can provide you with the CBT package you've designed.

Figure 10-3. Response analysis form.

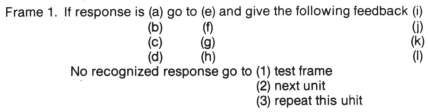

Frame 1. If response is (a) go to (e) and give the following feedback (i)
(b)   (f)   (j)
(c)   (g)   (k)
(d)   (h)   (l)
No recognized response go to (1) test frame
(2) next unit
(3) repeat this uhit

Summary

In this chapter we have looked at the growth and recent development of state-of-the-art technology in training. We have defined each of the stages that make up the evolution of technology and examined some of the state-of-the-art applications and also some of their major limitations. The four main hot technologies are virtual reality, computer-based training, multimedia presentations, and distance learning. We explored each of these, what it does, and how best to use it. In order to counter limitations, we examined the elements that make each technology effective, in particular, what happens when the technology incorporates random accessibility to data, conditional branching of the process, and manipulable variables.

Integration of these principles was examined, and we discussed ways in which you can make generic technology much more useful and viable for your trainees. The last of these is to write your own program. Of course, there is no intent here to make you a computer programmer, but, as a trainer, you can work closely with your own programmer to create excellent CBT, or even virtual reality. The steps for drawing up the necessary documentation to enable a programmer to develop CBT for you were also covered.

Applications

1. Find and explore a virtual reality program. A simple flight simulator will do, but an action-packed CD-ROM is better. If possible, try out a virtual reality headset. These are available for sale in toy stores and computer stores. They are also available to the public at the EPCOT Center at Disney World in Florida, and perhaps in some video arcades. As you experience it, make a list of at least six applications for your training that could benefit from this technology. (Note: you may have trouble coming up with six applications. This is part of the limitation of the technology.)

2. Attend a public seminar that will be using multimedia projections. Talk to the instructor about the medium. Ask yourself if, indeed, they are more than mere bells and whistles. List what benefits they may bring to your training. Explore software to develop multimedia presentations yourself. (They are fun to create.)

3. Following the diagrams and instructions at the end of the chapter, write a CBT lesson. Add a storyboard for animated or video graphics interface.

4. Contact your local school library or college library and arrange to sit in on a distance-learning session. Draw up a list of potential applications for such training in your organization. Draw up another list of ways to keep the training active and social.

Chapter 11

Setting the Physical Environment

I HAVE stressed that one of the keys to effective training is a positive learning environment. Although the physical situation doesn't teach us, it makes it easier or harder to learn. As a trainer you need to look at ways of making learning easier by managing the physical setting.

Comfort Factors

If your trainees are comfortable, they will be able to concentrate on what you are teaching them. Let's consider the five comfort factors:

1. *Temperature.* Few things kill a seminar faster than a room that is either too hot or too cold. If it is too hot, participants fight to stay awake. Even if your lesson is dynamic enough to keep them awake, they have to work at concentrating, so they miss vital points, are exhausted much too early, and generally feel dissatisfied with the training. A room that is too cold, on the other hand, keeps everyone awake but distracts terribly from the material at hand. People are too uncomfortable to learn. It has been found that 72° Fahrenheit is the optimum temperature for a training room in northern and temperate climates while 74° is most comfortable for those who live in warmer climates. The closer you are to these thermostat settings, the more comfortable participants will be.

2. *Chairs.* If you have ever attended a seminar where you had to sit on hard, wooden-slat folding chairs, you know how distracting it can be. Use the most comfortable chairs available, short of lounge chairs.

3. *Lighting.* A dingy room throws a pall over your training. Participants must always be able to see you, your visual aids, and their notes clearly and comfort-

ably, without effort. A room can be lit dramatically for effect, but participants still need to see those three elements. Be sure the lighting is sufficient before you begin your program. If necessary, bring in extra lights.

4. *Writing and work space.* A steady surface is a must for each trainee, so he or she can take notes. If you need to use an auditorium with chairs but no foldaway writing arms, make the sessions shorter. Most people can't remember a day's worth of instruction without notes to remind them; make it easy for them to take notes. If you are training in technical skills, each trainee must likewise have sufficient workspace to enable him or her to practice the skills and assignments you will be giving.

5. *Sightlines.* When a participant can't see you or your visual aids, he or she will move or shift to one side, or squint to see better—once, usually twice, sometimes three times. Each time, the person tries a little less than before, and after that, he or she simply gives up. You've lost a listener. Check the entire room before your program to be sure no one has even a partially blocked view. If there are such blocked views, correct them or suggest no one take those seats.

These five considerations are the basics, regardless of what you are teaching, where you are teaching, or whom you are teaching. Take care of these and you'll have an environment where learning can take place.

Room Setups

The seating arrangement of a room may vary, depending on the purpose of the training. Figures 11-1 and 11-2 show the most common ones.

Classroom Arrangements

Aptly named, these seating arrangements are formal settings familiar from school days. In the straight classroom arrangement, the tables or desks with chairs are in neat rows in front or alongside one another. There can be individual desks or tables seating two or more people. Usually there are aisles between the rows (see Figure 11-1). The classroom arrangement has one strong advantage. Because it is formal and isolates each participant, it is the most authoritative setup for training. This is especially so when you use a raised platform or stage at the front of the room. If you need this authority, the classroom style will help. In addition, you might need to use the classroom style if you have a large group. For example, I use it whenever I have a group of more than sixty or seventy people. It lends itself well to a blank-slate delivery.

The drawbacks of the classroom arrangement are strong, however. It creates

Figure 11-1. Classroom-style seating arrangements.

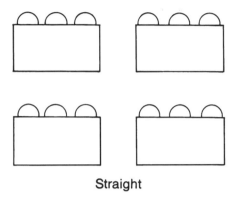

Straight

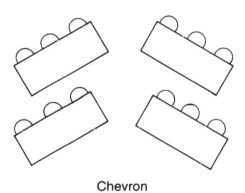

Chevron

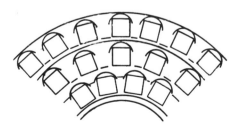

Theater

Figure 11-2. Other common seating arrangements.

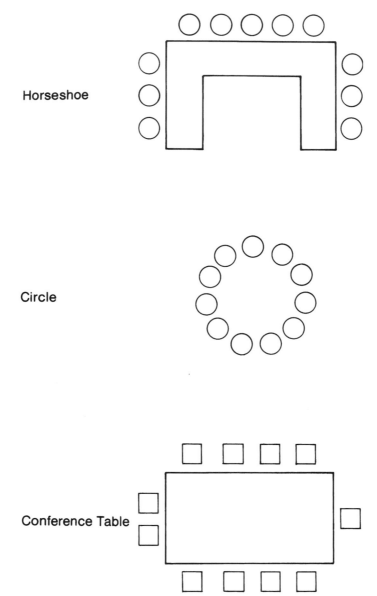

Horseshoe

Circle

Conference Table

a "school" environment, and unless your trainees loved school, this will be a negative. Soften the arrangement by using a chevron effect, whereby tables are slanted at an angle toward the center aisle (see Figure 11-1). Or use a theater, where everyone sits in anchored seats, raked so that everyone can see clearly (see Figure 11-1). But even these modifications do not break the isolation and formality of this setup. Each participant sees only you and the back of other heads. There is little chance and no inducement to interact with others. Use the classroom setup for large groups and when you need extra authority, but when you can, soften it with a chevron arrangement.

Horseshoe Arrangement

Any arrangement that seats participants at tables along both sides and across the back while leaving the front and center areas open for the trainer is usually referred to as a horseshoe. This is true whether the configuration is rounded or squared (see Figure 11-2). The horseshoe setup is excellent for demonstrations and role-playing. It has excellent sightlines and, because participants face each other, it fosters good interaction. Furthermore, participants can be broken into teams readily, and you have easy access to each participant. For these reasons, it is one of the most common training arrangements.

There are, however, some drawbacks to the horseshoe. First, the number of people it accommodates is limited. Twenty people is usually the maximum, although it can be pushed to thirty. After that, the horseshoe becomes too crowded and unwieldy. Second, participants really only interact with the two-thirds of the group they are facing. The closest people to them—those on the same side of the horseshoe—seldom get to see one another or interact. Third, if you work your way closer into the central area, you lose those trainees sitting on the ends. If you use this arrangement, make an effort always to include the end people.

Circle Arrangement

The circle setup is simply a circular grouping of desks, tables, or chairs (see Figure 11-2). The advantage of the circle is that it has the lowest authority position. If you want to encourage low-key participative leadership, the circle works well. If you still want some formality, use desks in a circle or a large round table. If you want complete informality, have just chairs. In other respects, the circle has almost the same advantages and limitations as the horseshoe. One word of caution, though; if you are working inside the circle or doing role-playing or demonstrations within it, take care to move around so no one is excluded. In the circle, there can be no "front of the room" for focus.

Conference Table Arrangement

We are all familiar with the rectangular conference table (see Figure 11–2). Perhaps the greatest asset of a conference table is its flexibility. It can be formal and authoritative when you sit at the head, or informal when you sit to one side. It allows you to use visual aids, yet keeps a feeling of intimacy among the group.

The major drawback of a conference table is its size. Few tables are workable with more than twelve people seated at them. In addition, conference tables are not particularly useful for role-playing, although they do foster discussion.

Team-Style Arrangements

I use team-style arrangements a great deal. Participants are seated at tables in groups of from four to eight. Tables can be round, square, or oblong and can be arranged casually or formally around the room (see Figure 11-3). There are several distinct advantages in these arrangements. First, the team-style arrangement is the least threatening environment for trainees. It creates small, intimate groups and makes no demand for interaction with the whole group. At the same time, it doesn't leave participants feeling isolated because it demands engagement within the group at each table. Second, from the trainer's point of view, it quickly fosters group spirit and encourages a relaxed atmosphere. It is very "unschool-like," yet formal enough to allow for strong leadership. Third, the arrangement provides ready-made teams for projects, and instills those projects with a pleasant degree of team competitiveness. In short, the team-style arrangement makes a pleasant yet businesslike atmosphere in which to conduct training.

There are several disadvantages, however. Size is a major consideration. I've handled sixty-five in one of these arrangements, but that is too large a group. You tend to lose the tables farthest away. The optimum number is about thirty to thirty-five people. Another possible problem is sightlines. Using square tables in a horseshoe arrangement, for example, puts the people in the middle with their backs to the trainer. It is possible for them to sit sideways, but without swivel chairs (say, in a hotel setting) it is awkward. If using round tables (usually available in hotels), everyone has to crowd together at one side of the table. Putting fewer participants at each table helps, of course.

I occasionally hear people in my team-style setups voice a desire to get to know others in different groups. You can help participants accomplish this by shifting the tables and the groups each day or each time period.

Workstations

Many trainers instructing machine operators and computer workers choose to seat participants at workstations. This arrangement is similar to school science

Figure 11-3. Team-style seating arrangements.

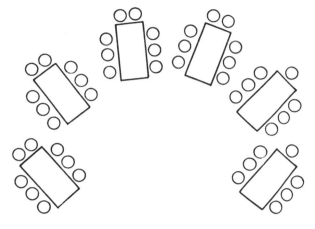

Horseshoe

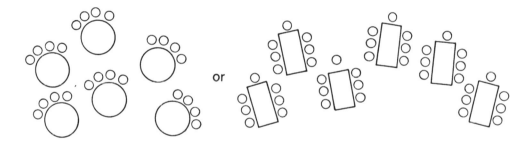

Random

labs, where each person has his or her own workstation to perform what is being taught (see Figure 11-4). Of course, the advantage of a workstation is the hands-on involvement it promotes. There are two problems: First, the arrangement usually is very expensive, so only small groups can be trained. Second, it leaves the individual working alone. An answer is to combine both problems for a single solution: Train groups of two or three people simultaneously. This approach achieves the feeling of group participation and accommodates more trainees; however, some hands-on opportunity is lost and it requires tighter task-scheduling.

The tradition is a classroom arrangement for workstations, but it needn't be for your training program. To have access to everyone's workstation, arrange the

Figure 11-4. Workstations.

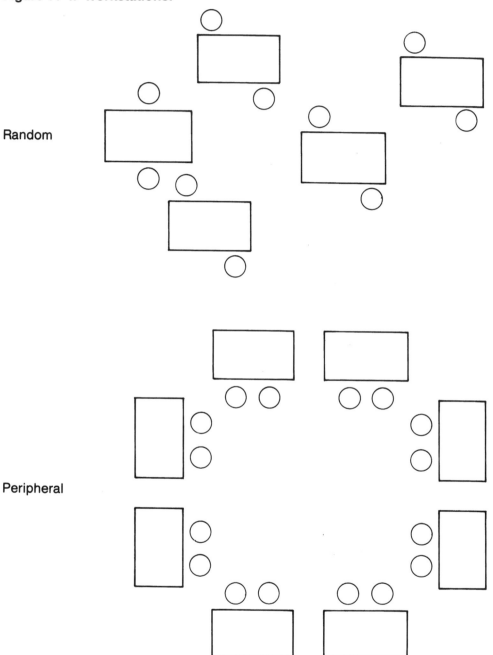

units around three or four walls, with you in the middle. Team feeling can be fostered by putting several units in a group or cluster. Finally, if there are several units or pieces of equipment to learn, use a sequential setup and rotate different teams working on different units at any one time.

Designing and Equipping a Training Room

We don't, unfortunately, often have the luxury of being able to design our own training facility. Sometimes, however, we do get that chance—or at least get an opportunity to redecorate one. Let's look at some prime considerations.

Design

Architects are not trainers. Even if your input is sought, it has been my experience that an architect will design a beautiful building, not a training facility. This is not to complain about architects; they are hired to create beautiful buildings, and they do so very well. But architects simply are not usually knowledgeable about training needs so their thinking is spatial and conceptual, not necessarily practical.

If you are given the opportunity, or have the political clout, insist upon working with the architect. Pay frequent visits to the construction site as your facility takes shape. Remember that you will have to live for a long time with whatever they build. Be sure they get it right. This is the case whether the company is building you a new complex or is remodeling or redecorating your existing facility. You are responsible for the effectiveness the facility will have. Work to make it right.

In the beginning of the chapter we discussed the importance of proper temperature in the training room. In your new facility, make sure each room has individual temperature control. You want a temperature control system with a maximum two-degree variation. That means that with the thermostat set at 72°F, the heat comes on at 70°F and turns off at 74°F (or the air-conditioning comes on when the temperature reaches that point).

If you have a say in design, go for broad rooms. Long and narrow ones feel constrictive. Unless you have very large groups or need them for other purposes, avoid amphitheaters and formal theater seating with a raised stage. Rooms need to be large enough to accommodate your largest training classes with several smaller breakout rooms located nearby. Flexible space is a consideration, too, but be sure you have fully soundproof dividers between seminar rooms. Breakout rooms could have half walls and could be *in* the seminar room, but that can create scheduling problems. Few things are more difficult than trying to teach when loud neighbors overwhelm your every word.

Be sure there is adequate power to run all conceivable audiovisual configurations. Locate controls at the front of the room, where you will have easy access to them. These controls should include a dimmer switch for the lights, remote controls for projectors, projector screen controls, audio system controls, microphone and sound system controls (if you use them), and video controls if you use a permanent installation such as a big-screen projector. Plan outlets, switches, and controls for your convenience, not to make the electrician's job easier. If your use of audiovisuals is extensive, consider creating an audiovisual station. Traditionally, projectors occupy a separate cubicle at the rear of the room. These are nice, but consider a modular unit (all electronics on one stand) that is self-contained and movable, or set up a central control room for all your audiovisuals except flip charts, overheads, and models. This means extra staff to work the room, but in a large organization, with several seminars going on at one time, a central control room with individual controls for slides, film, and video makes sense.

Put everything on videotape and use a large-screen video projector. The airlines use this approach with the projector attached to the cabin ceiling. If you do a lot of videotaping, consider installing a hidden or a remote-control camera to sidestep the participants' inhibitions about being taped. Whatever you decide, remember to allow for the convenient and safe storage of audiovisual equipment.

Provide for bright lighting (fluorescent is fine), with dimming capability for showing slides and films. Having some indirect incandescent lights to supplement is useful. What you want, however, is universal bright light throughout the room.

Windows, while nice, are distractions in a training room. You have better control of the lighting and of the trainees' attention without them. However, the absence of natural light for long periods can get depressing, so be sure there are windows in areas used for breaks or lunch.

As to room color, cool pastels are best. You and your materials should stand out, not the room decor. Grays, browns, creams, and perhaps pale greens could be used as a base color, with creams, pale oranges, yellows, or blues as highlights. Dark blue is very formal and authoritative, and could be used if that is your message. Gray is a very neutral color, associated with work. Brown is a warm color, and cream is neutral. Lastly, carpeted floors add a warm and comfortable touch while keeping noise to a minimum.

Furniture and Equipment

The importance of comfortable chairs was discussed earlier. The chairs you choose should swivel, tilt if possible, and be on wheels. The seats should be padded and textured for comfort. There should also be padded, comfortable arms. Lumbar support is excellent; height adjustment is a plus.

Tables should be designed for flexible use. They can be permanent rather than folding, but should have a drop leaf that lets you change them from narrow to wide. Tables should be rectangular, but able to be made into square or near-square configurations by extending one or both of the leaves and joining two tables together. They should also have a modesty panel across one long side.

Install an accurate wall clock on the back wall of each room, not in the front. You need to be able to see the time; your trainees don't.

Avoid artwork on the walls, but if you plan to use posters or to post sheets from your flip charts, cover the walls in a material that makes posting easier. The best is to run a two-inch-wide metal strip around the room within easy reach but above head level (say, six feet from the floor). Use magnetic vinyl strips to post anything you want.

Choose your audiovisual aids and other equipment with care. If you use whiteboards and chalkboards, get those on wheels so they are more flexible and you won't have to turn your back to use them.

See Chapter 9 for planning and purchasing audiovisuals. Minimally, you should have the following:

- At least two sturdy flip-chart easels and a selection of markers for your charts
- One overhead projector with scrolling attachment, pens for the overhead, and a stand, cart, or table for the projector
- A projection screen of sufficient size to be seen clearly from anywhere in the room
- A table (not a lectern) for your notes, supplies, and computer.

In addition, I recommend an electric projection screen (instead of the standard folding one) and a multimedia projector that allows you to project computer images onto a screen. You can use either the type that sits on top of your regular overhead projector, the type that projects directly (the most expensive, but also the best), or the type that displays your computer screen on a television monitor (the least expensive).

You will also need a complete videotaping package, including a camera, recorder (half-inch), monitor, microphone, necessary hookups, a cart or rack, and a tripod for the camera. If possible, get a second viewing unit with another monitor, tape player (recorder), hookups, and cart or rack. (See Chapter 9 for details.)

Beyond these minimums, however, you will want to purchase any other special equipment you favor. Obviously, if you don't like flip charts and prefer whiteboards, then substitute one for the other. If you train on computers, clearly you need one for each workstation. If you train *only* on computers, you probably won't need the video equipment but instead should consider a multimedia projection device that lets you project any computer screen in the room (including your own) onto a large screen in the front of the room.

Finally, be sure you have cupboard and shelf space for supplies like paper and pencils, handouts, and name cards. If you serve refreshments, have a table for them. If your trainees come from outdoors, have a closet either in the training room or just outside it. At the very least, provide a coatrack.

Multiuse Facilities

It would be nice if we could reserve our training rooms exclusively for our training programs. In the real world, however, this is not always possible. If you use rooms that are also used for other functions by other people, there are four considerations that might help you:

1. If you have input into the design or redecoration of the room, insist upon a closet for overnight storage of equipment. If possible, try for permanent storage space in the room.

2. Institute a monthly scheduling system for room use. Post the schedule outside the room and keep it up-to-date.

3. Reserve your room times early. If someone else wants the room and you can make other arrangements, make it a fair trade. In return, get other time you need. When people have to pay a price, they ask for fewer favors. Remember, however, that the room impacts heavily on trainees. Don't give up your time if the alternatives are not sound for training.

4. Always leave the room clean. Come early to be sure it is clean. Set it up the way you want it; don't assume cleaning personnel will do it. If need be, offer the cleaning people some small consideration to guarantee the room is immaculate when you want it.

In regard to the last item, a small gift at Christmas (for example, a bottle of cologne or liquor or several bars of nice soap) or an occasional lunch is usually enough to ensure cooperation, even special treatment, from maintenance staff. Be careful to make it appear as a grateful thank-you, not a bribe. Of course, what you give and how you give it depends on the people involved. Consider them, and be prepared to reward them for extra service.

Breaks and Meals

People cannot sit still and learn indefinitely. We talk about the need for breaks in Chapter 7, and now we discuss what to serve on those breaks. Heavy foods, high in protein and fats, are fillers. They do not energize us; they make us complacent and sleepy. Carbohydrates and sugars give energy, but only temporarily. For seminars, a temporary lift is excellent. The following suggestions should keep your trainees bright and active throughout the day:

- *Preseminar.* Coffee (regular and decaffeinated), tea, and hot cocoa are highly recommended. Fruit juices are an excellent plus. Fresh fruit is great, too (sliced is better than whole). Assorted danishes and doughnuts are good lifters but not as good as fruit.

- *Morning break.* Refill coffee (regular and decaffeinated) and tea, and provide more fresh fruit.

- *Lunch.* Light seafoods and salads are best. Cold cuts and cheese rank second, followed by sandwiches. Chicken is next best, then soups and stews. Avoid beef, pork, and other heavy meat dishes. Avoid pasta (except in cold salads), baked potatoes, and other heavy starches. Avoid heavy desserts like pies and puddings. Fresh or stewed fruit, cake, cookies, or tarts are possible.

- *Afternoon break.* Coffee (regular and decaffeinated), tea, and cold soda—especially diet soda—make good afternoon refreshers. Many appreciate bottled spring water as well. One of my clients serves an assortment of cheese and crackers. These make an excellent afternoon snack.

Off-Site Facilities

Although it is excellent to have good training facilities at your plant, there are many advantages to going off-site for training. Foremost among these is that a new place lends a festive air to the training event. Just as dimming the lights signifies entertainment, a trip somewhere means, at the very least, a pleasant change of pace, and, at the most, a working holiday. The second advantage is that when you take people away from their workplace, you minimize, even eliminate, interruptions. Furthermore, if you choose carefully and follow a few simple precautions, you can take advantage of superior training environments. Finally, depending on the place, an off-site seminar can be a welcome change of pace for you, too.

Usually the best sites for training are those built as training-conference centers. Many hotels have jumped onto the conference-center bandwagon with varying degrees of success. However, full training-conference centers do not admit the public. They take in only those who are being trained (although some don't have housing). They specialize in handling training, and most are excellent. Look for these centers in your area or in the areas where you wish to travel.

As indicated, this has become a highly competitive business. Hotel chains like Hyatt and Marriott offer the public special weekend discounts because so much of their regular business is weekday seminars and conferences. You are in a buyers' market. Shop around and look for the best facilities at the lowest cost. I have found most hotel staffs ready and willing to deal.

Although you may be in a favorable position, don't buy sight unseen. Facilities differ, and even in glamorous hotels the training facilities can be minimal. Look over the facilities. Check for the following:

- Several rooms in the sizes you will need. Contract for specific rooms only.
- Soundproof walls, if the space is flexible with movable walls.
- Heating and air-conditioning controls. If need be, talk to the maintenance engineers to achieve the levels you want.
- Lighting and decor. These multipurpose rooms often are quite inadequately lit for training or too plush and overdecorated.
- The menus if you are supplying lunch or snacks. Use recommendations given earlier.
- The surrounding area. Is recreation available on premises or nearby? Is there too much recreation available?
- The sleeping accommodations and room rates.

Negotiate a package deal including seminar rooms, meals, accommodations, and services. Set up a master billing account so that the hotel bills you directly. This makes charging and subsequent payment easier; however, limit the charges or the number who have authority to charge to the account.

The hotel sales staff is not usually involved in setting up your room. A few hotels have people on the sales staff who personally oversee your needs, but that is rare. Talk to the banquet manager and the catering staff to be sure they have enough people to set up and serve your group. A few dollars or personal considerations can ensure the service you need.

Arrive a day early and let everyone know you are there, making sure everything is set. Check with the catering staff to be sure it has a copy of your needs, your schedule, and so forth. Large hotels, like any large organization, tend to standardize. If you don't want the standard setups, say so and make sure you don't get them. I've been charged $5.00 per bottle for Perrier water along with the sodas because "they always include it." The participants loved it but the boss didn't!

If possible, request full setup the night before your training. If you can't get that, insist the room be completely set up by 7 A.M. Specify exactly how you want the room set up. Hotels are used to setting up for banquets, not seminars, so make sure tables are at least four-and-a-half feet apart—double that if people are to sit on both sides of them. Check sightlines.

The standard tip is still 15 percent; however, different parts of a hotel may be billed separately. Catering and room service frequently add 15 percent automatically, so check before you add on a tip. If you make special demands, take special care of those who supply them. Praise people who do good work for you, especially to their bosses. It ensures good service next time around.

As a rule, you don't get better service because you pay higher rates. Some very expensive hotels provide minimal service and space. By way of contrast, I know of one company that uses the YMCA for off-site training because the facilities are excellent, the service (minimal, true enough) is adequate, the recreational facilities are first-rate, and the costs are very reasonable. You might look into such service organizations. Normally, however, large and well-established hotels that cater to well-to-do clients also provide the most considerate and tasteful service. Convention centers and conference centers are probably the most efficient, while international hotel chains are not consistent. I've had poor service and excellent service and everything in between from all the major chains. It seems to depend upon local management, staff, and facilities. Try before you buy, and take care to ensure you get what you need.

Before the Session

Whichever setup you choose, you need to check several things before beginning your program. If it is a multiuse room, check at least one week in advance to ensure that you *do* in fact have it booked for the correct time.

Arrive at least one hour ahead to make sure everything is in order. Check the temperature setting, and check the chairs to see that they are safe, comfortable, and attractive. Walk around the room and check sightlines. Are the room lights satisfactory? Be sure you can operate them if you are planning to do so. Also see to it that all audiovisual equipment (including the marking pens) is operating properly. Position and focus projectors; get other equipment ready to go.

If there are to be refreshments, see that the right ones will arrive at the right time. Be sure each participant has his or her workbook, name card, pencil or pen, writing paper, refreshments (including ice water, candy) if desired, and any other handouts.

Post your agenda and set up any other materials you plan to reveal later in the program. Arrange your notes, slides, charts, overheads, pointer, and clock (always have one) for your convenience, then recheck the sightlines. Check yourself for open zippers, loose buttons, dandruff, messed makeup or hair, loose coins in pockets, or distracting jewelry just before beginning.

Summary

This is one of the shorter chapters in the book, but it touches on many important aspects of effective learning. At the outset, we established the need for a comfortable learning environment, and we discussed five important factors that contribute to that comfort. The chapter then focused on the various setups or arrangements for effective learning, from the traditional classroom pattern to the popular horseshoe, from the familiar conference table setup to the different workstation arrangements.

With these considerations in mind, we explored the possibility of designing our own training facility, and elaborated upon various design considerations as well as furnishings and equipment for the training rooms. Multiuse facilities were also discussed, with suggestions for keeping this a smooth operation. We briefly discussed the types of food to serve at breaks and for lunch, then moved on to cover the ways of selecting and using off-site facilities for your training. The chapter concluded with a review of last-minute things a trainer should check before beginning a training session.

Applications

1. Assume that you have an unlimited budget. Design the perfect training room for your company. Don't forget decor, carpeting, and paint. Furnish it as you'd like. Equip it fully. Research the cost of each new improvement you'd like to make. Now create a plan and a budget for gradually acquiring the training facilities you dream of.

2. The next time your company sends you to an off-site location, take time to explore the facilities. Ask the sales staff about what arrangements were made and what costs were incurred. Ask for the persons in charge of setting up the rooms, the audiovisual aids, the food and break services. Make it a practice to explore public facilities whenever the opportunity presents itself.

Part 3

Special Applications in Training

Introduction to Part 3

In the spirit of this work, this section has been added to illustrate several specific applications of the training principles covered so far. Frequently in my training sessions trainers will say, "That sounds interesting, but I don't really see how I can use it in training my people to . . ." All of the principles here are intended to be translatable into every facet of training, and so, to save time and help those who train in these areas to focus on how to accomplish some of that training, I've devoted several chapters to expanding in some detail on how one would train in these fields.

In Chapter 12, we look at the special requirements for training in teams. The practice of breaking workers into self-empowered teams continues to grow in the United States. Unfortunately, it is often attempted without any, or at least very little, training and so is doomed to failure. In this chapter I outline some of the background that has led to the popularity and success of teams and look at several considerations mandated for training. Finally, the chapter lists specific ideas and suggestions for training workers in teams.

In Chapter 13 we tackle training first-line supervisors. Despite the great need for training at this level of management, many organizations are only just beginning to consider formal training. This chapter is a guideline for those who need to prepare and present training to supervisors, both in manufacturing and office environments.

The final chapter in this section, Chapter 14, addresses sales training, both retail and through representatives. Again, we consider the need for such training and discuss a number of factors that will help the trainer to create the most effective approach for this group of trainees.

Chapter 12
Training for Teams

THE team concept, the idea that workers can and will perform better in self-directed groups, springs from the seminal thinking of Douglas McGregor, one of the pioneers of modern management theory.[1] McGregor disagreed with traditional approaches to management back in the late 1950s and early 1960s. He asserted that most workers would rather do a job well than poorly. Traditionally managers took the view that workers only performed for specific rewards or to escape punishment. They assumed:

- It is management's role to plan and direct the efforts of the workers, motivating and controlling them as necessary.
- Workers do not care about the goals of the organization and will not work unless they are watched and closely supervised by management.
- By nature workers do as little work as they can get away with. In order to get workers to perform, management must either threaten them or reward them for each task.
- Most people dislike responsibility, are not ambitious, and actually prefer having the boss do their thinking for them.
- Workers lack creativity and would never be able to accomplish the myriad complex tasks required of them without direction.

McGregor called this viewpoint *theory x–style management.*

A Better Way: Theory Y

McGregor's view, which he called *theory y–style management,* is that people are not passive and lazy by nature. Rather, they are energetic, self-directed, and often strongly assertive. A quick look at how they spend their leisure time is proof. Images of "couch potatoes" notwithstanding, people can be very active and self-directed and usually are. Counterproductive workplace behavior is a learned trait, not an instinct. Workers learn to wait for and accept direction because managers insist on directing and controlling them. We are all self-motivated, willing and able to assume responsibility, with a need to develop and grow, and we are usually quite able and willing to contribute to the organizational goals of the workplace. In other words, people work because they want to work and will work harder and more responsibly when they have a say in what they will be doing and how it will be done.

There is still considerable controversy over whether or not McGregor was right. Several companies tried his self-directed approach to management in the 1960s and 1970s with varying degrees of success. The academic world, including most human resource practitioners, began teaching his principles and concepts, almost as soon as his work was printed, but the ideas McGregor put forth were slow to be accepted by most U.S. business organizations. It wasn't until our Japanese and European competitors in the 1980s showed us somewhat painfully the power of McGregor's ideas, especially when combined with the idea of teamwork, that he really became fully accepted. Since that time self-directed work teams have become an accepted and even desirable approach to management. Now such teams abound throughout U.S. industry, and more and more companies are turning to the concept as a response to the ever more rapidly changing face of business.

Yet for all its successes, there have been many team-oriented efforts that have failed. Usually management blames McGregor, saying, "I always knew you couldn't trust workers to work independently. They just don't care. They need to be directed with a strong hand."

They're quite wrong, of course. The problem is not the workers' motivation or ability. The problem lies with the quality and type of training that workers receive, and subsequent management to which they are subjected. If they are managed in a *theory x* mode from the time they start school, workers will learn to wait for management's direction. When they do work on their own they will constantly run back to management to ask, "Is this okay?" "What should I do now?" They have learned to work this way. To change them is a more complex process than merely cross-training them in the various tasks they will be responsible for and then telling them to form teams and proceed. They will fail because they don't know how to form teams or to function successfully in them. Yet, each worker almost instinctively functions easily in social groups. The interaction of group processes begins in early childhood and is well structured by the time the workers reach adult status.

Therefore, because group dynamics happen instinctively and group behavior patterns evolve whenever three or more people gather together, it is vital to instruct workers in positive skills for managing their group interaction. Left alone, each will respond in habitual ways, ways usually learned in the workplace under *theory x-type* managers or in school. It is likely that the natural group dynamics that will emerge will be counterproductive. Groups are natural; teams need to be taught. Just as there is a body of trainable training skills, so there is a necessary body of teachable teaming skills. Putting people in a group simply doesn't do it.

Teaming Skills

Team members must be trained to function in each of three separate but interrelated areas: technical skills, team-building function skills, and tactical skills. Let us look briefly at each one.

Technical Skills. The technical skills area encompasses, as its name would suggest, the actual job skills each member of the team will be expected to perform. Cross-training members of the team to perform the skills of other members is an important benefit of creating teams in the workplace. Workers who can perform all the tasks related to their functional environment are an important asset. In fact, many organizations decide to develop a work-team environment because they feel they will gain universally skilled workers who will be much more flexible than traditionally compartmentalized ones. Sometimes they can be, but it is this type of thinking that has caused the failure of many team efforts.

The problem is that if team training means only that all workers will learn how to do every job and will gain universal work skills so that each may replace any other, where does this leave the worker? What will become of workers if they can simply be replaced by equally skilled cross-trained members of their team? When companies meet resistance from labor unions when they suggest team efforts, this is usually the core objection. And rightly so. Management creates the resistance by demanding cross-training without training in the benefits to the worker of learning other jobs. Management gains much greater flexibility and perhaps efficiency while the workers lose autonomy, pride in specialization, uniqueness, and job security. If learning technical skills across job descriptions were all there was to team training, few workers would willingly accept such a deal. The unions properly resist this narrow and manipulative effort.

Yet in order for a team to work efficiently, there must be a considerable amount of cross-training. As in a professional baseball, soccer, hockey, or basketball team, almost any member can play any other member's position and does so when necessary for the team effort. They don't play their secondary positions as well as the regular players and they play their own positions better than anyone else, but in order to score a goal, defense men play forward, forwards play defense, outfielders play all three outfield positions, and most infielders can cover any base. All players can and must stand at bat, although some are far better at it than others. Even in American football, where players are specialized and require different physical attributes for different positions (strength for the line, agility for the backfield, dexterity for pass receiving, etc.), and while most players cannot play every position, every player on the field knows what is happening in every other player's position and knows how to play that position even if he will never be called upon to do so. All the players must know these things in order to coordinate their complex team moves with each other.

It is this level of understanding that is vital for team effort and that must be taught as cross-training to ensure team success. Far from making workers interchangeable, cross-training in my experience broadens each worker's ability to respond to his or her peers effectively. Time and again I discover that workers in one function have either no clue as to what other workers are doing or are completely off the mark in what they believe is happening elsewhere. In a recent survey I conducted for a client, it became apparent that there was intense bitterness among hourly workers because salespeople seemed to get many more perks than the hourly people did. The workers thought that they too worked hard, put in as many hours, sometimes more, and it was grossly unfair of management to lavish awards, bonuses, and even prizes on salespeople who didn't appear to work any harder than the line workers.

Two days of cross-training completely solved the problem. The training was designed not to make each group capable of taking over the other's "turf," but to allow each group to share what it was exactly that they did, what they were paid for, and how they earned that money, with a chance for each worker to experience the other's work environment and core skills in simulation.

Salespeople learned:

- What went into the services and products they sold
- Why rush orders took as long as they did
- How to address production problems that held up deliveries
- How to troubleshoot and solve problems rather than hindering solutions by ranting and demanding immediate attention
- Respect and admiration for the behind-the-scenes skills that helped them to serve their customers
- How challenging, complex, and demanding the manufacturing, scheduling, and shipping skills were that supported them

The workers learned:

- What went into the process of selling
- How challenging selling is
- The amount of time and effort that went into just one sale
- How many aspects of his or her work the sales representative was responsible for

- What it felt like to be on your own, face-to-face with a customer
- What the salespeople's commission and rewards structures were based on
- The degree of risk and lack of job security each salesperson had to tolerate on a daily basis

At the end of the two-day cross-training, the resentments were gone. Salespeople came away with a sense of appreciation for the support they received; line workers gained a sense of respect for the risks and pressures of the sales environment. Given the opportunity to change jobs and work at the other's craft, the salespeople felt they didn't have the skills and that it would take too long to gain them to do the line workers' jobs. Only one line worker said he would like to try sales. It turned out he was quite good at it and has happily made the transition to sales. But the bitterness and misunderstanding were no more.

How does cross-training improve technical skills for the worker? There are quite a number of benefits:

- Ability in skills related to their own, to step in and help a peer or other team member.
- Comprehension of what is going on in related areas.
- Appreciation for the work, efforts, and skills of others.
- A sense of belonging to a process, of contributing to a larger whole.
- A sense of interrelatedness, both with their working peers and other areas of the company. A lessening of "us versus them" thinking.
- The peace of mind of knowing what's happening, and the awareness that their role is one of "value added," that they contribute to a larger effort of the group (organization) as a whole and that their role in the process is significant.
- The comfort level necessary to speak up and the knowledge to do so meaningfully.

Team-Building Function Skills. Despite these gains from the technical skills aspect of team training, the main benefit to workers in the process of team training comes from learning the skills of interaction and how to get things done.

After a lifetime of having others—parents, relatives, peers, schoolteachers, and now supervisors and managers—make decisions and direct their activity from their childhood onward, is it any wonder that the role of self-directed responsible worker seems a bit foreign to many workers? They must be trained in skills that allow them to take on the responsibilities of directing and functioning in their teams. This is true whether they are in solely autonomous teams or in teams that are supervised and run by a manager. They must learn how to behave as a team.

According to Peter Scholtes in his seminal work *The Team Handbook: How to*

Use Teams to Improve Quality, there are eleven things that a work team must know and be able to perform:

- Quality improvement concepts and skills
- The scientific approach to problems
- Team decision-making skills
- How to conduct and run meetings
- Record-keeping skills
- How to evaluate meetings and quality performance
- How teams interact with each other
- Stages of team growth
- A recipe for a successful team
- A five-stage plan for process improvement
- The operation of team dynamics[2]

In addition, Scholtes stresses that there are several attitudes and processes that a team must maintain to remain functional and successful. These can (and therefore should) be included in any team-building curriculum:

1. *Communicate.* First, a team must foster and maintain communication within its membership to remain effective. All of us believe that we can communicate clearly, especially if we are managers. I believe that if I say something and it's clear to *me* then it must be clear to *everyone.* This of course is nonsense. In fact, I teach that anything you say (or I say) can and will be misunderstood, forgotten, or deliberately ignored. Psychologists now teach that most, if not all, of our interpersonal problems stem from misunderstandings and the inability to communicate clearly. This skill must be taught, trained, and practiced throughout all team-training efforts and activities. It is the core skill of working in a team.

2. *Fix obvious problems.* The second need is for the team to recognize and take responsibility for fixing obvious problems. If there is a breakdown in communication or two people do not get along or someone consistently fails to carry his or her share of the load, the team must address this problem immediately. If an obvious problem is allowed to slip by for more than a day, it will only become worse. We all know this, yet we continue to procrastinate. This is usually because we believe that to raise the subject is to create a confrontation. That is why every team-training effort must include training on how to provide constructive feedback and criticism, how to defuse confrontation, how to confront rationally, and how to control those who become irrational when confronted. Every problem that can be solved must be solved as quickly as possible in order for the team to maintain its equilibrium.

3. *Look upstream.* Managing crises consists almost solely of being prepared for them. If you drive on the highway and watch only the car in front of you, sooner

---

Team Function Skills

- Interpersonal communication skills
- Effective listening skills
- The operation of team roles and dynamics
- Conducting and running meetings
- Team decision-making skills
- Problem-solving techniques
- Performance measurement
- Performance evaluation techniques
- Team evaluation techniques
- Giving positive constructive feedback
- Record keeping and documentation
- Team roles and how teams grow
- How team members interact with each other
- A plan for team development

---

or later you will bump into it. Defensive driving classes teach that the most important car on the highway to watch, after your own, is the one in front of the one in front of you. I practice this skill diligently and can count at least seven times that I have avoided serious accidents by seeing the trouble coming in time to react calmly and avoid it. Frequently I find myself putting on my brakes or taking evasive action before the driver in front of me has reacted. A good team must learn to anticipate and monitor several tasks ahead of where it is. This is a trainable skill and must be incorporated into team-training efforts.

4. *Document problems and progress.* Progress without evaluation is impossible. Evaluation becomes nearly impossible over time without documentation. And, if you don't document a problem, it is very difficult to assess progress toward solving it. Documentation is a vital skill of group growth and must be included as a regular practice in all of your team-building classes.

5. *Monitor change.* This is a double-edged sword. The team must both anticipate the impact of changes that take place outside of its purview (that is, the marketplace) to be most responsive to them and, at the same time, constantly assess the impact that it (the team) is having on the tasks it is assigned and on the organization as a whole. In order to do this, members must be trained in the dynamics of change and its processes as well as how to respond appropriately and productively to change.

In the section of his book entitled "A Recipe for Team Success," Scholtes lists ten key elements for working well as a team:

1. Define, clarify, and set team goals.
2. Devise an improvement plan and follow it.
3. Define the roles of the team members clearly.
4. Insist on clear communication.
5. Define, list, and publish beneficial team behaviors.
6. Clearly define decision-making procedures and responsibilities.
7. Ensure balanced participation.
8. Establish, publish, and enforce ground rules.
9. Stress awareness of the group process through training, observation, and communication, and discuss it often.
10. Use the scientific approach in solving all problems.[3]

Clearly, each is a trainable skill, and yet few teams have been trained to model any of them. When you take on team training, your core curriculum must be built around these crucial skills. Without acquiring these skills, most teams will fail; but with them, most teams will succeed. Incidentally, the "scientific approach" is a four-step logical approach to problems:

1. Collect meaningful data before making a decision.
2. Identify root causes of problems. Try to avoid treating symptoms.
3. Develop appropriate solutions only after the first two steps have been taken.
4. Plan and make changes.

Team Killers

- False consensus
- Unresolved covert (or overt) conflict
- Underground conflict
- Inability to reach closure
- Calcified team meetings
- Uneven participation
- Not being accountable to others (excluding stockholders)
- Forgetting the customer[4]

"[T]here are eight signs to look for that will help you to identify real teams in your organization," wrote Oren Harari in *Management Review*.[5] While he is talking about existing teams, this list of attributes is a final checklist of what teaming skills must be accomplished by any group you want to make into a team:

1. *Consensus.* Team members must share the same vision, or goal, toward which all are contributing. This kind of mission statement needs to be brought out of the group itself, and can be achieved by a skilled facilitator/trainer. In addition, the group members must share a common set of values in relation to their work. This consensus is trainable if the group is guided in the development of its own set of values. Finally, group members need to develop a sense of ownership of their mission, their values, their tasks, and most important, their team.

2. *Trust.* Group members must be able to believe what each person in their team says. Through team exercises, special attention must be paid to developing the trust among team members. In their work, they need to feel safe and unthreatened within their team. Members must learn to depend and count on each other. This level of trust can only develop through proper training. The habit of using honesty rather than manipulation when working together must be instilled in members. They must develop confidence in each other's ability.

3. *Candor.* Apart from general honesty, members must develop candor. They must learn to be open about concerns and ideas and forthright in addressing problems. Hidden agendas and passive acceptance of what is not desired are underminers of group team building. Members must be taught to express their concerns directly, assertively, and without malice or anger. They must be taught to select language that is conducive to openness rather than to conflict and defensiveness. Finally, they must share the losses as well as the wins. Only by taking responsibility for failure can the thrill of success be fully realized by each member.

4. *Respect.* People must be taught to listen and to respect the right of others to be heard. Without instruction, most people never progress beyond the infant stage of demanding what they want, without regard for anyone else. Such infantile behavior undermines group process. The tools of respect need to be acquired by all would-be team members. Each member should become aware of the full range of the other members' skills. Each must learn to value other members' time and to hold agreements and promises sacred. These actions show respect and build trust and team spirit. Finally, all members must share in public recognition and honor when they are earned. Respect is earned, but the skill of showing it is learned.

5. *Caring.* One of the most difficult hurdles to cross in training teams is getting members to overcome their sense of codependency. Several years ago, a client of mine was getting very poor results from efforts to create self-directed work teams. The client was about to admit failure and return to a modified *theory x–style management.* Through a series of focus groups, we discovered the problem was that team members did not want to criticize each other. As one woman said, "I've known Edna for twelve years. Our kids are dating each other. I'm not about to go tell her that she's not doing a good job. She'd never forgive me!" Therefore, no one was giving constructive feedback. There was no realistic evaluation of performance, and naturally, production was the pits. Once we trained the work-

ers in good coaching skills and how to evaluate without confrontation, the team concept took off in this organization.

Workers must be trained to set high standards of performance and provide straight nonaccusatory feedback with regard to those standards. They must be taught to hold high, no-nonsense standards. Yet, at the same time, they need instruction in coaching and counseling with compassion. They must learn how to feel empathy and a desire to help each other to achieve a successful team.

6. *Collaboration.* Teams consist of members participating in a joint effort. When one or two stand out and do "star turns," the overall performance of the team suffers. This is frequently what happens on sports teams when the big name stars play for themselves and not for the team. The best of them are great team players and inspirations to their teammates. The worst are temperamental prima donnas. Talented, yes, but they don't help to create winning teams. Team process training teaches members that personal success is enhanced by group success. Individuality is rewarded for its unique contribution rather than for its egotistical efforts at self-aggrandizement. Collaboration means sharing tools, information, and resources. It means seeking win-win integrative solutions that incorporate everyone's ideas rather than pushing for distributive division of problems and solutions. Workers must learn to work as a group, avoiding traditional "cover your flank" attitudes. Problems need to be brought out and addressed in a cooperative way, not hidden for fear of repercussions. Such skills need to be taught. Old habits need to be changed to new productive methods.

7. *Recognition.* Rewards and recognition need to be tied to team performance, not individual achievement. The only valuable individual awards should be for helping and coaching other members of the team. Establish clear and desirable rewards for the team, as a whole, to strive for. This helps to create a climate for change and a willingness to learn and practice new skills.

8. *Connectedness.* Teams don't work in a vacuum. Successful teams learn to create their goals and mission statements with the help and input of both their key internal and even external players. The team must function within the company at large, and it needs the necessary skills to accomplish this. Authority and the skills to exercise it need to be established and learned. The team must be able to plan for and control the dollars, time, and company resources allocated to it. It must also earn the respect and trust of management at all levels, but particularly at the top.

These last two elements, while trainable, overlap into our third necessary team-training area: tactical skills.

Tactical Skills. As Harari points out, teams don't function in a vacuum. Not only must members learn to appreciate and perform each other's tasks—and to recognize and respond positively to the inevitable group dynamics they will expe-

---

Tactical Skills

- Presentation skills
- Persuasion techniques
- How to assess and manage internal politics
- Negotiating skills
- Networking tools and skills
- Project management
- Budgeting
- Report writing

---

rience—they must also learn to master the art of interfacing with the rest of the company and, in many cases, the customer base. At a minimum, they must gain expertise in project management, negotiation, presentation skills, persuasion, meeting management, budgeting, and most of the other tasks of management. They need to learn how to represent their team in the company, and so they must master diplomatic skills.

Of course, every team member doesn't need to be expert in all of these functions, but at least one member of the team needs to be very good at each of them. The rest of the team needs to know what is involved and what they are expected to contribute in support of those who interface with other teams and with management.

Training Teams to Perform

Proper team training is nearly equivalent to a master's degree in social skills, only it is made even more difficult because it also includes in-depth study in political science and training in specific job skills. How can a usually understaffed training department cope with such a vast curriculum? The answer lies in the principles of learning explored in Chapter 1:

1. Readiness versus resistance
2. Active versus passive
3. Association
4. Practice, trial and error, and feedback

- *Readiness vs. resistance.* We learn faster, better, and easier when we are ready to learn. Resistance must be addressed and removed in order to foster sound learning. New ideas and new ways of working can be very threatening to workers.

This is especially true when they are also being asked to learn each other's jobs in cross-training skills. A prime concern in team training, therefore, is to address this resistance very early in your sessions. Continue to stress it until a new culture of team sharing becomes the dominant mode of conduct among your trainees.

■ *Active vs. passive.* Because we learn through activity, most team training must actively involve the trainees. The more they perform, exhibit, and practice skills and activities, the faster and the better they learn. Team training must keep the teams active. The more they do, the more they learn.

■ *Association.* What is familiar to us is easier to learn than what is strange, new, or incomprehensible. The more we can build our team training around what is familiar, the easier and faster our people will be able to learn. Aside from familiar team metaphors (such as sports), it is possible to schedule lessons to gradually build on each other so that each new one is firmly couched in material learned in earlier ones and is therefore familiar.

■ *Practice, trial and error, and feedback.* Repetition and practice are the only way to build skill in performing most tasks. As we get better at doing the tasks, we become more skilled. In order for teams to learn, they must practice being teams in a controlled environment; if they make mistakes, their mistakes can be analyzed and corrected. But this evaluation must be a function of the teams themselves, not of an outside trainer intervention.

If we combine these six principles of learning and apply them to the range of topics and skill areas that must be mastered, several things become clear. First, group members must become comfortable as a team before they can experience any other meaningful learning. Therefore, the first element of team training must be the team function skills. Use team games and fun exercises to reduce resistance and to introduce key team elements. Such self-exploration of group dynamics is usually enlightening and enjoyable, and it initiates the process of building a team in a positive direction.

Second, because learning is active, the teams need to do as much of their own internal instruction as possible. Weave coaching and presentation skills into the fabric of the early team-development work. Once members can handle group projects and presentations from a coaching perspective, instruction shifts to the teams. Assign team members into job- or task-related subgroups. Assign each subgroup the responsibility for developing and conducting training sessions in the skills of the subgroup for the other members of the larger team. The trainer's team lesson sessions then become planning and presenting sessions that allow each member to help his or her team members to understand and, if need be, perform all of the skills of the group. The cross-training takes place as a team-project assignment. The role of the trainer is to act as a training guide and not as a subject matter expert.

Third, once the teams begin to understand and learn each other's tasks, they develop a strong sense of togetherness, of team spirit. They are accomplishing a task that, at first, none of them thought they would be able to do. Now you can introduce more challenging aspects of team training such as large project management, case histories of interaction with the politics of the organization, problems in team job functions, or problems in team-management functions. The teams will have their own positive association of early training success to build on and will gain many opportunities to practice and gain feedback. Throughout the process, they are constantly repeating the initial basic skills, deepening their understanding and experience as a team, and gaining more competence in handling their own affairs with skill.

This process can go on as long as you, the teams, and management feel that it is productive and beneficial. In my experience, a minimum of three weeks of solid training is needed. However, more weeks would bring the teams to an even higher level of competence. Or, conversely, after two weeks the teams could return to their work environment. Several months later, you need to conduct follow-up sessions in which team members can raise, address, and solve problems and practice solutions from their real-world environment. At these sessions, you can then begin to introduce increasingly challenging situations and projects in order to develop even higher levels of competence. Gradually, over time, these follow-up sessions will become less frequent as the teams become more independent and effective.

Summary

This chapter has explored the current trend toward self-directed work teams from a training perspective. We examined the origins of the movement and the rationale for joining it. We also explored the principal causes for failure and, as an antidote to these causes, we reviewed a series of checklists for the three main subject areas that teams must master. These subject areas are:

- *Technical skills.* These skills encompass the nonteam tasks that the members of any team need to perform. One of the frequent motivations for management to explore team efforts is to cross-train workers in each other's skills in order to gain greater flexibility and increased efficiency.

- *Team-building function skills.* These skills address the "how-to's" of becoming a functional team. This area is frequently handled poorly or inadequately, and yet it is key to creating effective self-directed work teams. People must be taught how to become team members and how to function in teams.

- *Tactical skills.* These skills are necessary because no team functions in a vacuum. To succeed, a team must become a working entity in the company that interfaces politically and functionally with all other entities. This chapter lists many of the skills that members must learn to become fully successful in the company. How to perform most of these skills is covered elsewhere in the book (see Chapters 5, 16, 17, and 20).

Finally, to help trainers structure the considerable amount of learning that must be acquired by most teams, we applied six of the principles of learning from Chapter 1 and demonstrated how they could be woven into a cohesive and detailed training sequence for developing functional work teams.

Applications

1. Assess the climate for team training in your organization. Interview three key managers and ask them what they've read about self-directed work teams, and how they feel such groups might function in your organization. Then interview five or six workers who might conceivably be trained to become team members. Ask them what they know and how they feel about self-directed work teams. Out of this exercise you should gain some degree of insight into both management's expectations and what direction, if any, worker resistance might take. It will also give you a direction to move when preparing persuasive messages for each of these two groups.

2. Using the guidelines in this chapter, select a work group or area for team training. List all of the required skills that will need to be cross-trained. Based on your findings in Application 1, prepare a list of the team function skills in which you will need to train this group. Finally, within the political structure and management hierarchy of your organization, list the tactical skills that this team will need to master.

3. Using the three lists of topic areas you devised in Application 2, prepare a tentative sequence for instructing your new team. Be sure to use the six principles of learning and the suggested outline I've provided in this chapter.

Chapter 13
On-the-Job Training

NEARLY 75 percent of all training in the United States is done on the job. Despite the fact that more and more companies are turning to formal training and are realizing the value and importance of it, the bulk of all training is still done one-on-one by line supervisors. Even in companies that have formal training classes, once the trainees have graduated and left the training room, they must actually perform their new skills under the direction of their immediate supervisors.

In my classes on how to improve supervision, I ask participants how many have ever received formal instruction in how to coach or train their people. Usually no more than 10 percent of them have. Yet these people are expected to train their workers, or in many cases, become the backup for formal training. The situation becomes even more critical when senior managers, who are pressured by budget crunches that limit funds, often feel that they cannot afford to have formal training, leaving their supervisors with the sole responsibility for training.

In some companies there simply are not enough employees to justify either hiring a full-time trainer or bringing one in for on-site training. By default, the supervisors are the only ones left to do training. However, companies have two other alternatives:

1. Send their employees to one-day "information" meetings.
2. Buy off-the-shelf packages for the employees to teach themselves.

Both of these work, but only in a limited fashion. Given a bit of luck, most learners can muddle through and, by doing the job, discover ways to get it done well enough. But this is hardly acceptable training.

The problem with one-day "quickies" is that, while the information is usually sound and the presenters are generally very good, there is little or no application of the skills being explained. Consequently, very little of what is covered will actually be retained and transferred to the job when the learners return from the session. The best of the one-day seminars will use memory-enhancing techniques, such as repetition and small hands-on group assignments, to allow the participants to at least become familiar with how it feels to perform the tasks being taught—but this is seldom full training.

There are, however, two safeguards that can ensure that at least some of the material covered in the one-day seminar will be applied by those who attended. First, the supervisor can be trained to use the principles of learning to coach the workers as they apply the material from the seminar on the job. In such an approach, the seminar becomes only the preparation and presentation steps of the lesson. The practice and evaluation, where the learning will in fact take place, will be under the guidance of the supervisor.

The other safeguard is for the supervisor to assign work to the learners to be done immediately upon their return from the seminar, which will engage them in performing, or at least exploring, the skills that have been covered in the session.

On-the-Job Training at Home and Abroad

I once overheard two managers in an electronics firm arguing over whether or not to fire a young man they had just hired a week earlier. He was fresh out of high school. This was his first job, and he was hired to be a shipping clerk in the warehouse. On his first day, the warehouse supervisor spent nearly two hours showing him how to do all of the tasks involved in the job. When he was asked from time to time if he understood or if he had any questions, the young man replied that he had understood and didn't have any questions. It all seemed clear to him. The supervisor was pleased and told the young man to go ahead and do the job. He then left him to perform the tasks he thought he had trained him to do.

Five days later, the young man had cost the company nearly $150,000 in misshipped orders, lost materials, and customer dissatisfaction. He seemed totally incompetent, and the warehouse supervisor wanted him fired. The personnel manager was reluctant because time and effort had been devoted to paperwork necessary in hiring the young man and selection of another person would take time and money. So the two were arguing about how best to proceed when I happened to hear them.

I suggested that, as there was a cost factor involved with termination and the issue might well revolve around training, they give the young man five days of probation. On each of those days the supervisor would need to spend no more than ten or fifteen minutes explaining one—and only one—new task to the youth. The young man would then be expected to perform that task—and only that task—on the first day. On the second day he would be responsible to continue performing his first day's task but would also be responsible for the new task he'd learned that day. On the third day, likewise, he would perform the two already learned tasks plus the new one for that day, and so on for the five-day probationary period. If, at the end of that time, he still could not do the job satisfactorily, then they would have to let him go. On the other hand, it was my belief that, with this careful, step-by-step training, he would be able to perform his new job quite well.

The managers took my advice. The young man was trained in small increments. The result was that he not only learned to do the job, but five years later, when the warehouse manager retired, the company gave the lad the manager's job. He turned out to be an ace at warehousing.

The problem was that this young man, like many young people who grew up in the MTV generation, had developed only a very short attention span. He had never learned to concentrate on listening for more than ten or fifteen minutes at a time. Yet all of the instruction he was initially given on his new job was dumped on him at once over a period of two hours. Everything that was said after the first ten minutes was a total waste of time and merely drifted through his mind—in one ear and out the other. This had nothing to do with his intelligence or his ability to perform or understand the job. Listening and paying attention were simply skills that he had never been taught in his school career. Lacking these skills, he was unable to grasp more than a few concepts at any one time and, therefore, could not possibly learn a whole set of job responsibilities by being told about them all at once.

Unfortunately, much of the on-the-job training in the United States today is closer to the first episode in this young man's warehouse career. When I was in high school I got a part-time job that involved working skillfully with an electronic control panel on which a wrong move would have quite serious consequences. The man who was instructing me would explain what to do and then tell me to do it. However, the instant my hands touched the controls, he would scream at me, swipe my hands away from the panel, and take over himself.

There was a duplicate panel in the next room. It was a backup for the main one and was rarely in use. I could practice on it, but my instructor never coached or explained things to me on that one. He worked only on the live one and only by refusing to let me actually *do* anything with it. Because I could practice on the spare, I eventually taught myself how to run the board, but it was not because of any instruction I received. In fact, if I hadn't been stubborn and determined, my instructor would have discouraged me from ever learning how to operate the controls.

I'm sure you can recall tales similar to these two that you've seen or experienced. Sadly, such procedures make up the bulk of informal training in the United States.

Training in Germany

It doesn't have to be so. Arguably the best on-the-job training in the world takes place in Germany. There, 67 percent of young people between the ages of sixteen and twenty-three are working apprentices, learning a craft on the job while going to school. At age sixteen, young men and women choose whether they want to complete an academic education, pushing on through college, or a technical one. If they choose the latter they enter an apprenticeship, which is a formal work-study program.

For the next seven or so years, they attend school for part of the year and work in industry for the other part. While they are in the work environment, they are trained by supervisors who have received special instruction and are qualified as training supervisors. These people are paid at a higher rate than regular supervisors because of their advanced training skills and extra responsibilities. They work closely with each student-worker to develop his or her skills and to teach good work practices.

The students are given an academic education and skill training while they are working at a productive job and earning their way. When they complete the full course, they are tested and can qualify for full journeyman status. The skills training is standardized, tested, and regulated. It is taught by trained professionals who are themselves skilled at administering on-the-job training. The academic training is not college-focused but rather work-focused and relates more to skills, information, and technologies the apprentices will face in the work world. This system works.

Contrast this with our system where young people attend a school with a college-bound curriculum, whether they need it or not (or can master it or not), and then are expected to find a job and learn a craft or skill on their own. The most progressive companies provide training by removing their workers from their tasks for a period of intense training and then expecting them to transfer that learning to the job when they return. Unfortunately, when they return, many of them are subjected to the infamous greeting from their supervisors, "Forget all that stuff you learned in training. Here's how I want you to do the job."

Surprisingly, this system also works, but not as well. In our approach, the learner must be self-motivated to overcome the obstacles the system presents and to succeed despite them. The German system makes it much easier both for the learner to succeed and for industry to standardize and assess the worker's skills.

How to Make On-the-Job Training Effective

Clearly, we do not have the German system, and some would argue that—like many Japanese systems—it wouldn't work well in our culture anyway. However, most Japanese approaches have proved adaptable to our culture and, consequently, have been made to work in a uniquely American way. Many of the existing work-study programs in this country approach the German system, and quite a few of the cooperative programs between industry and schools (see Chapter 18) are providing both high school and college students with opportunities to learn work skills while they are still in school. But assuming such options are not available to you, what can you do to ensure effective on-the-job training?

Steps for the Trainer to Take

It is imperative that the trainer maintain as much control over the learning as possible. At a minimum, you must provide the framework for the training. You should also provide:

- *Training for the supervisors in how to train their people.* Clearly, if you can establish key techniques and develop key skills among the supervisors, they will be able to train much more effectively. I have worked with several organizations to help them achieve this result.

- *Objectives.* Since these are the building blocks of effective training (see Chapter 2), it is essential that you provide supervisors with clear learning objectives, even if you cannot train them to become trainers. Work with the supervisors to develop learning objectives that are both desirable and in tune with what the supervisors feel needs to be mastered by the learners.

- *Lesson plans for the supervisors to follow.* Whether or not the supervisors are trained by you, they will benefit by having clear lesson plans (see Chapter 2) to guide them and coach them into better training practices.

- *Sequence and structure.* Supervisors all have a different approach to any particular job. Standardize by providing an incremental sequence, a structure for the flow of new learning to the worker. As I explained in Chapter 2, a spool sequence will be effective for most tasks. Build it for the supervisor to help him or her train better.

- *Time frames and benchmark points.* Human beings tend to procrastinate. Supervisors are no exception. They are busy and have many priorities. Training is easily put off until a better time occurs (which it never does). Help your supervisors by giving them a tight time schedule, including deadlines and benchmark levels by which all people must be trained up to the agreed-upon standard performance levels.

- *Evaluation and testing materials (if possible).* This is the method our public school and college-entrance systems use to control what is taught in our high schools. By having standardized exams, educators control what topics and skills are covered in school. Unfortunately, standardized tests don't control how well these are taught. However, it is a means of maintaining standards when supervisors must back up or perform on-the-job training.

- *Off-the-shelf modules can standardize what's being taught.* If you don't have time to create lesson plans (although this is important enough to have a very high

---

Controlling On-the-Job Training

- Objectives
- Lesson plans
- Sequence and structure
- Time frames and benchmarks or target dates
- Evaluation and testing materials
- Off-the-shelf modules to standardize content
- Electronic personal support system
- Follow-up and coaching

---

priority) or there are none available, use off-the-shelf packages and break them into usable modules that the supervisors can then use as guidelines for instruction.

- *Electronic personal support system.* This is a high-tech computerized training system that would completely replace the supervisor as a coach (see Chapter 10 for details). It is an expert system that interactively walks the trainee through whatever task he or she is faced with, explaining how to perform the task and then asking the learner to do it. It is, in effect, a self-teaching work center and is the state of the art in computer-based training.

- *Follow-up and coaching.* Arrange with the supervisors to check on their workers' skill levels from time to time and actually coach each one where possible.

Steps for the Supervisor to Take

All of these steps are fine when you have a full-time trainer to provide them. But I know that many of you are managers or supervisors for whom training is only a part of your larger job description. What can you do when there are no guidelines prepared? Here are some.

These guidelines are all drawn from the first three chapters of this book. I advise you to first read these chapters carefully to fully establish the principles that will be discussed here. If you have already read them, this section may appear a bit redundant, but the principles I want to stress will act as a guideline for you as a supervisor and will select key elements to help you to achieve effective training and coaching of your workers.

Four Steps. It is most important that the four steps to good lesson planning (preparation, presentation, practice, and evaluation) are not forgotten when it comes to informal on-the-job coaching. Learners must be prepared to learn. You cannot expect a worker who is ten months away from retirement to want to learn a new skill. You must address the worker's need and bring him or her around to accepting the value of the training.

You can randomly train people whenever the right opportunity comes along. Sometimes it will work, and they will learn. But many times, if their minds are not focused or their mood is not right, the training will be a waste of time. Prepare them. Tell them why they need to learn what you're teaching them. Set a time frame for the training in advance. Give them at least one and preferably two days' notice that you plan to spend a specific amount of time training them on a particular skill. Let them get ready to learn. Assign a task or reading in the manual, if there is one, so that they will come to the designated time focused and ready to learn. If you give them a reading assignment, make sure they actually read it by asking them to write down six or seven questions they might have about the material when you begin the lesson. They will have to read the material in order to write and ask the questions.

Remember, attention spans are surprisingly short. If you only have five or ten minutes of someone's full attention (and this is all that you will have with many of your people), don't waste it by trying to cram as much material as possible into that tiny time frame. Break your material down into short segments and teach them only one segment at a time. We do not learn by listening to someone tell us how things work, no matter how golden tongued that person is. We learn only when we perform the skill. Keep your lectures and instructions to a minimum.

The human mind makes sense out of patterns, not random steps. Make patterns, or sequences, out of instruction to help the learner to remember it. This is how commercial packages like *Hooked on Phonics* succeed in increasing learning. This is how *Sesame Street* teaches three- and four-year-olds how to read. Make a pattern with a story or an acronym, something that will act as a memory hook for the learner.

Remember the 60/40 rule. Sixty percent of training time must be spent with the learner practicing and doing what has been taught. Instruction must be kept to a maximum of 40 percent of the total time available. You should instruct for five or ten minutes, and then give the worker the opportunity to try out what you've been explaining. Don't wait until they have heard it all; do it as you go. If you have only one hour for showing someone how to work a tool or machine, limit your instruction to twenty minutes. Let the person practice for forty minutes under your guidance. He or she will learn better and faster. After all, we cannot learn to drive a car by listening to someone tell us how. We must sit behind the wheel and drive it. Even demonstrations, which are excellent for preparing a learner and showing him or her the skill to be learned in operation, and which may be necessary in showing exactly how to hold or do something, are not as effective a learning tool as having the learner do the task. Keep learners active.

Evaluation and coaching as they develop skills are vital, too. Schedule future sessions once the trainees can perform the skill to help them get up to speed and to give them both encouragement and correction when needed. This will ensure that they learn to do the job the right way.

Principles of Learning. In Chapter 1, I discussed in detail what factors and behaviors enhanced learning.

- We only learn when we are ready to do so, so it is important to prepare people to learn.
- We learn by doing, not by just listening, so learning must be active.
- We learn by making mistakes and, therefore, we must be allowed to make them.
- Things make sense to us when they seem familiar. Create associations for new ideas so that we can say, "Oh, that's really just like . . ." and learn it easily.
- More than one sense gives us information at a time. The more senses that can be incorporated into the learning, the faster we'll learn and the longer we'll remember.
- Humans always look for shapes and patterns. Give us clear structure. Let us know where we are and where we are going at all times. Provide many street signs for your training. Don't confuse us with too much information. Keep it simple. Less is more effective.
- Everything isn't equally important. Let your learners know what level or depth of understanding and learning is expected of them.
- We learn only by practice, not really by instruction. We must have time for supervised practice.
- We must get feedback in order to know we are learning correctly.
- Each of us is a unique individual and needs to be treated with respect and consideration.

As a supervisor you can become an effective coach or trainer by combining the four steps and the ten principles of learning to organize each training or coaching session that you schedule. For each one:

1. Draw up three, or at the most four, clear learning objectives.

2. Think of a parallel situation that is similar to what you want your people to learn. Pick one that they will readily understand so that you can build a bridge from familiar ground to the new material or skill you want them to learn.

3. Develop the practice assignments you want them to complete so that you will know which skills they must learn in order to perform the task.

4. List the steps you want them to take to perform each task. Arrange the steps so that after every three or four they have a chance to practice or at least try them out.

5. When you actually teach the skill:

- Start your session with the clear learning objectives.
- Describe the parallel situation or association you've planned to relate the work to their familiar world.
- Explain and demonstrate the first three or four steps.
- Assign a practice exercise or task that demands that they use the three or four steps you've just covered, and coach them till they can do the steps easily.
- Continue in this fashion.
- From time to time, insert a larger task that allows them to combine all of what they've learned up to this point.
- Once they've mastered the skill set, assign them real work to do using the skills. Check with them frequently, at first, to encourage and correct as necessary. As they get better, check less often.

Supervisor's Tips for Good Instruction

- Set learning objectives.
- Create parallels to bridge unfamiliar material to the familiar.
- Decide on and develop practice exercises and tests.
- List the steps they need to learn and break them down into groups of no more than four at a time.
- Start with your objectives; then explain your parallel situation; then demonstrate and explain the first set of three or four steps.
- Give the learner a practice exercise in those steps.
- Continue with the next three or four steps, followed by an exercise for the learner to perform.
- After three or four sets of steps, give the learner a larger exercise that will challenge him or her to use all that has been learned up to this point.
- When the learner has mastered the skills, let him or her try them in the real world of work. Check back with the learner to coach or correct as necessary.

Summary

This chapter explored the state of on-the-job training in the United States and compared it with training in Germany. We looked at ways to enhance our system of on-the-job training, specifically the roles of the trainer and the supervisor.

Wherever possible, the training department must support supervisors with specific training in how to coach employees. In addition, they should provide supervisors with follow-up materials, lesson plans, and exercises to create more effective learning on the job, and to maintain a greater degree of control over the learning and skills-acquisition process.

Finally, we discussed how the supervisor might improve his or her coaching in organizations that do not have formal trainers, or that only bring in outsourced trainers for one day or so at a time. We discussed how the supervisor can plan and conduct effective training on the job.

Applications

1. Assess how on-the-job training is done in your organization. Go into the workplace and observe. Talk to several supervisors and workers. If necessary, gain managerial and supervisor approval to do so. Document the results of your informal survey.

2. Survey and interview supervisors to discover what they want their people to know and be able to perform when they return from training. Adjust your lessons accordingly.

3. Write a series of follow-up lessons or review discussion topics tied to key points from training and distribute these to supervisors to be used in regular meetings with employees.

4. If you are a supervisor or manager and must do your own training, pick a skill that you know will require you to train one or more workers. Using this chapter's guidelines, create a series of lessons for training your people in this skill.

Chapter 14

Special Considerations for Training in Technical and Sales Environments

WHILE there is considerable variety in the broad areas of technical and sales environments, they are frequently perceived as requiring different categories or types of training. By implication, each is thought to be somehow different from other types of training. Yet this is not really so. Although there are differences among all subjects of training, the principles of learning remain the same. Good solid training objectives are mandatory if training is to succeed. The purpose in all cases is to change job-related behavior. Lesson plans still need to contain four clear steps. Methods need to be dynamic; the learners need to be engaged; people learn better through active participation; and so forth. The rules of good training do not change. Each of these areas of training demands the same adherence to the procedures outlined throughout this book as all of the other areas. Yet, somehow, the myth persists that there are major differences and that these areas require completely different sorts of training.

Sources of the Myth

In the late 1980s, there was much discussion in the training press about what was eventually called the "woo woo" theory of training. The field of modern psychological practice had produced a number of very effective facilitative techniques for drawing people out, raising their consciousness, or modeling their behavior. Trainers, many of whom had taken a lot of psychology and pop psyche courses in college in order to prepare for their careers, adopted these techniques with great vigor. In fact, some are still doing so.

The result in the early to mid-1980s was a lot of trainees who had "got their heads straightened out" and, at the same time, a backlash of other workers who were dissatisfied with the "other world" stuff they were getting in training. It was usually fun, but not very practical. They called it "soft." As a result, current technical and skills training is often referred to as a separate category, from "regular" training categories, such as sales, customer service, retail, or management training. The American Society for Training and Development even has a separate membership section for technical and skills trainers. They have their own annual conference and exposition (at which nearly all of the same vendors exhibit mostly the same wares that they show at the regular sessions), and they consider themselves a breed apart, separate from those "woo woo" guys who train the managers and salespeople.

Such an unfortunate division is the price we pay for overindulging in one aspect of our craft.[1] The issue should not be whether one trains rank-and-file workers, managers, or salespeople, but rather how well one trains all of them. Each category or work type demands different skills and, therefore, different techniques for training. However, the principles of good training remain universally the same. Matching the method to the appropriate skill level and learner should dominate training's response to each group, not simple stereotypes, however well deserved they may have been in the past.

The main problem is one of credibility and identification. If my background is in engineering and I try to train salespeople, they might rightly question what I had ever sold and how I came to be teaching them something I had not experienced myself. When assembly-line workers are taught by motivational-emotional facilitators who have never worked a regular third shift in heavy industry, they are correct in questioning the relevance of what they are being taught to their actual working conditions. When a sales trainer who has never managed more than one or two sales at a time tries to teach me how to counsel and manage my employees, I must question the validity of the training he or she is trying to sell me.

But the problem here has little to do with the fact that each of these areas of training is different. The problem occurs when the trainer has done nothing to gain credibility in his or her trainees' field of reference. This is why, as we discovered in Chapter 1, the first question a trainer must ask when planning a lesson or course is "Who will be trained?" And it is why, having created the course or lesson, the trainer must then ask, "What do I have to do, given this lesson, to gain credibility and establish identity with this group of trainees?"

In today's rapidly changing work environment, with its increased demand for training in every field, it is very likely that you will have to confront this issue at some point. If that happens to you, the best solution is to take the necessary time to build your credibility and to gain a level of identification with your trainees. Chapter 6 will give you instruction on how to go about doing so. Remember, as well, that too much of any method is not good training. The method must be created to fit the learner and the skills being taught. Keep affective objectives to a minimum and concentrate on the skills-oriented ones. Keep the practice step as the major function in your training, and you should be fine.

Socratic facilitation is great. But nothing works if it is overused or doesn't fit. In Japan, with a group of multistatus workers, Socratic dialogue is a near impossibility. In France, it is unavoidable. In either case, it is not the technique you use that is important, but the purpose for which the technique is being used and the nature of the group it is to be used with. Facilitate, yes. But Socratic dialogue is not the only form of facilitation. For many skills-oriented jobs, it is the worst kind. The Japanese system of differing status may need to be brought slowly to dialogue (if it will help workers to perform a new skill), while the French may have to be carefully weaned into other facilitative activities like simulations and role-plays. We know that training works best when it is 60 percent or more practice. Oral facilitation is only one kind of practice. Balance all of them.

Training in a Technical Environment

How does one approach the training of technical skills? First, if you have a background in the technical skill in which you will train, you will simply be able to talk the talk. Your explanations and examples will come from your immediate experience, with which the trainees can identify because they face similar situations every day. Your challenge is to learn the arts of training in order to best convey your skills to your trainees.

But let's suppose you are asked to train a group of workers in a particular skill in which you have expertise, say a computer software program, but where the workers' application of the software is totally foreign to you. There are six things you can do to help the group accept you and your training.

Acquire Expertise

Make yourself a subject expert. Learn their application of your software. You don't have to be expert in its operation, but you must know how it works for them. Draw several examples from their tasks and challenges. Gather details on situations that relate to them. The purpose is to become conversant in their everyday tasks and problems and to demonstrate how your new software can help. It is also helpful to become familiar with their terminology so that you can establish early on a comfort level with them. Don't try to sound like an expert because you are not, but by making the effort to see the world from their perspective you establish a degree of credibility and the grounds for gaining identification with them. You should not try to be a know-it-all, but let them know that you've done your homework.

Avoid Stereotyping

Don't prejudge the trainees. There is a stereotype of the blue-collar worker being "all brawn and no brains," or very handy with his or her hands but not really a good thinker. This is utter nonsense. Although education levels tend to be higher among managers than among hourly workers, it has nothing to do with intelligence, ability, or even talent.

The jobs we hold usually come about through a combination of opportunity, economics, family, schooling, interests, cultural influences, and gender. Given the opportunity and the motivation, the great majority of hourly employees would succeed as well, or better, at management than most of those managing now. We know this by the track record of those who have done so. Consider how many of our current politicians and leaders take pride in claiming their humble origins. It is indeed a part of the American dream that any of us can grow and develop to our fullest abilities. The hourly employees whom you train are every bit as capable, intelligent, and potentially skilled as any group you will ever train. Do everything that you can to show them that you respect their intelligence and value their abilities.

Remember That Workers Enjoy Their Work

Don't assume that these workers will be any more resistant than any others. Somehow, we have come to accept the stereotype that workers hate their jobs and only work as hard as management forces them to. If they didn't have to make a living, they wouldn't work at all. Again, where do such outlandish ideas come from? I don't believe I have ever met a worker of any kind who didn't take pride in his or her job. Yes, there are jobs that are less pleasant than others. We look at people working at grueling manual labor and we feel sorry for them because we wouldn't want to have to do that work ourselves. But engage one of those workers in conversation and very quickly you'll find, despite some complaining about facets of the work or the lack of compassion in management, that each of them takes pride in some facet of what he or she is doing.

By far, most workers are pleased with their pay and proud of what they do. In my experience, they look forward to training. If their experience with school has not been a good one, they will be more hesitant at first to engage in training. However, once they discover the practical nature of your training and the amount of concern, feedback, and respect they receive, they will begin to look forward to it. As Joan Chesterton wrote in "Shattering the Myths of Hourly Workers":

> Managers and professionals generally have acquired at least 16 years of education with some degree of success. And most approach conference-room training with a minimal amount of apprehension.

Factory employees, on the other hand, frequently have negative memories of painful experiences in grade school or high school. A fair number of these workers will approach . . . training with real dread.[2]

However, dealing with this form of resistance is simply a matter of creating a learning environment that is different from any they experienced in school. Slowly and gradually increase their confidence in both your instruction and themselves.

There are four main fears that you may need to help them face:

1. *The fear of reading aloud.* Even those of us who read well feel extra pressure when we have to read aloud. Having had bad experiences with this in school makes people even more apprehensive. We don't read aloud the same way we read silently nor the same way that we talk. This is a particular skill that needs to be developed if one is to use it.

2. *Having to read, understand or outline, and complete a written assignment in a limited time frame.* If I don't read well or am slower than most, this kind of assignment puts tremendous pressure on me. It is compounded by not being able to write very well. I give many written assignments in my Training the Trainer classes, and I constantly find people who cannot finish such an assignment in the time allotted. This can be quite traumatic. If it is a problem, allow those who suffer from it other ways to express themselves. Give them more time to complete the work. Help them to gain a sense of success on these assignments to combat the sense of failure they carry with them from school.

3. *Speaking up in class.* Past experience has taught them to be quiet and let others speak up. Perhaps they have been wrong or ridiculed or simply overwhelmed by the vociferous ones in their past experience. It is unquestionable that, at one time, they were willing participants. A visit to any elementary school classroom will reveal a forest of willing hands who want to answer any and all questions. At some point they learned temerity. You must gradually bring your trainees out of this shyness. Give them ample opportunity to talk in small group projects and events.

This shyness is compounded even further by their fear of speaking in public in front of the group. This is a common fear for all of us. Bring them gradually into it in small increments if possible. Play games. Make it as much fun as possible and protect them from a threatening environment.

4. *That their shortcomings in written or spoken English, and inability to work figures quickly and accurately, will be noticed by the trainer or other trainees.* This is particularly noticeable with the foreign-born who may be struggling with the language, but it is just as prevalent among those who are native but whose skills are far below what they perceive are standard levels. They do not want to lose face and so they have developed many coping skills to hide their inadequacies. Wherever possible,

they will try to maintain these coping skills even when the skills prove inadequate. Chapter 18 covers in detail how to respond to literacy problems in the workplace, but as a trainer you must be aware that people are afraid of being judged and so they may want to hold back. It is essential that you create an accepting climate.

Remember There Is Life Outside of Work

Don't assume that workers are at their best only at work and then go home to idle, dull, empty lives. There are a few young people I know who work all day only for the chance to party all night. But they are very few indeed. For those of us who have gone to the best colleges and work in executive positions, it sometimes comes as a shock to realize just how rich and rewarding the lives of many hourly employees can be.

I recall a New York City cabdriver who was one of the principal fund-raisers for Carnegie Hall. He devoted all of his spare time to classical music. Many of the volunteers who work so hard during political campaigns are shift workers who are committed and care about their communities. The majority of workers will have deep, rewarding interests. Perhaps they are engaged in hobbies. I know many who are avid golfers and spend most of their spare time at the game. Others coach Little League, bowl, play jai alai, or do church work. In my experience, many of them take on leadership responsibilities and do a commendably better job of managing than many of the managers they work for. Some study, collect, innovate, and create. Every church, community theater group, town fair committee, or fund drive knows that it can depend upon these blue-collar workers to turn out and help. The term "do their eight and hit the gate" is a misnomer. It's catchy but inaccurate most of the time.

Gain Their Respect

You must plan to earn the workers' respect. Don't be misled. Workers do not automatically respect or look up to management. There are few more honest appraisals of management or management style than by those who are managed. Not only do workers not respect poor management, they do not respect poor management decisions. Respect is earned by managers exactly the same way it is earned among workers, through honesty, genuine care and concern, competence, loyalty, fairness, and the offering of respect to others. Managers who are perceived to have these traits are respected. To the extent they lack them, they are disrespected.

The greatest problem with gaining respect is communication. It is essential that managers beware of the *math teacher syndrome*. This is my name for the all-too-common tendency to assume that what is clear to you must be clear to others, that what is easy for you is easy for others, that whatever you have said is understood and clear to those you've spoken to.

As recently as the late 1980s, one could still buy books touting the old saw *information is power*. To gain power you must control information. This is still true, of course, if your goal is to gain power. However, if your goal is to manage, to lead, then sharing information is the only logical route to follow. Human beings need to know everything about what they are doing, often even the irrelevant things. This need runs very deep in our nature. We start to ask "why" as soon as we can speak. Respect comes from sharing information, not from withholding it.

Think About Special Requirements

Take into consideration special requirements of this group. If you are training shift workers, recognize that someone who has just put in eight hours of hard work is unlikely to be sharp and active, and at his or her best, for an additional eight hours of training. Either train in short bits of one or two hours, or arrange for the workers to be free from shift work on days when they are to be trained. Management training takes people out of their workstations—so should worker training.

Remember, too, that many hourly workers are on their feet most of their working day. It is very uncomfortable for them to have to sit through eight hours of cerebral and oral activity. Create more opportunities for them to stand. Call more frequent breaks. Develop games and/or assignments that allow them to be more active.

If your workers are unionized, consider the union. Don't fight it; you'll lose. Invite the shop steward to attend the training and ask him or her to participate and perhaps even handle a small aspect of the training. If necessary, consult a higher authority in the union hierarchy to invite guests to the training. Keep the union informed as much, or even more, than you keep management informed. This both minimizes union interference and gains support among the militant union members in your classes.

Always remember Joan Chesterton's advice: "What's in and what's out, what's funny and what's not, may vary sharply, depending on education, gender, class and income level of trainer and trainee. Becoming sensitive to cultural differences and respecting the preferences of others can build a bridge of trust between trainer and [trainee]."[3]

Principles of Learning in a Technical Environment

In 1985 the New York University School of Dentistry tried an experiment.[4] Traditionally, first-year dentistry students spent four months in the classroom studying

---

Gaining Credibility in Technical Training

1. Make yourself a subject expert.
2. Don't assume that because they are not managers they are not smart or capable. Don't underestimate their intelligence and ability to learn.
3. Don't assume they hate their jobs. Most love them.
4. Recognize that your trainees are not couch potatoes. Many of them are very active and talented outside of their work role. Respect and use this.
5. Realize they do not automatically respect management nor do they respect management's decisions. Respect is earned. A title doesn't confer it. Not even the title of trainer.
6. Take into consideration the special nature of their work and/or culture. Schedule around shifts. Let those who work on their feet use their feet. Don't condescend, but do make yourself aware of cultural humor patterns and language.

---

the theory and terminology of bridgework and prosthetics, then went to a two-month series of laboratory sessions to learn the mechanical and craft skills involved. Not that year. The school decided to start the first-year dentists in the lab and give them the theory later.

The dentists-to-be went into the lab knowing none of the terminology, theory, or background material. They were confused at first and made a number of mistakes (on models, not on live patients). Yet, they picked up the skills quickly. After two months of working in the laboratory, they were as skilled at working the various procedures and tools as any other class had been. Then they were sent to the theory and background section of the course to find out how what they had learned to do was supposed to be done, and how it worked medically. They finished this part of the course in less than two months, with higher average scores on final tests than preceding classes who had had the traditional four months of study.

By becoming active in the learning process, they had learned not only the traditional manual skills but had also cut the learning time of the necessary theoretical support material in half. They learned better because they learned actively. When you are training people in technical skills, whether they are prospective dentists at a prestigious university or high school dropouts learning to enter the world of work for the first time, the single most important principle of learning is *active versus passive*.

We spoke in detail about the principles of learning in Chapter 1. I'm now going to select the four most important ones for technical training so that you can build your training session around them.

Active vs. Passive

No one ever learned how to do something without actually doing it. People say to me, "Well, I read an excellent book that told me step-by-step how to do this." Fine. But they don't really know how to do it until they actually try it out, feel what each step does in their hands, see the results of each action they take. You cannot learn to cook without actually using a stove (or heat source of some sort). You cannot learn to operate a machine without actually running it. You cannot learn to use a tool without actually using the tool to perform its intended function. All technical training must be predominantly built around the activities of the learner performing the job being taught. Sixty percent of training time should be devoted to practice and coaching. Instruction should take no more than 40 percent of the time allotted. Follow these steps:

1. *Set your skills objectives first.* Then decide what actual hands-on practice will allow you to gauge how well they've learned. Decide how much practice and coaching they will need to get to that level. Build all of these factors into your training plan and then, not before, plan the instruction you will need to give them.

2. *Book the equipment for practice, or devise simulations or working models for them before you plan your lessons.* This way each event in your lessons will be practiced by the learners.

3. *If time is limited, cut the scope of the training down.* Do not cut the amount of practice. If anything, increase it.

4. *Train Socratically.* You will be surprised at how much they can tell you. Ask first. Lecture and explain only when they don't know the answers.

5. *Wherever possible, let the learners discover how things operate rather than telling them.* Position them at the controls and ask them how they feel they should proceed. Give them guidance as necessary but always ask first.

6. *Use a buddy system if possible.* Let them help each other.

Readiness vs. Resistance

Resistance can occur with any type of training. We all like to remain comfortable. As long as training is trying to change our comfortable patterns of behavior to new and possibly uncomfortable ones, we will tend to resist that training. It is vital, therefore, to give technical learners good sound reasons for why they are learning, reasons that make sense from their point of view. Fortunately, by building active hands-on experience into your training from the start, you create the opportunity for the learners to get comfortable with the new processes and to enjoy watching their own progress. This in itself tends to lower resistance. There-fore:

1. *Whenever possible, find out ahead of time how the trainees feel about the upcoming training.* Do this weeks before the training is scheduled. See Chapter 4 for details on needs analysis.

2. *Ask questions.* Respond to frowns. Take every opportunity to ventilate any possible resistance. (See Chapter 1.)

3. *Have the learners explain to you what they are doing while they perform the task.* Ask them to explain why these steps are important. Talking about what we are doing builds a sense of ownership and creates buy-in.

4. *Let the hands-on sessions work their magic.* It's hard to resist what we are gain-ing competence in.

Association

Most technical skills are very practical. This can be a tremendous help both in dealing with resistance and in creating bridges from what the learners already know to the new skills you want them to learn. In addition, many people in train-ing classes for technical skills will already have a technical aptitude in other non-job-related areas. These outside skills provide a rich source for using association to contrast a skill they already know with the one you are teaching them. There-fore:

1. *If you don't know the trainees' background skills, refer back to some common back-ground skills.* Nearly everyone drives a car. Most of us have played some sort of sport. Nearly everyone watches television (though not always the same shows). We have all shared relationships with families. We have all dated. We all eat out, etc.

2. *Try to match as closely as possible the steps, sequence, or key concepts in the two skills you are associating.* The bigger the gap, the less effective the association.

3. *Association doesn't have to be positive.* It can contrast desirable skills with un-desirable skills. It can also contrast more than two skills or events.

4. *Ask the trainees to provide examples you can build association on.*

Less Is More

In today's high-tech world, much technical training has its own insider's jargon, or scientific terminology, complete with acronyms and other aspects of technobabble. Few things will turn a learner away faster than a blizzard of terminology or a too rapid zip through a many stepped process. Information overload is a painful disease and quickly leads to frustration and loss of interest. To train technical people, you must simplify and use signposts for every step that you teach. Borrow from the New York University School of Dentistry. Your trainees will understand the reasons or theories behind their actions a great deal faster once they feel comfortable with the actions they will have to perform.

 - *Remember we organize all things into patterns.* Random information is useless. Create strong, simple, logical, visual, or artistic patterns to explain your information. The more technical it is, the more it needs this patterning. Use association.
 - *It is very easy to go too fast over complex new ground.* Beware of the math teacher syndrome. Provide many street signs and give ample warning when you are going to turn a corner.
 - *Review and summarize frequently.*
 - *Ask the learners to do the review and summary.* Help them to be active whenever possible.

Training in a Sales Environment

Training salespeople is one of the oldest areas of training. Long before we realized that managers performed better when they were well trained, we recognized the need to train salespeople. Technical training had begun with the guild system back in the Middle Ages, but aside from this one-on-one passing of mastery from generation to generation, very little training was done until the 1920s. With the advent of door-to-door selling, the need for training salespeople became apparent. So sales training has been around for a while. And that's part of the problem.

Newly hired sales representatives usually expect to be trained both in the knowledge of the product or service they are expected to sell and in the sales techniques that have been proven to work with this product or service. But once they are given the basics, there is a tendency for many salespeople to imagine that they have all of the training they need. Therefore, they resist any further efforts at formal training.

There are three common reasons for this phenomenon:

1. The quality of the initial training is sometimes so inadequate that it is unrelated to the real world the trainees will have to sell in. Hence, they resist further efforts to "train" them. They tried it once and it didn't do any good, so more would be a waste of time.

2. For commissioned salespeople, training takes them out of the field and, therefore, costs them time in which they could be earning money.

Sample Technical Skills Lesson Plan

Training Population: Four apprentice plumbers

Duration: One hour

Topic: Sweat-Soldering Copper Pipe

Objectives: Upon completion of this lesson each apprentice will be able to:
- Correctly clean and prepare copper surfaces for soldering.
- Light and properly adjust the torch.
- Correctly sweat-solder waterproof copper joins.
- Describe the following principles active in the soldering process: osmosis, thermodynamic gradients, and the use and function of catalysts.

Preparation
5 minutes: Each participant will be given a section of joined lead pipe and one of copper pipe. They will be asked to examine each one. Questions:
- "What differences are apparent to you?"
- "What advantages or disadvantages do you see for each of these differences?"
- "If I could show you a way to save time and effort on the job, would you use it?"

Presentation
5 minutes:
- Using diagram, real pipe, and (if possible) blow-up model, explain and show the thermodynamic gradient effect (differences in circumference create a microscopic space between smaller and larger units when each is expanded by heating).
- Using string and colored water in a cup, explain and show the principle of osmosis (liquid drawn into and filling a small space against gravity).
- Ask, "How do these two principles relate to the task in hand?"
- Explain the role of flux (catalyst).

Presentation and Application 20 minutes:	▪ *Step one:* Explain and demonstrate preparing the join. Apprentices then practice cleaning surface, applying flux, dry-joining the units. ▪ *Step two:* Explain and demonstrate lighting the torch and adjusting it to proper temperature. Apprentices then practice the procedure. ▪ *Step three:* Explain and demonstrate applying solder and creating a waterproof join. Apprentices then practice the procedure.
Practice Session 30 minutes:	▪ Each apprentice will perform three joins to be checked by the instructor. ▪ Each apprentice will then be assigned a segment of the actual plumbing in the training area (removed by instructor prior to the training session) and will be required to properly install that section. Each will be required to create a series of standard sweat-solder joins on the actual plumbing in the training area.
Evaluation:	Individual coaching and personal checking of each solder join immediately after it is completed. The final test will be to pass water under pressure through the plumbing.

3. The belief exists that as long as they are selling enough product or service, they must be doing something right and so don't need training. Of course, when they are not selling enough, their luck has soured or the market has turned down or they're just in a temporary slump, or some other such excuse keeps them from selling up to their potential.

In my experience, while new hires seldom resist training, seasoned sales reps are initially among the most resistant of learners. They are resistant because of all of the above reasons plus one more key one: They are shy about demonstrating their skill, or lack of it, in front of their peers. Selling is essentially a lonely task. The contact between the customer and the salesperson, whether face-to-face or by telephone, is largely a private one. Yet when they come to training, salespeople are usually expected to role-play their newly understood techniques. This is a traumatic experience for many.

The difficulty lies in the nature of the simulation. It is role-*playing*. Pretend is never real. They are salespeople, not actors. I have watched hundreds of skilled sales experts balk at the idea of role-playing in front of their peers. Frequently when I insist, they do not do well and need to resort to face-saving excuses, or worse, exaggerated buffoonery, which makes a mockery of the role-play. They must save face. They need to make it clear that the role-play is totally unreal and not at all like the real world they succeed in every day. Furthermore, when they fail in the role-play, they become more convinced that the old way they have been selling is better and that the new technique they have been exposed to in the training session will not work. This is the prime source of resistance to training among salespeople.

Responses to the Problem

There are four things you can do to address their resistance. Each of these responses works, but I find that a combination of several of them works best.

Set Goals and Standards for the Role Play. What frequently happens when salespeople role-play is that the one acting as the customer pulls out every dirty trick in the book and really beats up on the one playing sales rep. Don't allow this to happen. Describe in detail in a written assignment what the background and circumstances of each player are. Set minimum goals for both the customer and the salesperson so that each is challenged to strive to achieve something during the role-play aside from getting through it. Tell the customer that he or she must raise a particular objection or set of objections. Tell him or her that, if the salesperson responds as taught in the class, he or she must respond a certain way. Make the responses realistic but very specific.

By creating tighter scripts you guarantee each participant the opportunity to succeed using your newly taught instructions. You also have the opportunity to provide constructive feedback to help each of them become comfortable with the new responses. As they get better, you can increase the severity of the customer's response and make the selling task realistically tough. But don't let it start there. Build to it in controlled steps.

Be Real. Make the role-plays as realistic as possible. Base them on real situations from the field. If possible, use real-life customers to build your role-playing characters. Use traits that the salespeople can recognize and identify with. In this manner you make the simulation much more interesting and demanding at the same time.

If necessary, remove the salespeople to a simulated customer environment. I have had success with setting up a role-playing room as a typical customer office or home and videotaping the role-plays there. Then afterward, you can view the tape together and discuss in detail aspects that will help the salesperson to improve.

Remain Assertive. Role plays cannot deteriorate if you don't allow them to. Interrupt whenever the salesperson seems unable to handle the customer situation or gets offtrack. Remember, you must save face. Ask what else might be an effective response to the situation. Bring in class discussion. Let others suggest ideas, then go back to where the role-play got offtrack and start from there. If the customer is offtrack, interrupt and remind him or her of the rules for the role-play. The closer you keep them on track, the more they will learn.

Make It Fun. Two ways to engage the group are to make the role-plays a team effort and to make the effort a game. In the first case, your best salesperson can play the customer (with strong guidelines to help him or her stay on track). Then the rest of the group is divided into teams and each team is responsible for the role-play. Only one person at a time talks to the customer, but any team member can tag in and take the role-player's place at any time that they have a better idea of how to proceed or any time the role-player needs help. Of course, teams can compete with each other. I have found this type of role-play to be raucous fun, but you must keep a lid on it or it, too, will get out of hand and the learning experience will be lost.

I have also found the game system profitable. In this case, both the customer and the salespeople make up a team. Each team starts with a given number of points. Using certain key phrases or sales techniques will gain them more points. Each side wins points when it gets the other side to concede (the sellers sell or the buyers succeed in rejecting). Each side loses points for failing to do certain key things. In one particular game, each member of the team must take a turn in the actual role-play or the team loses points. In this way you get even the most shy ones into the act.[5]

Principles of Learning in a Sales Environment

Two principles are paramount in training salespeople: active versus passive and readiness versus resistance. Let's look at each one.

Active vs. Passive. All too frequently sales training consists of passive lecture sessions. Sales managers hold meetings to harangue their people and call it sales training. Companies buy audiotapes for their salespeople to play and listen to and call it sales training (see Chapter 9 for a more detailed discussion of the correct uses for audiotapes). Companies hire high-priced motivational consultants or sports figures to come in and deliver an hour or so of pep talk and call it sales training. These are all pleasant enough experiences, and may even have a legitimate place in preparing salespeople, but none of them is training. Remember, we learn only what we *do*. In order to be training, it must be active. However, all of these sessions are passive.

As I have indicated, role-plays are essential to get any kind of transfer of learning to take place. But there are other ways to create active learning:

1. *Use Socratic instruction as much as possible.* Seek input from salespeople and their experiences. Don't lecture.
2. *Let them figure out how to deal with problems.* Assign problems as group activities. They can give you the right answers.
3. *Don't tell, ask.* Ask them to describe the benefits that the customer can derive from your product's features. Ask them. They can figure it out.
4. *Let them define their own goals and quotas in groups.* One of the most exciting sessions I've conducted recently was to lead a group of top-end salespeople through the elements of creating a market plan. They brainstormed in small groups and as a class. Individuals gathered information and shared it in presentation sessions. And, at the end of two days, the company had a dynamic and ingenious market plan that was created with the help and input of the frontline salespeople who would have to carry it out. Because they had developed it, they could hardly wait to get out in the field and make it happen. Let them help to frame the company's marketing strategy. Everyone benefits.
5. *Allow them to create tests and develop role-plays for their own use.* You can assign team projects to create test questions that will be asked of, or role-plays played by, competitive teams.
6. *Create case situations that require them to work through a series of calls on a single customer.* Let them work out a strategy in their small groups to penetrate such an account.

Remember, the more active the participation, the more effectively the salespeople will transfer what they've learned in the classroom to the field.

Readiness vs. Resistance. As I've pointed out, salespeople do resist training. Like all of us, in addition to the special reasons for resistance we've discussed, they are loath to change their habits. Even habits that are counterproductive feel more comfortable than the new ways you are trying to get them to learn. Remember the seven sources of resistance (see Chapter 1), and be prepared to respond positively to each of them. Here are some ways to help them to make that change:

1. *Develop real and meaningful answers to the questions: "What's in it for me? Why should I?"* If salespeople can see a clear benefit to sales training, they will take it. Show them a dollar increase in commissions. Promise that the training will take care of a problem they face. Demonstrate that your training will make some facet of their work easier or more effective. If they can't see a benefit for themselves, they will resist the training and may even try to undermine it.

2. *If you need to, gain credibility.* Show them that you know your stuff. Don't brag. Be simple, but let them know that you have been where they are. If this is a problem for you (that is, you haven't been there), develop clear case examples that ring true for them. Learn to talk the talk. Show that you've done your homework. Start on time, create clear signposts and follow that agenda. Let them know they can count on your doing what you say you will do.

3. *Have them ventilate their understandings and doubts about the class.* Have a clear set of learning objectives and benefits to share with them. Reframe the purpose of the class in positive terms.

4. *Minimize change.* Build on what they've done in the past. Coach those that have a unique style. Don't try to force unnecessary change on them. Help them to remain as comfortable as possible while they achieve your training objectives.

5. *Create a climate where it is permissible to be wrong, to make mistakes.* Work to prevent efforts that judge, embarrass, or humiliate others. Create a positive climate that is supportive and yet objective-driven. I often tell people who are really good at a task to keep using their way if that is what they want, but, just to see how it feels, to try my new way a few times in practice. Then we discuss how it feels, not how well they did it. When they do well, they usually appreciate the new method and adopt it. If they don't feel comfortable or don't do well at first, at least you've made the situation nonjudgmental. They save face.

6. *Be aware that salespeople are very sensitive to their peers.* Because they face rejection every day in their work, they are supersensitive to it among their friends and coworkers. Work with the movers and shakers, the peer leaders, to get them to help you build a positive climate for them and their people. Solicit their input. Make them team leaders. Put them in charge of making the assignments real. If the leaders build it, the group will buy it.

7. *Start strong.* Make a dynamic first impression. These are people who are used to psyching themselves up and to being psyched up by others. They need to feel like professionals and so you need to come across as just that.

Finally, in my experience, most resistant salespeople will eventually come around. Some will recognize the value of your training sooner than others. The earlier you can get them to come along, the better.

Training in the Retail Sales Environment

Selling in a retail environment creates several additional problems for training. Active versus passive is still the operative learning principle, but resistance is usually much less in retail than in outside sales. The difference lies in the demographics. According to the Department of Labor and the National Retail Federation (NRF), turnover rates in retail are as high as 100 percent per year.[6] According to a 1993 study by the National Retail Institute (a division of the NRF), retail sales account for 25 percent of all part-time jobs in the United States. More than half of these part-timers are under the age of twenty-five, on their way to other jobs, and more than 60 percent are women who either do not need or do not have time for full-time employment. Nearly three-quarters of these retail salespeople work part-time by choice. Furthermore, retail selling accounts for an estimated 40 percent of all jobs in the United States.

The implications for training are obvious. These workers are there because they want to be there. They are new to the job. They know that they need to learn how to do it. Resistance to learning is low. However, because of the likelihood of short-term employment, companies are loath to carve out scarce funds for more than cursory training. Consequently, retail salespeople are more likely to be uncommitted to the job rather than resistant to training. Therefore, trainers must be more concerned when working with this group about morale and motivation than with resistance to training. Successful, large retail organizations such as McDonald's and Wal-Mart, therefore, regularly instill elements of evangelical fervor into their training. The goal is to motivate the learners and get them excited about what they are learning about the company and, most important, about serving the customers.

The NRF's Grant Management Committee spent two years developing job skills standards for the retail industry. The committee was made up of such retail giants as J.C. Penney Co., Federated Department Stores, Inc., Woolworth Corp., Nordstrom, Inc., Crate and Barrel, Toys 'R' Us Inc., and Kmart Corp., as well as representatives from labor, government, and education.

The standards they created are divided into six modules, each laying out minimum requirements for the best performance of the retail selling position. The six modules involve:

1. Providing personalized customer service, which consists of clear communication skills, elements of courtesy and good manners, responding appropriately to emotional customers, and so forth.

2. Selling and promoting products, which is a unit on basic selling skills including asking questions, listening, stressing benefits, cross selling, responding to objections, closing, and building future business.

3. Monitoring inventory, which involves learning record-keeping and organizing skills.

4. Maintaining the appearance of the store, which includes elements of display, arrangement, dress, and image.

5. Protecting company assets, which is a module on cash handling, equipment operations, and math skills.

6. Working as part of a team that, as the name suggests, consists of team-building skills and motivational training.

Each of these modules needs to be tailored and shaped to the specifics of the operation doing the training. However, the committee also identified a number of generic skills that need to be mastered in the context of the six main modules:

- Reading and understanding what is read
- Mathematical and number skills
- Listening
- Clear concise writing
- Basic cash register skills and computer and telephone skills, where they are needed
- Teamwork
- Developing and maintaining a positive attitude
- Elements of good manners
- Reliability
- Taking initiative
- Building self-confidence

These are the skills of retail sales. Note that there is a strong emphasis on personal development and motivational skills. Remember, too, that each of these skills must be practiced in a realistic environment. The more realistic the simulation, the better the likelihood that the learners will transfer the learning to their workplace. The Broyhill Company, for example, maintains a full showroom of its furniture, set up exactly as it would be in a retail store, which is used exclusively for training its salespeople.

Summary

In this chapter we explored the myths that cloud the attitudes of many trainers toward technical and blue-collar workers and the attitudes of those workers toward training. We traced the reasons for such attitudes and what you can do to combat them, both in your learners and in yourself. We examined how to apply the principles of learning to technical training and provided some pointers on how to gain credibility, create strong signposts for training, and keep training active. We also addressed resistance to training and gave some tips on how to respond to it.

In the sales environment, we talked about the two major attributes of sales training: keeping it active rather than passive, and dealing with the almost ever-present resistance of salespeople to training. We explored a special section on what standards are necessary for retail sales training.

Finally, we provided two lesson plans, one for technical skills training and the other for sales training.

Sample Sales Lesson Plan

Topic:	Features, Advantages, and Benefits
Time:	One hour
Trainees:	Twenty sales representatives
Objectives:	Upon completion of this lesson, sales representatives will be able to:

- Explain why people buy.
- Contrast and compare features, advantages, and benefits.
- Create benefit statements for the product.
- Use benefit statements in a sales role-play.

Preparation 12 minutes:

- Ask, "Why do we buy the things we buy?"
- Ask, "Who has recently purchased a major appliance? A car? A house?"
- Select two or three trainees to tell about their purchases.
- Probe by asking, "Why? What were the qualities of the things you bought that led you to make that choice?"
- Answers should be qualities such as style, capacity, color, price, service, etc.
- Ask, "Is it really the style (capacity, color, price) that made you buy? Wasn't it more that by buying a particular style you became stylish?

Presentation 5 minutes:

Explain that certain features of a product or service do things for us. It is these things that people buy the product or service to get, not the feature or any advantage that feature may give us over our competition.

Application 10 minutes:

- Break the group into small groups of four.
- Have groups brainstorm and list:
  - —The features of our product/service
  - —The sales advantages (if any) that each of these features gives us over our competition
  - —The benefits to the customer that each of these features provides the customer

Presentation 18 minutes:

Share these on flip charts. Ask each group for one and continue to rotate through the groups until they run out of answers.

Application 24 minutes:	▪ Break into groups of two.
	▪ Script effective phrasing of how to express each benefit (assign each pair two or three specific benefits).
	▪ Role-play, explaining each benefit using the key words and phrases they have created. Alternate sales and customer roles.
Evaluation 15 minutes:	(simultaneous with the Application step above)
	▪ Listen to each pair and provide coaching and feedback.

Applications

1. Make a list of five ways in which you can gain credibility with technical trainees.

2. Write a lesson plan to teach a technical skill. Remember to balance instruction and practice to create a minimum 60/40 percent ratio. When you have completed it, increase the practice time by 20 percent.

3. Write a role-play scenario. Create a personality, background, and point of view for the customer. Do the same for the salesperson. Add key demands, limits, and goals for each side. Write key phrases or skills that must be incorporated in the role-play.

Part 4

Managing the Training Function

Introduction to Part 4

This part addresses problems that training managers are likely to face, whether they are managers of large and active training departments or run small one-person operations. I've divided the problems into three broad categories: managing the training department (such as scheduling, budgeting, and handling subordinates); selling your training ideas to management and other departments; and negotiating with outside vendors, other departments, management, and subordinate staff. These tasks must be mastered by a training manager, whether experienced or just recently promoted to managing the whole training function. In essence, this material is a checklist on how to function as a training manager.

The approach here is consistent with the rest of the book in that it provides simple how-to information and avoids complexity wherever possible. There are more involved (perhaps even more accurate) systems available for accomplishing these tasks, but none is more effective for normal operations.

In Chapter 15, we look at the everyday tasks of managing people and money. Included here are general budgeting approaches and a specific budgeting format for a single seminar or training program. There is a breakdown of different training tasks and forms of employee (that is, trainer) performance evaluations, with discussion of familiar formats such as management by objectives. Approaches to praising, motivating, and criticizing subordinates are discussed along with Hersey and Blanchard's situational leadership system for developing employee skills and abilities.

Chapter 16 describes the steps to take in putting your training programs on the map in your organization as well as maintaining a high profile once you've achieved that. Because the marketing of training involves written communication, some guidelines for good writing are also included.

Chapter 17 presents some general principles of negotiation and then applies those principles to specific situations such as working with vendors, negotiating with subordinates, and arranging agreements with peers to train their people. Negotiations are viewed in terms of variables: time, information, and power. A set of questions is provided to help you prepare for negotiations along with a list of specific tactics to use.

As with the rest of the book, this section can be used as a convenient reference to refresh your memory and as a basic textbook of fundamental techniques and issues. It is also a resource for developing training personnel so they can eventually accept management responsibility on their own.

Chapter 15

Managing the Training Department

THE duties of management can be broken down into three arenas of activity: physical resources, human resources, and financial resources. Most managers tend to be good at one or two of these and regard the remaining one as a chore—something to struggle through when the time arises. We've discussed the importance of physical setting in Chapter 11. And being a trainer, you know that the human resources arena is paramount. If you are like most trainers, you probably concentrate on these two arenas and save financial management for budget time. This chapter discusses both human and financial resources, but begins with the often neglected topic of financial management.

Managing Your Financial Resources

Are you one of those managers who neglects the financial aspects of training? It needn't be so. Nothing gains the respect of financial people (for whom training personnel are a liability, remember) like careful allocation of financial resources. It's a good way to develop political friends.

In fact, budgeting benefits you in several ways. It promotes an analysis of existing activities, forcing you to take stock. It places your focus on the future and on future planning. And it provides a reference point for measuring performance (yours and your subordinates'). Budgeting also motivates you by forcing you to set goals and inspiring you to reach them. It focuses attention on priorities and makes you work for what is most important. Lastly, it fosters timely action to deal with upcoming operations.[1]

The first thing to recognize is that anyone can make up a budget. The challenge lies in making a budget that reflects your circumstances and that plans

---

Benefits of Budgeting

- Promotes analysis of existing activities
- Focuses on future planning
- Establishes reference points for measuring performance
- Motivates you to achieve your goals
- Focuses your attention on priorities
- Fosters timely action

---

accurately for future needs. As with computers, if you put garbage into a budget, you'll get garbage out. So the first step in making a budget is to gather accurate information.

The budget information you gather should answer three questions:

1. What is your cost history?
2. What is the present state of affairs?
3. Where do you want to go?

Based on the answers to the first two, you can determine how much you will need to get there.

There are two recognized types of costs to be budgeted: fixed and variable. Every budget format takes both into consideration, but they don't all do it equally well. If you mainly have fixed expenses (that is, wages, contributions to overhead, amortization of equipment, material costs, or scheduled maintenance), then a fixed-cost budget format is best. On the other hand, if you have a large number of variable costs (that is, new equipment, off-the-shelf package purchases, last-minute consultants, off-site locations, responses to management's reactive training requests, unscheduled maintenance, or equipment rentals), you'll need a budget format that accommodates variables and makes them easier to predict.

Fixed-Cost Budgets

There are two common formats for a fixed-cost budget. The first is planning, programming, and budgeting; the second is zero-based budgeting.

The Planning, Programming, and Budgeting System. In this approach there are five steps to preparing a budget:

1. Define and analyze your objectives. Trace last year's performances and compare them with current levels of performance. Determine what changes you want to achieve in the next year.

2. Analyze anticipated output in light of each objective. In effect, list the benefits to the company, in terms of money saved or increased dollars earned; that is, show the impact of each objective.

3. Using items 1 and 2 above, project the anticipated total costs for several years ahead (say, five years).

4. Put forward and analyze the alternatives to achieving your objectives. This is a vital step. It helps you develop convincing reasons for accepting your budget and training plans. It also encourages you to create contingency plans; these are vital because, in the event your budget isn't approved, you may have to accept one of these alternatives.

5. Break down dollar figures into interim and total costs. If approved, this will be your budget.

The Zero-Based Budgeting System. This approach was made popular in the late 1970s by the Carter administration. It assumes that there was no last year. You start from scratch (base zero). There are three rather simple, direct steps:

1. Break down all your activities into *decision packages;* that is, define and list the activities, clustering the related ones.

2. Evaluate each decision package and rank it on a scale from most important to least important.

3. Allocate your resources according to your rankings. If you want to accomplish all of them, it will cost more, and so you must ask for more money.

This system forces you to set clear priorities and then fund items in accordance with those priorities. The most important things get done; the least important are not so costly if they don't get done.

Variable-Cost Budgets

The greatest problem with fixed-cost budgets is that they usually can't handle contingencies. The variable-cost budget does deal with contingencies, but for that very reason it is less accurate. There are four approaches to variable-cost budgeting:

1. Direct estimates
2. Minimum-maximum

3. Correlation standard
4. Cost per unit

Direct Estimates. This is actually contingency planning. You base your estimates on past years' operations. If you are just beginning and have no past history to draw upon, use industry standards, data from your training network, or information from similar departments in your company. You can estimate flexible costs within a range, and budget for the top of that range. For example, this approach is used by some city governments to budget for snow removal. It works best with a carryover fund to draw against in shortfall years and to contribute to in surplus ones.

Minimum-Maximum. In this system, you address the problem of variable costs by creating two budgets: a minimum budget to keep you afloat and a maximum budget to allow you to grow. You ask for the minimum, but are allowed to draw up to the maximum as conditions dictate. Monthly operating expenses are figured on a formula based on the difference between the minimum and maximum amounts divided by the degree of fluctuation (such as changes, training days, travel costs, or off-site location expenses). You use the minimum budget as the baseline and the maximum as the limiter.

Correlation, or Historical, Standard. This is perhaps the most common type of variable-cost budget. You take the cost for each month and compare it to the equivalent month last year. Desired changes are forecast and accounted for. You are, however, linked to last year's patterns, which your training may change. It also assumes that while there are month-to-month variations, the monthly patterns themselves are not variable. As you know, this is not always the case.

Cost per Unit. A variation on the correlational format is to break all costs down to a per-unit measurement. For training, that breakdown would be a cost-per-person amount. Based on past costs, it is possible to project a fairly accurate budget by estimating the number of employees to be trained. This offers the added advantage of backup evidence from attendance records to show that you are on target. Such systems are used by public seminar organizations, by advertising agencies, and by direct mail marketing groups.

General Budgeting Considerations

The following four budgetary considerations should be helpful to the new training manager and may be food for thought for experienced managers, too:

1. Keep closer tabs on expenses by segmenting budgets into weekly, monthly, and quarterly goals. Thus, a very costly month can be balanced by a frugal one to keep the year in line.

2. In setting interim goals, use past data to predict where you should be at any given period. However, adjust the data and your goals to reflect projected trends and changes. This is especially useful when planning long-range, gradual growth.

3. Build attainment of major objectives into these interim milestones. Equipment purchases, for example, can be spaced out in planned intervals to look less costly in the annual budget.

4. Consider the budgetary impact of leasing versus outright purchase. Your accountant and company purchasing people can help you here. Purchase is a one-time variable capital expense. Leasing is a constant fixed expense that comes out of the operating budget.

Program Budgeting

So far we have talked only about budgeting for the department. Another separate, and vital, budget is the one drawn up for each training program. There are two sets of information you need: direct training costs and company costs. (See Chapter 4 for additional considerations.) The first we refer to as raw costs, and the latter as both gray-area costs and hidden costs. Which costs you include in your budget depends upon how you want to use the budget.

Raw Costs. In all cases you need to look at the raw cost—or training budget—first. This is the simplest budget format, and it is a tally of the costs to your department of a given training program. For comparison, it is also useful to divide the total cost by the number of participants you will be training. This gives you a cost-per-person figure that can be used to justify alternatives, prove the bottom-line value of training, call for departmental budget increases, and so forth.

The raw costs may include the following variables:

- Developing new programs
- Setting up and carrying out evaluations
- Preparing and duplicating handout materials
- Creating new audiovisual aids
- Obtaining outside materials (such as consultants or off-the-shelf packages)
- Renting off-site facilities
- Providing service setups on site or off site (coffee breaks, plus tips for serving personnel)
- Trainer travel

Gray-Area Costs. These don't usually come out of a training department's budget but are, nonetheless, important factors for the company. Gray-area costs usually come out of budgets for those departments or divisions sending people for training. Costs may include the following:

- Trainee travel (including transportation, room, meals, and entertainment)
- Lost work time of trainees

Hidden Costs. These are usually limited to the overall costs of maintaining training. For example, putting on a seminar involves a portion of the training department salaries to cover both actual training and preparation time. In addition, the costs of space (such as heating, furnishing, or lighting) are a percentage of company overhead. Such costs are monitored by the accounting department, so you should be aware of them.

For purposes of comparison and persuasion, all training program budgets should contain a list or breakdown of the costs per trainee. Whether you include gray-area costs depends upon the purpose of the budget. If it is to be seen by managers upon whom those gray areas impact, then by all means you must address them. If management looks at larger costs, then you will have to include those larger costs.

Hidden costs are usually of little direct concern outside the training department. In cases of cost justification, however—particularly if you are under fire from cost-cutting movements—it pays to be able to detail the costs of maintaining any training function. It is most effective to be able to compare these costs (raw, gray-area, hidden, and total) with the costs of not training or of less training.

Managing Human Resources

For the rest of this chapter, we look at the management of human resources—those who work for you. The content is designed as a way of approaching management problems as a series of workable answers to those problems and as a refresher on creative resources for the experienced training manager.

The management of human resources requires overseeing the process of getting things done by other people, motivating people to enjoy doing things well, and developing those people into more competent workers for the company—in short, preparing them for management themselves. The first of these functions we call staffing; the second has two parts, assessment and motivation; and the third is development. Let's look at each in turn.

Staffing

Staffing is simply the division of labor.[2] When the job becomes too large for you to handle or, preferably, when you can predict that it will be, it is time to hire one or more subordinates to take over some of the tasks. Coordinating and controlling their efforts—that is, knowing who is doing what and when—is the manager's task.

The question of when to hire is answered by asking what you are hiring that person to do. In training, there are twelve categories of jobs. In very large organizations several people may work at the same job, with a supervisor or manager for each category. In many organizations only some of the twelve categories are pursued; however, as a rule, a training manager hires others (either on staff or as consultants) to perform one or more of these jobs.

Most trainers wear many of these hats. Only in the largest organizations is it possible for each job to be a separate position. But each is a separate task and should be viewed as such when bringing in new staff or dividing the workload among the current staff.

Technical Training. This division of training involves teaching skills to technical personnel. Skills can range from safety training or heavy equipment operation to word processing, from teller training to telephone skills and computer operation. These are the basics of your company's operations, and they are taught to entry-level, clerical, skilled, and production employees. We covered the how-to details of technical training in Chapter 14. This training often makes up the entire training effort. When the task is large, it is best subdivided into logical divisions of labor such as clerical, production machine, or customer service.

Sales Training. Selling is a frontline skill. It is also a specialized skill (see Chapter 14). In many cases, a make-or-break marketing approach results in a

---

Twelve Divisions of Training

1. Technical training
2. Sales training
3. Supervisory training
4. Management training and executive development
5. Instructional systems design
6. Internal consulting
7. Human resources planning
8. Career development
9. Training administration
10. Audiovisual management
11. Organizational development
12. Training management

---

high turnover rate. So most organizations that depend heavily on sales have regular sales training. All too frequently, sales training is handled by the sales department itself, on the theory that only a sales rep can teach sales. You may want a specialist to handle it for you.

Supervisory Training. Most companies promote employees, yet skilled laborers moving into a supervisor's position may know nothing about supervising others. They need training in this field. Much of what must be covered is explained in Chapters 12 and 13. Often the answer is to rely on a professional service organization such as the American Management Association, which has a course for first-time supervisors. But if your company is large or has special supervisory problems, this situation is usually best handled in-house.

Management Training and Executive Development. As managers are promoted, new problems and new responsibilities demand new training. Courses such as budgeting, planning, systems design, management by objectives, presentation skills, and negotiation are needed. As the management level gets higher, the pool of trainees becomes smaller, and fewer courses are required. In these instances, professional organizations and consultants are used more heavily.

Instructional Systems Design. Someone has to plan and write new training programs. Much of Part 2 was about how to perform this function. In large training organizations, planning new programs can be a full-time job. In smaller operations, the alternative may be to relieve a staff trainer of regular work so that person can perform this function or hire a consultant.

Internal Consulting. Many organizations are shifting to a profit-center accounting system for their training departments. In this way, the training department acts as a consultant to design programs and supply training services. Other departments that use this service are charged back for it, so training realizes a profit. To make this work, usually there should be someone to act as liaison, sales rep, marketing planner, needs analyzer, and—most often—program designer.

Human Resources Planning. This is the job you are doing when you read this chapter. It involves long-range planning and staffing for the whole company, particularly with regard to pay scales, work hours, enforcement of Equal Employment Opportunity Commission regulations, and pensions and benefits.

Career Development. A special, relatively new area for training, this involves helping management candidates achieve their career goals. It includes both serving as a learning resource for these fast-track executives as well as creating assessment standards whereby they are selected and tested for advancement.

Training Administration. This is the job of running the training plant, scheduling the courses and personnel, and registering the attendees. It is just one more task if you train only three people a year, but it is a major job if you have an active and complex department. Usually this job is performed by an administrator who need not necessarily be a skilled trainer.

Audiovisual Management. As demands for training expand and technologies for training continue to grow, so do audiovisual needs. Frequently, there is sufficient demand for a manager and a staff of four to five people just to acquire, maintain, and schedule audiovisuals. It is an important task, but one easily assigned to others. Of course, if you are producing your own audiovisuals, this becomes an even more demanding job.

Organizational Development. These people are the change specialists. When a company undertakes a corporatewide change, it is wise to hire a full-time organizational development specialist whose job it is to plan and administer the innovations desired. An organizational development administrator would be advisable, for example, if you were installing a companywide quality circle procedure. Such a staffer would also be useful in planning or instituting unpopular changes such as new work rules, downsizing efforts, or new labor-saving equipment.

Training Management. This is the boss—the person who does the planning for, coordinates, and staffs all other divisions of training. Depending on the size of the training organization and the importance of training to the company, this position can vary from a firstline managerial or supervisory responsibility to a fourth- or even fifth-level senior vice presidency. The training manager is responsible for all training and is the person to whom all other training personnel report.

Assessment

Assessment, which is one of the tasks in the second function of human resources management, is often seen as a chore by management and as a trial by subordinates. It should be neither. Subordinates are hired to relieve you of some duties so you can perform others. Unless they are very good at what they do, you will spend far too much time helping or correcting them or even redoing their work. That is self-defeating. The purpose of assessment is to measure how well subordinates do their work and to provide positive feedback to encourage them to improve their performance. They benefit from knowing how they're doing; you benefit by being able to trust more and more their ability to get results on their own.

To evaluate job performance you must specify precisely what the job entails. Your analysis doesn't have to be as detailed as for a formal task analysis (Chapter 6). However, you do need to break each subordinate's assignment into specific tasks, then categorize those tasks to evaluate the performance on a scale from excellent to unacceptable. To do this, first analyze the duties, responsibilities, and behaviors of the task to set up criteria, then identify the desired performance level for each specified task—in other words, the performance standards.

It is best to work these out with your subordinates so that they become mutually acceptable goals and measurements rather than imposed ones. The assessment process is then viewed in terms of job requirements rather than individual performance. When the focus is on the job requirements, the assessment process is removed from the difficult and subjective interpersonal arena.

With the job requirements established, you must decide how often you will assess your subordinates, what methods and what scale you will use to evaluate their performance, and what you will do with the data you collect. The question of how often to assess your subordinates depends upon:

- The maturity of your people (see the section on development later in this chapter) and how actively you wish to develop their capabilities
- Available time
- Company policy (if there is one)

Many companies assess employees only once a year, some every six months. If you are active in developing your subordinates' skills and abilities, you will need to evaluate much more frequently—at least quarterly, perhaps every six weeks or once a month.

The question of assessment methods depends on the performance standards you've set. Presumably you've worked out the job requirements together and are keeping a performance record to compare development. The areas traditionally measured are as follows:[3]

- *Personal traits.* These are individual qualities such as initiative, leadership, positive attitude, or competitive attitude. Exercise great care to ensure that each trait is clearly job-related. You need those assurances to comply with EEO regulations.

- *Job performance behaviors.* These are skills required of the job. How well do the subordinates perform them? Measure their performance against agreed-upon standards.

- *Job results.* Sometimes doing the job "right" with the "right" attitude isn't enough. Job results are an important check on the accuracy of your assessment standards.

Approaches to Setting Standards. There are four approaches commonly used to rate employee performance, as follows:

1. *Comparative standards.* In the comparative approach, each employee is ranked in comparison with his or her peers. In each job category the evaluation will reflect top performers, middle-range performers, and those needing help. Our school system uses this approach almost exclusively. It is also used when you engage in motivational ploys like performance bonuses and sales contests. Those who do best win; those who don't, don't win.

2. *Absolute standards.* In this approach, the company or management—sometimes with employee input—sets the performance standards. Standards are an objective description of the job. Workers are measured on how close they come to meeting or exceeding the standards. Training objectives (see Chapter 2) are of this type. Our school system uses this method when it sets passing and failing grades. But within this approach, there are two types of standards:

   ▪ *Qualitative standards* measure employees for correct (established) behavior on the job, in real or simulated circumstances. Critical incidents are recorded and analyzed in the real performance of the job. Simulations (such as fire drills, airline flight simulators, war games, or role-playing) are run periodically in training. Judgment here is much more subjective, but clearly defined standards can keep the simulations meaningful. We'll look directly at such an evaluation system, which you can incorporate into your training department.

   ▪ *Quantitative standards* are specific goals that each employee strives to meet or surpass. These are defined criteria similar to the points used by judges in some sporting events: the time, speed, or distance records athletes try to break; the sales quotas set by sales managers; the admission standards established by schools and colleges. In effect, they are the level or standard to achieve or surpass.

3. *Set goals.* This approach uses a system called *management by objectives,* whereby an employee and manager jointly set performance goals to be achieved by the employee within a certain time.[4] Job standards can be used as one measure of achieving these goals. Assessment takes place at the end of that time, and performance is measured by whether or not the goals were achieved. This approach can be combined very effectively with quantitative absolute standards, which were just described. In essence, you use this system whenever you conduct training to produce a change in behavior. You specify your goals (training objectives), train them, and either fail or succeed depending on whether those goals were met. As a training manager, this is one of the easiest measurement tools to use.

4. *Direct indexes.* This approach is the system discussed in Chapters 2 and 5 for measuring your own effectiveness as a trainer in achieving affective learning objectives.[5] You relate attitudes to specific job behaviors and then observe those

behaviors down the line. Measurements such as absenteeism, turnover rate, sales volume, customer complaints, and use of time are the means of gauging how well employees are doing their jobs.

I know of a training department that assesses its trainers solely by measuring trainee performance after training. If trainees have failed to change, to improve, or to meet new standards, then their trainer is viewed as having failed also. It's a tough system but a logical one. The principal drawback is that there are many factors beyond a trainer's control that can impact on trainee behavior. It is unfair to hold a trainer completely responsible, but this limitation can be balanced by using trainee performance back on the job as just one measurement of trainer performance. Used in this way, direct indexes are valid for training assessment. After all, isn't this how an entire training department is measured? Senior management asks what the impact of training is. They answer that question with the direct index of results.

Behaviorally Anchored Rating Scales. In discussing absolute standards I mentioned using qualitative ratings. This approach has a motivational aspect as well as an evaluative one. It is called BARS, which is both an acronym for *behaviorally anchored rating scales* and a description of the system.

To make an assessment system for your trainers' work, you need to devise a checklist—a way of objectively quantifying the incidence of correct (desired) behavior. To do so you need to:

■ Isolate a group of behaviors, traits, or characteristics that reflect each level of performance.

■ Arrange them in a simple checklist or devise a differential scale by which the behavior can be judged. Your scale could be along the line of always does, usually does, occasionally does, seldom does, rarely does, or never does.

With this checklist or scale you can evaluate performance insofar as it approaches the preset standards. While the observance is not totally objective, the standards you've set are, and the checklist or scale focuses your assessment sessions on performance of the job rather than on subjective evaluation.

The BARS system adds a motivational dimension to this basic structure. Because subordinates are measured against a standard, it is always best to engage them in setting those standards. If they have helped set them, they cannot later claim the standards are unfair. In addition, with BARS you don't just set one standard but, rather, a series of ascending layers or "bars" of behavioral standards, each for a level of performance superior to the one below. The final result will be descriptions of the following BARS levels:

- Behaviors that constitute excellent performance
- Behaviors that constitute very good, or far above average, performance
- Behaviors that constitute good, or a little above average, performance
- Behaviors that constitute average performance
- Behaviors that constitute nearly average performance, but that are still in need of improvement
- Behaviors that constitute below-average performance that will require a lot of work to correct
- Behaviors that constitute unacceptable performance

All of these "bars" are performance levels toward which the participants can strive. Use positive as well as negative descriptions and work each one out carefully with the employees. To standardize the achievement levels for all employees, have them also reflect the input of other subordinates but negotiate until the standards are acceptable to all involved. Once you have agreed upon standards, you can contract with each trainer to achieve or maintain a desired level. Each trainer's assessment is a measure of his or her success in reaching the BARS level chosen.

The key to BARS is using descriptive anchors to delineate the performance levels. Write these in much the same manner you wrote your training objectives (see Chapter 2). That is, they should be:

- Very specific examples of behavior.
- Realistic examples of behavior (avoid qualifying adjectives and adverbs such as good, acceptable, and so on).
- Measurable, observable behaviors; avoid assumptions about knowing or understanding.
- Descriptive rather than prescriptive to avoid quantifying the behaviors; describe the behaviors rather than call for how often they should be performed (save that for a related rating scale, if you like).
- Neutral; specify the behavior but make no demands and set no performance limits.

To describe an acceptable performance level, you would not say, "Trainer moves well, has good posture, and gestures effectively most of the time." This is not specific enough and has too many qualifiers. Instead, you might describe these behaviors as, "Trainer does not wander or pace idly. He (or she) stands with both feet on the floor about two feet apart and stands still and erect while doing so. He (or she) uses both hands above the waist with elbows extended and wrists firm when gesturing."

Goal Setting. BARS also can be used as a developmental tool. It fits well with management by objectives, a highly successful system of employee development and evaluation that has become very popular in recent years.[6] The system, which is treated briefly here, is concerned with output rather than "how to." That is, this system aims solely at end results; within reason, the ends justify the means. Manager and employees jointly frame the results employees will achieve in an agreed-upon time frame. Employees are free to try whatever methodology they can to obtain the result, and their success or failure is measured by that result.

Management by objectives is a very pragmatic system. It appears on the surface to be very mechanical, but the human side is obvious when you realize that the end result can (and, indeed, should often) be positive behavioral and skills goals. In my experience, this system is best when it is project-oriented. That is, a task is identified and then the results are agreed upon by management and subordinates. A time frame (perhaps in terms of a series of plateaus) for completion is decided upon and management contracts to supply the needed resources while employees contract to deliver the finished task in the agreed-upon time. Notice that the manager is responsible for supplying resources and help and, if requested, coaching to achieve the goal. The contract is not a one-way street. The manager is a resource; the subordinates get the job done.

As suggested earlier, the frequency of assessment sessions depends upon company standards, employee motivation, the developmental nature of the job, and the needs of the managers and the subordinates. On a project basis, assessments can be at every plateau. On an overall job basis, they can be annual. Final assessment standards can be based on self-improvement, on BARS, or on direct indexes.

Motivation

As I've said, this chapter is intended to give initial direction to newly appointed training managers and to provide food for thought for the experienced ones. Consequently, I touch on only one or two aspects of motivation. The main concern in motivation is that you need to motivate yourself and your employees every day, whether or not you have a formal motivation system. People need to feel good about what they do. They don't feel good when the job dissatisfiers outweigh the job satisfiers or when they aren't receiving the recognition they would like. Let's look at both the nature of satisfaction and personal recognition as the keys to motivation.

Satisfiers and Dissatisfiers. Many readers are familiar with the brilliant concepts of Frederick Herzberg.[7] Herzberg's landmark study of motivation in the early 1960s was the first to look at the things most managers felt motivated the workforce. His findings showed that these factors only motivated behavior in some limited circumstances and then, usually negatively. He called these *hygiene motivators* because, like dirty hands, they motivate us only when negative enough to come to our attention. We wash our hands to get rid of dirt, but we seldom set washing our hands as a goal. Among the hygiene motivators, Herzberg listed such things as wages (only important when we get less than someone else doing the same job), working conditions, and hours.

What Herzberg believes is that there are a number of other factors that move us in positive, purposeful directions. People work hard for something they believe in (a verification of self-worth), for a sense of achievement, and for the sheer pleasure of the task. These he called *real motivators*.

In my seminars I like to ask which participants have hobbies. I select a hobby that requires a great deal of time, and I ask why that person puts such effort into doing that after a long day or week of work. The answers are always the same:

- A sense of personal satisfaction
- A sense of achievement
- A potential for growth and mastery
- Recognition among peers
- A perception of the task as pleasurable and challenging rather than work
- A sense of personal responsibility

These things truly motivate us. Of course, other things do, too, or there would be no television game shows. But these reasons just given are triggers often left untouched by management.

Management by objectives, combined with Hersey and Blanchard's situational leadership and BARS, can foster a sense of personal development on the job rather than a feeling of being worn down by the daily grind. If emphasis is on growth and development—on mastery to succeed—rather than on assessment and evaluation for their own sake, then the perspective shifts to a motivational one. Objectives become personal challenges, and evaluations are merely checkpoints to measure progress.

To achieve this perception, make your standards a point of pride (as the Marines do). Create rewards and recognitions for achievement on all levels. Set personal goals as challenges rather than as being for the good of the company. Load work horizontally, not vertically.* Express pride and disappointment appropriately and use management by objectives to gain a commitment to improve. Challenge employees with realistic objectives and make them a team by developing esprit de corps. Lastly, create formal ranks or levels of aspiration and celebrate the rite of passage from one to the next. These actions will build a sense of worth and create a need to grow, a motivation to improve and excel. One word

---

*Horizontal loading means giving work assignments that broaden skills and responsibilities. Unfortunately, most of us have worked for managers who loaded vertically—that is, who increase the workload for the same task. We only grow more efficient or tired; there is no challenge, only drudgery.

of caution, though. Be careful not to overwhelm newcomers. Lay out a path by setting objectives and letting them achieve before escalating to a full motivational program.

Recognition. The other key to motivation is recognition. No one ever gets enough recognition. Even top achievers, who get most of it, want more. Unfortunately, we usually wait until people have done really outstanding jobs before praising them. Or we do the opposite and praise people so often and for no reason that our praise becomes devalued. Using the assessment systems discussed in this chapter, you can set up a schedule as follows:

1. To praise highly successful people whenever they *surpass* their goals
2. To praise moderately successful people whenever they *reach* their goals
3. To praise less successful people whenever they *almost reach* their goals

I realize this goes against common practice, but if you never praise the people who don't ever quite reach their goals, they have no incentive to try. By praising their efforts, you can raise them to the level of those people who quite often reach their goals. They gain a sense of growth, accomplishment, and self-worth, and you gain more skilled and happier subordinates.

In giving praise, refer to the standards or objectives you've set. Be specific in your praise, and refer positively to a trait or personal characteristic that led to that success (perseverance, effort, and so forth). Express pride—show how you feel—and refer, if possible, to how far they've grown from last time.

The other side of the coin is criticism. When you need to criticize, make it constructive. Too often, managers throw the baby out with the bath water. Being disappointed, we rant and rave, criticizing everything. Yet in nearly every performance—even a bad one—there is some part that was done well. Praise that part. It doesn't lessen the criticism, but it makes it less personal and more job-oriented. To criticize fairly, follow these five tips:

1. Confirm the undesirable behavior with subordinates so you agree on what happened.
2. Express what you feel was good about their performance.
3. Explain the problems you have (make them problems, not faults).
4. Describe specifically what you think should be done to correct or solve the problems. This is best if subordinates can suggest what they think should be done.
5. Gain a commitment from the subordinates to make a change. This is to be their next objective.

Development

Using a few basic principles of motivation and assessment, you will be able to build an effective, tightly knit, loyal group of trainers. But there is a third function of human resources management: development.

Routine jobs get dull. For example, teaching the same course twenty times a year eventually becomes tedious. Stagnation results when someone does the same task over and over again. It is hard to motivate a workforce that feels its job is monotonous. The answer is to create a developmental program that tracks each trainer through the full range of tasks your department performs.

Instead of simply increasing the workload of each trainer as you become busy (vertical loading), set up a series of challenging tasks. Design the program so each task contributes to the overall effort of your department, each utilizes different training skills, and each challenges the trainer to whom it is assigned. Then assign these jobs so that each subordinate gets to perform nonroutine tasks as often as possible (horizontal loading).

Suppose that, following our proactive principles (Chapter 4), you detect an area you think mandates a new training program in the next twelve to eighteen months. You can assign the needs analysis to one subordinate, the program development to another, the proposal to a third, the writing of lesson plans to a fourth, and the creation of audiovisual aids to a fifth. These tasks would all be in addition to regular training duties. You would act as coach and coordinator—as a resource for them.

Notice that this way each trainer gains experience in a different facet of training. Each time a new project comes along, a different trainer performs a new task. This is development. Eventually, several trainers will become experts in all phases and are then promotable. Of course, if the only job to be promoted to is yours and you aren't leaving or being promoted yourself, you will probably lose at least one valuable employee to another company. But not really. You are a trainer, and you will have trained trainers. Be a mentor and help their careers. You'll develop loyal friends and build an effective training network.

To conduct such a development program, follow these five procedures:

1. Divide the overall project into specific tasks that can be segmented.
2. Arrange these tasks in a developmental sequence.
3. Have resources available to aid and instruct trainees (for example, this handbook).
4. Develop individual flowcharts for each trainer to help him or her through the developmental phases.
5. Use developmental coaching techniques that encourage each person to succeed.

Setting detailed times for completion may be useful, but since most of the tasks don't follow predictable schedules, the program should be task-oriented—that is, framed within a broad time, but with no set completion date. This is truly continuing education. Of the items just listed, most are straightforward, easily worked to suit your tasks. However, the matter of developmental coaching needs to be addressed. Paul Hersey and Kenneth Blanchard's situational leadership model is excellent for this purpose.[8]

Situational leadership is based on two dimensions of a job situation: task maturity and leadership response. The first dimension considers whether the employee is able and willing to do the job. The second dimension involves the type or level of approach the manager uses to assign and assist the subordinate to complete the task. The second dimension is a reflection of the first. Immature employees need a great deal of attention, while mature ones need very little help. Let's look at each in turn.

Task Maturity. Task maturity has nothing to do with employee age or longevity of service. It relates, instead, to the task and is a reflection of whether the employee is able to do the job. To decide this, you must answer three questions:

1. Does he or she possess the skills for the task?
2. Is he or she able to set and achieve realistic objectives to complete the task?
3. Is he or she able to take on the responsibility for completing the task?

In the situational leadership model, an employee who is strong in all three areas is fully mature, described as being at maturity level 4. In contrast, an employee with none or few of these requirements is task immature, at maturity level 1. Maturity levels 2 and 3 are judgment calls between levels 1 and 4. Notice that it is not the difficulty of the task that defines these levels but, rather, the ability and attitude of the subordinate.

Leadership Response. Each maturity level demands a different management style or approach: telling, selling, participating, and delegating. At maturity level 1, employees need instruction and close supervision. They are not able to set objectives, do not know what to expect, lack the necessary skills, are not yet able to take on full responsibility for the job, or fail at any combination of these. Such people need to be told how to do the job, be taught how to set goals, and be helped with the responsibility. This approach is *telling*, and it involves a lot of task-oriented communication and much less relationship-oriented communication.

As the employee matures to maturity level 2, however, the situation changes and demands a different style of management or leadership, hence the name *situational leadership*. Skills improve, the ability to set and reach objectives increases, and the sense of responsibility grows. This situation needs encouragement; relationship messages are very high, as well as task-oriented ones. You are *selling* the task to subordinates.

As employees master the job skills, become comfortable with setting and meeting objectives, and are, as a result, more responsible, they reach maturity level 3. You need not spend time on the how-to's of the job, but can relax and enjoy working with the subordinates. *Participating* is the mode of leadership style—high levels of relationship communication and little or no task-oriented direction. This is the team phase of development.

Finally, when employees reach maturity level 4, they are fully skilled, fully competent to achieve results, and completely responsible for completing assignments. Now you are *delegating* tasks, and you leave subordinates alone to achieve them. Communication of any kind is much less because employees are busy doing their jobs, and you are free to work with others on other tasks.

Hersey and Blanchard bring in a few abbreviations to simplify matters (see Figure 15-1). M1 to M4 show maturity levels, and S1 to S4 show management approaches. When you have a subordinate at M1, you match that with the S1 approach: *telling*. If your employee is at M2, respond with S2: *selling*. In the case of an M3 employee, respond with S3: *participating*. And, finally, with M4, use an S4: *delegating*. Which response you use depends upon an individual's maturity at a particular task, so one person may require all four leadership styles in the same day. Furthermore, as an individual grows, the style for a particular task must change, too. If you rush ahead and delegate too soon, a subordinate will fail, and you will need to go back to the next lowest S level to bring that person up to par again.

Situational leadership is a flexible, dynamic theory. In practice, however, there are usually three problem areas:

1. Few managers can remember all this all the time. Treated casually, the system tends to fall apart because it is easier to lose your temper when things go wrong than it is to adjust your S level.

2. Maturity levels tend to be guesswork, so the system doesn't always work.

3. It is easiest to categorize people at a certain maturity level and leave them there. You simply load them vertically at the same level, rather than advance them through horizontal loading.

The system *will* work for you, however, because I have solved each of those problems. As we discussed earlier, break down the tasks of your training department and organize them into a developmental hierarchy. Then flowchart each subordinate's progress through that hierarchy. That solves the first problem. You know exactly when to use which level of leadership with whom. If you forget, you can go back and look it up. Using the BARS system and management by objectives for assessment, you can solve the second problem. Gauge maturity to standardized levels and areas of performance. By creating a hierarchy of tasks and scheduling people to move through it with horizontally loaded tasks, you will see growth and development. In fact, you'll be hard-pressed to maintain a static judgment in the face of dynamic employee growth.

Figure 15-1. Situational leadership.

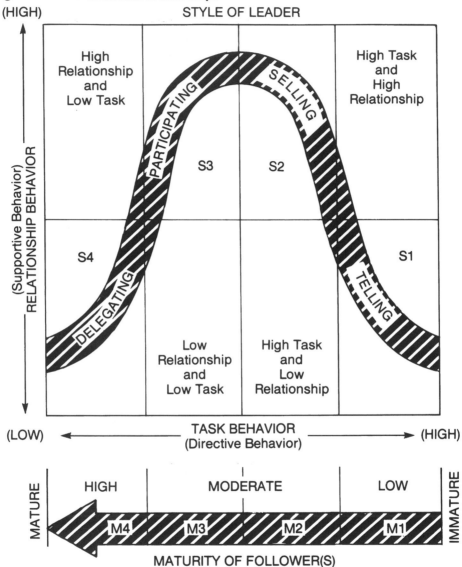

Source: Paul Hersey and Kenneth H. Blanchard, *Management of Organizational Behavior: Utilizing Human Resources,* 4th ed., © 1982, p. 200. Reprinted by permission of Prentice-Hall, Incorporated., Enhglewood Cliffs, New Jersey.

The purpose of situational leadership is employee development. The end result is a staff of highly skilled, first-rank trainers. As nothing remains static, however, you will also create a dynamic learning environment for your trainers, which they will carry over to their trainees, who, as a consequence, will become highly motivated achievers.

Summary

This chapter was about two of the three spokes of management: financial and human resources management. Financial management in the training function consists of budgeting accurately and then staying within that budget. We examined the value of budgeting and gave three formats: planning, programming, and budgeting systems; zero-based budgeting; and different kinds of variable-factor budgeting.

The balance of the chapter was devoted to human resources management. We covered three areas: staffing, assessment and motivation, and development. Within the realm of staffing we looked at the twelve traditional divisions of a training department to see in which areas you need help and to assist you in assigning staff to tasks in your organization.

For assessment and motivation we concentrated on ways to develop your employees' sense of satisfaction. Using goal-directed assessment tools such as the behaviorally anchored rating scales (BARS) and management by objectives, you can inspire employees toward self-improvement. Other contributing factors are horizontal loading of work assignments and recognition. We also provided a format for giving praise and constructive criticism. Finally, we looked at employee development and used situational leadership as a way to build trainer skills.

Applications

1. Based on your existing training responsibilities, work up a detailed zero-based budget for next year. Include all activities of the department and your hidden costs but exclude the gray-area costs. Also include new acquisitions of equipment and any new programs that will be developed over the next twelve months. Prioritize everything.

2. Select one training program you are currently offering or plan to offer in the near future. Prepare a full program budget for this training using a variable-cost format.

3. Select one employee. If you are the only trainer, work up this assignment for yourself. Create a BARS scale to assess improved performance.

4. Apply Hersey and Blanchard's situational leadership model both to your own performance and, if possible, to your coworkers' or subordinates'. Apply the model to your trainees' performance.

Chapter 16
Marketing the Training Function

IN the first chapter training was defined as the means for bringing about a change. A company creates a training department to bring about that change, and they hire or assign a trainer to produce the change. The trainer then becomes an agent for change, a management resource to be called upon when the need arises. It is at this point that we need to look at the marketing of the training function.

As a trainer, you are a management resource—a possible solution to an immediate problem. However, you are called upon only when the need arises, creating the all-too-common reactive stance—the "putting out fires" situation discussed in Chapter 4. It is part of your job to keep management aware of your position as a constant and important resource. Some managers realize this, but others don't; it is those who don't whom you need to inform.

This is not empire building, although I have seen several executives use the training function to do just that. I am talking about marketing your services in-house. As a consultant I am often brought in by the training department to serve as a resource. I occasionally work for other departments because they don't know their training department could help. I am always a little sad when this happens, because it means that the training department has failed to market itself successfully. Like any good salesperson, you, as a training manager, cannot wait for people to come to you; you must go to your customers and ask to solve their problems.

Steps to Marketing

There are six steps to a marketing effort:

1. Define the target market.
2. Define the product or service to be sold.

3. Research the target market.
4. Choose the most effective channel in which to market.
5. Sell the product or service.
6. Follow up on your sale.

Let's look at each from a training point of view.

Defining the Target Market

Do you know, as you read this, how every department or division in your company feels about you? If not, you need to do some marketing. Draw up an organization chart of the company (and of your division, if you work in a large organization). Check off the departments for whom you train or circle those for whom you don't. Of the latter group, fill in the names of executives from senior levels on down to supervisory ones. These individuals are your target market.

Defining the Product or Service

Once you have targeted your market, ask why you are not currently servicing their needs. There may be excellent reasons, such as lack of expertise in that area or insufficient staff to justify training. At this point ask what it is you can sell them. Your choices are among the following:

- Seminars tailored to identified needs
- Seminars tailored to needs of which they are unaware
- Seminars currently offered to others from which they or their people might benefit
- Expertise in hiring outside consultants for training
- Needs analyses
- Recommendations for outside seminars and self-study programs
- Audiovisual resources

Select one for now and two more as long-range goals for each area you've targeted.

Researching the Target Market

Find out about your market. Ask those who interface with these divisions and levels of management to glean information about their operations. Also talk to the personnel department. You want to discover:

- How do they feel about training?
- How do they feel about you (not personally, but as a training department)?
- What, if any, outside seminars have they sent people to or attended?
- Have they brought anyone in from outside to train?
- Are they informed about courses you offer?
- Are they affected by any current or proposed corporatewide changes?
- What is their political position in the company?
- Do they have a training budget?
- Are their counterparts in other companies doing any training?

The answers to these questions will give you a handle on how best to present your proposals. It is also advisable to assess the corporate climate for change as described in Chapter 4 in the section on needs analysis.

Choosing the Best Channel

There are many ways of approaching people. Be imaginative and have fun. For example, make appointments to ask what people's needs are. Be up-front about your request. Say that you are assessing your role as trainer (which indeed is true). Add the names on your targeted market list to the circulation list or "copies to" list for your memorandums. Then create new memorandums notifying all personnel of completed training programs. Each time a program is completed, tell everyone.

Ask for five minutes at key meetings to present a talk on what your training department has been doing. Start a word-of-mouth campaign by asking those you've trained to talk up their programs. Start a poster campaign, too, and write articles for the in-house press. In fact, volunteer to write a column.

For those who regularly send trainees to you, get together to sponsor a guest speaker and then invite target market personnel. Lastly, create a companywide survey of future training needs. Ask questions such as:

- What are your current needs?
- What do you perceive as your future needs?
- If we offered *xyz*, would you send people?
- Are you aware that we train in *abc* areas?
- Which of the following seminars or courses have you attended or sent people to in the last five years?

Selling the Product or Service

Choose one or two channels and mount your campaign. Be careful. You don't want to become a pain in the neck, but you do want to make people aware of you—to put your training on the organizational map.

Following Up on Your Sale

Once you've gotten people to your sessions, follow up. Three months down the line, ask them what they found useful from the seminar. Or ask how their people are using the information. Even if you've only sent a survey, follow up and ask for responses. All of these build the image of training throughout the company.

The Art of Gentle Persuasion

A major element in marketing your training function is persuasion. Persuasion is defined as gaining the willing cooperation or agreement of another. The important word is *willing*. You can force someone to do almost anything if you have enough power. Although coercion may get people to do what you want, it will never gain willing compliance. People hate to be coerced and fight back when even an attempt is made. If you rise to a position of power in the organization, always remember that you will get better work, cooperation, and results with persuasion than you ever could with force.

The Elements of Persuasion

There are probably many ways to persuade people and many successful approaches to use. There are, however, three elements that you can include in any message to ensure that it will be persuasive. There is no guarantee that the other person will agree with you, but you will exert great pressure for him or her to do so. The elements of persuasion are:

1. Logical appeal
2. Emotional appeal
3. Ethical or authoritative appeal

Let's look at each.

Logical Appeal. Whatever you are asking must make sense. And it must make sense from the other person's point of view. A persuasive argument should be well thought out, with solid, logical reasons to back it up. Define the problem and lay out your plan of action as the most logical possible solution to it. The person you are persuading must see that you have weighed alternatives, and have chosen this one only after careful thought. Explain your reasoning, and answer questions before there's a chance to ask them. Cover the facts; make them real, not puffed-up data for the sake of argument. When you discuss alternatives, track them down to their logical outcomes but show that your answer is better.

General Rules of Persuasion

1. People are persuaded by solutions to their own needs or arguments that satisfy their own attitudes.
2. People won't change opinions by 180°. Break your persuasive arguments into smaller ideas and make them appear familiar.
3. People never give more than they are willing or able to give.

Emotional Appeal. Don't rant and rave or become hysterical, but do show some excitement about what you say. Remember Albert Mehrabian (Chapter 3) and the three basic relationship messages. You must exhibit a high degree of involvement, and the other party must know that the topic matters to you—that you care. Show that you like the other person; people are seldom, if ever, persuaded by those they think don't like them. You must show you care and that you are working in that person's best interests. On the other hand, be authoritative and exhibit a degree of assertiveness—perhaps it is best called confidence. The people you are persuading must believe you expect them to agree with you, not that you expect them to say no.

Ethical or Authoritative Appeal. To be persuaded, people must feel that what you are asking them to do is the right thing. They need to believe they are making a good decision. An ethical appeal underlines or stresses those elements of your argument that affect broader aspects of the situation: The greatest good for the greatest number; justice and fairness; those who've been deprived will benefit; help the underdog. These are strong appeals because they reach people's sense of proportion, their desire for fair play, and, indeed, their perception of ethical conduct.

An authoritative appeal, on the other hand, gains its sense of correctness from references to powerful or respected others. The president of the company wants it, the competition must be met or matched, government agencies have proved, and so on. Such approaches apply pressure on people to agree with you, and they give both you and your argument an authoritative stance.

There are no guarantees, but a request that appeals on all three levels is hard to resist. Logic provides the rationale for the decision, emotion provides the desire to go with the decision; and ethics or authority provides the justification for making the decision. If people have a good reason to, want to, and are justified in doing so, they will make the decision you want them to make.

These are the persuasive elements; however, there are a few other factors you can use to enhance your persuasive powers even more:

- *Credibility.* This is a combination of belief and trust. If people believe you are an expert, they will trust what you say. You have credibility with them. If, on the other hand, they don't believe you know what you are talking about, you have no credibility. According to psychologist Jerome Brunner, there are two ways in which we gain belief, and hence credibility, in the eyes of another: authority and sincerity.[1] Cite your authorities. Let people know you know what you are talking about. Use a sincere, concerned manner (not as though you were showing off), and you'll build credibility for yourself.

- *Identification.* To be persuaded, people must feel you know their situation firsthand. They must be able to identify with you, and for that to happen, you must identify with them. Do your homework. Address their problems from their point of view. Let them know that you know where they are coming from, that you "done took into account what hills and valleys [they] come through befo' [they] got to wherever [they] is."[2]

- *Uniqueness.* Every commercial shown on television began with a conference of advertising writers to decide on the product's "unique selling proposition." They have considered what makes the product unique, different from everything else on the market. And the commercial reflects that difference. No one will be persuaded by "just another one of xyz." To persuade people, you must show your position, approach, or solution as unique.

- *Data.* People believe in numbers. Gather numerical proof and they will be swayed. Everyone knows that computers make mistakes, but look at the power of a computer printout. Do people doubt it? Use statistics, facts, and data to enhance your credibility and make it almost impossible to disagree with you.

- *Specifics.* Don't deal in broad generalities like politicians do. Tie your position down with facts, examples, and solutions.

- *Consistency.* Don't be too flexible. If you bend with every opposing request, you lose credibility. How can a good solution be so wishy-washy? Stick to your guns.

- *Scope.* One of the strongest ethical appeals you can make is to say that what you are asking is for the good of everyone, that it is bigger than both of us.

By using these elements of persuasion, you can gain power over other people's decisions. There are also a few other tactics for trying to persuade others. For example, people are best persuaded by approaches that fulfill their recognized needs or that grow out of attitudes they already possess. To persuade another person, find out what his or her needs and attitudes are, then couch your argument in those terms. You can find out about these attitudes and needs by talking to other people who know that person; by checking company performance records (as we suggested you do for the needs analysis covered in Chapter 4); by surveying needs or attitudes; or by simply talking to the person.

If you can avoid it, never ask for a 180-degree change. Almost no one will do a complete about-face. If someone believes your pen is blue, you will be very hard pressed to convince that person it is yellow. Instead, try for lesser degrees of change. For example, compromise your position to calling it a light-blue or a greenish-blue pen. Couch your arguments in what is familiar to people, and accentuate the familiar while minimizing the differences.

Lastly, if the request looks too big to tackle, the answer you'll get will be no. Don't ask for more than what those you want to persuade can or are willing to do. You can create the willingness, but don't ask for decisions they dare not make. Keep your requests within the range of what the other people's positions allow, what their character makeup will grant, and what the political pressures will permit.

As a final note on persuasion, here is a set of nine ground rules for making persuasive presentations to management:

1. *Talk from management's point of view.* Your boss doesn't want to approve things for your reasons, but only for his or her own reasons. This is human nature. Yet how often do we ask favors of others or request help or approval solely for our own reasons? Such requests carry no weight at all. When this type of request does work, it is because the person feels obliged or sees a personal gain. You can use these tactics, but be careful; they smack of poor ethics and can undermine your argument. It is best to allow the other person to discover a personal gain rather than pointing it out. It is fair and right, however, for you to point out how your request will help the boss achieve corporate goals. Couch your arguments in terms of management's goals; as a cost reduction or containment; as reducing inefficiency; as part of a larger company thrust; or as aiding the competitive position.

2. *Base recommendations on demonstrated needs.* You must prove that there is a significant enough problem to demand attention. It can't be a general problem, either; make it specific. I like the EASE formula:

E *Example:* Cite a specific incident.
A *Amplify:* Enlarge on how this affects others, how big or widespread the problem is, the number of cases involved, and so on.
S *Specify:* Tell what you think should be done; make your proposal; ask for money, more staff, new materials, new space, and the like.
E *Execute step one:* Plan an immediate first step that, once taken, locks everyone into your solution. Say, "If you approve, I'll go ahead and . . ." or "I have already completed the needs analysis and can create a new course for you within *xyz* weeks of your approval if I can start today," or some other dynamic statement. It means that you've gotten the ball rolling and it is up to others to either let it go on (the easiest thing to do) or stop it (usually too much bother).

3. *Describe the anticipated results.* What will happen if management approves your new, much larger budget? What will it gain by giving you the go-ahead? Describe it. Give solid estimates of exactly what benefits will accrue and how what you propose will solve management's problem. Again, be precise and specific.

4. *Describe costs.* You must bring up costs and discuss them realistically. Costs are a constant concern of management because they minimize profits. Just as your function is to create change, management's function is to manage costs to produce a profit. Sometimes trainers hide costs or sneak them timidly into their proposals. Don't do that. Put them in front and then justify them! Costs, regardless how great, are small if the benefits to be derived from them are greater. Besides, detailing your costs gains you credibility (you've obviously done your homework) and ensures that you are talking the boss's language.

5. *Do your political homework.* A perfectly acceptable proposal can be rejected solely for political reasons. It may not be pleasant, but a large part of management is politics. The higher you go, the more high-pressured the politics are. Do your homework; know who are your allies and who are your enemies. Talk to both sides before you make a proposal. Go to those who oppose you and ask what you can do to gain their approval. Even if their answer is an adamant "nothing," you've gained in trying. Be open to their suggestions. If your proposal is to be judged by several people, keep your allies close, avoid offending those who are opposed, and concentrate your efforts on the ones who are undecided. Strike deals for their cooperation. In Congress, this is called arm-twisting, and even the president does it. If your proposal matters to you, work at it. You ought to know the outcome of your request before you ask for it.

6. *Answer unasked questions.* An excellent way to head off opposition is to answer questions before they are asked. If you know someone will ask you a certain question, provide an answer ahead of time. That person will see that you've thought your proposal through from their point of view (identification), and that you're fully prepared (credibility). It's hard to argue with someone who anticipates your objections and satisfactorily lays them to rest.

7. *Describe other instances of what you are asking.* Only 7½ percent of the population is truly innovative; the rest need to be reassured to a greater or lesser degree that something will work because it has in the past. Cite pilot studies (if need be, sell a pilot study as your first step), research findings, industry parallels, and, if you can, what the competition is doing. I just recently sold a seminar on the strength of having also given it to my new client's major competitor. The thinking was, "If it helped them, it should help us." Nobody wants to give the competition an edge, not even in training.

8. *Go with realities.* People will not give what they do not have. If you have been persuasive, but get management approval for only three-quarters of your proposal, accept that. If it agrees, you've been persuasive; if it restricts you, it

probably feels it must. If you think management is restricting you merely for knee-jerk reasons, try negotiating but be prepared to go with reality.

9. *Keep management informed.* Let management know how you will report the results of your project. You accomplish several things when you do. First of all, often just after people have approved something they suffer "buyer's remorse." They wonder if they made the right decision. Being told that you will keep them up-to-date on developments has the effect of a ninety-day warranty. It makes them feel they are still in control; although they have made a decision, they aren't totally locked into it.

Second, it affirms and reassures that you expect solid results. It underlines the deferential relationship, saying you are acting on their behalf. It is a way of saying thank you without appearing desperate. In addition, knowledge is power, particularly at executive levels. By defining how you will keep them informed, you are letting them know that you are working to give them information (power) and are not building your own empire. Management seldom likes people who play their cards close to their chests. It wants team players. Lastly, you cement the relationship and make your next proposal much more likely to be accepted.

Writing Skills

Many aspects of marketing the training function involve writing. In fact, effective writing is one of the most important skills a training manager can master. I know several executives who save samples of atrocious (and often very funny) writing that crosses their desks. If these samples were meant to be funny they would be a few bright spots in a long day. But frequently such poorly written documents are incomprehensible and fail to communicate the writer's message. There are no overt penalties for unfocused memos, unclear proposals, or badly written evaluations. I've never heard of someone being fired for writing a confusing memo. But there are direct rewards for sharpening your writing skills. Among them is that you become an important source of information (power) for your superior. Trust is a two-way street, and you enhance your position considerably just by writing effectively.

Management communications consultant Beverly Hyman points out that schools do not teach how to write to communicate.[3] We are taught to write correctly (spelling, grammar, penmanship); to produce a quantity of writing (a paragraph, a page, ten pages); to express random thoughts (what we did last summer, who we want to be)—but never to communicate with each other.

Clear writing is very much like good training, and many of the same rules apply. Like teaching, good writing is a direct result of the planning that you put into the job. You can no more write effective memos off the top of your head than you can train extemporaneously. If you don't address the reader's interests and needs, it is unlikely he or she will respond as you intend. Furthermore, you can't burden your reader with unduly long pieces. We've all received (but I hope have never written) long, rambling essays that must be read five or six times before we can glean the writer's intentions. Unclear and clumsy memos are almost epidemic in the corporate world. Proposals filled with trite or legalistic language proliferate. Don't let your training materials reenforce these practices.

The Four-Step Recipe for Good Writing

Good writing requires personal discipline to eliminate such problems. Beverly Hyman suggests a four-step "recipe" for keeping your writing on track:

1. *Think before you write.* Don't write off the top of your head; first decide what you want to say. Collect your thoughts. After all, as Dr. Hyman points out, every time you prepare a memo, a proposal, or a report, you are writing your resume. While such documents usually don't go into your personnel file, they leave an impression of your capabilities with everyone who reads what you've written.

2. *Consider your audience.* First, ask yourself, "To *whom* am I writing?" Who do you want to reach? As in training, your potential audience controls to a large extent what you say and how you say it. Ask yourself what your reader knows about the subject. Obviously, there is no point in wasting time rehashing what people already know. A few words to set the context or refresh the memory are ample.

Second, ask yourself, "What does XYZ want to know about the subject?" When you write your memo, start with this premise. XYZ will read your memo, report, or proposal only if you include the information that's wanted. Hiding the information or saving it until the last ensures that your message will be discarded in disgust, frustration, boredom, or anger.

Finally, when you've established what XYZ knows about the subject and what he or she would like to know, you can concentrate on what he or she needs to know about it. That is the heart of communication; anything else is extraneous. If all this sounds familiar, that's because these are the same questions asked in Chapter 2 in connection with writing the lesson plan.

3. *Determine your objective.* Now ask yourself, "What action do I want my reader to take?" You've established what you need to say, but now you decide how you will say it. In effect, you are determining your objective. Never write a memo, report, proposal, lesson plan—in fact, any document—without an objective. If you can't think of an objective, don't write the document.

Have you ever received a memo and said, "What on earth am I supposed to do with this thing?" Hyman's third step—setting a clear, personal objective—eliminates this problem.

4. *Organize your information.* You know what you don't have to say; you know what your readers want; you know what you have to tell them; and you know the results you want. Now you can structure your presentation. Once again, as in a good lesson plan, you must consider almost the same structures described in Chapter 2.

Remember the primacy-ultimacy principle. Put your most important message in the beginning, then repeat it in your summary. For your overall structure, try a problem-solution format or a cause-and-effect arrangement. A straight topical arrangement is workable, but requires some additional organization. Avoid a strict chronological presentation, because it provides too much detail and nearly always moves too slowly. Use this arrangement only to describe a sequence or process whereby something is done. (A cookbook recipe is an example of such use.)

Break up large blocks of writing with headings and subheadings. Headings keep the reader on track and also show your train of thought. They are signposts to your meaning. Further highlight key points with bullets, but don't overuse them lest they lose their impact.

Remember always that *less is more.* Say what you want to say and then end it. In training, it is up to you to communicate with the learner. In writing, it is the writer's responsibility to communicate. If you follow Hyman's four steps, you will declare war on inconclusive and confusing writing.

"Wordsmithing": The Power to Say What You Want to Say

The essence of effective marketing is positioning—that is, defining and describing what you are selling in a way that appeals to those you are trying to reach. This principle is also at the heart of persuasive writing.

The words that you choose limit and control the responses others make. How you talk about something defines how we should behave toward it.

General semanticists use an interesting metaphor to describe this phenomenon. They say that the words people use are a map of what they mean.[4] I like this metaphor because it shows how language functions. We all know that a map is only a representation of the actual territory. We don't drive on a road map, we drive on the road. But the map tells us which road to take and where it leads. The map, therefore, directs and controls what road we travel on.

There can be many different maps of the same area. How you travel depends to a very large extent on which map you are using. For example, the area where you live has been described in street directories and on road maps, topographical maps, political subdivision maps, and survey maps. There probably also are demographic maps, aerial maps, navigational charts (if you live near water), geologic contour maps, and, if you live in a city or the suburbs, sewer maps.

Furthermore, there are state maps, regional maps, country maps, continental maps, and globes of the world, all of which cover the area where your home is.

Each of these maps allows us to behave in certain ways. In my seminars I explain how a sewer map shows a different way of getting from point A to point B than would a street map. In fact, the map can control the route one travels. When you write a memo, proposal, report, or any other document, regard it as a map and realize that those reading it will use the map to make decisions. Construct your map so that your readers end up where you want them, not lost, confused, or bored.

Another general semantics tool is the "ladder of abstraction." If you look at an object—for example, a ballpoint pen on your desk—you can describe it in a number of ways. Same pen, different words. If you arrange those words or phrases in a hierarchy (a ladder) starting with the most specific at the bottom and moving upward toward the abstract, you would climb the ladder of abstraction. For example, with the ballpoint pen, you might have the following list:

- Gross national product
- American affluence
- Planned obsolescence
- Total net worth
- Cheaply manufactured artifact
- Carelessly owned artifact
- My property
- Messy house
- Clutter in room
- Clutter on desk
- Writing instrument
- Pen
- Cheap ballpoint
- XYZ Co. medium-carbide clear plastic ballpoint pen
- XYZ Co. medium-carbide clear plastic ballpoint pen with black ink

If this were a listing for a chemical or design engineer, it could be even more specific with formulas for polymers. If it were a listing for a commission on international trade, the abstractions could extend to the world economic environment. But each of the expressions refers to the pen. If you send a memo about clutter on my desk, I may leave the pen there and move something else. If you address me about paying more attention to my artifacts, it is unlikely I will think of the pen. If you want me to understand that I shouldn't leave cheap ballpoint pens lying on my desk because it creates a bad image, say so!* Be specific. Come down

---

*"Bad image" is fairly high up the ladder, too. It would be better to say, "because those passing by might jump to the conclusion that you were messy, careless, and cheap."

the ladder of abstraction whenever there is any chance people will not understand what you've said. In my experience, 80 to 90 percent of the disagreements I've had with others cleared up when we exchanged abstractions for specifics. This is what *less is more* means. Keep it simple.

Writing Training Documents

As mentioned earlier, good writing skills are essential for marketing the training function. There are many documents a training manager must write. For example, reports to keep management informed are a vital part of persuasion. Training manuals and handouts are also critical to training and should be written well. Memos should always be very simple, very direct. Articles for in-house publications are challenging but one of your best marketing channels available. Beverly Hyman's four steps and the other semantic tools apply to these, too. Finally, personnel records and documents are far more useful when written clearly.

Foremost among a training manager's writing assignments, however, are training proposals. A proposal is written to gain permission, get a budget approved, or build support for something you'd like to do. The proposal combines elements of marketing, persuasion, and writing. There are four parts to any proposal:

1. Introduction
2. Rationale
3. Description
4. Conclusion

The Introduction

Remember that your audience governs much of what you write. Your objective is to get a go-ahead, so your proposal must start with the answer to the question, "Why should I approve?" Begin by telling your reader what will be discussed. Your first statement is the name of the program, whom it will involve (number and level of participants to be trained), and the length and frequency of the training. These should be simple statements; you don't need to elaborate yet.

The Rationale

Here you get to the heart of the proposal, the reasons why the plan should be adopted. Describe the problem from management's point of view. To do this you will have already found out what management knows, what it wants to know, and, therefore, what it needs to know. Management must recognize that you see the problem clearly, and your rationale should let managers see the problem as well.

Demonstrate the need for your plan by showing how badly the company needs the solution you propose. If you need support data, however, don't put it here. Include it as an appendix. If the plan is corrective action to solve an existing problem, state the problem, detail the costs that problem incurs (in dollars, if possible), and project the savings (again, in dollars) your solution will bring about. If the plan is preventive action or is aligned with an ongoing management thrust or master plan (always a good idea, if you can), then state the problem you foresee, project how that problem will interfere with the proposed operation or project, and describe how your plan will eliminate that problem.

End your rationale with a list of the management goals your proposal will satisfy. Management's goals are always cost reductions, more efficient operations, and higher profits. There also may be personal goals among managers, such as pet projects, promotions, or increased political power. Don't address these last three directly as such, but imply them through the other, more legitimate concerns.

The rationale is the heart of your proposal, yet it should not take more than five minutes to read. If this section doesn't grab attention in five minutes, the proposal probably never will, either. Keep it short and simple.

The Description

Once you have your readers interested, you will want to tell exactly what you are proposing and what it will cost. Start with a list of your training objectives (see Chapter 6) and follow with a fairly detailed agenda of what will be taught. This

---

Training Proposal Format

1. State what is to be taught, who is to be trained, and the length and times for training.
2. Create a rationale for training from management's point of view.
3. List management goals that will be met.
4. Describe training objectives that will be met.
5. Present a sequential outline of the training subject matter.
6. Explain how trainees will be evaluated, on both short- and long-term bases; tell how you will keep management informed of evaluations.
7. State the costs of the program and justify each aspect.
8. Restate the main points of your proposal and ask for approval.

---

material doesn't have to include timings but must be given in sequence. (See Chapter 8.) At the end of the agenda describe how you will evaluate trainee performance, from both short- and long-range perspectives (see Chapter 5). Let management know how you will report that information back to them. Finally, detail your costs. Spell out the cost of each item and justify it.

The Conclusion

Close the proposal by stating, in one or two sentences, what you plan to do. Ask for immediate approval by restating your objective (to get approval) and giving your best argument.

If your proposal is not for a specific course but rather for a training thrust into a new area that will eventually evolve into several courses, describe your plan of action instead of providing an agenda for what will be taught. If the proposal is a repeat budget request with no new course or plan of action, state last year's performance, describe your planned activities for this year, and then justify both (see Chapter 15 for budgeting procedures). If the proposal is a request for money to acquire new audiovisual equipment, describe how you will use the new equipment, what advantages you will gain, and how, with those advantages, you will address management's problems with even better results.

Summary

The training function needs good public relations because it is usually on the wrong side of the corporate ledger. This chapter considered the role of training manager as a person marketing the advantages of training to the company. Too often training is considered only in terms of its cost. It was shown how training managers need to adopt a proactive stance and let the corporate world know what training can achieve. To do this, we examined how to put together a marketing plan and what channels are available for spreading the word.

Because much of marketing is selling, we examined the art of persuasion, including the three types of persuasive appeal and some factors and tactics for persuading management. Since marketing also involves good writing, we looked at how to improve writing skills. We concluded with a discussion of a format for writing proposals.

Applications

1. Set up a marketing plan to further training in your organization. Follow each of the six steps outlined in this chapter to market your training plan.

2. Choose a training issue that you need to persuade management to buy into. Follow the three principles of persuasion and incorporate as many of the other factors that influence persuasion as you can. Compile these to create a persuasive document. Use the steps to clear writing covered in this chapter.

3. Prepare a proposal for training. Use the market analysis, persuasion, and writing techniques we've covered in this chapter. Follow the outline steps for writing a training proposal.

Chapter 17
Negotiations and Training

GERARD I. Nierenberg, often called the father of modern negotiation, defines it as "any interaction to change a relationship."[1] As a trainer you are in the business of change. You bring about changes in behavior through your classes. While marketing your services, you are engaged in changing other people's perceptions of your function. You sometimes need to convince your boss to accept your budget, plan, or proposal, and that involves a change, too. Most often, it is relationships that are changed. For example, training managers need to develop their staff, and they change their relationships with subordinates as they do so. Of course, as you buy services or equipment you change your relationship from being a sales representative's prospect to that of a vendor's client. Everyone is constantly engaged in changing situations, and many of these changes require negotiation. Let's look at a few pointers and procedures for negotiating.

Three Variables of Negotiation

No matter what is negotiated, there are always three variables that influence that negotiation:

1. Time
2. Information
3. Power

If you put these three variables to work for you, you'll be in a strong position.

Time

Ecclesiastes says, "To every thing there is a season." Timing your negotiation efforts properly is paramount. The best time to ask for a budget increase is during an excellent year when senior management has just expressed concern about employee training, not during a loss period when employees are being laid off. Notice that labor contracts nearly always expire just at the most difficult time. Vendors have sales with limited-time offers or upcoming price increases, which if you order immediately you can just avoid. The time you choose (or are compelled) to negotiate greatly influences the dynamics of the negotiation.

A second aspect is that negotiation is not a single event. It is a process that takes place over time and is never really completed. In my negotiation seminars people sometimes respond to this with, "But once you sign the contract it's over. You've agreed." True, you've agreed, but it's not over. The negotiation has just begun. Now comes the stage of negotiation in which both parties comply (or fail to comply) with the provisions of the contract. A mortgage, a purchase order, a disciplinary hearing, a court case, an employee assessment session, parent and child agreements, marriages—every one is an example of a negotiation that doesn't stop when agreement is reached. For example, a difficult participant may agree to attend a seminar session but may remain a problem participant for the whole time. Failure to live up to an agreement causes a renegotiation of the relationship, thus no negotiation is ever complete.

If these two points are combined you can see that it is much easier to wait for the right time to concede a point or make an offer when you realize that the whole process is an ongoing negotiation rather than a final event.

The third point about time is the most common one: The person who feels under the gun is more likely to concede or deal than the person with no time pressure. It is the nature of our culture to feel the pressure of deadlines. Most of our laws are passed just before Congress recesses. What student ever turns in a term paper early? Why do we rush to catch a plane? People get more things done when they have deadlines; they need a defined time frame to make their task an event. Negotiation is not an event, so we set time limits to make it one. The time limits are, however, arbitrary, and recognizing this fact will allow you to gain an advantage. Set the deadlines for yourself and for those with whom you negotiate, and at the same time, keep free of other people's deadlines.

As a rule, never let the other side know your real time pressures. Instead, set deadlines that pressure them. In addition, defer the toughest issues to last because, by then, time is pressuring both of you and there is stronger motivation to compromise.

Information

Professional negotiators agree that the single most important step in successful negotiations is to prepare thoroughly. The more you know about those with whom you will negotiate, the better. This includes both technical background (past history, prior negotiating behavior, goals, and social or economic status) and personal attributes (office politics, emotional needs, and personal foibles). The more you know, the stronger your position becomes because you can address what they know, what they want to know, and what they need to know. If that sounds familiar, it should. Both needs analysis and the Socratic method provide this kind of information. And, indeed, training is a form of negotiation, a contract to learn.

Probably the single most important thing you need to know is how badly the other party wants what you have. Do you go into a negotiation knowing your own needs and pressures? Are these foremost in your mind? Naturally, you are worried about getting what you want from the negotiation, but thinking this way puts pressure on you. To ease that load and give yourself leverage, ask yourself, "How badly does he or she want what I have?" Instantly, your position is stronger. If the answer is that the other party doesn't want what you have at all, then perhaps this is not the time for a negotiation. Or find a way to create a desire for what you are offering. This is why you must provide a management rationale for every proposal you make. It gives management something to buy into—a reason to create (or change) a relationship with you—to give you approval or support.

Power

A negotiation can also be defined as a power struggle, certainly in cases in which either or both parties perceive it as a win-lose situation. A negotiation is not a win-lose situation, however, if for no other reason than because there is no reason to comply with the contract if either party fails to gain enough of what they want. Because a negotiation is never really ended, you must always be sure that the other side has enough of what it wants to continue to supply you with what you want. Both parties *must win*, or both will lose together.

Unfortunately, managers who have not learned to examine the needs and wants of the other side play to win because they are afraid to lose, and they see only those two mutually exclusive outcomes. They create a power struggle by viewing a win only in terms of making someone else lose. Your job as a trainer, then, is to see that management benefits from the training you provide, that supervisors and others for whom you train have enough input to your training to make them feel it is beneficial to them to support you, that trainees see the value in learning from you, and that vendors and consultants recognize your training expertise and strive to truly satisfy your needs rather than just sell their products and services to you.

Negotiating power, therefore, is not a flexing of muscle. Far from it. It is exerting subtle control over the negotiating climate. As with training (in which, for example, you are negotiating a learning contract with your trainees), the environment in which you negotiate is a major key to success. You can create a win-win climate by being open and frank about what you want. Be honest and ethical.

Do not accept what is unacceptable to you but explain why the unacceptable is so. Make your offer in good faith. Appeal to the other side's sense of fairness (more on this later), and remain calm and unruffled. Remember, you lose only when you allow the other side to win without winning anything for yourself. When you get much of what you want and the other side gets much of what it wants, you've both won.

There are several other subtle ways of assuming power in the negotiations, which you can then use to reach a mutually satisfactory conclusion:

• *Precedent.* It is nearly impossible to strike out on a new path when precedent stands in your way. "Things are done the way they are done because that's the way they are done." If you align your negotiating appeal with the way things have always been done, or company policy, or an ongoing companywide thrust or program according to procedures and guidelines, you'll gain tremendous authority.

• *Legitimacy.* A negotiating appeal based on a demonstrated need will always appear as a legitimate position. In any negotiation, you need to have credibility, a contributor to such legitimacy. Establish your expertise if you feel those with whom you are talking are unfamiliar with it (see Chapter 3). In addition, anything in print gains legitimacy; a written proposal is considered legitimate merely by being printed. Use forms, contracts, documents, and computer printouts to enhance your power by holding a legitimate position.

• *Risk.* Anyone who has ever played poker with a skilled bluffer knows the power that can come from taking risks. Every time a union calls a strike, it is taking a risk to make a bid for power. If management can't run an equal or greater risk, the union will win. If management can risk having the strike run indefinitely, however, the union will lose. Unfortunately, a strike is a win-lose situation. Once the union goes on strike, everyone runs the risk of losing and the situation for both sides can become one of minimizing losses rather than making gains. As in the stock market and in the gambling casinos, however, the high rollers—those who risk the most—command the greatest respect, have the potential for earning the highest rewards, and gain the greatest power.

• *Persistence.* There is power to be gained merely by continuing to ask for what you want. I can recall very successful negotiations that came about after years and many tries. By realizing the nature of the negotiating process and treating it as a part of a long-range process, you gain leverage from persistence. If you've ever been called on repeatedly by the same sales representative, you know it gets harder to keep saying no.

• *Patience.* Closely related to persistence is patience. In fact, patience on your part may be the best antidote for persistence on the part of the other party. If you can wait patiently for the right time to ask (proper timing, remember), you can get most things you want.

▪ *Decisiveness.* In contrast to patience, when opportunity presents itself—when the time is right—you must seize it. Merely being patient allows the world to pass you by. Be patient with a purpose, but move when it is right to do so. Decisiveness at the right time gives you power and commands respect. This is particularly true when dealing with trainees. As shown in Chapters 1 and 3, decisive leadership in the training room is vital.

▪ *Morality.* To reject an ethical appeal is to risk being thought of as unethical, and few of us would do that. By announcing that you are seeking "fairness" or a "mutually equitable" or an "ethical" solution, you force the other side either to agree to do so also or to deny that it is fair, equitable, or ethical. Use phrases like "doesn't that seem fair?" to call your offer equitable.

▪ *Space.* As was shown in the material on training techniques (see Chapter 3), where you place yourself in the room and how you use the space around you reflect power. Sitting behind a desk lends a feeling of authority; sitting away from it, or to one side, creates a friendlier, equal-to-equal image. When each side of a negotiating team sits facing each other on opposite sides of a long table, there's an atmosphere of confrontation rather than cooperation. You gain power by meeting with people in your office or sitting at the head of a table, but you soften your authority by meeting with them in their office or sitting alongside the table. You also can exercise authority by taking over someone else's office or using all the space in their room. This is why formal negotiating sessions are often scheduled in neutral territory at round tables.

These three variables—time, information, and power—are at play in every negotiation. Recognize them as your first step, then use them to your advantage for more successful negotiations.

Negotiation Skills

There are five skills for effecting negotiations. These skills are the ability to:

1. Discover integrative solutions and discard distributive ones
2. Avoid positions and address interests instead
3. Understand the other person
4. Plan your strategy
5. Apply appropriate tactics

The consummate negotiator is expert at all five. Most of us are better at one or two than we are at the others; consequently, we do some parts of our negotiating very well and hope we'll get by for the other phases. This may have been enough in the past, but your negotiations will improve greatly if you develop your skills in each of these areas.

Seeking Integrative Solutions

When two or more parties want the same thing, traditionally they squabble among themselves and then each settles for an equal part of it. Although it may appear to be fair, this is seldom a satisfactory solution because each party gives up some of what it wants and is likely to be dissatisfied with the outcome. The classic example is that of children attempting to divide a pie. To give each an equal share is distributive—it distributes the existing assets. A much better solution would be to find another pie. Or better still, one pie for each child. This is an integrative solution—it seeks a larger picture that can encompass more solution options and integrates them into the negotiation.

In my negotiation classes I play a game in which I divide the participants into groups of two. I say that I will give one member of the pair $1,000 (hypothetically, of course) and he or she must share it with the partner. The possessors may give any portion of the $1,000 they choose but they must give something. There is no negotiation. This is a one-time, nonnegotiable offer. The partners have the opportunity to refuse or accept the amount offered, but they cannot counteroffer, nor can the giver change the offer once it is made. However, if a partner refuses the offer, I take the money back and both participants lose. The game assesses the participants' inclination toward win-win behavior.

The givers try to give as little as possible, attempting, without conversation, to divine how much their partner will settle for. The partners, on the other hand, must decide at what point they will throw away the whole deal rather than accept what they consider an unfair sum. It is a distributive trap.

Over the years, the most creative solution I've run across succeeded in turning the offer into an integrative solution. One participant offered his partner the whole $1,000, provided the partner agreed to pay him back $1,500 at the end of twelve months! The partner accepted, because both parties ended up with more than either could have gotten by distributing the original amount equally. Of course this solution involves a usurious rate of interest, but that was apparently acceptable to the recipient in order to gain the full $1,000. Truly an integrative solution.

The great skill here is to look beyond the obvious distributive alternatives and seek larger solutions that bring the parties together, integrate them, rather than separate them.

Responding to Issues Rather Than Positions

There is a TV commercial for a famous aftermarket replacement automobile muffler firm that features various customers striding into a dealership, pounding their fist on the counter, and shouting, "I'm not gonna pay a lot for this muffler!" That's a strong position. Many negotiators adopt a strategy of assuming a hard-line position at the outset, with the intention of gradually backing down from that position if the other side forces them to. This is positional bargaining.

We see such positional stances frequently in management and labor disputes. A lockout and a strike are both very extreme positions. Once either side has called their strong position, usually they will "negotiate" an end to the hostilities and back away from that position. This is the traditional approach, but it is time-consuming. It also creates and fosters hard feelings and much saber-rattling. A much better approach is for each side to address the interests behind the position, to seek out and negotiate the causes that gave rise to the strong position.

A skilled negotiator will ignore the strong "I'm not gonna pay a lot . . ." position and realize that what motivates the person making the demand is the fear that he or she will be overcharged or taken advantage of in some way. This person lacks trust and is behaving very defensively. An appropriate response to this type of insecurity is much gentler and much more likely to result in an amicable agreement than an equally tough counterposition.

Understanding the Other Person

This is such a vital skill that, in my two-day seminar on negotiating, I devote an entire day to discussing how to read and influence the behavior of others. Unfortunately, this is not a book about negotiation, and we cannot take the space here to delve into this all-important aspect. Throughout this book, however, are suggestions that you will find useful. For example, the ten principles of adult learning apply to negotiation because, after all, you are teaching the other person your position and learning his or hers. Check yourself on Chapters 1 and 3, which address aspects of human behavior. The material on active listening, question asking, and uniqueness will be of particular help to you. You can also benefit from the discussion of nonverbal communication, especially semantics, in shaping the perceptions of those with whom you deal.

In the context of negotiations, the purpose of understanding others is to motivate them to work toward a mutually satisfactory goal. To be successful at this, you should acquire a background in motivation theory. A good place to start would be books by Abraham H. Maslow, in particular his *Motivation and Personality* (Harper & Row, 1970). Check also *Games People Play* by Eric Berne (Ballantine, 1978); *I'm O.K., You're O.K.* by Thomas A. Harris (Avon, 1982); *Transactional Analysis at Work: A Guide for Business and Professional People* by Maurice Villere (Prentice-Hall, 1981); *TA and the Manager* by Dudley Bennett (AMACOM, 1976); *The Presentation of Self in Everyday Life* by Erving Goffman (Doubleday, 1959); *Work and the Nature of Man* by Frederick Herzberg (Crowell, 1966); and *Leadership and Decision-Making* by Victor H. Vroom and Philip W. Yetton (University of Pittsburgh Press, 1976). You will find these books fascinating reading, and you will come away with a much deeper understanding of why people do the things they do and how to change their behavior.

Planning Your Strategy

In any negotiation, your strategic plan is the basic approach you intend to take. In effect, you draw up the plan simply by doing your homework and preparing to negotiate. Of course, your plan is a *preliminary* one. I have seen many professionals give up strong negotiating positions because they locked themselves into plans that became out of step with the negotiation. A strategic plan is only good as long as it reflects the reality of your negotiation. As soon as the circumstances change, you must reevaluate and revise your strategy.

Here are seven questions to consider when preparing your strategic plan. Once you have the answers, you can use them to create your plan:

1. *What are the power bases?* Ask yourself how badly you want what they have. Then ask how badly they want what you have. If you don't know the answers, find out. In addition, ascertain what the time pressures are and what sources of power (if any) they are most likely to use. What sources of power are likely to work for you?

2. *What are the causes of the problem being negotiated?* Often, removing a cause of a problem eliminates the need to negotiate. Track the situation back to its roots so you'll understand it thoroughly. It can often reveal the issues that will be behind the other side's position. Get a grasp on the causes of the problem and you may turn up more creative alternatives, more integrative solutions, especially if both parties can't agree on some issues.

Are there any other solutions available besides negotiation? This question is also important. Investigate whether there is a better way to safeguard against spending time and energy negotiating something better solved another way. For instance, if you have an employee with a drinking problem, negotiation will not solve it. An alcoholic will agree to anything but cannot be held to it; he or she cannot control the addiction on the strength of a negotiation. Answering this question also gives a different slant on the pressures at work. If alternatives to negotiation are unacceptable, then both parties will feel pressured to negotiate. The more unacceptable, the greater the pressure. For example, ask yourself what the alternatives are to negotiating a nonproliferation treaty with all nations capable of creating nuclear weapons. Your answer should explain at least one reason why the United States continues to press for such a treaty.

3. *What personal and psychological needs are involved?* Here's where your study of motivation theory pays off. Regardless of what business matter you are negotiating, people are deeply affected by their personal needs. Major corporate deci-

---

Seven Questions for Planning Your Strategy

1. What are the power bases? How badly do they want what you have?
2. What causes the need to negotiate? Are there other solutions?
3. What personal and corporate needs are involved?
4. What are the other party's dominant behavior characteristics?
5. What is your minimum-maximum range?
6. What strategies are available to address the problems?
7. What tools will you need?

---

sions are often based on whims and pet projects or are made out of spite and for childish reasons. People are psychological beings, and we function within our mental and emotional networks. Understanding the other party's needs as well as your own is essential for an effective conclusion. Of course, you must also know what his or her corporate needs are and address them in the negotiation. But answering this question about less obvious factors is a tremendous help in reaching a win-win negotiation. If you don't know the other party's needs, you can't work to help to achieve them.

4. *What are the other party's dominant characteristics?* How does he or she behave? Ask around if you don't know. Find out if the other person is a hard-driving, success-oriented overachiever or more analytical in style, weighing alternatives and delaying decisions until all the facts are in. Your approach with these two types must be completely different. The hard-drivers seldom care about all the facts; they want results—action now. They are always pressured by time. The analytical types use time to their advantage; they don't want to make snap decisions and balk when pressured.

There are several personality inventory systems, and all are about equally effective. Choose one and figure out how you should respond to each personality type. I recommend *Please Understand Me: Character and Temperament Types* by David Keirsey and Marilyn Bates (Prometheus, 1978). You'll also find *Type Talk at Work* by Otto Kruger (Bantam Doubleday Dell, 1993) good, fun, and informative.

Transactional analysis is another tool for categorizing behavior, especially useful because it provides directions for handling each personality type.[2] Analysis of the other parties involved in a negotiation pays off handsomely in the end.

5. *What is your minimum-maximum range?* Have you known people who gambled away more money than they could afford to lose? Or who got carried away at auctions and bought things they couldn't afford? These are fairly common occurrences, but they shouldn't happen to you. Prevent this by setting maximums for yourself and don't exceed them. For negotiations I recommend three lists:

    a. The things you have to have

    b. The things you'd like to have but could live without

    c. The things you can afford to give away

These are your minimum-maximum limits.

Here's how the lists work. You will have already determined your objectives and decided what you must have and what you cannot compromise. You will have listed some key items for which you will fight but could compromise if pressed hard. And you will have a list of negotiables—things that, if others fight for them, you can give up without losing. Develop these three categories with thought and you'll have more successful negotiations.

6. *What strategies are available to you?* Using your three minimum-maximum lists, decide what concessions you can make and draw up a tentative sequence in which to make them. Decide what you will do and how you will respond when the other party takes a strong position or asks for concessions you cannot give. At this point, think through your alternatives and decide on several possible approaches. Use "What would probably happen if . . ." questions.

At this stage also weigh your credibility. If you think the other party may try to take advantage of you (either because he or she feels you don't know enough to spot it or you don't know enough about the business), you need to plan how you will gain credibility. There was a southern senator who used to say, "As far as I am concerned, the negotiation is over when the small talk ends." He used the introductory small talk to measure his opponent. Make your first moments count by establishing your credibility early on.

Your final step in answering this question is to consider what forms of resistance you are likely to meet when asking for each of the things you want. Consider also how you'll respond to the resistance; this is a form of cost-benefit analysis, and the format answers the following questions:

- What are your requests?
- What are the likely responses to each?
- What will each of these responses cost you (in concessions, climate, relationship, and so on)?
- Is it worth it to you?
- If not, what less costly alternatives are there?

Again, remember at this point in your planning that you are only examining alternatives. Nothing is final, yet.

7. *What tools will you need to implement your strategies?* There are three tools: language, skills, and tactics. To begin, what language—what words and maps—will you need to shape your point of view? Are there any language or word barriers that you will need to work around or that will cause you to redefine your

terms? What you must do is decide how to present your arguments in terms that will be understood by all involved.

With regard to skills, we've already mentioned the power of asking good questions and the corollary skill of active listening. One week before the negotiation, practice your questioning and listening skills, and brush up on reading nonverbal behavior. When the meetings begin your skills will be tuned to performance pitch.

Applying Appropriate Tactics

Consider which tactics you need for your negotiation to best influence the individuals involved. The pages that follow describe some standard tactics. Some you will have already used often or you will recognize as having been used on you. See how they work for you and choose those that get you the best results. Every time you negotiate with a new person, come back to this list and consider which tactics might work well this time.

For more information on negotiating tactics in general, read Gerard Nierenberg's *The Complete Negotiator* (Nierenberg-Zeif, 1986) or his earlier book, *The Art of Negotiating* (Cornerstone, 1981). Both are excellent, with the best coverage of the subject. For more of a "how-to" approach, consider Steven Samuels's cassette/workbook program *How to Negotiate*, available from AMACOM.

Salami Slices. Large issues sometimes are so monolithic they seem impossible to resolve. Slice large topics into pieces (like a salami), and they become manageable.

Trial Balloons. Couch your suggestions or offers in terms of "What if . . ." This allows both sides to consider an idea without really deciding on it. It's an exploratory statement rather than a crystallizing one. And, as you explore, you can learn a great deal about the other person.

Deferred Issues. To engage in an up-front struggle on the biggest issue usually means you'll never get past that issue. Let both sides start on what is easily agreed upon. Then, as the list grows longer, it gains momentum and begins to pressure both parties to compromise (if need be) on the big issue. Furthermore, the longer the negotiation process takes, the more those huge issues start to shrink. With success, everyone gains confidence that they can be solved, too.

First Concession. Many negotiators won't agree with me, but you gain several important advantages when you concede first. For instance, you establish yourself as a "good guy"—someone who is ready to deal to work out a solution. It gives you a moral edge. Also, fair is fair. You've given one, now the other side owes you a concession. You have a right to it. Lastly, you establish the turf. By making the first offer, you set the direction for the entire negotiation.

Straw Issues. This is a sneaky ploy, in which you make a large issue of an unimportant point. You make it seem important by fighting hard for it, only to give in at last and then demand a large concession in return.

Feinting. This is a variation on straw issues, whereby you make an issue of one aspect to hide a weaker point, in the hope of slipping that weaker point by unnoticed while everyone is upset about the false issue.

Fallback. Plan your retreat. If you anticipate having to concede, don't do it easily. Make them work for it. Don't give in without demanding concessions in return. They will value something they had to work for far more than an easy victory. By the way, when you concede, pay them a compliment. Give credit for good negotiating; it may lull them into early satisfaction.

Trade-Off. This is an offer to trade one-for-one so as to avoid or break a deadlock.

Deadlock. This is usually regarded as a negative result but can be an excellent tactic to use when you need more time or if you suspect the other side is pushing too hard because of time pressures.

Bland Withdrawal. I have seen this tactic used most effectively by simply agreeing with the other side and moving on. If the other party is anticipating tough opposition or a denial from you, by simply giving in, you completely throw them off base.

Reversal or Turnabout. This one is a very tough defensive ploy. I advise using it *only* when you perceive the other side has or is taking advantage of you. Simply say, "I've changed my mind. I don't agree to anything we've agreed on so far. Let's start over from the beginning." The usual response is to cater to you and make an important concession to avoid risking the entire agreement so far. But to use it for any reason other than a defensive one is unethical and predisposes a win-lose situation.

Temper Tantrum. In my experience lawyers are fond of throwing temper tantrums to intimidate others. Many managers keep employees in line this way, too. I deplore it as a management tool because it intimidates some and antagonizes others. The best response to anger is to remain calm and logical, and to thank the person for being honest with you. Or calmly remark that the person seems very upset, that you don't understand what's so upsetting, and ask for an explanation of the outburst. This forces them to discuss the issues rationally, in a win-win manner.

Walkout. A walkout is when you draw a line—you say you can go no further—and then walk away. It doesn't have to be done in anger, though it often is. A walkout is a way of implying you can't concede more, that you're not getting what you want, and that you're leaving. If the other side has invested time and effort, it will concede rather than give up all that's been invested. On the other hand, if the other side can't give anything more, then your walkout is appropriate because there is nothing more to negotiate. If someone walks out on you, it implies that the next move is yours, but you don't have to do anything about it. If they still want to negotiate, sooner or later they will come back. When they do, you have an advantage—they are coming to you. If they don't come back, of course, that is the end of that round of negotiation.

Fait Accompli. This is a frequently used and powerful tactic. In fact, much of our legal system is built on it. The term is French and means "the thing is done." In a negotiating sense, it is when one side takes some unilateral action and then presents the other with a finished event, take it or leave it. A subpoena is a fait accompli; so is a traffic ticket, a court order, a police raid, and many other such events. This is also what hijackers and terrorists do, what suicides do, what nations often do when they invade another country. You do it first and ask questions later, but there really is no answer. You must respond in some manner, either weak or strong. Because the tactic is so manipulative, use it with great care, if at all. If it is used on you, respond as calmly and rationally as possible.

Some Negotiating Situations

Now let's look at several direct applications of these negotiating principles to situations involving training managers.

How to Negotiate With the Boss

Working out an agreement with your boss brings us back to the three variables: time, information, and power. Usually the boss controls time by preempting it or by terminating interviews. You can gain control of the situation by using your time well. Be prepared, and express your arguments in crisp, concise language. Use time as the boss does. If he or she is a driver, be brief, factual, and action-oriented; if the boss has a slower style, cover *all* the issues and help guide his or her thinking.

In this negotiating arrangement information is your strong suit. If the boss

Negotiating With the Boss

(Be a team player with company's best interests at heart.)

Time

Controlled by the boss.
Minimize your use of time.
Use time the way the boss does—slow, fast, and so on.
Wait out the decision; bide your time.

Information

Your strength; do your homework.
Phrase your appeal in terms of company goals or benefits.

Power

In the boss's hands.
Use precedent and support from others.
Align your proposal with the boss's pet project.
Back up your appeal with facts; demonstrate the need for what you suggest.
Use fait accompli—if it is not too risky.

Strategic Plan

1. Clearly define your strengths and weaknesses. Find something the boss wants badly and offer it in *exchange.*
2. Clearly define the real problems. Show how your solution is better than any others.
3. Analyze your boss's personal, political, and organizational needs.
4. Determine the boss's personality type (using TA, Maslow, or some other system) and work out your best way of dealing with it.
5. Make a list of your minimum needs and your maximum desires.
6. Show the boss how he or she and the company will gain from your proposal.
7. Be prepared to justify the maps you have chosen.

---

has more or better information, you are not likely to win. Your information should point out company or personal benefits for him or her. Make them tangible benefits, on the lowest rungs of the ladder of abstraction (see Chapter 15).

Overt power is largely in the boss's hands, so you'll need to be as subtle as possible. Align yourself with precedent (if possible) or with larger ongoing campaigns. Write a persuasive proposal. Gather political support. If you have a boss who respects a "can do" attitude, try a fait accompli for part of your proposal. Use statistics and computer printouts, but don't take the time to go over them in detail; just submit them as backup evidence and summarize them if need be.

Answer the Seven Questions in Strategic Planning. Consider the seven questions discussed earlier in planning your strategy, and present your appeal in terms of what your proposal can do for the company. Avoid appeals to what you want, but emphasize those that produce results for the company. Work on this win-win approach. In short, follow the guidelines for marketing to management in Chapter 16. Become thoroughly familiar with the problem and *all* other possible solutions. Have indisputable reasons why the other solutions are less effective than yours.

Define for yourself what your strengths and weaknesses are. What are your psychological needs? What "face" do you have to save? Ask yourself how badly the boss wants what you are offering, then find something he or she wants and offer it. Analyze your boss's personal and political needs, too, and structure your negotiation to appeal to them. Define, on paper, what kind of person your boss is. Decide on a distinct personality type, then structure your approach to complement those characteristics.

Create a minimum-maximum range for your appeals. Assuming you want to keep your job, it's hard to maintain a "must have" position, but go for it because that's what you want. Look persuasive; you should be committed to your idea. Include your "must haves" in your "would like to haves" and then work to get them all.

In planning your strategies, remember that you are both on the same side. You gain credibility whenever you use these four strategies:

1. Show an understanding of the boss's point of view.
2. Present a successful track record or show how what you want has been successful elsewhere.
3. Align your proposal to his or her current interests.
4. Demonstrate real benefits to the company rather than personal benefits.

One of the problems in presenting proposals to management is that it is often an either-or situation. They either approve or disapprove. Period. If yours is such a situation, then you will need to build concessions into your proposal. Create two or three alternate plans, with separate budgets and separate results. Have one plan at a must-have level; it would be least costly but would also produce minimal results. Have another at a like-to-have level, which would produce much better results for a marginally increased budget. Finally, have yet another at an even more like-to-have-but-can-live-without level, for an ideal budget producing still more benefits. Present all three and let management choose. The key is to scale the benefits and make them real. If the first plan, which addresses the problem but doesn't solve it (merely holds the line), is accepted, at least you'll be able to maintain status quo. The second plan can then solve the problem but will cost more, and the third can solve it and provide additional benefits. By tying your costs into the boss's goals, you'll gain greater leverage.

Of course, you must anticipate any resistance. For best results, answer questions before they are raised. Do your political homework and speak with those who may oppose you. Give them what they want, if you can; deal before you present your package.

Choose your arguments carefully and be prepared to justify them. Practice your negotiating skills, and plan which tactics will be most effective. Obviously, high-handed methods are out of place here because they encourage win-lose situations. Since you're dealing from a subordinate position, you lack the leverage to keep them win-win situations.

Over the years I have successfully used the following tactics in negotiating with superiors:

- Trial balloons
- First concession
- Straw issues
- Feinting
- Fallback
- Deadlock (to wait for time and events to prove me right)
- Bland withdrawal
- Fait accompli

I've also made the first concession in negotiations with management to gain higher pay, acceptance of programs, promotions, and budgets including an expanded staff. Whatever tactics or approaches you use with management, make sure you are a team player, with the company's best interests at heart. You will come out ahead.

How to Negotiate With Subordinates

Again, let's begin a review of this negotiating situation by examining the variables of time, information, and power. In this instance time is officially in your hands, but be careful. There are subordinates who will waste a good deal of your time by begging to have their hands held.

Remember that negotiation is a process, not an event. You need to give them enough time to ensure that their performance doesn't waste your time. Review Chapter 15 for ways to do this.

Be informed. The more you know about the subordinate and his or her job performance, as well as what he or she wants to negotiate with you, the greater

---

Negotiating With Subordinates

(Create a win-win situation.)

Time   You control it.
                      Beware of stalling and hand-holding ploys.

Information   Be fully informed.
                      Know the people involved and the circumstances of
                      the negotiation.

Power   Be subtle, not overt.

Strategic Plan   1. What power do your subordinates have? What are
                         the real limits of your power? What things can you
                         offer easily that they want?
                      2. Why are they negotiating? Is this a serious problem
                         or is it routine? Are there any other solutions?
                      3. Define their corporate and personal needs, and
                         your own.
                      4. What is their dominant personality type?
                      5. Define your minimum-maximum range of what
                         you can give them.
                      6. Anticipate resistance and plan a response to it.
                         Keep negotiations on a friendly, relaxed basis.
                      7. Use verbal maps.

---

your leverage in getting what you want and, if need be, in arguing against giving too much.

Use the subtle forms of power. Choose the location to suit the individual and your intent, and prepare documents, if need be, to legitimatize your position. Show your knowledge of the facts—be a source of information. Show parental concern for the individual's well-being, and approach the subject from his or her point of view.

Answer the Seven Questions in Strategic Planning. When negotiating with subordinates, ask yourself what their power bases are. How badly do they want what you have and vice versa? What are the *real* limits of your power? Begin by giving them something they want. It doesn't have to be something they are asking for at this time, but it must be something they want and appreciate.

Ascertain why they are coming to you to negotiate. Are there other, better options? Is this a problem or is it merely routine? If it is a problem, what are the causes (not the symptoms)? Can negotiation solve the problem? If not, what else is needed?

Define what their personal needs are. Do the same for yourself. This will give you the opportunity to be personal, to discuss the situation informally. It also will prepare you to save face, both theirs and yours, if need be. Also, what are their dominant characteristics? This step, coupled with the last one, will tell you what your subordinate's "hot button" is (an expression used by salespeople for the thing that gets a prospect excited and ready to buy).

Define your minimum-maximum range. Unless you are an autocrat, be prepared to give something. Know what you must have from your subordinates, what you'd like to have, and what you are willing to give in on. Never give more than you can afford, and gain something from every concession you make. To anticipate what they will ask, examine what you know about them and decide how much more you need to learn. Then ask yourself how you can use that information to gain personal credibility and support. Anticipate what they will resist and prepare to deal with that resistance. Work up a scenario for each anticipated resistance, detailing your tactics for handling it.

Finally, decide on the approach you will use and which negotiating skills, if any, you will need to practice ahead of time. In considering tactics, here are a few more to add to those given earlier in this chapter:

▪ *Look at the record.* Examine both your past performance and that of the subordinate. A sense of what has happened in the past will put the present negotiation into perspective.

▪ *Needs search.* Both parties should specify their needs at the outset. Agreement is nearly always possible on several items and the tougher issues become more defined.

▪ *Ultimatum.* Never make an ultimatum right at the start. It is meaningless then and can lock you into a position that you later might want to shift. When you make one, do it gently and with empathy. Allow the other side to save face and withdraw with dignity.

In summary, these are recommended tactics for negotiating with subordinates:

▪ Salami
▪ Trial balloons
▪ First concessions
▪ Bland withdrawal
▪ Anger (only if needed)
▪ Look at the record

- Needs search
- Ultimatum

How to Negotiate With Outside Vendors

Time is on your side. It is a buyer's market, and even if you are pressured by your own deadlines (budgeting, for example), you can set an artificial deadline that puts pressure on the vendor. Anticipating your needs and early planning helps, too. Most vendors create time pressures by forecasting price increases or offering special deals for a limited time. If you feel pressured by them, either ignore them or turn them down flat. The time pressures may be real and you will have to pay more later, but you'll know it's fair. If the limited offer was just a hype, they'll make another one. With salespeople, get them to invest time and effort in you. It puts pressure on them to close the sale, and you can gain concessions. With consultants, however, this usually doesn't work because they have only time to sell. If you take that time, they will charge you for it; you may get some concessions, but you'll pay a higher fee overall.

Information is vital. Always ask for lists of current and satisfied subscribers, then check them. Network with other trainers to find out how good the service is, or see consultants at work, or try packages before you buy them. Remember that catalogues and salespeople, while required by law to be honest, take great pains to present their wares as favorably as possible. To a lesser extent this applies to consultants, too. You can hire them for one job to see how they work; if you like what you've bought, hire them for more. If you have a lot of work for them, after the trial project offer them a retainer. Remind yourself that vendors need your business probably more than you need what they offer. In the case of a consultant whom you really need, this situation is lessened but there are always other consultants, possibly many who are better than the one with whom you are dealing.

Power is always in your hands; they are coming to you. True, you have a need, but you have identified that need and they need you, too. Use all the tactics discussed earlier, not in a high-handed way but in a confident manner. Refer to precedent, be decisive, and use space to your advantage. Be prepared to risk not closing the deal, but persist on the points you need and stress fairness and ethical conduct. As a rule, have a higher power who must approve whatever you negotiate. This enables you to postpone requests for instant commitments.

If the negotiation is not going well, it is good to be able to shift to other solutions. Know what your options are before you begin to negotiate.

Answer the Seven Questions in Strategic Planning. Needs are of particular importance in this type of negotiating situation. Aside from your training needs, whatever purchase or contract you make reflects back on you. Good consultants

Negotiating With Outside Vendors

(This is a win-win situation.)

Time	Make it your strength. Allow enough lead time to avoid feeling pressured. Ignore offers designed to hurry a decision. Be realistic. Book consultants early, not at the last minute.
Information	Know exactly what you want. Ask for information—successful customers and references. Network with other trainers. Try before you buy.
Power	Use it subtly. Always have a power out—a higher authority to check for approval.
Strategic Plan	1. They need you more than you need them. 2. Be prepared to drop negotiations and try another solution. 3. Needs are paramount in these negotiations. Identify yours specifically and consider vendor's needs for more business and for more time to deliver. 4. Vendor will probably tailor his or her behavior to yours. 5. Know your minimum-maximum range and be creative in what you can offer them. Work to get what you want at a fair price. 6. Establish your credibility and prepare for resistance to strong demands. 7. Pay special attention to word maps—theirs as well as yours.

or sales reps are aware of this and do everything in their power to make you look good. You can measure their interest and confidence in their wares by their attitude toward you.

On the other hand, the vendors have needs as well. They look for sales that can be enlarged or expanded to cover several wares or services. Salespeople are concerned mainly with sales volume; consultants are concerned mainly with time.

Both have egos and both respond to compliments. Consultants, for example, need to know they are the best and that their advice is acted upon. If money is a problem, very often a package can be worked out at a lower fee in exchange for more work, commitment to future work, or expense packages that include families. For salespeople, almost the only cost reducer is a volume purchase that lowers the cost per item.

Look at your vendors' work needs and personal needs. To warm people up, take them into your confidence, listen attentively, take their advice, and treat them with respect. Take them to lunch and return their phone calls. Give them tough problems to solve and let them show you how good they are; give them a reputation to live up to. By speaking to their ego needs, you'll gain leverage in negotiations.

When dealing with vendors, remember that dominant behavior characteristics are less important because, as good salespeople, they are usually willing to match your behavior. Still, if you want to influence them, give some thought to how they behave. If you can accurately predict their behavior, you can better plan your negotiations.

Know your minimum-maximum range. This is vital when you are negotiating with a consultant. Most are independents and have flexible fees. If you know what you need, what you'd like, and what you can give, you can afford to be flexible as well. As a consultant, I've found that some of my most satisfying arrangements have been negotiated around unusual perks, payment formulas, business partnerships, royalties, or barters. If you really know your needs and limits, you can afford to be free within them.

To negotiate effectively you will need to demonstrate your competence and knowledge of what you are buying. Research the subject. Being knowledgeable will give you credibility. Review Chapter 8 for the questions or demands you can make of outside vendors. Be prepared for resistance, of course. Try to predict the responses to your demands and then ask yourself what that response will cost you. Can you afford it? If not, don't make a demand that provokes that response. If you can, then you are free to demand.

Pay special attention to your words—and theirs. All vendors will be happy to talk, but you will need to ask questions that probe to prevent deception or misunderstanding. What an off-the-shelf package sales rep means by "tailoring" his or her material is completely different from what a consultant means. Demand specifics. Keep the discussion on the lowest rungs of the ladder of abstraction. Define your meanings and be sure that you both understand. Saying exactly what you mean is important, as are listening and reading nonverbal behaviors.

Remember that vendors are not enemies. They are folks who need to work with you to make a living. Your negotiations with them should frame a partnership that:

1. Gives you the service you need at a cost you can afford
2. Allows the vendor to enjoy a livelihood commensurate with his or her abilities

All of the positive negotiating tactics are appropriate, but the confrontational ones usually are not.

How to Negotiate With Political Peers

Time is a factor in this negotiating circumstance only in that it is wise to recognize the other people's pressures and stay out from under any yourself. In essence, you both have infinite time. Do remember, however, that whatever engagement you develop, you will both have to live with for that infinity. The negotiation is a process, so take it easy. Aim small, but build for the future.

Information is vital in this situation. It is often beneficial to have subordinates who have friends who work for your peers. Of course, this smacks of a spy network, and if you are not comfortable with such an arrangement, don't do it. Otherwise, monitor the performances of your peers so you can know their positions and be aware of how you can help them when you need to work together.

Power is a treacherous element in negotiations with peers. Because of the insecurity of interoffice politics, neutrality is usually the best stance. To exercise power is to make political enemies. On the other hand, to give your power away seems foolhardy. Work at neutrality. Guard yourself against power plays, not to win them but to maintain a mutually winning stance.

Answer the Seven Questions in Strategic Planning. You must know how badly your peers want what you have. If they don't want it, bide your time; one day they may. If you need their support, devise something that they could want from you. Otherwise, you negotiate without a position.

As you talk, listen for their solutions. If possible, go along with their ideas—it puts your peers in your debt. Perhaps you can align yourself with someone so powerful that you can bypass them, eliminating the need to negotiate at all. In other words, analyze the political climate before you offer to negotiate.

The heart of peer negotiation is needs satisfaction. You need not love your peers, but both of you have ends to achieve and personal needs to fill for affiliation, support, esteem, and recognition. Finding your peers' needs and helping to achieve them put you in a strong bargaining position. This is a win-win approach; it is a How can I help? not a How can I get back at you? attitude.

Because, as peers, you are working together for the same organization, you should strive to complement each other's styles. Psychologist Jard DeVille presents interesting approaches to peer struggle in his book, *The Psychology of Leadership: Managing Resources and Relationships*.[3] DeVille suggests ways of matching and complementing behavior patterns to minimize friction.

Your minimum-maximum range is probably less important in peer negotiations than in other forums, but you should still list exactly what it is you want and precisely how much you are willing to pay for it. Then stick to your decision. Be

---

Negotiating With Political Peers

(Remember, you both work for the same organization.)

Time	Infinite. Don't let time pressure you. Use others' pressures to your advantage. Build to gradually gain what you want.
Information	Set up spy networks if possible. Keep track of others' activities.
Power	Can be treacherous; try to be neutral. Maintain a win-win stance.
Strategic Plan	1. You must know how badly they want what you have. Be prepared to exchange something they want for something you need. 2. Give their solutions a try. Perhaps you can leapfrog over them. 3. Need satisfaction is the key consideration. Strive for a win/win result. 4. Define their personality types and strive to complement their style. 5. Minimum-maximum ranges are not a key issue, but set a firm limit on what you can give. 6. Make sure you get something in exchange for each concession and anticipate resistance. If there is nothing for you to gain, don't negotiate. 7. Maps may be the key to success. Use your diplomacy and language skills.

---

careful of the price you pay, and set strict limits for yourself to prevent others from taking advantage of you.

As advised, guard your concessions. Give them generously, but only if you get what you need in return. Don't worry about credibility or identification unless the problem comes up. Your position gives you the credibility and identification, but if others have a mistaken view of either, you can demonstrate (don't tell or inform them) the truth. Don't rub it in—let it be discovered. Remember, also, that no one willingly switches position 180 degrees. Be patient and prove your points a little at a time. Resistance will be a problem, but recognize that most is personal and should be resolved at that level. If you anticipate very strong resistance, you have three choices:

1. Offer something irresistible
2. Negotiate only for the moral purpose of having made the effort
3. Postpone the negotiation until a better time

The words and expressions you use can be the key to success with peers. Nearly all disagreements with peers usually stem from how each party perceives the other's intentions or behaviors. Perceptions are nearly always controllable by your choice of words. Choose the expressions that both parties can accept and many difficulties will disappear. Of course your approach must be accurate, too, or the agreement will be temporary and future disappointments will cause even more friction.

Chief among the negotiating skills to practice with peers is diplomacy. Good listening ability and an empathetic response are helpful, too. So are reading nonverbal behaviors and asking good questions. Useful tactics include the following:

- Trade-off
- First concession
- Trial balloons
- Straw issues
- Feinting
- Fait accompli

In addition, use two tactics mentioned in regard to negotiating with subordinates: needs search and looking at the record. At all costs, however, avoid ultimatums.

Summary

Negotiation is a blending of desires for a mutually satisfying result. It is an interaction to change a relationship. Three variables are always at play in a negotiation: time, information, and power. Each shapes the outcome of any negotiation.

Many people regard negotiation as a win-lose situation, but it isn't. Both parties must be satisfied for a contract to be enforced. This means you should always take care that other parties win at least some of what they need and want. This is also why no negotiation is ever really concluded.

One crucial element that influences the outcome of any negotiation is the preparation you put into it. To help, this chapter outlined seven questions for preparing a negotiating strategy. It also discussed common negotiating tactics.

The chapter concluded by showing how to apply these negotiating principles to four common situations for a training manager: negotiating with the boss, with subordinates, with outside vendors, and with peers.

Applications

1. Pick a negotiation situation. Create at least three alternate solutions from the one or two that are being discussed. Work to develop one of these three as an integrative solution to the problems that create the opposition.

2. Take a position on a negotiation issue. Assess the other side's position. Now work to discover the interests the other party has in this position. Why have they adopted it? What does it gain them? What would cause you to adopt a similar position?

3. Answer the seven strategic planning questions for an upcoming negotiation you expect to have.

Part 5

Moving Beyond Training

Introduction to Part 5

This part is an overview of what is happening in training and what the trends for the future are likely to be. There are three chapters, each dealing with a different aspect of the state of the art today, the problems you are likely to encounter, some workable, practical responses to these problems, and the direction the problems are likely to take in the next decade.

In Chapter 18 we look at problems facing training managers such as performing a literacy audit and creating in-house literacy programs. We discuss and provide an approach to training and managing a multicultural work force and some considerations for training workers and managers to handle international assignments. Finally we look at the special demands of retraining current employees to prepare them for new tasks.

Chapter 19 addresses the wholeness of training. There has been an awakening among trainers and in many companies to the fact that training must be integrated into the whole organization in order to reach its full effectiveness. Training is at its best when it can form a partnership with management to enhance worker performance. This means bringing training into the strategic planning phase as well as extending its tasks and influence still farther into the posttraining workplace. It is the process of making training more responsive to the bottom line. Chapter 19 is an exploration of the ways you can extend the impact of training beyond the classroom.

Many issues are current and will remain current for a number of years that impact on training and are constantly being addressed at conferences and in training literature. We close the handbook in Chapter 20 by looking at some major ones. Among those to be discussed are the distinct roles of skills training, management training, and organizational development; the problems created by a seemingly ever less competent pool of entry-level employees and the responses available to trainers; the impact of the new technology on training and what to do about it; and, related to all of these, some thoughts on the future of training and, in particular, careers in the field.

Chapter 18
Special Problems in Training

IN 1991 for the second edition of this handbook I identified two special areas that present significant problems for training. These problem areas are:

1. Illiteracy, an increasing lack of basic working skills
2. The growing multicultural nature of the workforce

I am saddened to have to say that events over the past five years have only made these problems worse rather than better. On the one hand it gives me satisfaction to see my predictions were accurate. But on the other hand it seems so unnecessary that solvable problems should continue and even grow.

In the intervening years, the education crisis in America has continued to plague us with unskilled graduates entering the workforce. Now federal and state welfare regulations will add increasing numbers of former welfare recipients seeking entry-level jobs with minimal or no skills and frequently very little experience. Yet only an estimated ten percent of companies are seriously creating literacy training. Politicians are elected on platforms that intend to control an apparent flood of illegal immigrants while we still struggle to train and work with the legal ones we hire. It seems that, more than ever, these twin problems of illiteracy and multiculturalism are destined to impact on your training through the next decade and beyond and so it is necessary to continue to devote a chapter to planning, preparing, and managing effective responses to them.

The Lack of Basic Skills

Several years ago, one of my clients invested several million dollars in automating the assembly lines at one of its heavy manufacturing plants. It was an exciting system that would allow much of the assembly work to function under the control of a powerful computer program created by the company's information systems division. Everything worked superbly during the testing stages when the engineers set up the system and worked out the final wrinkles. Then they showed the supervisors and foremen on the floor how to perform the necessary monitoring, documentation, and consequent inputting that the program required and then allowed the system to run.

It was a disaster! The program that had tested so well simply didn't work in actual practice. When it was adjusted and tried again, it still didn't work. It wasn't until the engineers talked to each of the supervisors, foremen, and workers responsible for interfacing with the system that they discovered 48 percent of them were unable to read the computer's outputs comfortably or accurately. Because the actual users were afraid to make mistakes, these long-term, skilled employees, many of whom had been with the company for twenty or thirty years, simply ad-libbed the data they had put in. At this late date in their careers, the inability to read and comprehend comfortably had caught up with them. A literacy program provided by the company corrected the problem and the system is now up and working very well.

In 1987, the NYNEX Corporation (the "Baby Bell" that provides telephone service for New York and New England) had to test 57,000 applicants to fill 2,100 positions for operators and repair technicians—a ratio of twenty-seven people tested to every one person hired.[1] The tests were on the applicant's ability to perform simple arithmetic, problem-solving operations, and to read and follow instructions.

Employees with substandard basic work skills are becoming an increasing problem in U.S. industry (I'll discuss the scope of the issue in more detail in Chapter 20). As this lack of skills affects how workers and managers handle their job-related skills, their deficiency sooner of later must be addressed by trainers. Two areas in particular will be discussed here: performing a literacy audit and developing in-house literacy programs.

Performing a Literacy Audit

A literacy audit is a specialized form of needs analysis. There are three key skill areas that constitute minimal literacy in the workplace:

1. The ability to read and comprehend necessary instructions, forms, and documentation.
2. The ability to perform basic arithmetical calculations and to make any such calibrations correctly on the job.
3. The ability to organize and solve logical sequence problems in appropriate job-related areas.

As with all aspects of training, in order to change behavior in the work-place—that is, to improve the job performance of basic literacy, numeric, and communication skills—the trainer must know the depth and scope of the problem. Closing any performance gap involves first of all defining the gap to be closed. The problem with literacy is that the potential trainees are frequently unwilling to admit they lack these skills. It is a sensitive emotional issue that must be approached with care and consideration.[2]

This situation is further complicated by the fact that one of the almost universal characteristics of those lacking basic skills is that they have developed terrific coping skills in order to compensate for their lack. Even those closest to them are often unaware of the lack. But sooner or later, they are asked to do something different—prepare a technological update, for example—and their old coping skills prove inadequate, as was the case when my manufacturing client attempted to automate the production line. Inadequate skills show up most clearly when change is required.

A literacy audit is performed to pinpoint the sources of problems, which include deficient skills in job-related reading, computation, problem solving, and communication. There are four steps for performing such an audit:

1. Observation
2. Collection and analysis of materials used to perform the job that require the competent use of basic skills
3. Interviews to verify your observations and analyses
4. Creating and administrating customized performance tests

The general techniques for handling each of these steps is detailed in Chapters 4, 5, and 6, but need to be adapted to the specific mode of a literacy audit. Therefore, let's look at each in turn.

Observe Job Performance. The purpose of observing performance is to document the skills needed to do the job. You will need to watch workers on the job for an entire day or perhaps two or three days to ensure that you are observing all of the tasks that need to be performed. Record each time the worker reads, writes, or performs an arithmetic calculation. As you do so, note also the setting, the materials used, and the purpose of using that skill. Notice, too, whether the skill is performed individually or in a group.

Obviously it is much easier to observe in such detail if you have first established a degree of rapport and a comfort level with the workers to be watched. If they feel they are being spied upon, they are liable to avoid tasks that they don't perform well. It is, therefore, mandatory that you create a relaxed and easy climate for your audit. Select only workers who are willing to be observed. Frame the observation as a learning experience for you rather than as a test for them. I don't recommend lying, but if the workers observed are likely to be suspicious of your motives or feel threatened because of their inadequacies, it might be necessary to couch the observations as a part of some other ongoing operation like formatting a practices and procedures manual or setting training standards by performing a normal task analysis.

Collect Materials Used on the Job. Collect materials that are written and read on the job. This is necessary in order to determine the degree of skill proficiency needed to do the job well. It is a step that is too often neglected. To be effective, a literacy course must address exactly both the precise nature of the job and the skill level necessary to do it. Include such things as memoranda, telephone messages, manuals, bills of sale, wall posters, safety procedures, and forms such as inventory lists, balance sheets, and requisition slips.

Examine these materials to determine the reading level or skill level they demand and the necessary vocabulary they require. Style is important as well. Frequently the problem is not really the reading or skill level of the workers so much as it is the inappropriate level demanded by the forms or documents themselves. Anyone but a lawyer would have trouble deciphering legal documents. In fact, I know a number of lawyers who have to fake it, too.

You must analyze the content of the documents and determine their function. At this point you are still focused on the skill of the user of the document, but later you may be able to simplify the documents themselves. However, in a literacy audit, you are determining skill levels in order to create both a test of those skills and any lessons that may be needed to improve worker performance.

Interview Workers and Supervisors. Often our perceptions of what we do are quite different from the actual behaviors we perform in doing work. It is necessary to take a reading on this potential discrepancy to ensure that, when you train, you are not training in the wrong skills or in unnecessary ones. In your interviews, note the skills that the top-performing employees say are the most important. Then ask them which skills they use the most and how and when they use them. Ask supervisors which skills they feel are needed to perform the job well and identify those that are deemed critical. You might ask both supervisors and workers how they would break in a new employee. Ask, "How do you decide what to do first? Next?" Finally, examine any discrepancies between their perceptions and your observations.

Set Standards and Determine the Skill Level of All Employees. Combine the information you have gathered from your observations, the materials you have collected, and your interviews and write up a job description or task analysis for each of the audited jobs in terms of the reading, writing, and computational skills necessary to perform the job *well*. Check and validate the description by reobserving workers performing it on the job. If problem areas emerge at this stage (that is, the performance varies significantly from your description), discuss your observations and the discrepancy with the workers and supervisors informally in order to pinpoint specific areas of difficulty or concern.

Once you have set your standards in this way, create tests or simulations that are related specifically to each job. Use the language of the particular job in framing any questions and couch both such questions and any skill demonstrations in actual situations and formats that occur on the job. Once you have your set of diagnostic tools, ask all employees who are responsible for performing those jobs to perform the tasks and answer the questions that simulate what they encounter on the job.

You can now compare the results of your audit with the written description or inventory of necessary skills you've built up in order to diagnose and pinpoint problems where skill levels fall short of those demanded.

Optional Training Responses to Literacy Problems

Once you have determined where skill levels fall short, there are three things you can do. Your first option is to redesign tasks and rewrite job-related materials to demand only the skill level that actually exists. It is best to perform this step in conjunction with any training intervention you might plan. It makes training easier and simplifies job procedures in general. It will also give you a built-in standard against which to monitor and measure skill levels in the future.

Your second option is to devise a full training program, based on the skill levels you have defined, targeted at all new employees who will be performing the jobs covered to ensure that they have the necessary skills. Such a response, combined with the first one, may solve existing problems and tends to ensure that the company could respond appropriately to the dwindling basic skill levels of potential new hires (more on this in Chapter 19).

Steps to Performing a Literacy Audit

1. Observe workers performing the job and note when they need to read, write or calculate.
2. Collect and analyze all of the materials they use to perform the job that might involve them having to use a basic skill.
3. Interview the workers and especially their supervisors to verify that what you have observed and collected is indeed the required material and activity.
4. Using these standards, create simulations and tests utilizing the documents and skills, and test all workers.

Your final option is to design specific training programs to bridge the skill gaps discovered in your audit of existing employees. In order to do so, there are three areas you will need to address:

1. As with all training, you will need to define exact workplace needs that will be addressed by raising the basic skill level of employees. You will need to set precise, job-related training objectives.

2. You will have to set up some system for identifying workers in need of your new training.

3. You will also have to specify the projected results of such training for both the company and the employees.

What you are creating by addressing these areas is a rationale to justify your intervention into the area of basic skills or literacy training. Such a move requires justification because many managers do not see the connection between lack of literacy and poor job performance. They need to be convinced that what you propose to do is worthwhile. Furthermore, those workers who most need the training are often the most reluctant to admit it.

Your rationale can be centered around the answers to the following questions:

- What goals or performance standards of the company are not currently being met?

- Are there projected changes in the business or the business environment that will add new goals or modify current standards (such as my client's computerization of the assembly process)?

- What are the skills needed to perform specific jobs over the next five years?

- Do specific employees or groups of employees lack some of these skills?

- What results in job performance would you expect from your literacy training and what impact do you predict it will have on the bottom line?

- How will you know when you have achieved these results?

Developing Literacy Programs

Several aspects of literacy training require special attention. We need to highlight some of the program development needs we covered earlier in Chapters 2 and 7. Then we need to look at the sensitive issue of selecting employees for training in a manner that helps them to maintain their dignity and minimizes resistance. We will consider how to best evaluate the effects of your literacy training efforts, and, finally, examine some of the features of two model programs.

Special Considerations for Developing Literacy Programs

- Material must be organized around job tasks, not basic skills.
- All examples should be in the form in which they will be found in the workplace.
- Include direction and instruction to help employees move toward their personal goals.
- Package and promote literacy training as a normal part of the regular training agenda. Give it a nonremedial title.
- Involve as many trainees and supervisors as possible in the development of the program so that it becomes theirs.
- Build and encourage a positive word of mouth for the program.
- Use fun and inexpensive incentives.
- Schedule training at the work site wherever possible.
- Use available courses offered by outside organizations such as colleges, etc.
- Create job-related evaluation materials of your own. Standardized tests do not correlate with workplace literacy.

Set Job-Related Objectives. It is vital that all of the instruction be organized around job tasks and not basic skills. The skills themselves are important, but only insofar as they enable the worker to perform the job more easily. It is the worker's ability to perform the job comfortably that we are addressing and so this must take precedence. One of the problems most semiliterate people encounter in formal schooling is that the skills are presented as skills to be mastered for their own sake and not as useful tools to help learners perform real-world tasks. Reversing this order of emphasis and instruction will go a long way toward ensuring that they learn the skills and put them into practice on the job.

This means that all of the problems you use for presenting skills or information and for practicing and evaluating them must be real, work-related examples presented as they would be encountered on the job. The problems and simulations, which call for the use of the basic skills being taught, are those that will be addressed on the job.

Several benefits emerge when you structure learning around the job like this instead of around the skills you want the workers to learn. Most important, it allows you to link basic skills to the process of thinking. The skills are learned transparently or invisibly in order to solve the job problem. The learners feel they are learning positive work-related solutions rather than being forced to undergo embarrassing remedial instruction.

Because everything is job-related, this approach builds on the employees' existing knowledge of the job's content and provides them with the opportunity to work together and to learn from each other as well as from you. As a result, the goals you work toward are linked to both the participating employees' personal goals and the company's overall performance ones.

At the same time, general literacy itself is often a strong motivator. Discuss employees' personal motives and then include as many of them as possible in the work-related instruction. Frequent areas of interest include the following:

- High school equivalency (GED)
- Gaining other credentials or licenses
- Current events
- Reading and writing fiction, autobiographies, and poetry
- Dealing with personal credit and other legal agreements
- Reading good literature
- Helping children with homework

Recruiting Trainees. For many adults there is a stigma attached to not being able to perform skills we expect of our children. Resistance to training can be very real, therefore, even when the worker deeply desires the knowledge being taught. As the trainer, you must make this barrier as minimal as possible.

There are several things you can do to help learners perceive literacy training as a positive benefit. First of all, package and promote it as a normal part of the regular training agenda. It is not, nor can it ever be, remedial or special. Give it a positive name. Call it Advanced Processing Skills, or Managing New Technologies, or Job Skills 2000 or some such upscale title.

When you are planning the courses and performing your literacy audit, involve as many of the workers and supervisors as you can. Seek their input and advice. Let the course you develop be as much theirs as possible. Whenever you can, encourage those they trust to talk up the course for you. There is no more powerful positive advertising than word of mouth. Find those who want it and ask them to help you sell it.

Make the goals of the program very clear to the employees and, whenever possible, tie the training program to incentive programs. These needn't be large or expensive. The opportunity to upgrade to a higher paying job is a fine incentive for many. So is the opportunity to transfer to a different one. You can take all graduates to Pizza Hut or some other reasonable, fun place. Incentives help to answer the question "What's in it for me?" and so help to make literacy training fun.

It is very helpful to schedule training on the work site wherever possible. This keeps it work related in the learners' minds. The training situation should be as unlike formal schooling as possible. It should be clean and comfortable and accessible. Finally, schedule as much of the training as you can on company time.

This lets the workers see that the company is serious about the training, expects it to have an impact on the job, and supports their efforts to improve.

Evaluate Your Literacy Program. Literacy as a problem in the workplace is such a recently discovered area that there are as yet no common criteria developed for evaluating the results of training interventions. Perhaps there never will be because such results must be tied, as must the training itself, to the specific tasks and responsibilities of each job. Improvement in standardized reading tests seems so far to have little or no impact on job performance and so cannot be used as an effective measure of improvement. Furthermore, most of the little research that has been done has been based on military data, which is not common to many jobs in the private sector.

So, in order to effectively evaluate the impact of your literacy training, you will need to create evaluation tools of your own. Those activities that you measured and set up as criteria in your literacy audit can be used to assess posttraining performance as well as pretraining status. Set up pre- and posttest situations and simulations to gauge employee improvement. Talk to graduates and supervisors to establish what they feel the results of your literacy training are. Set up a schedule like Polaroid's (described below) to follow up on trainees every so many hours by reassessing their performance with their supervisors. Look for changes in attitudes and work habits. Setting up affective training objectives will help you here (see Chapter 2). Finally, you can invite supervisors to sit in on the training and evaluate both your performance and that of the class.

Two Model Programs. The Polaroid Corporation has a literacy program in operation that is frequently cited as a model approach to the problem. It offers job-related training in four areas of basic skills that its employees need to perform at peak levels:

1. *Basic literacy,* which involves reading and writing

2. *Arithmetic,* including addition, subtraction, multiplication, division, and working with fractions, decimals, and percentages

3. *Mathematics,* including not only algebra and statistics but the making of scientific calculations, working with computers, and the reading and calibration of instruments

4. *Problem solving,* which also addresses study skills and speaking and listening skills

Workers are chosen for the classes by individual assessment sessions and by supervisory referrals. The assessments or referrals may be for training in-house or for training in specific courses offered by colleges or outside service organizations. In either case, attendance is voluntary. Assessors and supervisors may only recommend. It is up to the individual to take advantage of the recommendation. However, strong positive word-of-mouth from graduates and very real job improvement results are the main persuaders.

Newly hired or newly referred employees are given assessment tests to determine their level of expertise in those skills applicable to their jobs. Those who score below the minimum standard (the fourth-grade reading level in the case of basic literacy) are given tutorials for four hours per week, half on company time and half on their own time. Instructors walk through the job with the trainees to make the material job-related. All instruction is thus relevant to what the worker must do on the job.

The content of each course or tutorial is determined jointly by the employee, the supervisor for whom the employee will work, and the instructor. Usually, upon completion of the course or tutorial, the employee is given a pocket guide that he or she has been taught to use, containing the fifteen or twenty most commonly used words or procedures to be encountered on the job. Instructors follow up and check their trainees' performance with the supervisors every ten hours of instruction to ensure transfer of learning. Finally, there is a literacy support group for each basic skill, which meets bi-monthly for breakfast so each learner has a chance to relate to others with similar problems.

The Ideal Box Company is a privately owned, family-run manufacturer of corrugated boxes. It hires a large number of immigrants, mostly from Mexico. It has one of the best literacy programs I have ever seen, even though it is not tailored to Ideal's workplace. Complete high school equivalency programs are offered on site in a special classroom near the factory floor. Classes are taught by outside teachers who come on site to teach their regular curricula. The classes are two hours each, the last hour of one shift and the first hour of the next one, so that workers only miss an hour of any given shift.

Stress is given to English as a second language, but all general high school courses are taught. Furthermore, last year the company expanded its offerings to college-level courses so that employees can work toward a two-year associate's degree.

The method used to finance this program is what makes it such an exciting one. The company pays for only half the tuition costs. The employees are expected to pay the balance. However, when they graduate, the company refunds what the workers have paid in full as a cash bonus to reward them for completing their program. This program is so successful that it has virtually ended turnover in a high turnover industry. And worker loyalty to the company is remarkable.

The Multicultural Workforce

Two current trends converge to create another area of special interest to trainers. They are the trend to greater globalization of industry and the continuing growth of foreign-born nationals seeking and filling entry-level and skilled jobs in the United States. Together, these trends demand that training departments take on the role of preparing native employees—management and lower-level workers alike—to interact effectively with those from other countries, both at home and abroad. It also means that a short course in American customs and cultural differences may become standard for many new hires.

Clearly this is not a book about the specifics of handling each culture. But there are a number of universal considerations and recommendations that will help you with some of the crucial decisions you will have to make when you are confronted with the problems of a multicultural workforce.

The first and most important recommendation is that you train management first. The single best way to prevent cultural conflicts in the workplace is to train every native-born mid-manager and supervisor who might come into contact with nonnative workers in how to respond to the cultural differences they might be expected to encounter. Include the non-native-born managers and supervisors to help them cope. Once your managers and supervisors are prepared to reenforce the training, your second line of effort should be to present for all workers who will work with other cultures a series of training sessions on recognizing and responding appropriately to cultural differences. These sessions should include nonnative participants as well, especially if you have worked with them to develop all or a portion of the curriculum in much the same way as you would perform a literacy audit.

Defining the Problem

The mere existence of cultural differences does not create problems. In fact, many of the pleasures we take in traveling and meeting people from other cultures arise because they are different from us. The problem is created when differing cultures come into conflict with each other in the workplace.[3]

It isn't actually the cultures themselves that come into conflict but rather the values that the cultures pass on to their members. A value is any thing or behavior that is held to be special or normal by an individual or group. A value can be a way of doing things, a set of gestures, manners, beliefs, or even skills. When two groups do things differently, or believe differently, and are forced into contact or joint effort, frictions and resentments can occur. We usually call such a situation a culture clash, but it is really just the value systems of the parties that are in conflict.

Anthropologist Edward Hall has defined ten categories or aspects of behavior around which values are formed in all cultures. He calls them primary message systems (PMS). The first PMS is the way in which we interact with each other. How we talk, forms of address, nonverbal behavior rules, volume, music, slang, jargon, and responses to humor, joy, sadness, or emergencies would all fit into this cluster. Thus, some things are appropriate to laugh at, others are not. Smiling is an important way of expressing embarrassment for the Japanese. Opening the eyes widely expresses surprise for Americans but outrage for the Chinese. Clearly, there is room for both friction and resolution in cultural clashes that center around this primary message system.

Hall's second PMS has to do with hierarchy and how we associate with each other. Status is nearly always expressed through our message systems, but constitutes a core behavior of humans in all cultures; many of our other value expressions also carry strong status messages. Americans nearly always want to be equal, open, and fair (as they see fairness) to everyone. But most other cultures have much stronger and more clearly defined strata in their hierarchies of relationship, and so frequently discomfort Americans with either too much formality and respect or too little. We call each other by our first names even in a reporting relationship whereas in most other cultures much more value is placed on recognizing the status differences between superior and subordinate. I have seen American-born employees of foreign-born managers sue the company for discriminatory treatment because of this value clash. I have also seen European workers refuse to do work that was "beneath them," an infringement on or insult to their status. This is a crucial area in which training can help greatly to further understanding.

The third PMS is subsistence, which probably plays a much smaller role in work-related value conflicts. It is the behavior we condone in preparing and eating food, in finding and using shelter, and in dress. There are obvious areas here where "fun" can be made of differences, and indeed has been for centuries in all cultures, but such behavior in the workplace would appear to be more symptomatic of other, deeper differences. The one possible exception is cleanliness and personal hygiene, which fits in part in this system but which is more closely allied to the rules of interaction. Apart from hygiene, however, subsistence values are unlikely to come into conflict in the workplace.

Sexual behavior, the fourth PMS, is much more likely to be a problem. This is not simply a matter of courtship. It involves how each gender defines what is appropriate behavior: what is acceptable masculine behavior and what is acceptable feminine behavior. It defines the roles of each sex in the culture as well as the rules for contact between the sexes. Some cultures are scandalized by the freedom exhibited by American women. Others are appalled at the repressive and puritanical restrictions of our society. And we, in turn, are equally put off by their behaviors. Sexual behavior patterns are not a matter of morality in a cross-cultural context, but rather they are an indicator of cultural norms and values. Issues centered around the treatment of one sex by the other can emerge in the workplace, particularly when American-born women work with men or women from cultures that hold very rigid and strict roles as norms.

Territoriality, the fifth PMS, is usually one of the easier primary message systems to deal with because, although it can make us uncomfortable, it seldom causes an outright confrontation or even conflict. It is apparent in our choice of seating or work spaces, parking spaces, office size, distance between each other while communicating in different environments, and so forth. Only when it is used as an association message, that is, an assumption of space as an indicator of presumed superior status, is it likely to be troublesome. In fact, we covered one of its positive uses in Chapter 3 as a means of controlling difficult participants in seminars.

Hall's sixth PMS is time. The perception of time and how it is "used" is a major source of conflict between cultures, possibly because it is one of the most transparent message systems. We see our own expectations of time to be perfectly natural and the only possible attitude to have. Yet every culture does the same. Latin cultures tend to be what is called *polychronic*, which means that members are usually quite comfortable doing more than one thing at a time. Most Arabic peoples are not. Furthermore, in the Middle East much time needs to be given over to discourse and debate rather than instruction or mandate. In many cultures around the world, things don't happen "on time." Instead, they occur when the time is ripe for them to occur. The European/American concept of *on time* has little or no meaning in these cultures. In fact, it is usually a cause for much puzzlement and confusion. For them, what possible purpose is there in doing a thing before it is ready to be done? This can be a considerable source of value conflict and needs to be addressed in any cross-cultural training.

Learning is the next category and values about it and how it should best take place vary as much from culture to culture as do other value areas. This book is based entirely on Western European and North American research into how people of these cultures learn. Even when transferred to other cultures, the practices outlined throughout this work hold true. However, what constitutes practice and application varies from one culture to the next. In France, Spain, and most Arab nations, discourse is regarded as intense application and so much time needs to be allotted to it. In many countries activities like role-plays and case histories are regarded as games for children and would humiliate and mortify participants. People of whatever culture who have learned to study well and pay close attention to lectures almost always claim to learn better this way, despite the fact that most other people don't. They have developed a particular skill and enjoy using it. Conflicts in this area can be dealt with efficiently by anticipating them and adjusting assignments and class time accordingly.

Number eight is play and it can vary everywhere. However, it is almost always a source of union and potential sharing rather than one of possible friction. Even struggling to understand a joke from another culture is more positive than negative.

Number nine is centered around defensive behavior. Here it is important for you as a trainer to become aware and to teach those you train to be aware that defensive behavior is only symptomatic. We defend only when we feel threatened. It is usually some other value conflict centered on a different primary message system that is triggering the defensive response. In your preparation for working with any culture, learn how they acceptably express defensive behavior so that you can teach others how to read that behavior and use it to diagnose the real problem behind it.

Hall's final category is exploitation and it deals with how people from different cultures use the tools and artifacts around them. It covers things like hours of operation, traffic regulations (both pedestrian and vehicular), dress, budgeting, and treatment of the tools of work. Conflicts can occur over keeping tools in perfect operating order, cleanliness in the workplace, or safety regulations. This is an important and frequent source of cross-cultural difficulty.

Responding to the Problem

Hall goes further and describes three levels of cultural values delineated by the manner in which they are learned and how that learning is used. The easiest for trainers to address is the technical level, in which the learner masters skills, tool use, general competence, and so forth. This is the simplest for us because, of course, it most closely parallels the normal content of our skills-oriented training. However, do take into consideration the differences in values in learning message systems and adjust your activities accordingly while training those from other cultures. Also be sure to train supervisors to do so when they coach those from cultures other than their own.

The second most accessible category is those values and behaviors that the individual has learned formally, that is, has made a conscious effort to master. These values are largely those taught in schools or by one-on-one instruction and include language, manners, time use, and a number of other everyday skills. Because they have been taught more or less formally, they can be relearned or at least adapted to accommodate the demands of the American work culture. Certainly they can be discussed in a relatively calm manner and differences can be pointed out and adjusted.

By far the most difficult is Hall's third level of learning and acting, which he calls informal. This level is made up of all those ways and mores that have been learned unconsciously, that have been simply "absorbed" by immersion in a particular culture. To the practitioner these ways seem perfectly natural and obviously the "right" way to do things. Attempts to perform them differently or to "correct" them will at best be thought amusing and at worst, will be met with fierce and angry defensiveness. It is here that most value and cultural conflicts occur.

The response to cultural conflicts then is to ventilate the friction in order to discover which level you are dealing with. Any or all of the primary message systems may be involved at any level so deciding which ones are contributing is the next step. Now answer the following sequence of questions:

1. What values are actually in conflict on both sides?
2. At what level is the conflict and which PMS's are involved?
3. Which individuals and groups in the organization hold to each of the competing value systems?
4. How powerful politically are each of them?
5. What allies do they have externally as well as internally?
6. Which values are consistent with the larger values, the organizational goals and objectives?
7. What alternative resolutions to the conflict can be discovered?
8. What value sacrifices or adjustments would each resolution require of each side?
9. Are some problems insoluble at present because of irreconcilable value conflicts?
10. What other solutions (such as changed recruitment practices, training, or reorganization) are possible?*

Remember, there are no right answers to such value conflicts. Each side is certain, deep down, that its values are the right ones and that the other party is at fault. Ventilation, listening, and positive negotiation are the best procedures.

Cross-Cultural Training

Specific communication and behavioral management skills should be taught and practiced until participants tend to use them automatically when they are confronted with a cultural problem.[4] Here is a list of such skills, each of which is discussed in turn:

- Respect for other cultures, both verbally and nonverbally
- Tolerance of differences; acceptance of ambiguous behavior on the part of others
- The ability to build relationships slowly
- A nonjudgmental attitude
- The belief that the ways of other cultures are as good as our own
- Empathy—seeing the other person's point of view
- Patience and persistence when dealing with people whose ways differ from our own

Respect is the first and perhaps the most important skill. We will tolerate and forgive all kinds of social and cultural gaffes if we believe that the one committing

*These questions are adapted from Donald Weiss's article "Managing a Diverse Workforce: How to Deal With Value Conflicts" in the December 1987 issue of *Trainer's Workshop*.

them respects our ways. Managers and workers both need to learn the proper social rules for showing and receiving respect in the cultures that they manage or work with. They should master both the verbal and nonverbal forms of respect and use them when the situation calls for their use. Managers will also find such knowledge very helpful in diagnosing relationships among their charges.

Tolerance is second. Intolerance has no pace in multicultural work environments. This is not simply a lack of bias but is, rather, a habit of acceptance of ambiguity. People do not do things the way we want them done all of the time. Different work styles are still often very effective. Dogmatic managers will find themselves swamped with unnecessary problems. Successful multicultural management requires developing a comfort level for the new, surprising, and ambiguous behavior of one's subordinates.

Most Americans are viewed internationally as very rushed and highly driven people. The rest of the world, by and large, needs to spend more time developing relationships than they do in getting the job done. In fact, in most Arabic countries the relationship between the worker and his or her manager is far more important than the job. Who you work with is vital. What you do or how well you do it is immaterial. American managers must learn the specific skills of building relationships with their coworkers and subordinates.

Being nonjudgmental is one of the crucial skills in building a relationship. We cannot work comfortably when others are looking over our shoulders or when we feel constantly under pressure to perform. Snap judgments often lead to misunderstandings. This is particularly true when the judgments are made across cultures. Managers must learn to withhold judgment until they fully understand the cultural patterns surrounding problem behaviors on which they must act. So must everyone who works with others who have a cultural background different from their own.

All of us internalize the world around us. We see things and understand them in terms that are familiar to us, and so we regard our way as the only way, or at least as the right way. Internationally such an attitude is a disaster. Even within the same overall culture this attitude can cause problems. In parts of Florida contractors and other service workers proudly display a bumper sticker that states, "We don't care how they did it up North!" Cross-cultural managers must learn to guard against this tendency. Sometimes the other culture's way actually is better.

Empathy is a vital skill for communication in general and most especially for anyone working with multiple cultures. Developing the skill requires constant practice in seeing the other person's point of view. Games and simulations, case histories and role-plays are all very helpful in forcing managers to look at the problem from the other party's perspective.

Finally, your managers must learn persistence. If we are trying to change people's job-related behavior, we must realize that the behavior they now have is comfortable to them. As we have seen throughout this book, people behave in the way with which they are most familiar. For foreign-born workers, that way will almost always be different from the American-born manager's way. And the foreign-born worker will deeply believe that his or her way is not only the better way, but that the manager's way is probably ineffective. It will take much time, patience, and persistence to bring that attitude around. Managers must learn to become comfortable with patience and persistence.

Training for Foreign Assignments. If your company rotates a number of employees and managers to other countries, you should set up a twofold cross-cultural training effort. One step is to either create or adapt a short course on the material we've just covered here with specific modules on each of the countries to be visited. Use the techniques we've covered in Chapter 6 to learn about the specific cultures. The second tier is to create a library of culture-specific books (the travel section of most bookstores has an exciting selection) and then develop a series of self-study readings to highlight various aspects of each culture. Make sure you get multiple copies of each book so that several people can use each resource at the same time. These employees might also benefit from attending one of your regular cross-cultural classes. Finally, develop an outside resource list of college classes, symposia, cultural centers, and foreign consulates and schools in your area to which you can refer your charges.

Summary

This chapter addresses two of the most pressing issues in training today: the growing population of marginally literate new hires, which also relates to the growing need for retraining existing workers in upgraded skills, and the rapidly increasing influx of foreign-born workers.

To address the first, we looked at the requirements of performing a literacy audit and how it differs from a regular needs assessment. The emphasis here is that you are not merely defining the skill level but possibly refining the work-related material that demands literacy or basic calculation skills in order to simplify them. With this in mind, we outlined the steps necessary to creating your own literacy audit.

A training program will most likely grow out of any literacy audit, so we touched upon several of the special considerations in creating training in basic literacy. The principle concern is to make the training surgically job specific. Literacy skills are not as transferable as we would like to think. It is not merely the skills of reading, writing, figuring, and communicating that you need to teach, but rather *the application of each of those skills in the specific work environment* that the trainees will be using.

Selecting trainees for literacy programs presents the issue of reluctance on the part of many workers to admit to such a shortcoming, and so some special considerations must be given to positioning the training. Finally, evaluation of the impact of the literacy training is dealt with.

In outlining steps to take with regard to the increasingly multicultural workforce, we stress the need to train from the top down. It is management and supervision who need to be able to respond to cultural differences, not the workforce per se. Workers can and should be trained to work together, but such training is futile if their managers and supervisors cannot respond appropriately to cultural conflicts. Teach those in charge first.

Our approach to recognizing and planning for cultural change courses is based on the work of anthropologist Edward Hall, who analyzes cultural value systems according to ten primary message systems every culture uses to interact with its members and the rest of the world. These in turn are layered as three distinct levels of learning and behavior, which help the trainer to formulate an approach to training others in cultural sensitivity. We then provide a series of diagnostic questions that can be adapted as a core curricular approach to such courses.

The last section of the chapter is a brief discussion of how to adapt this material in constructing courses and other resources for employees who are assigned to work abroad and who need to better understand the cultures they will encounter.

Applications

1. Perform a literacy audit for your company. Follow the steps outlined in this chapter. If you are already conducting or planning to conduct a needs analysis, expand it to include the necessary elements of the literacy audit.

2. Select a task. Create a series of work-related skill practices around the literacy level involved in this task. Even if you don't have a literacy problem, incorporate these skill exercises into your regular training in that task area.

3. Using Edward Hall's PMS structure, create a cultural profile for each set of workers in your organization who are from a culture other than your own. Interview members of each of these cultures. Read books. Flesh out your profiles in full.

4. Using these analyses, write a full training program about understanding and working with cross-cultural behavior. Even if you don't need it now, you probably will one day and it is always best (and easiest) to be prepared.

Chapter 19
Enlarging the Vision of Training

TRAINING has always had the same goal: to change workers' job-related behaviors. That is why training was first brought into the workplace. It is why the ancient medieval guilds created apprenticeships and set up courses of study and skill practice. This requirement of a change in behavior or an improvement in skills is so basic to training that it is safe to say that if training is not improving the workers' job-related skills, it is not training. Yet a great deal of what passes for training today fails to meet this essential qualification. One study reports that "on average only 10 percent to 20 percent of training transfers to the job so that the performance of the employee has been enhanced and changed."[1]

The Nature of the Problem

This is a transfer-of-learning problem: Are the learners using what they've learned when they return to the job? The results of studies like the one cited earlier seem to be true. We can all think of "training" that had little or no impact on the job skills of those trained.

However, on reflection, most of us would agree that those sessions that failed to help the learners to acquire usable skills were really not training, as it is defined in this book, but rather what I have called *information meetings*. These sessions consist of one day or less of intense briefing on a subject. They are frequently presented by dynamic and professional speakers. Many use extremely well-produced visual aids. They are on job-related topics, and the best of them are challenging and informative. But they are not training. They are seminars. They provide little or no practice in the techniques described and almost no opportunity for feedback and coaching. As in college classes, learning is up to the learner. The information is presented and the learner can take it or leave it. With no immediate application opportunity, all but 10 percent or so leave it.

It is this state of affairs that has prompted the use of the phrase *going beyond training*, which implies that training as we know it has failed to deliver the promised changes in job behavior, and so we must go beyond mere training in the next era to ensure results. The difficulty I have with the proponents of this approach is that they lump all training in with the information-meeting type of presentation and cite massive failure statistics. They ignore the hundreds of thousands (perhaps millions) of workers and managers who have been successfully trained using the solid techniques covered in earlier sections of this book. Nearly everyone who uses a computer in their work learned their computer skills in training classes. Assembly workers in major factories are given intensive classroom instruction and practice to shorten the learning curve. Tens of thousands of managers learned how to manage well through training. Truck drivers need to pass rigorous training standards to drive. ISO 9000 and QS 9000 standards demand intensive and documented training. And the learners learn. They transfer their new skills to the workplace successfully. There is a problem with transfer of learning, but it is not the failure of training per se that is the root cause. Rather, it is the failure of management and theorists to distinguish between effective training and information meetings.

In fact, the corporate culture creates the response to training. The way in which a company is run, how it performs strategic planning, how it evaluates success, its corporate goals—these are the things that determine how training will be perceived and performed. Following is an example of the power of corporate culture to influence training.

Federal Express and United Parcel Service

Peter Cappelli and Anne Crocker-Hefter, two practicing organization development specialists, have made a detailed and careful study of the similarities and differences between these two giants of the package delivery industry.[2] For Cappelli and Crocker-Hefter, "the way in which human resource competencies are generated and the business strategies that flow from them" are an interwoven whole. They explore the relationship between business strategy and the human resources department, including the training function.

They point out that "organizations that move quickly to seize new opportunities compete through flexibility and do not develop employee competencies from within."[3] Consequently, Federal Express, whose whole thrust is rapid response to market conditions and the latest technologies, outsources a considerable amount of its training. This practice keeps the company flexible and responsive. To cite an example from my personal experience: a few years ago I was brought in to train several of the worker units on negotiation skills. Then, in the spring of 1997 several aircraft maintenance workers from Federal Express attended my public seminar on "Training the Trainer." The company does perform internal training, but on a limited number of core skills, preferring to use more flexible and rapid outsources for much key training. This pattern is a part of their strategic plan and is worked out with the cooperation of their highly regarded training department.

United Parcel Service, on the other hand, enjoys a strong union environment that has built up an enviable set of core competencies and standards of performance over the years. These are taught internally by the training department and used in employees' performance appraisals. Training is internal, thorough, and slow to change. But it is the backbone of the organization, helping UPS to compete by maintaining standards and core competencies at a very high level. When new technology is required, training is an integral part of the planning process for implementation.

Thus the personal competencies of the workforce and the training philosophies of each of these two large competitors help to create their marketing and business strategies and vice versa.

Opening the Doors

When I had just earned my bachelor's degree, I was summoned to the office of the head of the company I worked for. I had been working part-time, summers and weekends, for this company during three of my four years of college. I liked the work and my boss, and I revered his boss, the CEO, who was founder of the company and one of the true pioneers in the industry. It was this great and famous person that wanted to see me. I entered his large and imposing office feeling very confident and puffed up by my freshly minted degree.

He began by saying, "Well, I see you've completed the first step of your education."

I was stunned. I had just graduated! I had *finished* my education! This wasn't the ending of the "first step," this was the end, period, the completion of my learning. I was hurt and puzzled and deflated. He offered me a full-time job at an excellent salary, which was his purpose in calling the meeting. I turned him down because I wanted to work in the area that I had been studying for four years. I was now a teacher with a completed college degree to prove it. I was going to teach. And so I did, and still do.

What I had not realized then—and have since learned—was that my attitude was and still is a very common one. I had closed the door on my classroom learning. I was finished. I had walked out of the university believing that I had acquired an education, that it was over, complete, and that I was now a qualified and skilled practitioner. I wasn't worried by the fact that I had almost no experience in the work I thought I was qualified to perform.

When training goes wrong, it is frequently this attitude that creates the problem. If we see training as what goes on during the training sessions and that's it, then we deserve the criticism of studies like the Broad and Newstrom one cited earlier. If training starts and stops at the training room door, it will never succeed in changing behavior on the job. Training cannot be an isolated function in any organization. Rather it is a integral part of the company, tied to the company's vision, a process that produces improved job performance. What you do in the training sessions is only a step; it is never the completion of training, any more than graduating from college is the completion of learning. The doors of the training room must remain open and interactive with the rest of the company.

Remedies

Early in his book *Beyond Training and Development: State-of-the-Art Strategies for Enhancing Human Performance*, William J. Rothwell, one of the leading proponents of the "going beyond training" concept, sets forth a series of excellent questions. Asking these questions and answering them carefully will keep any training department tied to the company's strategy and will produce real training with on-the-job results. Rothwell challenges you to answer the following:

- How does the training and development department contribute to achieving the organization's strategic objectives? to meeting and exceeding customer requirements?
- How does the training and development department conduct needs analysis?
- How does the training and development department prove the return on training investment?
- How are problems that should be solved by training distinguished from problems that should be solved by management action?
- How do line (operating) managers hold employees accountable on their jobs for what they learn in training?[4]

Rothwell's purpose is to create training that is focused on achieving job-related changes in performance. I cannot fault him for this nor any other of the *human performance* promoters that have recently emerged. It is indeed what I have been saying for eighteen years. As performance consultants Dana and James Robinson define it, "[The] primary focus of [training] is to partner with management to identify and achieve performance excellence . . . [Training should be] valued as a partner to management in the achievement of performance and business needs."[5] This is inarguably the task of modern training.

What these authors are saying is that training needs to provide context and fight isolation within the company. Training that is simply training—a service that can be turned on and off—will probably not do well at creating transfer of learning to the workplace because trainees will close the training room door behind them as they return to work. Once it's done, then it's over with. Instead, we as trainers must expand our function into the work environment before training and into the work environment after training. Both are integral parts of the training process and so must be woven into it. How do we do this? The answers to Rothwell's questions can be found earlier in this book.

How Does the Training Department Contribute to the Organization's Goals? Within the discussion of needs analysis in Chapter 4 you will find a detailed outline for assessing the climate for change in an organization, who to contact and ally with, as well as how to approach various key players within the organization. In addition, Chapter 7 speaks of how to align the goals of training to those of management in the creation of a rationale for training. Later in this chapter specific examples of partnering with management to focus more closely on its goals and to use training skills as a creative management tool will be discussed.

How Does Training and Development Conduct Needs Analysis? Needs analysis is the focus of Chapter 4. The chapter explains how to document performance, assess and measure the current level of performance, and determine the desired level of performance you want the learners to change to. A section deals with feasibility of analysis and training that ties your work to the plans of management.

How Does Training Prove Its Return on Investment? Chapter 4 contains detailed procedures for assessing and justifying costs in training. In addition, Chapter 5 discusses how to assess the impact of your training on the company's profits in the section on level three, bottom-line evaluations.

How Are Management Problems Distinguished From Training Problems? Chapter 4 has a section on classifying the types of problems a needs analysis will uncover and how to respond to each type. Among them are organizational (management) problems, systemic (market and technology) problems, and training (skills) problems.

How Do Line Managers Follow Up on Training? Chapter 5 treats this problem in detail in the sections on immediate impact on the job and bottom-line evaluations. Chapters 13 and 14 deal specifically with tools for post-training evaluation and follow-up by managers and supervisors in order to hold workers accountable for performing what they have learned. In addition, later on in this chapter case studies will expand even further on ways to perform this function.

Training and Management Partnerships

More and more, senior managers are realizing the growing importance and influence of training on their bottom line and strategic and marketing plans. Companies are seeking training expertise to help them in earlier stages of change, prior to the actual training. Let me cite four examples.

Anchor/Darling Valve Company

Anchor/Darling manufactures valves for the nuclear power industry, both defense applications and public utilities. It is a dominant player in this market. However, in recent years, a combination of declining military budgets and greatly increased foreign competition has put considerable pressure on its marketing efforts. In 1995 management created a dynamic market plan based on clear forecasting and careful market analysis. Unfortunately, its market managers—operating in distinct and separate districts around the nation and the world—were slower to respond to the program than management had expected. They were not as familiar with the larger picture, the total data, the change in market demographics, and so forth; so the plan failed to achieve the results the company had hoped for.

Therefore, in 1996 the company tried a different approach. As we all know, people carry out their own plans with much more enthusiasm that they do those of others. Anchor/Darling wanted the market managers to develop a marketing plan that would encompass the findings and projections of senior management and, most important, would be put to use in the field. The company hired a training consultant, myself, to conduct a team building and planning session with the market managers to guide them in creating the 1996 marketing plan.

Together we worked through a number of team-building exercises, including several brainstorming sessions, problem-solving approaches, presentations, and group management projects. The company provided the data: market and forecast information. The market managers provided the work, the thinking, and the results. I provided the plan for the day, controlled the format, and facilitated the interaction. At the end of a long but highly charged and exciting day, Anchor/Darling had a market plan for 1996 that the managers couldn't wait to put into practice.

First Bank

First Bank in Minneapolis emerged in the mid-1990s as a major player in the credit industry. It did so both with managerial skill and through a series of acquisitions and mergers that greatly enlarged the scope of its operations. A problem every organization faces when making a number of acquisitions is that gaining new portfolios, operations, and outlets means taking in the marginal and questionable operations as well as the excellent ones. Particularly in banking, new acquisitions mean taking on the management of vast new portfolios of mortgages and credit card loans. As such, the management practices and risk standards of the acquired operations are invariably different from your own, and so the ratio of poorly performing loan pools and even bad debt increases at the same rate or one even greater than your rate of growth. Your collections function is faced with a tremendous upsurge in defaulted loans.

The collections division of First Bank was feeling the pressure. Management responded with new, state-of-the-art technology, increased staffing, and a new, full-time training department. However, with all of the new operations, staffing, and responsibilities and the increased work load, people were uncertain, ill at ease, and sometimes even working at cross purposes. What was needed was a clear sense of mission and a defining set of principles and practices that would act as a guide and anchor during the division's necessary changes. To that end, management brought in a training consultant, myself, to help frame a mission statement and a set of standard practices for the collections division. This is not a traditional role for training, but rather a part of the current trend toward partnerships of management and training to formulate policy and procedures.

Senior managers were each asked to frame what they would like the mission and standards to be. These statements became the core material for a focus group which I conducted with the frontline managers of the division. I framed the need and the situation for them. We explored each of the options that management had proposed and added our own preferences and input. In the process the group was able to air some of its concerns so that these could also be addressed in the final document. Using the information from the focus group and working closely with the head of the collections division, I was able to create a comprehensive mission statement and a set of performance standards that reflected First Bank's overall mission, the collections division's specific mission, management's desire for standard performance, and the frontline supervisors' concerns.

Finally, I met again with the focus group participants and senior management to present the mission statement and guidelines to them. With these in hand, we worked through a second focus group that allowed supervisors to express both concerns and commitment and allowed management to respond to the concerns and in turn make commitments. I facilitated the discussion. The entire project was a great success and went a long way towards solving the problem of unsettled conditions that the division was experiencing.

What had happened in both of these examples was the partnering of traditional training skills with the strategic planning function to create a specific, limited, but essential result. Note that the training function did not usurp any of management's power or privilege but rather supplied its normal service function. But the service was in a new direction. A joint effort of management and training was created to produce a change in employee performance. This is a new horizon for training and one that will become more and more important in the next few years.

Sun Life of Canada

In the examples I've addressed so far, the training/management partnership has occurred prior to or independent of actual training. As Rothwell has suggested, it becomes essential for training to reach out and create these sorts of pretraining partnerships in order for our function to keep pace and remain a central focus in the next century. But it is also important that we establish patterns of posttraining partnership as well. The best of these partnerships that I know of is at Sun Life of Canada, which I described in detail in Chapter 5.

During training participants are required to formulate action plans that will be carried out after the training is completed. At the end of the training session trainees are given time to coordinate their action plans for each topic covered into a master plan. Within two weeks of training they are required to sit down with their managers and gain the managers' input and help towards achieving their outlined goals. It is this last step that lifts the plan out of the mundane and into the world of transferring learning and ensuring beneficial change in job-related behavior.

In order for this system to work, several things must take place before the learners meet with their managers:

▪ There must be a partnership between management and training that is established before the training begins.

▪ The managers must be fully trained in the system so they will know how to provide meaningful feedback and coaching to their workers.

▪ Each department using this system must be developing staff performance on a management by objectives system where workers mutually set goals with their managers and then work together with those managers to achieve them. Sun Life's special wrinkle is that those goals are tied to specific training events that draw the learning far beyond the classroom and into the realm of everyday work.

▪ The posttraining meeting must be an initial meeting with regular follow-up meetings to be scheduled. In this manner, training objectives will become an integral part of the employee's regular working objectives and also a part of his or her performance assessment record.

This system works excellently in white-collar environments such as Sun Life's. In order to apply it to a blue-collar manufacturing or equipment operation environment, the action plans need to be changed to performance standards and operational checklists. The workers meet with their supervisors to go over and ensure compliance with the lists and standards. As the supervisors oversee the work performed, they give feedback in the terms of the standards and checklists.

In this way the concepts from training are moved to and applied to the work world. The system for doing this is described in detail in Chapter 13.

Standard & Poor's

This final example involves close partnering both before and after the actual training, and it illustrates the power of extending training to encompass the full spectrum of changing workplace behavior.

Several years ago my close colleague, Beverly Hyman, and I contracted with Standard & Poor's to train their technical analysts in clear writing skills. Standard & Poor's is a securities rating organization that assesses the investment quality of companies, municipalities, bank deals, and both state and national governments. Their analysts assign creditworthiness ratings to these organizations, which have a large impact on the organization's ability to raise funds in the bond markets of the world. Most organizations strive for a favorable S&P rating.

S&P has a number of weekly and daily publications to keep the investment community informed. Through a series of readership surveys the company conducted it discovered that most readers found its analyses very dense and its publications crowded with too much material and not enough white space, making them hard to read. This is hardly surprising as the analyses and articles are written by S&P's analysts, who are expert in the arcane science of credit analysis, but not in prose writing and layout design. S&P wanted to change this image by revamping its style rules and creating performance standards for its analysts' writing. To that end, Beverly and I were hired to develop a style manual and perform the necessary training in writing skills.

We began with a series of focus groups involving the end users of S&P's publications, its customers, to establish specific directions and guidelines to follow in making style choices. This was done with the participation of the publishing management group. Out of this step came the essentials of the house style and the key writing elements to be taught.

A unique feature of S&P's situation is that it necessarily has managers who are in charge of the analysis procedures and who consequently have an important say on how things are done and especially, from our point of view, how they are written up. In addition, as in any publishing situation, S&P has a staff of editors who also exercise considerable control over what gets printed and how it is written. It was clear that no change in behavior could take place without the full partnership and cooperation of both of these groups. Consequently we prepared and delivered two initial pilot programs, one for the editors and one for other senior analysts and managers. Our tasks were as follows:

1. Convince them to join our efforts
2. Help them to see the need for and approve of the changes

3. Convince them that we could make the changes work
4. Let them know we had the full support of their management and their customers
5. Help them learn and practice the skills we would be training their subordinates and analysts to perform

These events accomplished, for the most part, we launched the program. In each class we had at least one editor and usually several group or senior managers as well as experienced analysts and new hires. If stylistic disputes or excuses came up, we had a publisher's hot line directly to the editor in chief for verification, back-up, or clarification. Once the trainees left our two-day class, their work was subject at the editorial level—and in most cases at their individual managerial levels—to the standards the company had newly adopted and that we were teaching.

Within the first week the publications began to show the difference. Within a few months customers were commenting on how much improved the format and layout were and how much more clearly the analysts were describing their conclusions.

The remarkable achievement here is that the company was able to effectively change its style and image and the way its employees performed one of their most critical tasks. The company did so, not by merely training the employees, but rather by engaging fully in the process of setting standards, convincing others to accept them, backing up the training team, and rigorously reinforcing what had been taught in the training room. Beverly and I were successful, but we could not have been so if the learners had been allowed to mentally close the training room doors after they left. It was the total partnership before, during, and after training that made this project a success, that created a profound change in the employees' job-related behavior.

Summary

This chapter addresses the growing concern of many practitioners that the traditional view of training as a purely service function that cranks out orientations for new hires is ineffective. Writers are publishing materials in growing numbers that promote the need for trainers to become involved in the entire process of any change their organizations contemplate. In fact, many feel they should be involved in the selection of which changes to undertake, which is part of long-range strategic planning.

This is the view that I have taken throughout this book, but in this chapter we looked at exactly what this process involves, and how some have gone about achieving it. We explored and defined the concept of partnering with management throughout the entire cycle of planning, needs analysis, training, and follow-up.

Because it gets results, many managers are beginning to try the process. This chapter gave four clear examples of the principles in operation, all of them successful because of the partnership formed with management by the trainers to work throughout the multiple phases of the training sessions.

Applications

1. Set up at least two focus groups with former trainees to discover how well they are applying what you taught them and whether they met with resistance to the techniques you taught.

2. Set up a focus group of the supervisors and managers—or at least interview several of them—that send trainees to you to discover what in their opinion is best about what their people learn from you and where you might improve.

3. Conduct a needs analysis.

4. Seek out and approach a senior manager to become a mentor to you and to bring you into a partnership on planning.

5. Devise and implement a system like the one used by Sun Life of Canada to follow up training by involving management in the follow-up tasks.

Chapter 20

Issues in Training

MANY issues have been touched upon throughout this book. I'd like to devote the final chapter to providing a perspective on them and to delineating at least some of the potential for training as a career that the next decade holds because of these issues. Most training issues fall into three broad categories: the changing workforce, the growth of technology, and the changing marketplace. Let's look at each category in turn.

The Changing Workforce

The broadest issue is the amount of change in the workforce. Several years ago, the most often cited authority for these changes was an in-depth study conducted in 1987 by the Hudson Institute in Indianapolis called *Workforce 2000: Work and Workers for the 21st Century*. Here is a summary of key conclusions this study predicted that would have an impact on training:

- In the next decade, 27 percent of new jobs will demand only minimal, low entry-level skills. The present rate is 40 percent.

- In addition, for the first time in history, the majority of new jobs (over 50 percent) will demand some post-secondary education. High school graduation or a GED will no longer be a sufficient entry-level qualification for half of the new jobs.

- The middle or moderate skill level jobs of today will be the lowest minimal skill jobs of tomorrow.

- The percentage of the workforce made up by younger workers will decline from more than 50 percent today to around 40 percent.

▪ The average age of the workforce will increase from 36 years to 39 years. An older workforce with a need for new skills means a heavy demand for retraining.

▪ Many, if not most, workers will need to change jobs (not necessarily companies) five or six times in a career.

▪ 80 percent of new workers will be women, minorities, and immigrants. All three categories have always provided a vital labor pool for American industry, but historically have also received less education and training.

▪ By 1999 barely 10 percent of the entering workforce will be able to solve a simple algebraic equation.

In the intervening years since the Hudson Institute made these predictions, all of them appear to be, if anything, on the conservative side.

The American Management Association's annual survey on testing and training practices in 1995 reported that:

> 33.1 percent of job applicants failed basic skill tests at the 961 responding companies. That compares to a deficiency rate of 38.5 percent in 1994. . . . The survey defined basic skills as "functional workplace literacy, such as the ability to read instructions, write reports, and/or do arithmetic at a level adequate to perform common workplace tasks."
>
> Although the overall deficiency rate fell last year—and reached its lowest level since 1990—the study found an especially high failure rate on math tests. The deficiency rate was 48 percent among applicants tested for math skills only; among those tested for literacy only, it was 32 percent.[1]

If they are to remain competitive and continue to grow in the marketplace, companies are faced with having to choose one (or more) of six alternatives in order to respond to these predicted demographics:

1. They can continue to ignore the problem, hiring only those who can pass standardized basic skills tests.

2. They can increase salary levels at the lower echelons to attract more qualified applicants.

3. They can lower standards and accept more entry-level workers with less ability.

4. They can send work abroad to countries where entry-level standards are much higher (i.e., Barbados, Ireland, and Poland and several other former Eastern Bloc countries).

5. They can form partnerships with schools in order to improve the caliber and direction of the education their entry-level labor pool receives.

6. They can take on the task of providing training and full high school equivalency themselves. They would then be accepting many more applicants and molding them into an effective workforce.

Let's look at each of these in turn.

If companies continue to do nothing they will fall behind. As most studies today indicate, the number of those applicants who can pass the skills tests will decrease, requiring longer, more costly searches for fewer new hires while at the same time the skills requirements will be increasing. A 1996 survey of 105 human resources directors and trainers predicted that demand for training will grow in such technical areas as e-mail, computer competency, the Internet, sexual harassment issues, diversity, safety, and ISO 9000.[2] To do nothing is obviously self-defeating, and the organization will face a trend of increasing costs that cannot be reversed.

Increasing salary levels for lower echelon employees works only as long as a few companies do it. When everyone gets on the bandwagon (which must happen as qualified candidates become rarer), competition for new hires will be characterized by cutthroat recruiting practices. Obviously, this is a self-defeating strategy.

The effect of simply lowering the standards in order to keep up the numbers will be a considerable decline in worker efficiency as new hires take longer to get up to speed on the job; a further decline in efficiency as current workers are distracted by longer periods of time spent training new hires; and a severe decline in job performance standards as the quality of service sinks to the level of ability of the new unskilled work force. These declines cannot help a company stay competitive.

Many organizations have realized the futility of the first three alternatives and have chosen one or more of the other options. Sending work abroad, however attractive it may seem at first (not only are the entry-level workers more skilled, but they are willing to work for less pay), in the long run weakens the U.S. economy by exporting jobs. Sooner or later in an increasingly competitive global marketplace such a policy is self-defeating. If we weaken or destroy the infrastructure at home, we lessen the quality of life there, too.

This leaves only two truly viable responses to the problem: partnerships and in-house training. The lesser of these is partnerships simply because even the best of the many partnerships that have been tried have enjoyed only limited success. One of the model programs with which I have been involved, the New York Academy of Finance, was begun in 1984. New York's banking community needed entry-level employees with solid basic skills. They were not finding them among the high school graduates who were applying for work as tellers, clerks, and data-entry operators. A number of banks (now numbering a dozen) spearheaded by American Express Bank set up the Academy as a partnership with the New York City Public Schools.

In addition to their regular class work, students in the program are given extra classes two days each week in subjects such as finance, personal grooming, interviewing skills, and so forth. Most of these courses are taught by volunteer bank personnel. The core of the program, however, is that the enrollees serve as summer interns in the banking industry. Maurice Tandler, director of the Academy of Finance, says, "The internships are extraordinarily important to the success rate of the program. [They] bridge the gap between theory and the world of work."

Competition to get into the program is fierce. The sponsoring banks are very pleased with the vastly increased potential of the new hires. It is an excellent and very successful program, a model for other such partnerships around the nation. The problem is that, even after more than a dozen years of operation, there are only between 2,000 and 3,000 students enrolled nationwide in the New York Academy of Finance. Of the millions of students graduating from high school in any given year, this excellent program is able to help only a tiny fraction of them. Certainly it is worthy, but it cannot stem the tide, nor can it alone even begin to address the problems we've delineated above.

Still, partnerships work. And because they are a learning endeavor, trainers should legitimately be involved. It is an option that is open to us, and one in which we can have a clear leadership role in both our working organizations and in the schools and outside community. Most partnership programs are of the "adopt a school" variety where a corporation works closely with a single school or school district to provide whatever help it can.

Such help usually takes the form of financial aid, such as paid work-study programs for students (much like the Academy of Finance, but usually without the company-based instruction), teacher training at business locations to provide school personnel with a more realistic business outlook, grants to teachers for creative innovation in the classroom, sponsorship of students to business-oriented training sessions either in the company or at service organizations such as the American Management Association's excellent Operation Enterprise, general scholarship funds, purchase of equipment and materials, and even achievement prizes and team sponsorships.

Participation in some form of partnering with the school community must center around strong mutual trust, shared responsibilities, close cooperation, and some form of clear-cut evaluation. As a part of its Project Bridge program, for instance, Polaroid pays the full salaries of up to ten employees per year who go back to school to become math and science teachers.

To start a partnership, start at the top. Gain executive support in your company first. Then gain top level support from the school or school system. Here are some factors that you must consider if you hope to succeed:

1. *Be sure to provide training and monitoring assistance.* Even experienced teachers will need training in key areas. And monitoring is the only way to make sure you are on track.

2. *Require a partnership action plan to be drawn up in the planning stage.* Be sure to include measurable, SMART objectives (see Chapter 2).

3. *Create clear evaluation procedures.* The single greatest cause of failure in partnerships is that there is usually insufficient evaluation built into the program to allow the business half of the partnership to measure progress in ways that are compatible with its traditional monitoring systems.

4. *Create evaluation stages.* Remain flexible in order to make midcourse corrections.

5. *Keep records.* Plan and quantify the number of participants, activities, volunteers, and the length of service of volunteers. Determine timing and methods for recruiting new volunteers, renewing the partnership, and measuring, advancement and progress.

6. *Check perceptions and attitudes of participants as well as concrete achievements.*

7. *Be sure to report back to all of the audiences involved.* Use newsletters, meetings, fund-raisers, annual reports, and the media where possible.

8. *Hold celebration and recognition ceremonies.* People love them, and they keep your partnership alive and in the public eye.

Finally, companies can take on the task of training their employees themselves. Clearly, in-company training, as we have described it here, has proved itself and is still proving itself to be the most effective source of skill learning. This includes basic skills. Hoechst Celanese, in its large chemical plant in Rhode Island, has undertaken a program to provide all of its rank-and-file employees with training in basic chemistry and math beyond that which they use on the job.

Other companies that are leading examples of success in this area are Motorola, Polaroid, Ona Corporation, and General Motors (GM). GM is particularly interesting in that its program has been fully supported by and designed in conjunction with its unions. In fact, unions are an excellent source of support for training because they realize that their membership's contribution to the organization is considerably enhanced by solid basic training. It also protects job security and makes the unions more flexible on issues like job retraining.

One of the most popular union-sponsored programs is a return to the apprenticeship approach to training. This is intense one-on-one on-the-job instruction and practice, which first evolved in the Middle Ages in Europe. It is still very popular there, particularly in Germany (see Chapter 13 for details). It is a strong and viable approach to skills training and may well be one of the best answers to the problems of the next decade. The key to apprenticeship is strong training.

A totally different but frequently suggested answer to the problem of inadequately trained entry-level workers is that the school system be reformed to produce better results. Both major candidates for President in the 1996 elections had platforms on education. They were expressing a major concern of the electorate; we must do something to improve our schools. The current results of twelve years of schooling are simply unacceptable. Certainly much could be accomplished if we could redevise our entire curriculum so that children learned only specific skills and were taught from specific behavioral SMART objectives. This approach has proven itself superior for many years now in industry. It is time we incorporated it into our general education system.

I have two problems, however, with this solution. Such an approach would require every existing teacher to be retrained (a monumental task even if they were willing, which most are not), all teacher training schools to revamp their curricula accordingly, and all existing and future college professors to be instructed in sound training principles. A highly improbable situation. The second problem concerns me even more, however. Many of those "experts" who want to reform our educational system want to see this curricular revolution accomplished through the universal use of computer-based instruction and other advanced technologies, which brings us to the second issue in training.

The Growth of Technology

Trainers are surrounded by a plethora of technological goodies. Everywhere we look there is a new high-tech medium that promises to deliver training more compactly, more economically, or more efficiently over greater distances. And more seem to be coming every year. I talked at length in Chapter 10 about the four most promising ones (most promising meaning that those who develop and sell them promise that they will deliver the most). They are virtual reality, computer-based training (CD-ROM interactive), distance learning, and multimedia visual aids. In this chapter I'd like to provide a set of guidelines for training managers to help them keep up with the twenty-first century and at the same time to maintain the high quality of training I have promoted in this book.

There is little doubt that these four technologies are exciting and have been demonstrated several times over to be effective aids to learning. Each of them can be extremely effective, but each of them can be equally ineffectual and all of them are limited in what they can accomplish. The question isn't whether or not to use the technologies, but how best to use them.

Everything we know about learning, people, and how to instruct them points to the fact that people learn best when:

- They have the opportunity (or are mandated) to practice and use what they have learned.
- They can interact with each other as they learn.

- They can question, probe, and explore concepts with those training them.
- They are challenged realistically by what they are learning.
- They have the opportunity to explore unique and personal applications of what they are learning.

Keep in mind that all of these conditions are most effective when they are present at the time of and for a short while immediately after instruction.

To the extent that technology helps the learner to do these things, it is being used well. To the extent that technology does not help or hinders learning, it is a waste of money, and perhaps more important, a waste of effort, energy, and people's time.

Virtual reality is thrilling. It can allow the learner to explore at random or with direction. It is at its best fully interactive and so can build competence and correct errors. For a few, it can even do so without organized instruction. After all, people do learn to drive a car or ride a bicycle by just getting behind the wheel or mounting the saddle and doing it. Quite a large number of the computer literate never read a manual or take a class but accept the challenge of exploring new software on their own. This approach works—for some. But the majority cannot learn well this way. Formal instruction must be provided. The best virtual reality simulations are used to supplement face-to-face instruction as a means of applying principles that have been previously taught.

Computer-based training has been demonstrated to train well. But it can only do so when it can also provide real-world simulation and interaction. It works quite well with virtual reality. However, because computer-based training is frequently used as an impersonal coach prompting a learner through a set of test

---

Questions for Judging When to Use Technology

- How are the learners practicing what is being taught? When? Where?
- How are the learners able to interact and how often? How easily?
- How much opportunity is there for the learners to interact with and challenge the instructor? How easily?
- Are the learners challenged by what they are doing?
- What opportunity will the learners have to explore unique and personal applications of what they are learning? How? Where? When?
- How are all of these necessary preconditions woven into the fabric of instruction before, during, and after material has been presented? To what extent?

---

questions about procedures and asking a series of multiple choice questions, it fails to instruct adequately. When it is used to prompt action, as in Gloria Gery's Personal Support Systems, it is excellent. But even here, computer-based training is limited to granular skill levels at slower than full operating speeds and is helped tremendously by live instruction and coaching. Computer-based training that isolates the learner fails to take advantage of the social nature of people, and only those learners who prefer to work alone will shine in this mode.

Distance learning tends to be even more isolating. And boring. At its worst, it is merely a talking head, sometimes relieved by action video sequences, all seen on a video screen. This is still the most common form distance learning takes. It is like *NOVA* or some other science program on public television: informative, interesting (sometimes), and very colorful, but not at all likely to be absorbed by the viewer or remembered in any great depth. Of course, distance learning doesn't have to be this way. But all too frequently it is. Most of the college, high school and commercial courses available by satellite are of this sort. If your distance learning allows both visual and auditory interaction between learners and instructors and learners and each other, as well as providing learners with the opportunity to plan and work together in groups or in computerized networks (LANS or WANS or the Internet), it is probably doing a good job of training. If it is not doing all of these things, you are probably deluding yourself about the quality of the learning taking place.

As for multimedia, they are enlivening visual aids. They can add color and motion to a topic and can even illustrate complex flows or changes. But they cannot instruct on their own. They are good involvers of multiple senses and can make a lesson more lively and perhaps even entertaining, but they are a sideshow. If they are allowed to become the main event, your training is failing to improve performance because the learner is not actively involved. Learners may be delighted by the show and remember it as great fun, but they will likely learn nothing else. Unless they are involved and interactive with much time spent working on applying what they've been taught, the learners will forget more than they remember. Don't neglect this principle in the interest of jazzing up the presentation of information. Multimedia are fine and fun, but use them to support your presentation, not to train your learners.

Even in the United States and other highly technologized cultures like Japan and Germany, most training is still done live and will most likely continue to be done this way. This is not because of laziness, or poor organization, or dated training methods. It is because people learn better in discourse with other people. Learning is a dialogue. In cultures that are not highly technologized, American high-tech instructional methods—particularly instruction through computers—are still scoffed at. Such things are seen as toys and games for children. Learning is clearly a humanizing activity, and it therefore can only be supplemented by technology, not replaced by it.

At the same time, anyone reading this book will see clearly that training well takes a great deal of time, a commodity few trainers have. Therefore, they will have to rely more and more on technology in order to maintain their service in the face of increasing demand. Training trade shows are packed today with exhibitors selling every shortcut imaginable, from sound cassettes and slide makers to distance learning networks, virtual reality vendors, and computer-based training programs. Many of them are excellent; many more are much less than excellent.

In Chapter 9 we provided some guidelines for choosing which aids would work best for you, but what must always be kept in mind is that whatever means of training help you select, the bottom line against which you must measure every offering is how it contributes to your training objectives.

In Chapter 7 we examined methods and provided you with a set of guidelines for choosing them effectively. Use it to establish a balance of learning activity for your trainees. Remember that your task is to create an environment that is conducive to learning and that what is learned is far more important than what is taught or even how it is taught. If the demographics or the budget demand that you use high technology like distance-learning classes or computer-based training:

1. *Make sure that learners are as interactive with other learners and with live instructors as possible.*

2. *Use the media and technology to keep them active.* Remember that it is what the learner does that teaches far more than what the learner listens to or observes. Don't let the siren song of media foist passive inactivity on your learners.

3. *Create opportunities for providing personal instructor feedback wherever possible.* Keep learning a live experience, a dialogue.

Technology isn't wrong. What is wrong is using technology for technology's sake. If it can be soundly justified by learning objectives, use the technology. Work it in with human contact and you'll be able to handle the technological onrush of the twenty-first century with relative ease and, more important, excellent training. Even so mighty an exponent of technology as Bill Gates said on a David Frost interview on Fox Television in October 1996, "In no way will the electronic world ever replace real experience!"

The Changing Marketplace

Training today is on the threshold of its greatest growth spurt since the medieval guild halls institutionalized the practice of one-on-one apprentice training. It is in a position very much like the one in which public education found itself in the United States at the dawn of the twentieth century. The traditional ways of preparing workers for their jobs are failing. Skilled entry-level workers are coming to be more and more in short supply. The slack will be picked up increasingly by other, less traditional sources of new hires such as the disabled, women, and immigrants.

Furthermore, recent downsizing as a response to market pressures has created a huge demand for cross-training of employees who are now expected to pick up the work of several departed former workers. Even though an American Management Association survey in October 1996 found that the crest of the downsizing wave has passed and companies are now beginning to "up-size" again, there are still many companies that are only coming to the downsizing strategy now. They will continue to downsize well into the next century. Either way, whether downsizing or rehiring, these companies *must* train their people.

This is an exciting time. And training is at the core. More and more workers will need to be retrained, not just once but several times in their work lives. New hires will need new and better training. The economy is challenging U.S. companies to improve their service and performance in order to hold on to their market share. This struggle must demand greater and greater attention to human capital through training. Trainers are entering an exciting decade and a dynamic new century. United States training is still not as popular worldwide as U.S. technology is. But the demand will grow. Entrepreneurship, which no one does better than Americans, is in great demand in China, Eastern Europe, Africa, and in many other areas. Training is becoming more practical daily. Americans are maintaining the premiere position of state of the art in training and so the demand for all sorts of training will grow. As that demand for American training grows, more U.S. trainers are going abroad. That opens a career choice to most of us: either go abroad and help others or stay here and fill the gaps and growing demand at home. Either way, training is a wonderful career choice for the next two decades—and a great place to be for trainers with ambition.

Summary

We have taken a brief look at:

- The changing nature of the workforce
- The incredible growth of technology in training
- The final decade of the century and the impact on training of recent trends such as downsizing

Each of these issues is described from a training perspective and, wherever possible, some steps and considerations in response to each of them are provided. I conclude that the new century holds nothing but promise for the growth of training as an aspect of the business world and, consequently, it's a great place to be.

Applications

1. Set up and keep a scrapbook on articles about virtual reality, computer-based training, and distance learning. Build a library of books by the experts in these fields. Become knowledgeable about what's available, how it works, and how you might best take advantage of it.

2. Assess your existing training and ask yourself how technology might be used to improve aspects of it. Work up full-scale projections of costs and effectiveness. Be prepared.

3. Seek out opportunities for partnering with local schools in order to help public and private education. Contact and schedule internships for students. Discuss ways to help schools with the skills of training that you now have.

4. Begin a ten-year plan to help launch your training department (or your career) into the twenty-first century.

Appendix:
Training Resources

Associations

American Management Association
1601 Broadway
New York, NY 10019

American Society for Training and Development
1640 King Street
Box 1443
Alexandria, VA 22313

Publications

Bulletin on Training
The Bureau of National Affairs
1231 25th Street N.W.
Washington, DC 20037 (202) 452-4200
  Short five-page monthly summary of current training news.

Training
Lakewood Publications
50 South 9 Street
Minneapolis, MN 55402 (612) 333-1471
  Excellent magazine written mostly by professionals. Very "how-to" oriented.

Training and Development Alert
Advanced Personnel Systems
P.O. Box 1438
Roseville, CA 95661 (916) 781-2900
  Excellent detailed summary of all currently published articles and books on training worldwide. Isssued monthly.

Training and Development Journal
(included in ASTD membership)
   Good magazine written mostly by trainers. Some issues devoted to a single
   topic.

Evaluation Service

Seminar Clearing House International
630 Bremer Tower
St. Paul, MN 55101 (612) 293-1044
   An on-line collection of evaluations of training attended or purchased by its
   members.

Video Resources

Almanac/Catalogue of Video Equipment and Video Services: MPCS Video Industries,
   Inc., Bill Daniels Company, 1984
   A complete catalogue of video-related equipment.

Video User's Handbook, Peter Utz, Prentice Hall, 1981
   A useful nontechnical guide to producing video materials for the training
   process. Explains how equipment operates, what the production process
   involves, and how to evaluate and troubleshoot what results. Extensively
   illustrated.

Books*

Apps, Jerold W. *Teaching From the Heart* (Melbourne, Fla.: Kreiger Publishing,
1996).

Bird, Malcom. *How To Make Your Training Pay* (London: Business Books Ltd.,
1991).

Bowsher, Jack. *Educating America* (New York: Prentice Hall, 1990).
   Fascinating discussion of the problems in American Education and a straightforward training-oriented solution by the former head of education for IBM.

Brinkerhoff, Robert O. *Achieving Results From Training* (San Francisco: Jossey-
Bass, 1987).
   A nontechnical book written by managers for strengthening program impact.
   Step-by-step approach deals with design, operation, and evaluation.

Broadwell, Martin M. *The Supervisor And On-The-Job Training*, 4th ed. (Reading,
Mass.: Addison-Wesley, 1995).

*This section is derived from research done by David Kippen for Beverly Hyman Associ-
ates.

Brookfield, Stephen D. *Understanding And Facilitating Adult Learning* (San Francisco: Jossey-Bass, 1995).

Burnham, Byron R. *Evaluating Human Resources, Programs, and Organizations* (Melbourne, Fla.: Krieger Publishing, 1995).

Caffarella, Rosemary S. *Program Development and Evaluation Resource Book for Trainers* (New York: Wiley & Sons, 1988).

Carr, Clay. *Smart Training: The Manager's Guide to Training for Improved Performance* (New York: McGraw-Hill, 1992).

Casner-Lotto, Jill, ed. *Successful Training Strategies: Twenty-six Innovative Corporate Models* (San Francisco: Jossey-Bass, 1988).
   The editor discusses twenty-six detailed case studies from leading edge companies on reshaping training strategies. Covers classroom training, self-instruction, coaching, and rotational assignments. Extensively illustrated.

Clark, Ruth Colvin. *Developing Technical Training* (Reading, Mass.: Addison-Wesley, 1989).

Cohen, Norman H. *Mentoring Adult Learners: A Guide for Educators and Trainers* (Melbourne, Fla.: Krieger Publishing, 1995).

Coleman and Barrie. *525 Ways to be a Better Manager* (Hants, U.K.: Gower, 1990).

Craig, Robert L. *Training and Development Handbook*, 3rd ed. (New York: McGraw-Hill, 1987).
   Covers the role of training development methods and media, applications, and resources.

Dean, Gary J. *Designing Instruction for Adult Learners* (Melbourne, Fla.: Krieger Publishing, 1994).

Eitingoton, Julies. *The Winning Trainer*, 2nd ed. (Houston: Gulf Publishing, 1989).
   Almost an encyclopedia that targets basic training techniques. Practical concepts are compiled in more than one hundred pages of handouts, ready to photocopy. It consists of puzzles, exercises, and role-playing models. Includes chapters on needs analysis, team building, and evaluation.

Ellis, Steven K. *How to Survive a Training Assignment: A Practical Guide for the New, Part-time or Temporary Trainer* (Reading, Mass.: Addison-Wesley, 1988).
   A self-study guide for trainers. Included are chapters on designing training programs, the training process, and evaluation. Illustrations include worksheets and checklists for instructional preparation.

Galbraith, Michael W. *Administering Successful Programs for Adults* (Melbourne, Fla.: Krieger Publishing, 1996).

Gardner, James E. *Choosing Effective Development Programs* (New York: Quorum Books, 1987).

Gardner, James E. *Training Interventions in Job Skill Development* (New York: Wiley & Sons, 1981).

Guide for establishing and administering training programs for new employees. It applies principles of learning and techniques of instruction in an insightful way.

Gilley, Jerry W., and Steven A. Eggland. *Principles of Human Resource Development* (Reading, Mass.: Addison-Wesley, 1989).

Goldstein, Irwin L. *Training in Organization: Needs Assessment, Development and Evaluation*, 2nd ed. (Pacific Grove, Calif.: Brooks/Cole, 1986).
Covers needs assessment, evaluation, and instructional approaches. Also includes chapters on design and research issues. Addresses questions referring to organizational analysis.

Greenberg, Eric Rolfe, ed. *Basic Skills: An AMA Research Report on Testing and Training* (New York: AMACOM, 1989).

Hawthorne, Elizabeth M. *Evaluating Employee Training Programs: A Research-Based Guide for Human Resources Managers* (Westport, Conn.: Quorum Books, 1987).
Extensively evaluates all phases of employee training, research, and approaches to training employees.

Heron, John. *The Facilitator's Handbook* (London: Kogan Page, 1989).

Jordan, Dale R. *Teaching Adults with Learning Disabilities* (Melbourne, Fla.: Krieger Publishing, 1996).

Kirkpatrick, Donald L. *A Practical Guide for Supervisor Training and Development* (Reading, Mass.: Addison-Wesley, 1983).
Written to provide practical help for line managers as well as personnel and training directors. Gives detailed recommendations and guides to the experienced or inexperienced trainer.

Knowles, Malcolm. *The Adult Learner*, 4th ed. (Houston: Gulf Publishing, 1990).

Kohn, James P. *Behavioral Engineering Through Safety Training* (Springfield, Ill.: Charles C. Thomas, 1988).

Kubr, Milan, and Joseph Prokopenko. *Diagnosing Management Training and Development Needs* (Geneva: International Labour Office, 1989).
This step-by-step book includes practical information on needs analysis, training concepts, and training techniques.

Laird, Dugan. *Approaches to Training and Development*, 2nd ed. (Reading, Mass.: Addison-Wesley, 1985).
Offers practical and informal information on training methods, cost of training, and selection of staff by one of the great names in training. Illustrations include a bibliography.

Lambert, Clark. *Secrets of a Successful Trainer* (New York: Wiley-Interscience, 1986).
This book explores step-by-step objectives for evaluating training methods and gives practical tips and techniques. Several case studies are discussed.

London, Manuel. *Managing the Training Enterprise* (San Francisco: Jossey-Bass, 1989).

Mailick, Sidney, Solomon Hoberman, and Stephen J. Wall. *The Practice of Management Development* (New York: Praeger, 1988).
> Written to provide useful advice for senior executive decision-makers. An analysis of case studies pertaining to management training approaches, organization changes, and determining development needs. Includes a bibliography.

Materka, Pat Roselle. *Workshops and Seminars: Planning, Producing, and Profiting* (Englewood Cliffs, N.J.: Prentice Hall, 1986).
> An informal book covering all phases of the training program, useful to all types of organizations. Also includes practical ideas on marketing and promoting workshops.

Mellander, Klas. *The Power of Learning: Fostering Employee Growth* (Homewood, Ill.: Business One Irwin, 1993).

Moore, Allen B., and R. L. Brooks. *Transforming Communities* (Melbourne, Fla.: Krieger Publishing, 1995).

Moore, Allen B., and James A. Feldt. *Facilitating Community and Decision Making Groups* (Melbourne, Fla.: Krieger Publishing, 1993).

Moxon, Peter. *Building a Better Team: A Handbook for Managers and Facilitators* (Brookfield, Vt.: Gower, 1993).

Mumford, Alan, ed. *A Handbook of Managment Development*, 2nd ed. (Brookfield, Vt.: Gower, 1986).
> Offers useful information for managers and consultants for improving management development. Chapters cover planning the process of management development, learning methods, and needs analysis.

Munson, Lawrence. *How to Conduct Training Seminars: For Management, Marketing, Sales, Technical and Educational Seminars* (New York: McGraw-Hill, 1989).
> Highlighted throughout with illustrations and stories, this book covers the complete training process. Also covers needs analysis, planning and development, and budgeting for seminars.

Nadler, Leonard, and Garland D. Wiggs. *Managing Human Resource Development* (San Francisco: Jossey-Bass, 1986).
> A practical human resources guide in design, organization, and policies for HRD. Also covers strategic HRD planning, supervisory programs with staff conclusions at the end of each chapter.

Nilson, Carolyn. *How to Manage Training: A Guide to Administration, Design, and Delivery* (New York: AMACOM, 1991).

Nilson, Carolyn. *How to Start a Training Program in Your Growing Business* (New York: AMACOM, 1992).

Nilson, Carolyn. *The Trainer's Complete Guide to Management and Supervisory Development* (Englewood Cliffs, N.J.: Prentice Hall, 1992).

Nilson, Carolyn. *Training for NonTrainers: A Do-it-Yourself Guide for Managers* (New York: AMACOM, 1990).

Nordhaug, Odd. *Human Capital in Organizations: Competence, Training, and Learning* (New York: Oxford University Press, 1993).

Odiorne, George S., and Gary Rummler. *Training and Development: A Guide for Professionals* (Chicago: Commerce Clearing House, Inc., 1988).
   A guide suited for all levels of management that includes program design, curriculum, and learning theories. Practical information is also given on classroom effectiveness, technologies of training, and organization skills.

Orlin, Jay M. *Training to Win: Strategies for Today's Industrial Challenges* (New York: Nichols Publishing, 1988).

Pike, Robert W. *Creative Training Techniques Handbook* (Minneapolis: Lakewood Books, 1989).

Piskurich, George M. ed. in chief. *The ASTD Handbook of Instructional Technology* (New York: McGraw-Hill, 1993).

Quick, Thomas L. *Power, Influence and Your Effectiveness in Human Resources* (Reading, Mass.: Addison-Wesley, 1988).
   Stresses being an effective trainer, building power, and becoming influential. Chapters cover developing strategic relations, overcoming resistance to projects, and improving the organization's perception of training.

Rae, Leslie. *How to Measure Training Effectiveness* (New York: Nichols, 1986).
   A how-to book on evaluating individuals and clients. Analysis and interviews using questionnaires, repertory grids, and measurement methods.

Rae, Leslie. *The Skills of Training: A Guide for Managers and Practitioners* (Aldershot, England: Gower, 1983).

Rece, R. Wayne, and Brent D. Peterson. *Analysis in Human Resources Training and Organizational Development* (Reading, Mass.: Addison-Wesley, 1988).
   A comprehensive guide in analytical approaches to training and organizational development. Included are chapters on task analysis, needs analysis, and systems analysis. Illustrates and evaluates the usage of gathering data.

Reynolds, Angus, and Ronald H. Anderson. *Selecting and Developing Media for Instruction*, 3rd ed. (New York: Van Nostrand Reinhold, 1992).

Ricard, Virginia B. *Developing Intercultural Communication Skills* (Melbourne, Fla.: Krieger Publishing, 1993).

Robinson, Dana Gaines, and James C. Robinson. *Selecting and Developing Media for Instruction*, 3rd. ed. (New York: Van Nostrand Reinhold, 1992).

Roscow, Jerome M., and Robert Zager. *Training—The Competitive Edge* (San Francisco: Jossey-Bass, 1988).

Detailing case studies of corporation's training programs and policies. Discusses cost of training, program design, and delivering training to geographically dispersed employees.

Rothwell, William J., and Dale C. Brandenburg. *The Workplace Literacy Primer: An Action Manual for Training and Development Professionals* (Amherst, Mass.: Human Resource Development Press, 1990).

This is an examination of the problems of literacy in the workplace. It features an excellent resource list for off-the-shelf programs in literacy.

Silberman, Mel. *Active Training* (Lexington, Mass.: Lexington Books, 1990).

Spaid, Ora A. *The Consumate Trainer* (Englewood Cliffs, N.J.: Prentice Hall, 1986).

Tracey, William R. *Designing Training and Development Systems*, 3rd. ed. (New York: AMACOM, 1994).

Tracey, William R. *Human Resource Development Standards: A Self-evaluation Manual for HRD Managers* (New York: AMACOM, 1981).

This manual offers more than 140 sets of detailed standards for effectively evaluating the various programs of an organization. Contains helpful selected readings at the end of each section.

Utz, Peter. *Video User's Handbook* (Englewood Cliffs, N.J.: Prentice Hall, 1995).

A useful, nontechnical guide to producing video materials for the training process. Explains how equipment operates, what the production process involves, and how to evaluate and troubleshoot your results. Extensively illustrated.

Van Wart, Montgomery N., Joseph Cayer, and Steve Cook. *Handbook of Training and Development for the Public Sector* (San Francisco: Jossey-Bass, 1993).

Vaught, Bobby C., Frank Hoy, and W. Wray Buchanen. *Employee Development Programs: An Organizational Approach* (Westport, Conn.: Quorum Books, 1985).

Ward, Gary. *High-Risk Training: Managing Training Programs for High-Risk Occupations* (Houston: Gulf Publishing, 1988).

Written for managers and trainers to apply to any field of training. Processes, tools, and techniques for training programs combine with simulation management development. Extensively illustrated.

Wexley, Kenneth N., ed. *Developing Human Resources* (Washington, D.C.: BNA, 1991).

Wheelan, Susan A. *Facilitating Training Groups* (New York: Praeger, 1990).

White, Bren. *World-Class Training* (Dallas: Odenwald Press, 1992).

Wilson, Donna L., and Donna A. Amstutz. *Educating Learners to Become Informaton Literate* (Melbourne, Fla.: Kreiger Publishing, 1996).

Zaccarelli, C.S.C., and Herman E. Brother. *Training Managers to Train: A Practical*

Guide to Improving Employee Performance (Los Altos, Calif.: Crisp Publications, 1988).

   This easy-to-follow manual offers extensive illustrations describing the total training process. Written for all levels of management and employees, covering strategies, basic techniques, and objectives.

Zimmerman, A. L., and Carol J. Evans. *Facilitation: From Discussion to Decision* (East Brunswick, N.J.: Nicholas Publishers, 1993).

Other Publications

Becker, Stephen. "The Ten Sequential Steps for the Training Process." *Training*, January 1980.

Byrd, Richard E. *Creativity & Risk Taking*, University Associates, Inc., 1995.

Forbes-Greene, Sue, L.M.S.W. *The Encyclopedia of Icebreakers: Structured Activities That Warm-up, Motivate, Challenge, Acquaint and Energize.* University Associates, 1996 current inventory.

Fournies, Ferdinand F. *Coaching for Improved Work Performance.* University Associates, 1996 current inventory.

Gorlin, Harriet. "Guide for Designing Training Programs." *Training and Development*, 1981.

Hall, J. *NASA Moon Survival Task.* University Associates, 1996 current inventory.

Jones, John E. *Team Development Inventory Trainer's Package.* University Associates, 1996 current inventory.

Learning Materials from Telemetrics International. University Associates, 1996 current inventory.

Lost at Sea. University Associates, 1996 current inventory.

McNamara, J. Regis. "Why Aren't They What We Trained Them to Do?" *Training*, February 1980.

Mill, Cyril. *Activities for Trainers: Fifty Useful Designs.* University Associates, 1996 current inventory.

Molly, William F. "Making Role Plays Pay Off in Training." *Training*, May 1981.

Pfeiffer, William J. *Developing Human Resources: The Annual Series Set, 1972–1989.* University Associates.

Pfeiffer, William J., and John E. Jones. *A Handbook of Structured Experiences—The Boxed Set.* Volumes I–X. University Associates, 1996 current inventory.

All of the following references are published by University Associates:

The Encyclopedia of Group Activities: 150 Practical Designs for Successful Facilitating; William J. Pfeiffer.

The Encyclopedia of Icebreakers: Structured Activities That Warm-up, Motivate, Challenge, Acquaint and Energize; Sue Forbes-Greene, L.M.S.W.

A Handbook of Structured Experiences, Vols. 1–10, William J. Pfeiffer and John E. Jones.

The Team-Building Source Book; Steven L. Phillips and Robin L. Elledge.

Understanding and Managing Stress: Instruments to Assess Your Lifestyle; John D. Adams (includes a facilitator's guide).

Notes

Chapter 1

1. Edward L. Thorndike, *Human Learning* (New York: Century, 1931).
2. Edward DeBono, *New Think* (New York: Avon, 1971).
3. Beverly Hyman, "Managing Change," in *How Successful Women Manage* (New York: AMACOM, 1981).
4. Jard DeVille, *The Psychology of Leadership: Managing Resources and Relationships* (Rockville Centre, N.Y.: Farnsworth, 1984).
5. Solomon Asch, "Effects of Group Pressure Upon the Modification of Distortion of Judgment," in H. Guetzkow, ed., *Groups, Leadership, and Men* (Pittsburgh: Carnegie Press, 1951).

Chapter 2

1. J. R. Anderson, "Arguments Concerning Representation for Mental Imagery," *Psychology Review* 85 (1978): 247–249.

Chapter 3

1. Based on Stanley L. Payne, *The Art of Asking Questions* (Princeton, N.J.: Princeton University Press, 1980); John McConnell, *AMA Conference Leadership Manual* (New York: AMACOM, 1973); and "Effective Strategies for Platform Speaking," a manual for a 1981 AMA seminar.
2. Based on the categories of questions developed by Gerard I. Nierenberg in *The Art of Negotiating* (New York: Hawthorn, 1968).
3. Ray L. Birdwhistell, *Kinesics and Context: Essays on Body Motion Communication* (Philadelphia: University of Pennsylvania Press, 1970); and Birdwhistell, *Introduction to Kinesics* (Louisville, Ky.: University of Louisville Press, 1952).

4. Paul Watzlawick, et al., *Pragmatics of Human Communication* (New York: Norton, 1967).
5. Albert Mehrabian, *Nonverbal Communication* (Chicago: Aldine-Atherton, 1972).
6. Edward T. Hall, *The Silent Language* (Westport, Conn.: Greenwood Press, 1980); and Hall, *The Hidden Dimension* (New York: Doubleday, 1966).
7. Beverly Hyman, "The Dominant Models and Metaphors With Which Teachers Report They Function in the Classroom Environment" (Ph.D. diss., New York University, 1980).
8. This material, used with permission, is taken from Glenn Pfau's sessions of the AMA seminar "Projecting a Positive Executive Image," which is given frequently at many locations throughout the United States and Canada.

Chapter 5

1. Elton Mayo, *The Human Problems of an Industrial Civilization* (New York: Macmillan, 1922).

Chapter 7

1. B. F. Skinner, *The Behavior of Organisms* (New York: Appleton-Century, 1938); Skinner, *Walden Two* (New York: Macmillan, 1961); and Skinner, *About Behaviorism* (New York: Random House, 1974).
2. This comparison is based on Tom Kramlinger and Tom Huberty, "Behaviorism versus Humanism," *Training and Development Journal* (December 1990).
3. Beverly Hyman, trainee's manual from "Training the Trainer," a 1987 AMA course, © 1980 Beverly Hyman, Ph.D., and Associates.

Chapter 8

1. Karl R. Popper, *The Open Society and Its Enemies* (Princeton: N.J.: Princeton University Press, 1966).
2. Based on Beverly Hyman, "Advanced Training the Trainer," a 1987 AMA course.

Chapter 9

1. This treatment of equipment is based on the working operations of Uniforce Temporaries, New Hyde Park, N.Y., and on research conducted by Beverly Hyman for "Advanced Training the Trainer," a 1987 AMA course.

Chapter 10

1. This approach to the evolution of training technology was created by Dr. Deborah Steele of Corporate Management Services and is described in her AMA course "How to Use Multi-Media in Training."
2. Conceived and promoted by Gloria Gery in her book *Electronic Performance Support Systems* (Medford, Mass.: Ziff Institute, 1991).
3. Maureen Minehan, "Virtual Reality: The Next Step in Training," *HR Magazine* (August 1996).
4. © 1989, Brøderbund Software, Inc.
5. See *Multimedia & Videodisk Monitor* (March 1992).
6. Gloria Gery, "The Ten Most Important Lessons I've Learned About Computer-Based Learning," in *What Works at Work: Lessons From the Masters,* George Dixon, ed. (Minneapolis: Lakewood Books, 1988), p. 212.
7. Floyd H. Allport, *Social Psychology* (Boston: Houghton Mifflin, 1924).

Chapter 12

1. Douglas McGregor, *The Human Side of Enterprise* (New York: McGraw-Hill, 1960).
2. Peter R. Scholtes, *The Team Handbook: How to Use Teams to Improve Quality* (Madison, Wisc.: Joiner Associates, 1995).
3. Ibid., pp. 6–11.
4. Deborah and Alan Slobodnick, "The Team Killers," *HR Focus* (June 1996): 22–23.
5. Oren Harari, "The Dream Team," *Management Review* (October 1995): 29.

Chapter 14

1. Of course, I believe that skills trainers should indeed have a special interest group within ASTD if they want one. It is their concomitant dismissal of the rest of trainers as "airheads" that I find sad, especially since the epithet has occasionally been deserved.
2. In addition to the quote, this entire discussion is based on Joan Chesterton's article "Shattering the Myths of Hourly Workers," *Management Review* (September 1995): 56–60.
3. Ibid.
4. Anecdote related by Michael P. Seidman, DDS, PC, in August 1996.
5. This game is the creation of Cathy and Peter Chartier of CommTech Communications in Toronto, Canada.
6. This entire section is based on Barbara Solomon's article, "Retailers Agree on Educational Priorities," *Management Review* (June 1995).

Chapter 15

1. Section on budgeting based on Paul E. Guilmette, "Budgeting," a 1987 Dun & Bradstreet seminar; and Grover M. Clark and Jeanette Pearlman, "Budgeting for Human Resource Systems," in William R. Tracey, ed., *Human Resources Management and Development Handbook* (New York: AMACOM, 1985), pp. 111–122.
2. Section on staffing based on David W. Brinkerhoff, "The HR Professional Staff," in William R. Tracey, ed., op. cit., pp. 174–178.
3. Based on Richard W. Beatty and Craig E. Schneier, *Personnel Administration: An Experiential Skill-Building Approach* (Reading, Mass.: Addison-Wesley, 1981).
4. George S. Odiorne, "Management by Objectives for HR Managers," in William R. Tracey, ed., op. cit., pp. 101–110.
5. Beatty and Schneier, op. cit.
6. Odiorne, op. cit.
7. Frederick Herzberg, *Work and the Nature of Man* (New York: Thomas Y. Crowell, 1966).
8. Paul Hersey and Kenneth H. Blanchard, *Management of Organizational Behavior: Utilizing Human Resources,* 4th ed. (Englewood Cliffs, N.J.: Prentice Hall, 1982).

Chapter 16

1. Jerome Brunner, "Credibility in the Media," paper delivered at Media Ecology Symposium, Saugerties, N.Y., April 1984.
2. Lorraine Hansberry, *A Raisin in the Sun* (New York: New American Library, 1961), act II, scene iii.
3. Beverly Hyman, "Writing," course offered by Beverly Hyman Associates.
4. S. I. Hayakawa, *Language in Thought and Action,* 4th ed. (New York: Harcourt Brace, 1978).

Chapter 17

1. Gerard I. Nierenberg, *The Complete Negotiator* (New York: Nierenberg-Zeif, 1986).
2. Dudley Bennett, *TA and the Manager* (New York: AMACOM, 1976).
3. Jard De Ville, *The Psychology of Leadership: Managing Resources and Relationships* (Rockville Centre, N.Y.: Farnsworth, 1984).

Chapter 18

1. Cited in *AMA Basic Skills: An AMA Research Report on Testing and Training* (New York: AMACOM, 1989).

2. Materials on literacy are based on *The Bottom Line: Basic Skills in the Workplace,* a joint publication of the Department of Education and the Department of Labor (Washington, D.C.: GPO, 1988).
3. The discussion of cultural differences is based on Donald H. Weiss, "Managing a Diverse Workforce: How to Deal With Value Conflicts," *Trainer's Workshop* (December 1987); and Edward T. Hall, *The Silent Language* (New York: Fawcett, Premier Books, 1959).
4. This material is based on Philip R. Harris and Robert T. Moran, *Managing Cultural Differences* (Houston, Tex.: Gulf, 1990), pp. 95–96.

Chapter 19

1. M. L. Broad and J. W. Newstrom, as cited in Dana Gaines Robinson and James C. Robinson, *Performance Consulting: Moving Beyond Training* (San Francisco: Bennett-Koehler, 1996), p. 1.
2. Peter Cappelli and Anne Crocker-Hefter, "Distinctive Human Resources are Firm's Core Competencies," *Organizational Dynamics* (Winter 1996): 21.
3. Ibid., p. 19.
4. William J. Rothwell, *Beyond Training and Development: State-of-the-Art Strategies for Enhancing Human Performance* (New York: AMACOM, 1996), p. 4.
5. Ibid., pp. x, xi.

Chapter 20

1. "The Dearth of Basic Skills Continues," *HR Focus* (August 1996): 16.
2. "Tomorrow's Training," *HR Focus* (August 1996): 16.

Index